RACIAL DISPROPORTIONALITY
IN CHILD WELFARE

Racial Disproportionality in Child Welfare

Marian S. Harris

 COLUMBIA UNIVERSITY PRESS   NEW YORK

COLUMBIA UNIVERSITY PRESS
Publishers Since 1893
New York   Chichester, West Sussex

cup.columbia.edu
Copyright © 2014 Columbia University Press

Library of Congress Cataloging-in-Publication Data

Harris, Marian Sabrina.
  Racial disproportionality in child welfare / Marian S. Harris.
    pages cm
  Includes bibliographical references and index.
  ISBN 978-0-231-15046-0 (cloth : alk. paper) — ISBN 978-0-231-15047-7 (pbk. : alk. paper) —
  ISBN 978-0-231-52103-1 (ebook)
  1. Child welfare—United States. 2. Social work with minorities—United States.
  3. Social work with African American children. 4. Social service and race relations—United States.
  5: Race discrimination—United States. I. Title.

HV741.H339 2014
362.7'7800973—dc23

                                                           2013047696

Columbia University Press books are printed on permanent and durable acid-free paper.
This book is printed on paper with recycled content.
Printed in the United States of America

c 10 9 8 7 6 5 4 3 2 1
p 10 9 8 7 6 5 4 3 2 1

COVER IMAGE:
COVER DESIGN:

FOR JIM,

LOVE OF MY LIFE,

FOR MY PARENTS AND DAUGHTER, TRINA

CONTENTS

AT LEAST AS FAR BACK AS THE MIDDLE of the nineteenth century, would-be child protectors in the United States have sought to "save" children from what they perceived to be unfit families and communities. The savers were generally established members of European American political and economic elites, whereas the children being saved generally came from socially excluded communities, including immigrants and, later, after coming to be seen by the white majority as fully human and therefore worthy of salvation, Native Americans and African Americans. Given this history it should not be surprising that children of color, particularly African Americans and Native Americans, are much more likely than their white peers to end up in the care of the state. Nevertheless, a debate continues over the extent to which this disproportionate representation of races within the child welfare system should be a cause for concern and, if so, what actions should be taken to reduce disproportionality.

I am not at all surprised that my friend and colleague Marian Harris has succeeded in moving this debate forward in a practical way with her new book, *Racial Disproportionality in Child Welfare*. I have known Dr. Harris since the 1990s, when she came to the University of Wisconsin–Madison on a National Institute of Mental Health postdoctoral fellowship at the School of Social Work, where I was a faculty member at the time. While I was supposed to be her postdoc mentor, I learned at least as much from Dr. Harris as she could have possibly learned from me. She immediately impressed me as a thoughtful scholar whose work was informed by a comprehensive knowledge of the research literature combined with her own

extensive clinical practice and ongoing dialogue with other practitioners. We
shared the perception that much more could be done for families involved
with the child welfare system, particularly families of color, who often seemed
particularly ill served by the kinds of help offered by the system.

When I had the opportunity in 2002 to help organize the first national
research conference on children of color in the child welfare system, Dr.
Harris was on the short list of scholars I made sure to involve in planning for
the meeting. She contributed there to a spirited discussion of the potential
contributors to racial disproportionality, and we ended up collaborating
on a study of how race, ethnicity, and family structure interact in complex
ways to influence the likelihood that children are able to return home to
their parents from foster care. Since then I have had many opportunities to
exchange ideas with Dr. Harris about racial disproportionality in the child
welfare system and have always come away from those exchanges with new
insights. That I am not the only one impressed with her insights regarding race is evidenced by her involvement over the years in leading efforts of
scholars and policy makers to grapple with the subject. Most impressive in
this regard is Dr. Harris's leadership of the Washington State Racial Disproportionality Advisory Committee, the first body of its kind created by
a state legislature.

Racial Disproportionality in Child Welfare provides much food for
thought for policy makers, practitioners, and researchers interested in taking action to address racial disproportionality in the provision of child
welfare services and the outcomes experienced by children and families
affected by the child welfare system. Dr. Harris begins with a thorough
overview of U.S. child welfare policy dating back to the federal government's first significant forays into that realm in the 1970s. She describes
how the policy framework can work to the advantage, and disadvantage, of
racial minorities. Dr. Harris also wisely draws attention to the importance
of the nation's core antipoverty programs, such as Temporary Assistance
for Needy Families, in helping low-income parents safely parent their children. In her review of research on and policies to address disproportionality abroad, Dr. Harris rightly points out that racial disproportionality is an
international issue, with black and indigenous children being particularly
likely to find themselves in the care of the state.

Dr. Harris begins her discussion of best and promising child welfare
practices by examining the five key decision points that determine whether

children enter the child welfare system and how long they stay involved. She deftly reviews the research on how each decision contributes to disproportionality, providing guidance to those interested in crafting effective policy and practice reform. Dr. Harris also provides practitioners with theoretical frameworks to inform culturally competent child welfare practice. Reflecting the ecological perspective that she brings to her analysis of disproportionality, Dr. Harris devotes considerable attention to the potential impact on disproportionality of changing the organizations that deliver child welfare services, improving the training provided by the nation's schools of social work, and conducting rigorous research and evaluation. Through selected excerpts from interviews she conducted, Dr. Harris also gives voice directly to key participants in the child welfare system, including those the system is supposed to help, as well as the potential helpers. Importantly, *Racial Disproportionality in Child Welfare* is chock-full of practical tools for administrators and practitioners to use to assess their own efforts to address disproportionality.

Race is often a difficult subject to discuss in the United States, but it is also a subject that generally cannot be avoided without doing terrible injustice to those disadvantaged by the history and ongoing evolution of racism in the United States. Dr. Harris deserves much credit for challenging us to continue to wonder why children of color are more likely than white children to become the children of the state and to recommit ourselves to making that a thing of the past.

Mark E. Courtney

ACKNOWLEDGMENTS

THERE ARE MANY INDIVIDUALS to thank for their help and support on this project and many others who have contributed to this book as a result of my work with them throughout the years. I am enormously grateful to the numerous children and families that were my clients during my work in the child welfare system and in my private practice over the past thirty years. The case study presented in this book has been completely disguised to protect client confidentiality. All interviews in the book have also been disguised to protect the confidentiality of the interviewees. Throughout my career in social work education I was mentored by two exemplary individuals, Dr. Dolores Norton and Dr. Mark E. Courtney. From the time I met them many years ago, they have willingly shared their knowledge, time, expertise, and wisdom. Our relationship evolved from one of mentoring to great friendship. I am truly blessed to have both of these individuals in my life today.

I appreciate everyone at Columbia University Press for their high degree of professionalism, support, and guidance in this process. I am enormously grateful to my colleague Dr. Rich Furman, who introduced me to Lauren Dockett, the former social work editor, who encouraged me to write my book. Another colleague and friend, Dr. Jerry Finn, has provided support and encouragement from the time I signed a book contract until the present time. I am most fortunate to have my friend Tasha Pritchett, whom I thank for her kindness, love, and support as well as her technical knowledge and skills in making sure all illustrations were completed in a quality manner. I want to thank Terry L. Cross, executive director of the National

Indian Child Welfare Association, for granting permission for the inclusion of the Cultural Competency Continuum.

On a personal note I have received an overwhelming amount of love, encouragement, and support from my dear friends Drs. Jose Rios, Kathryn Basham, Joyce Everett, Ada Skyles, and Lovie Jackson. Sandy Lapham, Delois Brown, Babette Beckham, Billie Johnstone, Ted Johnstone, Beth Van Fossan, Bernice Morehead, Deborah Purce, Daryllyn Harris, Shirley Bonney, and Stephen Wilson are friends that have been loyal, kind, and caring as I worked to complete this book during a most difficult time in my life. It was their love, faith, humor, constant encouragement, and reminders about the significance of this book that helped me keep writing during those times when I felt like abandoning the project.

THE U.S. CHILD WELFARE SYSTEM is currently facing a crisis involving race and poor outcomes for children and families of color. As a result of this crisis children of color continue to enter the system in disproportionate numbers and encounter extreme difficulty exiting the system. Racial disproportionality is evident when the percentage of children of color in any system, including the child welfare system, is higher than the percentage of children of color in the general population. Racial disparity occurs when the rate of disproportionality, poor outcomes, or deficient services of one group (e.g., African Americans) exceeds that of a comparison group (e.g., European/White Americans). Data have repeatedly shown that children of color are disproportionately represented in the child welfare system in the United States. For example, according to the Annie E. Casey Foundation (2007), African American children comprised 15 percent of the total U.S. child population under the age of eighteen; however, African American/black children accounted for 32 percent of the children placed in foster care. Although racial disproportionality is most severe and dramatic for African American children, American Indian children also experience higher rates of disproportionate placements in foster care than do children of other races or ethnicities. In 2004 American Indian children represented less than 1 percent of the total child population in the United States; however, 2 percent of children in foster care were American Indian. Hispanic/Latino children are 19 percent of the child population and 17 percent of the children in foster care.

Race is a significant factor in the decision to place a child in foster care. Research has shown that children of color, when compared to white children, are more likely to be removed from the care and custody of their birth parents and placed in foster care. Once in foster care, they remain longer, and they receive fewer services; they also have less contact with child welfare caseworkers while they are in care (Barth 1997; Child Welfare Watch 1998; Harris & Skyles 2005; Harris & Hackett 2008). According to the U.S. Department of Health and Human Services (2009), there were 463,000 children in the foster care system on September 30, 2008; the race/ethnicity of these children is as follows: Alaska Native/American Indian 8,802; Asian 2,631; black 142,502; Hawaiian/Other Pacific Islander 877; Hispanic (of any race) 92,464; and white 183,149. Children of color continue to exit the system at slower rates than white children. In fiscal year 2008, 124,688 white children exited the system compared to 5,605 Alaska Native/American Indian children, 2,316 Asian children, 75,441 black children, 763 Hawaiian/Other Pacific Islander children, and 56,741 Hispanic (of any race) children (U.S. Department of Health and Human Services 2009). Children of color have suffered for decades from racism that exists in the child welfare system.

Addressing and reducing disproportionality and disparities in the child welfare system were placed on the national agenda several years ago. In September 2002 the U.S. Children's Bureau convened a research roundtable of national experts/researchers in Washington, D.C., to explore the extent and ramifications of "Racial Disproportionality in the Child Welfare System." Seven papers were commissioned for the roundtable and subsequently published in the May/June 2003 issue of *Children and Youth Services Review*. The papers explored explanations for racial and ethnic disproportionality and examined the ways in which children enter and exit the child welfare system. Among the findings are the following:

- Disproportionality may be more pronounced at some decision-making points (e.g., investigation) than at others (e.g., substantiation) (Fluke, Yuan, Hedderson, & Curtis 2003).
- Family structure is significant. Race and ethnicity have a different effect on family reunification rates in two-parent families than in single-parent families (Harris & Courtney 2003).
- Changes in policy and practice may be effective in reducing racial and ethnic disproportionalities, particularly those arising from differences in duration of out-of-home care (Wulczyn 2003).

The impetus for this book emanates from the strong need to take a hard look at the complex and ongoing problem of racial disproportionality and disparities in the child welfare system. Research studies in other countries have demonstrated the extent and ramification of this problem; yet the child welfare field is still perplexed about what needs to be done to eradicate the problem. This book illuminates a serious problem that continues to prevail in the child welfare system.

CHAPTERS OF THE BOOK

Chapter 1 (Social Welfare Policy and Child Welfare) provides a succinct overview of existing social welfare policies that have a direct impact on children and families in the child welfare system (the Child Abuse Prevention and Treatment Act of 1974, the Indian Child Welfare Act of 1978, the Adoption Assistance and Child Welfare Act of 1980, the Multiethnic Placement Act of 1994, the Personal Responsibility and Work Opportunity Reconciliation Act of 1996, the Adoption and Safe Families Act of 1997, the Fostering Connections to Success and Increasing Adoptions Act of 2008, and the Child and Family Services Improvement and Innovation Act of 2011). Included are a critique of each policy and a discussion of how these policies affect disproportionality.

Chapter 2 (An International Exploration of Disproportionality) examines disproportionality from an international perspective. This chapter looks at the disproportionate number of children of color in the child welfare systems in Australia, England, New Zealand, and Canada.

Chapter 3 (Best Practices/Promising Practices) consists of four sections. The first section examines five key decision points in the child welfare process: (1) reporting child abuse and neglect; (2) referring the report for investigation; (3) investigating the referral; (4) removing the child from the home, including the court process; and (5) exiting the system. Research has demonstrated that European American/white children fare better at each of these decision points than children of color (Caliber & Associates 2003; Bowser & Jones 2004; Lemon, D'Andrade, & Austin 2005; Harris & Hackett 2008; Washington State Racial Disproportionality Advisory Committee 2008). The second section discusses what children need for optimal growth and development. The third section focuses on ecological systems theory and attachment theory, as well as factors in the microsystem that impact outcomes for disadvantaged children of color in the child welfare system. Best practices/interventions that are needed at key decision points when working with children and families of color are explored. There is also a discussion of risk factors, particularly the risks for those children of color who enter the system with histories of insecure attachment, severe maltreatment, and early trauma and loss, and what these families don't have and need vis-à-vis policies and interventions; in addition, protective factors are examined. Section four focuses on the significance of ongoing cultural sensitivity and competency training for child welfare practitioners, supervisors, administrators, and child protective services workers. Examples of a cultural competency training module and cultural competency self-assessment instruments are included. The cultural competency continuum is also discussed. This section culminates with the presentation of a best practice case scenario.

Chapter 4 (Child Welfare System Change) critiques the child welfare system and provides proactive steps that can be taken to address institutional racism, resulting in disproportionality and disparities, in any child welfare organization/agency whose goal is equitable treatment for all children and families. A measurement instrument is included to assess disproportionality in child welfare organizations/agencies. Narrative interviews from a variety of individuals who discuss their experiences with the child welfare system conclude this chapter. Interviewees include a birth mother, a birth father, a former foster parent and kinship caregiver, a former juvenile court judge, an executive director of a private child welfare agency and adoptive mother, an adoptive mother, and two alumni of the foster care system (one female and one male).

In Chapter 5 (Social Work Curriculum) the reader learns why curriculum is significant for students planning to work in the child welfare system. Syllabi for five courses are presented. These courses should be required in schools of social work that are training students to work in child welfare organizations/agencies. Information for field instruction, including the importance of home visits and respect for family cultural practices, is also explored.

Chapter 6 (Future Directions for Research and Policy) highlights areas of research that need to be explored, including referrals by mandated reporters. Future research is especially important in this area because the largest percentage of children of color continues to enter the child welfare system because of child neglect; however, the definition of *child neglect* continues to be quite nebulous. Changes to current social welfare policy that are needed, as well as new policies that appear to be warranted, are also addressed.

It is my hope that *Racial Disproportionality in Child Welfare* will be a powerful resource for social work educators, students, practitioners, policy makers, and researchers, as well as others in communities across the country, who are working/advocating to end racial disproportionality and disparities in the child welfare system in this country, as well as in other countries, and to achieve equitable treatment for all children and their families who become involved in the child welfare system.

REFERENCES

The Annie E. Casey Foundation. (2007). *The 2007 kids count data book.* Baltimore, MD: Author.

Barth, R. (1997). Family reunification. *Child Welfare Research Review, 12,* 109–122.

Bowser, B. P., & Jones, T. (2004). *Understanding the over-representation of African Americans in the child welfare system: San Francisco.* Hayward, CA: Urban Institute.

Caliber & Associates. (2003). *Children of color in the child welfare system: Perspectives from the child welfare community.* Washington, DC: U.S. Department of Health and Human Services.

Child Welfare Watch. (1998). *The race factor in child welfare.* New York, NY: Center for an Urban Future.

Fluke, J. D., Yuan, Y. Y., Hedderson, T., & Curtis, P. A. (2003). Disproportionate representation of race and ethnicity in child maltreatment: Investigation and victimization. *Children and Youth Services Review, 25*(5/6), 359–373.

Harris, M. S., & Courtney, M. E. (2003). The interaction of race, ethnicity, and family structure with respect to the timing of family reunification. *Children and Youth Services Review, 25*(5/6), 409–429.

Harris, M. S., & Hackett, W. (2008). Decision points in child welfare: An action research model to address disproportionality. *Children and Youth Services Review, 30*(2), 199–215.

Harris, M. S., & Skyles, A. (2005). Working with African American children and families in the child welfare system. In K. L. Barrett & W. H. George (Eds.), *Race, culture, psychology, and law* (pp. 91–103). Thousand Oaks, CA: Sage.

Lemon, K., D'Andrade, A., & Austin, M. (2005). *Understanding and addressing disproportionality in the front end of the child welfare system*. Berkeley, CA: Bay Area Social Services Consortium.

U.S. Department of Health and Human Services. (2009). *The AFCARS report*. Washington, DC: Author.

Washington State Racial Disproportionality Advisory Committee. (2008). *Racial disproportionality in Washington State*. Olympia, WA: Author.

Wulczyn, F. (2003). Closing the gap: Are changing exit patterns reducing the time African American children spend in foster care relative to Caucasian children? *Children and Youth Services Review, 25*(5/6), 431–462.

*RACIAL DISPROPORTIONALITY
IN CHILD WELFARE*

1

Social Welfare Policy and Child Welfare

FOR DECADES FEDERAL, state, and local governments have been consistently involved in developing and implementing laws, agencies, organizations, and other means to protect children in this country when their parents are unable or fail to protect them. In this chapter the reader will be familiarized with the major social welfare legislation that affects children and families involved in the child welfare system, especially children of color. Research consistently demonstrates that children of color when compared to their white counterparts continue to be disproportionately represented in the child welfare system (Bowser & Jones 2004; Lemon, D'Andrade, & Austin 2005; Harris & Hackett 2008; Washington State Racial Disproportionality Advisory Committee 2008; U.S. Department of Health and Human Services 2009; Crofoot & Harris 2012). The following social welfare laws are succinctly discussed and critiqued in this chapter: the Child Abuse Prevention and Treatment Act of 1974, the Indian Child Welfare Act of 1978, the Adoption Assistance and Child Welfare Act of 1980, the Multiethnic Placement Act of 1994, the Personal Responsibility and Work Opportunity Reconciliation Act of 1996, the Adoption and Safe Families Act of 1997, the Fostering Connections to Success and Increasing Adoptions Act of 2008, and the Child and Family Services Improvement and Innovation Act of 2011. There is also a discussion of how these laws affect racial disproportionality in the child welfare system. The appendix contains a synopsis of each piece of legislation for readers.

THE CHILD ABUSE PREVENTION AND TREATMENT ACT OF 1974

The Child Abuse Prevention and Treatment Act of 1974 (CAPTA; Pub. L. No. 93–247) was the first major child welfare law to establish federal guidelines for states to use in passing child abuse and neglect reporting laws; each state is responsible for defining child abuse and neglect based on the minimum standards stipulated by CAPTA. However, CAPTA does not provide a federal definition of child abuse or neglect. Consequently, there is ambiguity and variation among the states in their definitions of child abuse and neglect. According to the Child Welfare Information Gateway (2009), CAPTA, as amended by the Keeping Children and Families Safe Act of 2003, defines "child abuse and neglect, at a minimum, as any recent act or failure to act on the part of a parent or caretaker which results in death, serious physical or emotional harm, sexual abuse or exploitation, or an act of failure to act which presents imminent risk of serious harm" (1). The primary types of maltreatment recognized by most state statutes are physical abuse, neglect, sexual abuse, and emotional abuse. Many states also include child abandonment and parental substance abuse in their statutes as types of child abuse and neglect.

These definitions are important because child protective services (CPS) uses them in addressing allegations of child abuse and/or neglect. Any person who has knowledge or suspects that a child is being abused or neglected may contact a CPS office to report an allegation. It is the responsibility of CPS to initially assess the allegation and, using the state definitions of child abuse and neglect, to determine whether or not an investigation is warranted. Frequently, impoverished children and families of color seem to be at the forefront of these allegations, and the result is an acrimonious investigation that often results in the removal of children from the care and custody of their birth parents and placement in out-of-home care (King County Coalition on Racial Disproportionality 2004; Johnson et al. 2007; Harris & Hackett 2008; Washington State Racial Disproportionality Advisory Committee 2008). Disproportionality tends to be quite prevalent at the decision points of CPS investigation and substantiation (Fluke, Yuan, Hedderson, & Curtis 2003; Lemon, D'Andrade, & Austin 2005; Harris & Skyles 2005; Harris & Hackett 2008).

Other provisions of CAPTA include the following:

- State grants: Formula grants to states and territories to help improve their CPS systems, in exchange for which states must comply with various requirements related to the reporting, investigation, and treatment of child maltreatment cases
- Discretionary activities: Federal data collection, dissemination, and technical assistance efforts related to child abuse prevention and treatment, as well as competitive grants to a range of eligible entities for research and demonstration projects or other activities related to the identification, prevention, and treatment of child abuse and neglect
- Community-based grants: Formula grants to states and territories to support community-based activities and services to prevent child abuse and neglect
- Children's Justice Act grants: Formula grants to states and territories to improve investigation, prosecution, and handling of child maltreatment cases, particularly those cases related to child sexual abuse or exploitation (Child Welfare Information Gateway 2008)

CAPTA also requires the appointment of a guardian ad litem (GAL) in any child abuse or neglect case; the GAL may be an attorney or a court-appointed special advocate (CASA) or both. The GAL is responsible for making recommendations to the court about the best interests of the child.

The following legislation subsequently amended and/or reauthorized funding for CAPTA: Pub. L. No. 95–266 (1978); Title VI, Chapter 7 of Pub. L. No. 97–35 (1981); Pub. L. No. 98–457 (1984); Pub. L. No. 99–401 (1986); Pub. L. No. 100–294 (1988); Pub. L. No. 102–295 (1992); and Pub. L. No. 104–235 (1996). On December 20, 2010, President Barack Obama signed the CAPTA Reauthorization Act of 2010 (Pub L. No. 93–247). The act received funding of $1.039 billion and spans a five-year period. The following are its three major goals:

- Improve program operation and data collection over time
- Improve systems for supporting and training individuals who prevent, identify, and respond to reports of neglect, abuse, and maltreatment of children
- Strengthen coordination among providers who address the challenges associated with child abuse, maltreatment, and neglect, as well as dating and domestic violence (National Conference of State Legislators 2010, 1)

The act stipulated that GALs should be trained about early childhood, latency, and adolescent child development; that CPS should collaborate with agencies providing domestic violence services; and that CPS should conduct research on and be encouraged to use the practice of differential response. According to the National Conference of State Legislatures (2010), differential response is "a state or community-determined formal response that assesses the needs of the child or family without requiring a determination of risk or occurrence of maltreatment. Such response occurs in addition to the traditional investigatory response" (1). Differential response would result in CPS finding ways to protect children other than removing them from the home and care of their birth parents. The use of differential response has been shown to have a positive effect on children and families (Institute of Applied Research 2004).

THE INDIAN CHILD WELFARE ACT OF 1978

The Indian Child Welfare Act (ICWA; Pub. L. No. 95–608) is a federal law that regulates child abuse and neglect cases, as well as adoption cases, involving Native American children; specifically, it mandates that Native American Nations and Tribes have jurisdiction in cases of abuse, neglect, and adoption of these children. Congress passed ICWA because of the high number of Native American children who were removed from their families and placed primarily with European American families in foster care, boarding homes, or adoptive homes. ICWA laid the foundation for child welfare practice with any "Indian child," which it defines as "any unmarried person who is under age eighteen and is either (a) a member of an Indian tribe or (b) is eligible for membership in an Indian tribe." Because ICWA takes precedence over state law in cases involving Native American children and families, it is important for state child welfare agencies and courts to always determine if any child coming into care is Native American. Native American Tribes have legal and cultural interests in their children.

In 2005 the U.S. Government Accounting Office collected data from states via a survey to determine ICWA's impact. Although the data collected from states were limited, it was very clear that problems were still prevalent in some states when Native American children entered the foster care system.

ICWA created important protections to prevent state child welfare agencies and courts from inappropriately separating American Indian children from their families. More than 25 years after it was enacted, however, we know very little about the effect of this law on moving American Indian children in foster care to permanent homes in a timely manner, while ensuring their safety and well-being. The scarcity of data on outcomes for children subject to the law, along with variations in how individual states, courts, social workers, and tribes interpret and implement ICWA, make it difficult to generalize about how the law is being implemented or its effect on American Indian children. Our discussions with tribal officials, as well as our review of the limited information on ICWA implementation from the CFSRs [Child and Family Services Reviews], indicate that some problems with ICWA implementation are occurring, although we cannot estimate how extensive such problems are.

(U.S. Government Accounting Office 2005, 58)

It is ironic that problems that were highlighted with ICWA in some states in 2005 have continued to be prevalent since that time. For example, in Washington State Native American children are less likely to exit the foster care system within two years compared to European American children; they are also less likely to have one or two placements and more likely to have four or more placements compared to European American children (Washington State Racial Disproportionality Advisory Committee 2008). In addition, Native American children are twice as likely to remain in foster care for over two years, less likely to be adopted, and less likely to be reunified with their birth parents when compared to European American children (Washington State Racial Disproportionality Advisory Committee 2008). In Washington State the Washington State Racial Disproportionality Advisory Committee worked with tribal leaders and other community partners for passage of a Washington State Indian Child Welfare Act and continues to engage the community in its initiatives to reduce the disproportionate number of Native American children in the child welfare system. Finally, although ICWA is the major federal child welfare law that provides protection for Native American children and families, it is the only child welfare law without regular federal child and services reviews.

THE ADOPTION ASSISTANCE AND CHILD WELFARE ACT OF 1980

In an effort to have children exit the foster care system and to facilitate family reunification, the permanency planning movement of the 1970s was started. When one examines the child welfare system of the 1950s, 1960s, and early 1970s, one sees few attempts to offer services to facilitate reunification of children with their families and to keep children from languishing in out-of-home placements. However, the permanency planning movement of the mid-1970s served as the major impetus to expedite either the return of children to live with their families or the legal adoption of children in order to become members of new families. Several demonstration projects developed ways to facilitate family reunification or adoption (Emlen, Lahti, Downs, McKay, & Downs 1978; Stein, Gambrill, & Wiltse 1978). The practice principles and methods developed through these projects were incorporated into the Adoption Assistance and Child Welfare Act of 1980 (Pub L. No. 96–272).

The enactment of the Adoption Assistance and Child Welfare Act was the most significant affirmation of the intent of foster care to be a short-term, temporary service to children and families. This law provided fiscal incentives to states to (a) take steps to implement permanency planning in foster care, (b) reduce the child's length of stay in foster care, (c) promote the return of children to their own homes whenever feasible, (d) demonstrate "reasonable efforts" to prevent unnecessary out-of-home placements, and (e) encourage adoption as an exit from the foster care system. It further mandated that reasonable efforts be made to remedy the harms to children that require state intervention and that children be reunified with parents whenever possible.

The Adoption Assistance and Child Welfare Act also mandated that when children are removed from the care of their birth parents, they should be placed in the least restrictive (most family-like) environment available and as close as possible to their birth parents in accordance with the best interests of the child. This mandate was interpreted by many states to mean that kinship care was the placement of choice when children must be removed from their birth parents (Gleeson & Craig 1994). Placement of children in kinship care was a frequent child welfare practice in the late 1980s and early 1990s in large urban states such as New York, California, and Illinois; the majority of these children were members of economically disadvantaged families of color (Barth & Berry 1990; Kusserow 1992; Testa 1992, 1993; Wulczyn & Goerge 1992).

The intent of this law was good because no child should languish in the child welfare system; however, there was evidence that permanency planning did not dramatically reduce the number of children in foster care (Barth, Courtney, Berrick, & Albert 1994). In fact African American children continued to be overrepresented in the child welfare system after this law was passed (Wulczyn & Goerge 1992). According to an eight-year study by Goerge (1990), African American children in Cook County (Illinois) had a median length of stay of fifty-four months; however, the median length of stay for all children in placement was eighteen months. The weight of the evidence demonstrated a major problem with permanency planning: i.e., failure of the child welfare system to provide needed services to birth parents to facilitate family reunification and continued failure to provide services to children and families after family reunification (Fanshel 1981, 1982; Hubbell 1981; Maluccio 1981; Besharov 1986; Hartman 1993; Tatara 1994). According to Turner (1984), "It is noteworthy that community services were infrequently rendered to parents or children, either while the children were in care or following their return home" (502). This practice is still prevalent today in work with children and families in the child welfare system, especially with children and families of color.

THE MULTIETHNIC PLACEMENT ACT OF 1994

Another significant federal law affecting children in the child welfare system is the Multiethnic Placement Act of 1994 (MEPA; Pub. L. No. 103–382). This legislation was a response by Congress to address permanency for the large number of children in the foster care system. For example, in 1994 there were 468,000 children in the foster care system in this country; approximately 60,000 of these children were waiting for adoption (U.S. Department of Health and Human Services 1994). A large percentage of these children were children of color, especially African American children, whose stay in the foster care system and waiting period for adoption were substantially longer when compared to those of European American children.

MEPA was amended by the Inter-Ethnic Adoption Provisions of 1996 (IEAP; Pub. L. No. 103–382) to include the following provisions:

- It prohibits states and other entities that are involved in foster care or adoption placements and that receive federal financial assistance under Title IV-E, Title IV-B, or any other federal program from delaying or denying a child's foster care or adoptive placement on the basis of the child's or the prospective parent's race, color, or national origin.
- It prohibits states and other entities from denying to any individual the opportunity to become a foster or adoptive parent on the basis of the prospective parent's or the child's race, color, or national origin.
- It requires that to remain eligible for federal assistance for their child welfare programs, states diligently recruit foster and adoptive parents who reflect the racial and ethnic diversity of the children in the state who need foster and adoptive homes. (U.S. Department of Health and Human Services 1994)

There has been much controversy regarding this legislation. Proponents state that race and ethnicity should not be factors in placement decisions for children in foster care who are legally free for adoption; they emphasize that it is more important for children of color to have permanent homes than to languish in foster care waiting for a same-race home. However, many opponents state that it is emotionally harmful for children of color to be placed transracially with foster and/or adoptive parents. Some opponents have expressed concern that children of color will not be exposed to their racial and cultural backgrounds. Others state that children will experience identity and self-esteem problems, especially when they enter the adolescent phase of development. For example, the position statement of the National Association of Black Social Workers (1994) clearly affirmed the following:

- Stopping unnecessary out-of-home placements
- Reunifying children with parents
- Placing children of African ancestry with relatives or unrelated families of the same race and culture for adoption
- Addressing the barriers that prevent or discourage persons of African ancestry from adopting
- Promoting culturally relevant agency practices
- Emphasizing that "transracial adoption of an African American child should only be considered after documented evidence of unsuccessful same

race placements has been reviewed and supported by appropriate representatives of the African American community" (1)

It is highly important for child welfare professionals to be proactive in their recruitment efforts to increase the number of foster and adoptive homes in communities of color. At the same time professionals have a legal mandate to work with European American families who want to become foster and/or adoptive parents.

THE PERSONAL RESPONSIBILITY AND WORK OPPORTUNITY RECONCILIATION ACT OF 1996

Welfare reform is generally thought of as the government's sweeping attempt to change social welfare policy in the United States. Its primary goal is to decrease the number of individuals and families dependent on public assistance and to facilitate efforts of individuals and families to become independent of government assistance and self-sufficient. As a result, welfare reform impacts children and families involved in the child welfare system. The 1996 Personal Responsibility and Work Opportunity Reconciliation Act (PRWORA; Pub. L. No. 104–193) was welfare reform legislation designed to decrease the number of children growing up in poor single-parent families by mandating that women move from welfare to work; there was also increased emphasis on promoting marriage. The 1996 act reformed welfare by eliminating the Aid to Families with Dependent Children (AFDC) program and replacing it with the Temporary Assistance for Needy Families (TANF) program. State governments were given broad latitude to develop and implement their own welfare programs. Although many women have left welfare for work since the passage of PRWORA in 1996, most working poor women have been unable to move their families out of poverty because of low-wage employment. Higher rates of child neglect, as well as higher rates of foster care entry, have been linked to maternal moves from welfare to work (Paxson & Waldfogel 2002). However, Courtney, Pilliavin, Dworsky, and Zinn (2001) reported a negative correlation between workforce involvement and CPS investigation.

Poor women are particularly vulnerable to chronic poverty. Many chronically poor women are sometimes dependent but often are working poor. They find themselves in chronic poverty for a multitude of reasons that form a matrix of interrelated factors. These factors include lack of access to education and employment, as well as constraints on human and social capital; these factors are key barriers to moving out of poverty. "An estimated 3.1 million families live in poverty after welfare reform, including 1.5 million who live in dire poverty (income less than 50 percent). In addition, the poverty gap for poor single parent families does not decline in the post PRWORA period" (Peterson, Song, & Jones-DeWeever 2002, 3).

One might ask, Are there other connections between welfare reform and the child welfare system? The answer is yes. First of all, public welfare was the main source of income for many of the children and families involved in the child welfare system prior to TANF. Needell, Cuccaro-Alamin, Brookhart, and Lee (1999) studied a sample of California AFDC recipients and found approximately 27 percent were reported for child maltreatment, 21 percent were investigated, 8 percent of cases were opened, and 3.2 percent entered the foster care system. The U.S. Department of Health and Human Services (2000b) reported another 2.0 to 2.6 percent of children entered the foster care system during the years of 1995 and 1996; these children were recipients of AFDC in California, Illinois, and North Carolina.

Second, poverty rates tend to be higher for children of color, who are disproportionately represented in the child welfare system (Bass, Shields, & Behrman 2004; Bowser & Jones 2004; Roberts 2002).

Third, children of color from single-parent families, especially African American children, remain in foster care longer and have difficulty reunifying with their families (Harris & Courtney 2003; Bowser & Jones 2004; Harris & Hackett 2008). Harris and Courtney (2003) studied children in the California child welfare system; their findings demonstrated the following: "African American children were reunified at slower rates than other children and children from two-parent families were returned home faster than children from single-parent homes" (423). A policy that focuses on reducing poverty among female-headed families of color, especially African American families, would go a long way to decrease the disproportionate number of children of color who continue to enter and remain in the child welfare system in this country. Although there is evidence that caseloads have decreased since the passage of PRWORA and the implementation of TANF, the weight of the evidence still shows that a large number of working poor women have not become self-sufficient and continue to vacillate between welfare and work. Many of these women are mothers of color; they and their families are still in poverty and disproportionately involved in the child welfare system.

Finally, many children of color are cared for by grandparents or other relatives in formal kinship or relative care. Kinship care/relative care placements have become the preferred placement option of child welfare agencies (Urban Institute 2001). "Public [formal] kinship caregivers are more likely than non-kin foster parents to be older, African American, single, and never married. They are also more likely to live in poverty and to be less well educated" (U.S. Department of Health and Human Services 2000a, 44). If kinship caregivers do not meet the requirements to be formal foster parents, TANF can be provided for the children or for the kinship caregiver and the children. Kinship caregivers who receive TANF for themselves and the children must adhere to TANF regulations, including work requirements and time limits. "Most kin caregivers receive the inadequate Temporary Assistance for Needy Families payment, which averages $200 per month, depending on the number of children, and are not eligible to receive the much-higher foster board payments for nonrelatives that range from $356 to $431 per month, depending on the age of the child" (Hill 2004, 69–70). African American children continue to be disproportionately placed in kinship care when compared to white children (Harris 1999, 2004; Harris & Skyles 2008; Minkler & Fuller-Thomson 1999; Ross & Alday 2006).

Many children of color and their families, especially African American children, are adversely affected by PRWORA in other ways. For example, the law has a lifetime ban on TANF and food stamp benefits for any person convicted of a felony due to the possession, use, or distribution of drugs. A large percentage of African American children enter the child welfare system because of child neglect by birth parents who are abusing drugs (Cross 1997; Harris & Hackett 2008; U.S. Department of Health and Human Services 2009); parents who abuse drugs experience an extreme hardship if they try to get the financial assistance needed to provide care for their children from programs that are funded via PRWORA, such as TANF (Geen & Boots 1997). Although one of the most widespread effects of PRWORA was a dramatic decrease in caseloads for public social service agencies, the adverse effect for poor families was a change in the type of financial assistance that could be received from the federal government.

THE ADOPTION AND SAFE FAMILIES ACT OF 1997

Another major social welfare law is the 1997 Adoption and Safe Families Act (ASFA; Pub. L. No. 105–89). ASFA mandated that the health and safety of children were the most significant factors in placement decisions; it established new time lines to expedite permanency for children by reunification, adoption, or legal guardianship. One of the controversial mandates in ASFA is that a petition to terminate parental rights shall be filed for birth parents whose child has been in the foster care system fifteen of the most recent twenty-two months. ASFA stipulates that case plans and case reviews shall always consider the safety of children and encourages child welfare workers to engage in concurrent permanency planning for children in foster care: i.e., plan for family reunification but also plan for adoption or legal guardianship.

ASFA further mandated the development of a rating system and outcome measures known as the Child and Family Service Reviews (CFSRs). ASFA also

- continues and expands the Family Preservation and Support Services program;
- continues eligibility for the federal Title IV-E adoption assistance subsidy for children whose adoption is disrupted;
- authorizes adoption incentive payments to states;
- requires states to document efforts to adopt;
- expands health care coverage to non-IV-E adopted children with special health care needs;
- authorizes new funding for technical assistance to promote adoptions;
- addresses geographic barriers to adoption;
- establishes kinship care advisory panels;
- includes a sense of Congress provision on standby guardianship;
- establishes new time lines and conditions for filing termination of parental rights;
- sets a new time frame for permanency hearings;
- modifies the reasonable efforts provision in the Adoption Assistance and Child Welfare Act of 1980;
- requires states to check prospective foster and adoptive parents for criminal backgrounds;

- requires notice of court reviews and opportunity to be heard for foster parents, pre-adoptive parents, and relatives;
- directs states to establish standards to ensure quality services;
- requires assessment of state performance in protecting children;
- directs development of a performance-based incentive funding system;
- expands child welfare demonstration waivers;
- requires study on the coordination of substance abuse and child protection; and
- authorizes the use of a federal parent locator service. (Child Welfare League of America 1997, 1–4)

In terms of racial disproportionality the ASFA mandate that child welfare workers must file to terminate parental rights for children who have been in foster care fifteen of the most recent twenty-two months poses several issues of concern. Although it is highly important for all children who enter the child welfare system to achieve permanency as soon as possible, this time line is unrealistic when one considers that the largest number of children enter the child welfare system because of neglect by birth parents who abuse alcohol or other substances.

> Among confirmed cases of child maltreatment, 40% involve the use of alcohol and other drugs. This suggests that of the 1.2 million confirmed victims of child maltreatment, an estimated 480,000 children are mistreated each year by a caretaker with alcohol or other drug problems. Additionally, research suggests that alcohol and other drug problems are factors in a majority of cases of emotional abuse and neglect. In fact, neglect is the major reason that children are removed from a home in which parents have alcohol or other drug problems.
>
> (Prevent Child Abuse America 2005, 1)

In this country African American and Native American children continue to enter and remain in the child welfare system in disproportionate numbers. Many of these children have parents who have alcohol and/or other substance abuse problems and are unable to get treatment (Child Welfare League of America 2001; Harris 2011). According to Cross (1997), approximately 90 percent of child neglect cases and 60 percent of child abuse cases can be linked to parents with alcohol and/or drug problems. It has been repeatedly shown that African American women who abuse substances are more likely to be reported to CPS than white or Hispanic women with substance abuse problems (U.S. Department of Health and Human Services 1999). Many birth parents try to get treatment for their substance abuse problems but are put on waiting lists; while they wait for treatment, the permanency planning time clock is steadily moving. The U.S. Department of Health and Human Services (1997) stated that approximately half of families with substance abuse problems in their study received no substance abuse treatment; although another 23 percent with substance abuse problems were offered treatment, no treatment was provided to them; and no substance abuse treatment was offered to 23 percent of the cases identified in this study.

In addition to the limited number of treatment facilities and the failure to provide treatment, there are several other barriers to treatment, especially for women whose children are in the child welfare system. Child care is a major barrier. Many alcoholic and drug-dependent women are single parents and do not have the resources to get the care needed by their children. In a multicity survey of services for alcoholic women conducted by the Woman to Woman Program of the Association of Junior Leagues, the most frequently mentioned institutional barrier to treatment was the lack of child care service for women needing residential care (Association of Junior Leagues 1987; see also American Association of Family and Consumer Services 2013; Friedman n.d.). Among the other obstacles to participation in treatment for women who abuse substances are the following: distrust of the social services system, as well as treatment providers; financial hardship; social isolation; and greater physiological complications (Nelson-Zlupko, Kaufmann, & Dore 1995).

It makes sense to reassess ASFA in light of the fact that large numbers of children are entering the child welfare system due to child neglect because their birth parents abuse substances and are unable to care for their children. The severe shortage of substance abuse treatment facilities greatly hampers efforts to reunify families, especially the disproportionate number of families of color; this problem is a continuous one.

THE FOSTERING CONNECTIONS TO SUCCESS AND INCREASING ADOPTIONS ACT OF 2008

The Fostering Connections to Success and Increasing Adoptions Act of 2008 (Pub. L. No. 110–351) was enacted to improve outcomes for children and youth in foster care, provide support for kinship caregivers, provide access to foster care and adoption for Native American children, and increase incentives for adoption, as well as increase adoption assistance. To facilitate a positive transition to adulthood and exit from foster care for youth in foster care who have not reached age nineteen, twenty, or twenty-one and are still in school or working, states also are given an option to extend Title IV-E assistance. This act mandates the following:

Promoting Permanent Families for Children in Foster Care with Relatives

- Notice to relatives when children enter care
- Kinship care navigator programs
- Subsidized guardianship payments for relatives
- Licensing standards for relatives

Promoting Permanent Families for Children in Foster Care with Adoptive Families

- Incentives for adoption
- Adoption assistance

Promoting Permanent Families for Children in Foster Care with Birth Families and Other Relatives

- New family connections grants
- Efforts to keep siblings together

Improving Outcomes for Children and Youth in Foster Care

- Foster care for older youth
- Educational stability
- Health care coordination

Increasing Support for Native American and Alaska Native Children

- Direct access to federal support for Indian Tribes
- Technical assistance and implementation services

Improving the Quality of Staff Working with Children in the Child Welfare System

- Extended federal support for training of staff (Center for Law and Social Policy 2008, 1–2)

This federal legislation has several mandates that positively impact the disproportionate number of children of color and their families in the child welfare system. For example, extending Title-IV-E assistance to youth after they reach age eighteen is a positive provision; most youth in foster care continue to need support and services long after their eighteenth birthday. Child welfare professionals certainly can never get too much training, especially training that is specifically geared to their work with the disproportionate number of children and families of color—African American and Native American children, in particular—that continue to enter the child welfare system and are adversely affected by longer placements and service disparities when compared to their white counterparts. Findings from a study by Olsen (1982) demonstrated that when compared to all ethnic groups, Native American children and families had the least chance to be referred for services. According to Harris and Skyles (2005), "Research on delivery of services to children and families in the child welfare system consistently demonstrates that African American children are at a disadvantage regarding the range and quality of services provided, the type of agency to which they are referred, the efficiency with which their cases are handled, the support their families receive, and their eventual outcomes" (95).

Effective implementation of this legislation by states can result in positive outcomes if child welfare professionals work proactively to provide services and supports to children, birth parents, and relatives to preserve families and to facilitate family reunification for children who are currently in out-of-home care. This legislation is about maintaining connections of children and families rather than terminating these connections and can be viewed as a positive effort to decrease the disproportionate number of children of color who are removed from the care of their birth families and placed in the child welfare system.

THE CHILD AND FAMILY SERVICES IMPROVEMENT AND INNOVATION ACT OF 2011

On September 30, 2011, President Obama signed into law the Child and Family Services Improvement and Innovation Act (Pub. L. No. 112–341). This law requires states to develop protocols and monitor the use of psychotropic drugs for children in foster care. According to Congressman Jim McDermott (D-WA), "This new provision in the law will better protect this vulnerable population from medications that may be harmful to them, especially medications that could have extremely harmful effects" (2011, 1).

This law strengthened provisions in the Fostering Connections to Success and Increasing Adoptions Act of 2008 that mandated states to develop a health coordination plan for children in foster care and oversee prescription drugs.

The Child and Family Services Improvement and Innovation Act authorized extended funding for the Promoting Safe and Stable Families Program for five years—i.e., from 2012 through 2016. The services provided via this program will make a difference in the lives of many children of color who are disproportionately represented in the child welfare system, especially through the family support services. Among the purposes of family support services are the following: strengthening and stabilizing families, improving parenting skills, promoting child safety and well-being, and enhancing child development. This law mandates that states spend no less than 90 percent of federal funding received for children and their families in the following service areas: (a) family support, (b) family preservation, (c) time-limited reunification, and (d) adoption promotion and support. As noted throughout this chapter, research has demonstrated that children of color have longer stays in out-of-home care when compared to their white counterparts (Harris & Skyles 2005, 2008; Harris & Hackett 2008). The revised definition of "time-limited family reunification services" is intended to impact children of color in a positive way and reduce their long stays in out-of-home care.

> These are services and activities intended to safely permit a child and his/ her parent(s) to be reunited within the first 15 months after the child was removed from the parent's home and placed in foster care. The services and activities are now stipulated as counseling, substance abuse treatment, assistance to address domestic violence, services to provide temporary child care, and transportation to and from any of these services. The new measure adds the following to these activities: peer-to-peer mentoring, support groups for parents and primary caregivers, and services and activities aimed at facilitating visits and other connections between children in foster care and their parents and siblings.
>
> (Stoltzfus 2011, 3)

The U.S. Department of Health and Human Services received reauthorization to grant waivers to states that want to develop and implement new programs for the purpose of improving services to children in the care and custody of the child welfare system. It is hoped that all children involved in the child welfare system, especially the disproportionate number of children of color, will have improved outcomes as a result of these new and innovative programs. This law also requires states to have policies and procedures to ensure that children in the foster care system are visited by their caseworkers once each month and provides that most of these visits should occur in the homes where the children are placed during their time in out-of-home care. These visits will allow child welfare caseworkers the opportunity to interact with, observe, and assess these children in their home environments.

REFERENCES

American Association of Family and Consumer Services. (2013). *Child care for the 21st century*. Alexandria, VA: Author.

Association of Junior Leagues. (1987). *Highlights of the women to women survey: Findings from 38 communities in the U.S. and Mexico*. New York, NY: Author.

Barth, R. P., & Berry, M. (1990). A decade later: Outcome of permanency planning. In The North American Council on Adoptable Children (Ed.), *The Adoption Assistance and Child Welfare Act of 1980: The first ten years*. St. Paul, MN: The North American Council on Adoptable Children.

Barth, R. P., Courtney, M. E., Berrick, J. D., & Albert, V. (1994). *From child abuse to permanency planning: Child welfare services, pathways and placements*. New York, NY: Aldine de Gruyter.

Bass, S., Shields, M. K., & Behrman, R. E. (2004). Children, families, and foster care: Analysis and recommendations. *The Future of Children, 14*(1), 5–29.

Besharov, D. (1986). The vulnerable social worker. *Children Today, 15*(5), 34–37.

Bowser, B. P., & Jones, T. (2004). *Understanding the over-representation of African Americans in the child welfare system*. Hayward Hills, CA: Urban Institute at California State University.

Center for Law and Social Policy. (2008). *Fostering Connections to Success and Increasing Adoptions Act will improve outcomes for children and youth in foster care*. Washington, DC: Author.

Child Welfare Information Gateway. (2008). *What is child abuse and neglect?* Retrieved from http://www.childwelfare.gov/can/defining/federal.cfm

Child Welfare Information Gateway. (2009). *Definitions of child abuse and neglect: Summary of state laws*. Retrieved from http://www.childwelfare.gov/systemwide/laws_policies/statutes/define.cfm

Child Welfare League of America. (1997). *Summary of the Adoption and Safe Families Act of 1997*. Washington, DC: Author.

Child Welfare League of America. (2001). *Alcohol, other drugs, and child welfare*. Washington, DC: Author.

Courtney, M., Pilliavin, I., Dworsky, A., & Zinn, A. (2001, November). *Involvement of TANF families with child welfare services*. Paper presented at the Association of Public Analysis and Management Research Meeting, Washington, DC.

Crofoot, T. L., & Harris, M. S. (2012). An Indian child welfare perspective on disproportionality in child welfare. *Children and Youth Services Review, 34*, 1667–1674.

Cross, T. (1997). *Understanding the relational worldview in Indian families*. Retrieved from http://www.casanet.org/program-services/tribal/relational-worldview-Indian-families.htm

Emlen, A., Lahti, J., Downs, G., McKay, A., & Downs, S. (1978). *Overcoming barriers to planning for children in foster care*. Portland, OR: Portland State University, Regional Research Institute for Human Services.

Fanschel, D. (1981). Decision-making under uncertainty: Foster care for abused or neglected children. *American Journal of Public Health, 71*(7), 685–686.

Fanschel, D. (1982). *On the road to permanency: An expanded data base for service to children in foster care*. New York, NY: Child Welfare League of America.

Fluke, J. D., Yuan, Y. Y., Hedderson, T., & Curtis, P. A. (2003). Disproportionate representation of race and ethnicity in child maltreatment: Investigation and victimization. *Children and Youth Services Review, 25*, 359–373.

Friedman, M. (n.d.). *Almanac of policy issues: Child care*. Retrieved from http://www.policyalmanac.org/social_welfare/childcare.shtml

Geen, R., & Boots, W. (1997). *The impact of welfare reform on child welfare financing*. Washington, DC: Urban Institute.

Gleeson, J. P., & Craig, L. C. (1994). Kinship care in child welfare: An analysis of states' policies. *Children and Youth Services Review, 16*(1/2), 7–31.

Goerge, R. M. (1990). The reunification process in substitute care. *Social Service Review, 64*(3), 422–457.

Harris, M. S. (1999). Kinship care: Reunification vs. remaining in care. In J. P. Gleeson & C. F. Hairston (Eds.), *Kinship care: Improving practice through research* (pp. 145–166). Washington, DC: Child Welfare League of America.

Harris, M. S. (2004). Best practices in kinship care for African American mothers and their children. In J. E. Everett, S. P. Chipungu, & B. R. Leashore (Eds.),

Child welfare revisited: An Africentric perspective (pp. 156–168). New Brunswick, NJ: Rutgers University Press.

Harris, M. S. (2011). Adult attachment typology in a sample of high-risk mothers. *Smith College Studies in Social Work, 81*(1), 41–61.

Harris, M. S., & Courtney, M. E. (2003). The interaction of race, ethnicity, and family structure with respect to the timing of family reunification. *Children and Youth Services Review, 25*(5/6), 409–429.

Harris, M. S., & Hackett, W. (2008). Decision points in child welfare: An action research model to address disproportionality. *Children and Youth Services Review, 30*(2), 199–215.

Harris, M. S., & Skyles, A. (2005). Working with African American children and families in the child welfare system. In K. L. Barrett & W. F. George (Eds.), *Race, culture, psychology and law* (pp. 91–103). Thousand Oaks, CA: Sage.

Harris, M. S., & Skyles, A. (2008). Kinship care for African American children: Disproportionate and disadvantageous. *Journal of Family Issues, 29*(8), 1013–1030.

Hartman, A. (1993). Introduction: Family reunification in context. In B. Pine, R. Warsh, & A. Maluccio (Eds.), *Together again: Family reunification in foster care* (pp. xv–xxii). Washington, DC: Child Welfare League of America.

Hill, R. B. (2004). Institutional racism in child welfare. In J. E. Everett, S. P. Chipungu, & B. R. Leashore (Eds.), *Child welfare revisited: An Africentric perspective* (pp. 57–76). New Brunswick, NJ: Rutgers University Press.

Hubbell, R. (1981). *Foster care and families: Conflicting values and policies.* Philadelphia, PA: Temple University Press.

Institute of Applied Research. (2004). *Minnesota alternative response evaluation: Select interim evaluation findings.* Retrieved from http://www.arstl.org

Johnson, E. P., Clark, S., Donals, M., Pedersen, R., & Pichott, C. (2007). Racial disparity in Minnesota child protection system. *Child Welfare, 86*, 7–17.

King County Coalition on Racial Disproportionality. (2004). *Racial disproportionality in the child welfare system in King County, Washington.* Seattle, WA: Author.

Kusserow, R. P. (1992). *Using relatives for foster care* (OEI-06-90-02390). Washington, DC: U.S. Department of Health and Human Services, Office of the Inspector General.

Lemon, K., D'Andrade, A., & Austin, M. (2005). *Understanding and addressing disproportionality in the front end of the child welfare system.* Berkeley, CA: Bay Area Social Services Consortium.

Maluccio, A. (1981). Casework with parents of children in foster care. In P. Sinanoglu & A. Maluccio (Eds.), *Parents of children in placement: Perspectives and programs* (pp. 15–31). New York, NY: Child Welfare League of America.

McDermott, J. (2011). *Obama signs child welfare law today, includes McDermott provisions.* Retrieved from http://mcdermott.house.gov/index.php?option=com_content&view=article&id=524:obam

Minkler, M., & Fuller-Thomson, E. (1999). The health of grandparents raising grandchildren: Results of a national study. *American Journal of Public Health, 89,* 1384–1389.

National Association of Black Social Workers. (1994). *Preserving families of African ancestry.* Retrieved from http://www.nabsw.org/mserver/PreservingFamilies.aspx

National Conference of State Legislators. (2010). *Child Abuse Prevention and Treatment Act (CAPTA) Reauthorization Act of 2010.* Washington, DC: Author.

Needell, B., Cuccaro-Alamin, S., Brookhart, A., & Lee, S. (1999). Transitions from AFDC to child welfare in California. *Children and Youth Services Review, 21*(9/10), 815–841.

Nelson-Zlupko, L., Kaufman, E., & Dore, M. M. (1995). Gender differences in drug addiction and treatment: Implications for social work intervention with substance-abusing women. *Social Work, 40*(1), 45–54.

Olsen. L. (1982). Services for minority children in out-of-home care. *Social Services Review, 56,* 572–585.

Paxson, C., & Waldfogel, J. (2002). Work, welfare, and child maltreatment. *Journal of Labor Economics, 20*(3), 435–474.

Peterson, J., Song, X., & Jones-DeWeever, A. (2002). *Life after welfare reform: Low-income single parent families, pre- and post-TANF.* (#D446, Research-In-Brief). Washington, DC: Institute for Women's Policy Research.

Prevent Child Abuse America. (2005). *Fact sheet: The relationship between parental alcohol or other drug problems and child maltreatment.* Chicago, IL: Author.

Roberts, D. E. (2002). *Racial disproportionality in the U.S. child welfare system: Documentation, research on causes, and promising practices.* Baltimore, MD: The Annie E. Casey Foundation.

Ross, M. E. T., & Alday, L. A. (2006). Stress and coping in African American grandparents who are raising their grandchildren. *Journal of Family Issues, 27*(7), 912–932.

Stein, T. J., Gambrill, E. D., & Wiltse, K. T. (1978). *Children in foster homes: Achieving continuity of care.* New York, NY: Holt, Rinehart & Winston.

Stoltzfus, E. (2011). *Child welfare: The Child and Family Services Improvement and Innovation Act (P. L. 112–34).* Washington, DC: Congressional Research Service.

Tatara, T. (1994). Some additional explanations for the recent rise in the U.S. child substitute care population: An analysis of national child care flow data and future research questions. In R. Barth, J. D. Berrick, & N. Gilbert (Eds.), *Child welfare research review* (Vol. 1, pp. 126–145). New York, NY: Columbia University Press.

Testa, M. F. (1992). Conditions of risk for substitute care. *Children and Youth Services Review, 14,* 27–36.

Testa, M. F. (1993). *Home of relative (HMR) program in Illinois: Interim report (Revised).* Chicago, IL: University of Chicago, School of Social Service Administration.

Turner, J. (1984). Reuniting children in foster care with their biological parents. *Social Work, 29*(6), 501–505.

Urban Institute. (2001). *Kinship care: Prevalence, benefits, challenges.* Washington, DC: Author.

U.S. Department of Health and Human Services. (1994). *A guide to the Multiethnic Placement Act as amended by the Interethnic Adoption Provisions of 1996.* Washington, DC: Administration for Children and Families.

U.S. Department of Health and Human Services. (1997). *Study of protective, preventive and reunification services delivered to children and their families.* Washington, DC: Children's Bureau.

U.S. Department of Health and Human Services. (1999). *Blending perspectives and building common ground: A report to Congress on substance abuse and child protection.* Washington, DC: Administration for Children and Families.

U.S. Department of Health and Human Services. (2000a). *Report to Congress on kinship foster care.* Washington, DC: Children's Bureau, Administration on Children, Youth, and Families, Administration for Children and Families.

U.S. Department of Health and Human Services. (2000b). *Temporary Assistance for Needy Families (TANF) program: Third annual report to Congress.* Washington, DC: Administration for Children and Families, Office of Planning, Research, and Evaluation.

U.S. Department of Health and Human Services, Administration on Children, Youth and Families. (2009). *Child maltreatment 2007.* Washington, DC: U.S. Government Printing Office.

U.S. Government Accounting Office. (2005). *Indian Child Welfare Act: Information on implementation issues could be used to target guidance and assistance to states.* Washington, DC: Author.

Washington State Racial Disproportionality Advisory Committee. (2008). *Racial disproportionality in Washington state.* Olympia, WA: Author.

Wulczyn, F. H., & Goerge, R. M. (1992). Foster care in New York and Illinois: The challenge of rapid change. *Social Service Review, 66*(2), 278–294.

2

An International Exploration of Disproportionality

THE UNITED STATES IS not the only country that is faced with the complex problem of racial disproportionality in the child welfare system. Readers will learn that this problem is also pervasive in other places around the world. This chapter will explore the disproportionate number of racial minority children in the child welfare systems in Australia, England, New Zealand, and Canada. These countries were selected for a discourse about disproportionality as a result of communication about this problem with colleagues from the aforementioned areas and availability of data for these geographical locations.

DISPROPORTIONALITY IN AUSTRALIA

In Australia Aboriginal and Torres Strait Islander children, also referred to as Indigenous children, are disproportionately represented in the child welfare system. Aboriginal children and youth are over nine times more likely to be in out-of-home care (Yeo 2003), and Indigenous children as a group continue to be disproportionately represented in out-of-home care placements (Valentine & Gray 2006; Tilbury 2008; Zhou & Chilvers 2010).

Aboriginal and Torres Strait Islander children are also disproportionately represented in all areas of the Australian child protection system and are more likely to have substantiated reports of child maltreatment than other children. "Across Australia, Indigenous children were 7.7 times as likely as other children to be the subject of substantiation in 2009–10. This is a slight increase in the level of over-representation from 2008–09 when

Indigenous children were 7.5 times more likely than other children to be the subject of a substantiation" (Lamont 2011, 5).

Reports of alleged child abuse and neglect are called *notifications* in Australia. However, there is no standardized definition of child abuse and neglect, so there are variations in definition across states and territories. More than one notification may be received for a child. Notifications are most often received from police officers, hospital/health center staff, and school personnel (Lamont 2011). According to Lamont (2011), there were 286,437 reported cases of child abuse and neglect across Australia in 2009–2010; this total represented a 16 percent decrease from the 339,454 reported cases in 2008–2009. In 2009–2010 child protective services (CPS) investigated 131,689 reports of child abuse and neglect and substantiated 46,187 cases (Lamont 2011). The number of substantiated cases of child abuse and neglect declined from 2007–2008 through 2009–2010 (see table 2.1).

The main types of child maltreatment substantiated in Australia are neglect, emotional abuse, physical abuse, and sexual abuse, with the first two being the most common (see table 2.2). Although in the United States it is difficult to substantiate cases of emotional abuse, there is a high rate of substantiated cases in Australia. Australia includes a wide range of behaviors in its definition of emotionally abusive maltreatment (terrorizing, verbally abusing, isolating, rejecting, ignoring, and causing the witnessing of domestic violence), and Holzer and Bromfield (2008) attribute the country's high rates of substantiated cases of emotional abuse to the inclusion of children who witness domestic violence. "When children are exposed to domestic violence, their safety and well-being are at risk; however, there is much controversy among policy makers, child welfare professionals, domestic violence advocates, and service providers regarding whether exposure to domestic violence is considered child abuse or neglect" (Harris 2007, 45–46). Approximately 275 million children worldwide are exposed to domestic violence (Carvel 2006), and evidence does indicate that it is deleterious to any child to witness such violence:

- Children who live with domestic violence not only endure the distress of being surrounded by violence but also are more likely to become victims of abuse themselves. An estimated 40 percent of child abuse victims also have reported domestic violence in the home.

TABLE 2.1   Total Number of Notifications, Investigations and Substantiations Across Australia, 2000–2001 to 2009–2010, and Total Number of Children on Orders and in Out-of-Home Care, June 2000 to 2010

	TOTAL NOTIFICATIONS	TOTAL FINALIZED INVESTIGATIONS	TOTAL SUBSTANTIATIONS	CHILDREN ON ORDERS	CHILDREN IN OOHC
2001–01	115,471	66,265	27,367	19,917	18,241
2001–02	137,918	80,371	30,473	20,557	18,880
2002–03	198,355	95,382	40,416	22,130	20,297
2003–04	219,384	(a)	(a)	(a)	21,795
2004–05	252,831	121,292	46,154	24,075 (c)	23,695
2005–06	266,745	137,829	55,921	26,215 (c)	25,454
2006–07	309,448	(b)	60,230	28,854 (c)	28,379
2007–08	317,526	148,824	55,120	32,642 (c)	31,166
2008–09	339,454	162,259	54,621	35,409 (c)	34,069
2009–10	286,437	131,689	46,187	37,730 (c)	35,895

Notes: (a) Due to the implementation of a new information management system, New South Wales could not provide data for investigation, substantiations or children on orders in 2003–04. (b) Due to the implementation of a new information management system, Queensland was unable to provide investigation data in 2006–07. (c) The data from Victoria for previous years were updated in 2009.

Source: AIHW 2011. Permission to reprint from the Commonwealth of Australia, Australian Institute of Family Studies, Level 20, 485 La Trobe Street, Melbourne VIC 3000, Australia.

TABLE 2.2   Primary Types of Substantiated Maltreatment in Australian States
and Territories, 2009–2010

	NSW	VIC	QLD	WA	SA	TAS	ACT	NT	AUSTRALIA
Emotional abuse	8,984	3.137	2,773	346	793	478	330	251	17,092
Neglect	7,999	472	2,230	646	721	286	282	639	13,275
Physical abuse	4,980	2,468	1,505	330	200	122	89	246	9,940
Sexual abuse	4,285	526	414	330	101	77	40	107	5,880

Source: AIHW 2011. Permission to reprint from the Commonwealth of Australia, Australian Institute of
Family Studies, Level 20, 485 La Trobe, Melbourne VIC 3000, Australia.

- Even when children are not physically abused themselves, their exposure
  to domestic violence can have severe and lasting effects. The impact begins
  early: studies show that younger children are more likely to be exposed to
  domestic violence than older children, and this can impair their mental and
  emotional growth in a critical stage of development.
- As they grow, children exposed to domestic violence continue to face a
  range of possible effects, including trouble with schoolwork, limited social
  skills, depression, anxiety, and other psychological problems. They are at
  great risk for substance abuse, teenage pregnancy, and delinquent behavior.
- The single best predictor of children continuing the cycle of domestic
  violence—either as perpetrators or as victims—is whether they grow up
  in homes with domestic violence. Research shows that rates of abuse are
  higher among women whose husbands either were abused as children or
  saw their mothers being abused. Many studies also have found that children from violent homes show signs of more aggressive behavior, such as
  bullying, and are up to three times more likely to be involved in fighting.
  (UNICEF 2006)

In Australia there appears to a pattern of intergenerational removal of
Indigenous children from their birth families and placement in out-of-
home care compared to other children. The Western Australian Aboriginal
Child Health Survey (completed in 2002) collected data on 5,289 caregivers

and their children, who ranged in age from newborn to seventeen years. Its findings revealed that 20.3 percent of the mothers of the primary caregivers (grandmothers of the children in the survey) and 12.6 percent of the fathers of the primary caregivers (grandfathers of the children in the survey) had been in out-of-home placements and that approximately 12.3 percent of the primary caregivers and 12.3 percent of the secondary caregivers reported being separated from their birth families (Australian Human Rights Commission 2008). Another finding was that 35.3 percent of all Aboriginal children and youth living in Western Australia were living in homes where a caregiver or a caregiver's birth parent had been "forcibly separated" from his or her birth family (Australian Human Rights Commission 2008). Similar intergenerational patterns of removal of children of color from their birth parents and placement in out-of-home care is found in the United States' treatment of its African American and Native American children.

Most (94 percent) of the children in Australia who are removed from their birth families are placed in home-based care. There are three types of home-based care: foster care, relative/kinship care, and other home-based care (private home care that is not foster care and/or relative/kinship care). According to Lamont (2011), there were 11,468 Aboriginal and Torres Strait Islander children in home-based care as of June 30, 2010. Indigenous children were ten times more likely to be placed in such care than other children.

DISPROPORTIONALITY IN ENGLAND

Disproportionality in the child welfare system is also problematic in the United Kingdom. Black and minority ethnic (BME) children are disproportionately represented in the child welfare system in England. According to a Department for Children, Schools and Families report (2009), in England 27 percent of the children in care had BME backgrounds. Owen and Statham (2009) analyzed three datasets of BME children and found as follows: "The patterns of over- and under-representation that have long been reported in national level statistics are also reflected at local authority level. Children from black and minority ethnic groups are represented in these statistics at rates different to their presence in the local population (disproportionality) and at rates different to those for White children locally (disparity) which broadly match the pattern at the national level"

(44). BME families are also disproportionately represented when family group conferencing is offered to families in the child welfare system (Barn, Das, & Sawyerr 2010).

Other findings on children in the child welfare system are as follows:

- All "mixed" (dual/mixed parentage/heritage) ethnic groups are overrepresented (and especially the "other mixed" category).
- Asian children and young people are underrepresented (particularly the Indian group).
- All black groups are overrepresented.
- BME children are more likely than white children to have long-term foster care, rather than adoption, specified in their care plans.
- Children of mixed parentage experienced severe placement disruption compared to their minority ethnic counterparts.
- Over 20 percent of Asian children are considered to be in need due to disability compared with 14 percent of white children, 9 percent of Caribbean children, and 7 percent of mixed parentage children. Asian families, however, are less likely to receive support services, and they have limited knowledge of direct payment assistance.
- BME families report fewer than average support networks compared to white families.
- Social workers may be more likely to think of temporary foster care as the first stage in compulsory care when they provide it for BME children.
- Placement breakdown rates for BME children are no different than those for white children, although the breakdown rates for children of mixed parentage are higher than those for white children.
- There are no significant differences in placement breakdown between BME children placed with carers from a background similar to their own and those placed with white families. When black boys were placed with white families, the relationship was less likely to break down, but the opposite seems true for girls.
- Because ethnicity is very important to black and Asian children, white carers face extra challenges in providing them with necessary support.
- Because many BME foster carers empathize with parents from their own culture who have struggles with adversity, they want to help both parents and child. They often prefer to offer a permanent foster home rather than to adopt. (National Children's Bureau 2009, 1–2)

Race has also been a major factor in services to children and families of color in the child welfare system in the United States. According to Harris and Skyles (2005), "African American children are at a disadvantage regarding the range and quality of services provided, the type of agency to which they are referred, the efficiency with which their cases are handled, the support their families receive, and their eventual outcomes" (95).

There appear to be some discriminatory practices in the care provided to BME children and families.

> Whether we have evidence of "systematic" discrimination or not, we do have plenty of anecdotal and research evidence from service users that discriminative practices are present in children's social care and given that this is incongruent with social work and social care values we have an individual and collective responsibility to work to redress the balance. Uncertainty among children's social care professionals about how to respond appropriately to the needs of BME families compounds other forms of discrimination experienced by BME children and young people in care.
>
> (National Children's Bureau 2009, 2)

There have also been reports that ethnic minority children receive less support and fewer services to help them remain at home and therefore enter the child welfare system earlier (Barn, Sinclair, & Ferdinand 1997; Hunt, Macleod, & Thomas 1999).

DISPROPORTIONALITY IN NEW ZEALAND

The disproportionate number of Maori children in the New Zealand child welfare system has been a major problem for many years. New Zealand law does not require reporting of allegations of child abuse and/or neglect. However, annual notifications to CPS in New Zealand dramatically increased from 6,000 in the 1980s to 71,927 in 2007; these rates surpassed rates in the United States, the United Kingdom, and Australia (Ministry of Social Development 2008). The Children, Young Persons, and Their Families Act of 1989 is the government's major legislation to address this problem. "The driving force behind this legislation—and the implementation of FGDM [family group decision making]—was to address issues of institutional racism experienced by Maori, the country's indigenous people" (Connolly 2004, 1). This legislation focused on the significance of child well-being in the context of family, including the role of the *whanau* (Maori extended family), *hapu* (clan, descent group, or subtribe), and *iwi* (tribe).

Prior to passage of this legislation the Maori extended family and other kinship networks were not recognized or supported by the New Zealand child welfare system. A common practice during the nineteenth century was to place Maori children in residential institutions or in industrial schools if they were destitute, homeless, neglected, or maltreated; if they lived in undesirable surroundings or with "unsavory" companions; or if they were unable to be controlled or committed offenses (Dalley 1998). The industrial schools had the authority to keep children until they were twenty-one years of age. This practice seems parallel to the practice of placing Native American children in boarding schools, "often far from their homes, where they were taught Christianity and vocational skills to assimilate and to 'civilize' them" (Weaver 2005, 87). Even during the 1980s it was common practice to remove Maori children from their families and place them outside their kinship network.

There were approximately 6,000 substantiated cases of child abuse in New Zealand from January through April 2006 (Newman 2006). In 2009 the Department of Child, Youth and Family Services received over 125,000 allegations of child abuse and/or neglect and substantiated over 21,000 of these (Bennett 2010).

A major concern continues to be the disproportionate number of Maori children and children of Pacific Island background who are in the child welfare system. Although Maori children are 24 percent of the child population, they are 35 percent of the children in out-of-home care. In 2005, approximately 76 percent of the children in out-of-home care were in some type of family care placement: specifically, 35 percent in kinship care placements (46 percent of these were Maori children and 48 percent were Pacific Islander children) and 41 percent in nonkinship foster family placements. In that same year over 46 percent of the children in out-of-home care had been in placement for two years or longer. Asian and European children and white (*Pakeha*) children are not disproportionately represented in the child welfare system in New Zealand, but once white children are in care, they tend to remain there longer than Maori children (Department of Child, Youth and Family Services 2005). There has been a concerted effort in New Zealand to move to a "differential response" system in CPS; the goal of this system is to assist families in getting the services and supports they need when a notification/allegation is reported without having an investigation by a social worker (Waldegrave 2005). An integral part of the child welfare system in New Zealand continues to be the family group conference. It is mandated in the 1989 Children, Young Persons and Their Families Act that family members be actively involved in caring for and protecting their children; according to Section 13(b):

> The primary role in caring for and protecting a child or young person lies with the child's or young person's family, whanau, hapu, iwi, and family group, and that accordingly (i) . . . that family should be supported, assisted and protected as much as possible and (ii) intervention into family life should be the minimum to ensure a child's or young person's safety and protection.

It is clear that this law recognizes the significance of the birth family and extended family, as well as the cultural values inherent in the Maori children and families who continue to be disproportionately represented in the New Zealand child welfare system.

DISPROPORTIONALITY IN CANADA

In Canada First Nations children are disproportionately represented in the child welfare system. Disproportionate numbers of these children entered the child welfare system by being victims of the "rescue" movements that were prevalent in Canada. According to Sinclair (2007), during the "Sixties Scoop" many First Nations children were taken into the care and custody of the Canadian child welfare system and adopted by non–First Nations families. First Nations children were also sent to boarding schools as part of the "rescue" movement. MacDonald and MacDonald (2007) state that the children were sent to boarding schools in an effort to provide them with a "better" life than they had in the past. "There can be no doubt of the racist and assimilation underpinnings of the placement of Aboriginal youth in the residential schools." "Even in a racist society most 'helpers' are not openly racist. They can usually justify their actions as contributing to what they consider the common good" (Sullivan & Charles 2010, 3). Although Aboriginal children are only 8 percent of the children in British Columbia, they represent 51 percent of the children in that province's child welfare system (MacDonald 2008).

Research has also shown that as far back as the 1880s and even in the 1930s thousands of "Children of the Empire" were transported from England to Canada via "orphan boats" because they were labeled as poor children (Kohli 2003; Charles & Gabor 2006). Supposedly these children were rescued from their poverty-stricken environments to be placed in the homes of "good" families; however, the "good" families used them as farm workers and as servants.

It is crystal clear that racial disproportionality in child welfare is not a problem unique to the United States. Children of color are also represented at disproportionately high numbers in child welfare systems in other countries. This problem will not be abated until these countries stop blaming children of color and their families for being poor, with the myriad of issues associated with being poor, and get them the resources and services required to preserve their families.

REFERENCES

Australian Human Rights Commission. (2008). *A statistical overview of Aboriginal and Torres Strait Islander peoples in Australia.* Retrieved from http://www.hreoc.gov.au/social_justice/statistics/index.html

Barn, R., Das, C., & Sawyerr, A. (2010). *Family group conference and black and minority ethnic families: A study of two community-based organizations in London.* London, England: The Royal Holloway, University of London.

Barn, R., Sinclair, R., & Ferdinand, D. (1997). *Acting on principle: An examination of race and ethnicity in social services provision for children and families.* London, England: BAAF.

Bennett, P. (2010, August 23). Why you should care about child abuse. *New Zealand Herald,* p. 1.

Carvel, J. (2006, August 14). 1m children in Britain at risk in violent homes. *The Guardian.* Retrieved from http://society.guardian.co.uk/children/story/0,,1844784,00.html

Charles, G., & Gabor, P. (2006). An historical perspective on residential services for troubled and troubling youth in Canada revisited. *Relational Child and Youth Care Practice, 19*(4), 17–26.

Connolly, M. (2004). *Family group decision making: A solution to racial disproportionality and disparities in child welfare.* Englewood, CO: American Humane.

Courtney, M. E., Barth, R. P., Berrick, J. D., Brooks, D., & Parks, L. (1996). Race and child welfare services: Past research and future directions. *Child Welfare, 75*(2), 99–137.

Dalley, B. (1998). *Family matters: Child welfare in 20th century New Zealand.* Auckland, New Zealand: University Press.

Department for Children, Schools and Families. (2009). *Children looked after in England (including adoption and care leavers) year ending 31 March 2009.* London, England: Author.

Department of Child, Youth and Family Services. (2005). *2005 Annual report for the year ending 30 June 2004.* Wellington, New Zealand: Author.

Fanshel, D. (1981). Decision-making under uncertainty: Foster care for abused and neglected children? *American Journal of Public Health, 71*(7), 685–686.

Harris, M. S. (2007). Silent victims: Issues and interventions for children exposed to violence. *Protecting Children, 22*(3/4), 45–53.

Harris, M. S., & Skyles, A. (2005). Working with African American children and families in the child welfare system. In K. L. Barrett & W. H. George (Eds.), *Race, culture, psychology, and law* (pp. 91–103). Thousand Oaks, CA: Sage.

Holzer, P. J., & Bromfield, L. M. (2008). *NCPASS comparability of child protection data: Project report.* Melbourne, Australia: Australian Institute of Family Studies, National Child Protection Clearinghouse.

Hunt, J., Macleod, A., & Thomas, C. (1999). *The last resort: Child protection, the courts and the Children Act.* London, England: The Stationery Office.

Jeter, H. (1963). *Children, problems and services in child welfare programs.* Washington, DC: U.S. Department of Health, Education and Welfare.

Katz, M. R., Hampton, R., Newberger, E. H., & Bowles, R. T. (1986). Returning children home: Clinical decision making in child abuse and neglect. *American Journal of Orthopsychiatry, 56*(2), 253–262.

Kohli, M. (2003). *The golden bridge: Young immigrants to Canada, 1839–1939.* Toronto, Canada: National Heritage.

Lamont, A. (2011). *NCPC resource sheet: Child abuse and neglect statistics.* Melbourne, Australia: Australian Institute of Family Studies, National Child Protection Clearinghouse.

MacDonald, K. A. (2008). *The road to Aboriginal authority in child and family services.* Vancouver, Canada: Canadian Centre for Policy Alternatives.

MacDonald, N., & MacDonald, J. (2007). Reflections of a Mi'Kmaq social worker on a quarter century work on First Nations child welfare. *First Peoples Child and Family Review, 3*(1), 34–45.

Maluccio, A., & Fein, E. (1989). An examination of long-term foster care for children and youth. In J. Hudson & B. Galaway (Eds.), *The state as parent* (pp. 387–400). Dordrecht, The Netherlands: Kluwer Academic.

Ministry of Social Development. (2008). *The statistical report for the year ending June 2008.* Retrieved from http://www.msd.govt.nz/documents/about-msd-and-our-work/publications-resources/statistics/statistical-report-2008.pdf

National Children's Bureau. (2009). *Black and minority ethnic looked after children.* London, England: Author.

Newman, M. (2006, July 2). Maori child abuse crisis. *Newman Weekly,* p. 1.

Olsen, L. (1982). Services for minority children in out-of-home care. *Social Services Review, 56,* 572–585.

Owen, C., & Statham, J. (2009). *Disproportionality in child welfare: The prevalence of black and minority ethnic children within the "looked after" and "children in need" populations and on child protection registers in England.* London, England: Thomas Coram Research Unit, Institute of Education, University of London.

Sinclair, R. (2007). Identity lost and found: Lessons for the Sixties Scoop. *First Peoples Child and Family Review, 3*(1), 65–82.

Sullivan, R., & Charles, G. (2010). *Disproportionate representation and First Nations child welfare in Canada.* Vancouver, Canada: University of British Columbia, School of Social Work.

Tilbury, C. (2008). The over-representation of Indigenous children in the Australian child welfare system. *International Journal of Social Welfare, 18*(1), 57–64.

UNICEF. (2006). *Some of the biggest victims of domestic violence are the smallest.* Retrieved from http://www.unicef.org/media/media_35151.html?q=printme

Valentine, B., & Gray, M. (2006). Keeping them home: Aboriginal out-of-home care in Australia. *Families in Society, 87*(4), 537–545.

Waldegrave, S. C. F. (2005). A differential response model for child protection in New Zealand: Supporting more timely and effective response to notifications. *Social Policy Journal New Zealand, 25,* 32–48.

Weaver, H. N. (2005). *Explorations in cultural competence: Journeys to the four directions.* Belmont, CA: Thomson Brooks/Cole.

Yeo, S. S. (2003). Bonding and attachment of Australian Aboriginal children. *Child Abuse Review, 12,* 292–304.

Zhou, A. Z., & Chilvers, M. (2010). Infants in Australian out-of-home care. *British Journal of Social Work, 40*(1), 26–43.

3

Best Practices/ Promising Practices

THIS CHAPTER WILL EXAMINE BOTH BEST PRACTICES and promising practices in the child welfare system. The first section will provide a discussion of five key decision points in the child welfare process: (1) reporting child abuse and neglect; (2) referring the report for investigation; (3) investigating the referral; (4) removing the child from the home, including the court process; and (5) exiting the system. Prior work has demonstrated that European American children have better outcomes at each of these decisions points than children of color (Caliber Associates 2003; Lemon, D'Andrade, & Austin 2005; Harris & Hackett 2008). The second section will discuss what children need to achieve optimal growth and development. Section three will focus on ecological systems theory and attachment theory, as well as factors in the microsystem that impact outcomes for disadvantaged children of color in the child welfare system. Best practices/interventions that are needed at key decision points when working with children and families of color will be explored. There will also be a discussion of risk factors, particularly the risks for those children of color who enter the system with histories of insecure attachment, severe maltreatment, and early trauma and loss, and what children of color and their families don't have and need vis-à-vis policies and interventions; in addition, protective factors will be examined. Finally, the fourth section will focus on the significance of ongoing cultural sensitivity and competency training for child welfare practitioners, supervisors, administrators, and child protective services (CPS) workers. Examples of a cultural competency self-assessment instrument and a cultural competency training module are included. This section will culminate with the presentation of a best practice case scenario.

KEY DECISION POINTS IN THE CHILD WELFARE SYSTEM

Research has shown that children of color are disproportionately represented and have disproportional outcomes at key decision points in the child welfare system (Hill 2001; Caliber Associates 2003; Bowser & Jones 2004; Hines, Lemon, & Wyatt 2004; Harris & Skyles 2005; Harris & Hackett 2008). The initial key decision point is a call to CPS raising an allegation of child abuse and/or neglect.

Reports of Child Abuse and/or Neglect

The call to CPS to report child abuse and/or neglect can be made by a family member, friend, neighbor, or one of the individuals designated as a mandated reporter (teacher, school counselor, school principal, emergency medical personnel, nurse, physician, psychologist, psychiatrist, medical examiner, dentist, police officer, district attorney or assistant district attorney, substance abuse counselor, social worker, and child care worker). Most reports are made by mandated reporters, who are required by law to report any suspected cases of child abuse and/or neglect to CPS; however, laws vary from state to state. In 2007 approximately 57 percent of child abuse reports came from teachers, lawyers, police officers, and social workers (Iannelli 2010).

Children from any racial or ethnic group can be victims of child abuse and/or neglect. "In 2007 one-half of all victims of child abuse and neglect were white (46.1%), one fifth (21.7%) were African American and one-fifth (20.8%) were Hispanic" (Iannelli 2010, 1). The preponderance of evidence demonstrates that cases involving children of color are reported, investigated, and substantiated and result in the ultimate placement of these children in out-of-home care at higher rates than in cases involving white children; however, rates of child abuse are not higher for children of color when compared to white children.

At the crux of the process for mandated reporters is the legal mandate to report suspected cases of child abuse and/or neglect; the focus is on reporting. There are obviously objective criteria (bruises, slap marks, welts, lacerations, bite marks, scald burns, contact burns [e.g., from cigarettes, irons], and bone injuries) that can be utilized in deciding to make a report to CPS. However, subjective criteria (e.g., family isolation, attitude of parent, lack of financial resources, delays in seeking medical attention for a child due to lack of health insurance) also play a major part in the decision to report allegations of child abuse and/or neglect. The utilization of subjective criteria opens the door for other factors—such as stereotypes, racial biases, prejudices, false assumptions, and misconceptions—to influence the decision to report suspected cases of child abuse and/or neglect to CPS. Exposure/visibility bias has also been identified as a reason for the high rates of reports to CPS by mandated reporters for children of color (Chand 2000).

> According to this view, because children from African American and Native American families are more likely to be poor, they are more likely to be exposed to mandated reporters as they turn to the public social service system for support in times of need. Problems that other families keep private become public as a family receives Temporary Assistance to Needy Families (TANF), seeks medical care from a public clinic, or lives in public housing.
>
> (Cahn & Harris 2005, 6)

Referral of Reports for Investigation and Investigation of Referrals

The second and third key decision points are referral of the report for investigation and investigation of the referral by a CPS worker to determine whether or not to substantiate the allegation after completion of an investigation. Cases involving children of color are opened for investigation and substantiated at higher rates than cases involving white children (King County Coalition on Racial Disproportionality 2004; Lemon, D'Andrade, & Austin 2005; Johnson et al. 2007; Harris & Hackett 2008; Washington State Racial Disproportionality Advisory Committee 2008). There is also evidence of higher substantiation rates of child abuse and/or neglect for Latino or Hispanic children than for non-Hispanic white children (Church, Gross, & Baldwin 2005; Church 2006). Lemon, D'Andrade, and Austin (2005) examined cases in five states and found that African American children had a 90 percent investigation rate versus a 68 percent investigation rate for white children; the rate for Hispanic children was 53 percent, and children of "Other" ethnicities had an investigation rate of 67 percent;

white children always had lower investigation rates in all five states when compared to African American children.

Placement in Out-of-Home Care

Another key decision point in the child welfare system is placement in out-of-home care once a suspected case of child abuse and/or neglect is substantiated. Research has consistently demonstrated that children of color have higher rates of placement in out-of-home care, multiple placements during their time in out-of-home care, and longer stays than white children in out-of-home care. According to the U.S. Department of Health and Human Services (1997), 57 percent of African American children were placed in out-of-home care, but 72 percent of white children remained in their homes and received in-home services. In Washington State African American children and Native American children were more likely than white children to be removed from their homes and placed in out-of-home care, and they remained in out-of-home care longer than white children (Washington State Racial Disproportionality Advisory Committee 2008). Findings from a study in Illinois revealed that 38 percent of white children were placed in out-of-home care compared to 53.7 percent of African American children (Lemon, D'Andrade, & Austin 2005).

The Court System

The court system plays a major role in all child abuse and neglect cases. Dependency court, also referred to as juvenile court and family court, typically has jurisdiction over cases of child abuse or neglect. This court's primary focus is the safety, stability, permanency, and best interest of the child. Judges in dependency court have a responsibility to make decisions that will protect children from risk of future abuse or neglect.

> The initial hearing is the most critical stage in the child abuse and neglect court process. The main purpose of the initial hearing is to determine whether the child should be placed in substitute care or remain with or be returned to the parents pending further proceedings. The critical issue is whether in-home services or other measures can be put in place to ensure the child's safety. At the disposition hearing, the court decides whether the child

needs help from the court and, if so, what services will be ordered. Placement is the key issue at the disposition hearing. The child can be:

- Left with or returned to parents, usually under CPS supervision
- Kept in an existing placement
- Move to a new placement
- Placed in substitute care for the first time if removal was not previously ordered
- As part of its reasonable efforts inquiry, the court needs to scrutinize carefully any CPS recommendation that the child be placed outside the home

(Jones 2006, 4)

Some children and families of color have encountered problems in dependency court. For example, many fathers have been marginalized or ignored. The following is a response from a caseworker who participated in a research study conducted by Johnson and Bryant (2004):

I find amongst African American fathers, even if they have a criminal record that is even fifteen years old, judges will shut down. Whereas if the man [father] is white, the court is more likely to overlook the criminal record, look at his family as well, and think about the resource that the father could be. (178)

There have also been reports of racist practices by judges. For example, a judge in a Texas court threatened a young Latina mother with removal of her child and placement of the child in the father's care unless she agreed to speak only English in her home (Verhovek 1995). Several participants in the King County, Washington, racial disproportionality study (King County Coalition on Racial Disproportionality 2004) said they felt intimidated when interacting with judges, attorneys, and other court officials.

The National Council of Juvenile and Family Court Judges has been proactive in its work to determine what changes need to be made in dependency court to reduce racial disproportionality, as well as disparate treatment for children and families of color.

The complexity and significance of this issue points to the critical need for collaborative efforts to not only further study the factors that contribute to racial disproportionality and disparities in the child welfare system, but to also design and implement specific actions that courts and child welfare system stakeholders can take to reduce these inequities and ultimately improve outcomes for all children and families. The Courts Catalyzing Change: Achieving Equity and Fairness in Foster Care Initiative (CCC) brings together judicial officers and other systems' experts to set a national agenda for court-based training, research, and reform initiatives to reduce the disproportionate representation of children of color in dependency court systems.

(National Council of Juvenile and Family Court Judges 2011, 1)

National studies have repeatedly shown that a large percentage of children enter the child welfare system because of neglect by parents who abuse alcohol and/or drugs. In 1994 Family Dependency Treatment Court was started in Reno, Nevada, to handle cases of child abuse and neglect that involved a birth parent or caregiver who had a substance abuse problem. This model has been replicated in other states across the country. Many of the disproportionate number of children of color involved in the child welfare system have a parent who has a substance abuse problem; the implementation of this model has resulted in lower recidivism rates, decrease in the use of drugs, increase in reunification rates for families because parents are able to regain or able to get custody of their children, increase in education as well as vocational training and job placements for parents involved in family drug court. "Family drug courts emphasize treatment for parents with substance abuse disorders to aid in reunification and stabilization of families affected by parental drug use. These programs apply the adult drug court model to cases entering the child welfare system that include allegations of child abuse or neglect in which substance abuse is identified as a contributing factor" (National Criminal Justice Reference Service 2013, 1).

There have also been issues with state and tribal courts regarding Native American children and families (e.g., variation by state courts in their interpretation of the Indian Child Welfare Act [ICWA] and failure to transfer ICWA cases to tribal courts). "Some state courts have modified the definition of 'Indian child,' in contradiction to the language contained in the federal ICWA, thereby creating exceptions to who is an 'Indian child' and to whom federal protections under ICWA apply" (Horne et al. 2009, 5).

The Pew Commission has made the following recommendations to strengthen dependency courts in this country:

- Courts are responsible for ensuring that children's rights to safety, permanence and well-being are met in a timely and complete manner. To fulfill this responsibility, they must be able to track children's progress, identify groups of children in need of attention, and identify sources of delay in court proceedings.
- To protect children and promote their well-being, courts and public agencies should be required to demonstrate effective collaboration on behalf of children.
- To safeguard children's best interests in dependency court proceedings, children and their parents must have a direct voice in court, effective representation, and the timely input of those who care about them.
- Chief Justices and state court leadership must take the lead, acting as the foremost champions for children in their court systems and making sure the recommendations here are enacted in their states. (Horne et al. 2009, 8–9)

These recommendations have resulted in improvements in dependency courts in many jurisdictions across the country (Edwards 2011; Office of Children & Families 2009; U.S. Children's Bureau 2006); however, there is still work to be done because children and families of color continue to have a disproportionate number of cases in dependency courts in states throughout this country and also continue to receive disparate treatment in many dependency courts.

SERVICE DISPARITIES

Disparities in services are another major challenge for children and families of color once a case has been substantiated for child abuse or neglect and a child is removed from the care and custody of a birth parent and placed in out-of-home care. The weight of the evidence continues to show that race impacts the quantity and quality of services for children and families of color once they enter the child welfare system (Olsen 1982; Close 1983; Maluccio & Fein 1989; Harris & Skyles 2005; Harris & Hackett 2008). According to Olsen (1982), Native American families had the least chance of being recommended to receive services when compared to all other ethnic groups. Courtney et al. (1996) reported a prevailing pattern of racial and ethnic disparity in the provision of child welfare services. According to Cross (2008) and Rivaux et al. (2008), children of color are more likely to be removed from their homes and placed in out-of-home care and less likely to receive services once they enter out-of-home care.

Exiting the Child Welfare System

The final key decision point is exiting the child welfare system. Children of color easily enter the child welfare system in disproportionate numbers when compared to white children. However, they encounter extreme difficulty exiting the system. Johnson et al. (2007) found that when an African American child and a white child enter the child welfare system for the same reason, the odds of reunification for an African American child were 1.19 times the odds for a white child. Findings in a December 2011 Applied Research Center (ARC) report titled *Shattered Families* revealed that the detained or deported families of approximately 5,100 children currently placed in foster care were experiencing "insurmountable barriers" in their family reunification efforts (Cuentame 2011):

> Ovidio and Domitina Mendez lost their five children to foster care when the Georgia Department of Family and Children Services arrived at their home [and] claimed the kids were malnourished. The couple, who are both undocumented immigrants from Guatemala, says they did everything the child welfare agency asked them to do to get their kids back. . . .
>
> According to the family and to advocates in Georgia, the Mendez family are the victims of a biased child welfare system that denies undocumented and non-English speaking mothers and fathers their parental rights. . . .
>
> The ARC investigation . . . found that undocumented parents face bias in the child welfare system, even when parents are not detained or deported. This is partially a result of cultural and language discrimination against immigration parents. Wessler (2011) reports:
>
>> Questioning about English came quickly during the June termination-of-rights hearing, according to court documents. Then came questions about the parents' immigration status.
>>
>> "Describe for the court why even three years after [the children went into the state's custody] you cannot speak English without an interpreter,"

Bruce Kling, special assistant attorney general for Whitfield County Department of Family and Children's Services, said to Domitina Mendez.

"I cannot speak English, but I did—because I did not grow up speaking English," she said through an interpreter. . . .

Though the couple completed the child welfare department's reunification case plan tasks and even the children's attorney believed that the family should have been reunified, the judge who presided over the case ruled to terminate their parental rights. (1)

Findings from Harris and Hackett (2008) revealed that race impacted the availability and delivery of services, resulting in disproportionate numbers of children of color entering the child welfare system and remaining in the system longer when compared to white children.

African American and Native American children are often placed in kinship care when they enter the child welfare system. When children of color are placed in kinship care, these placements often last longer, and these children are impacted by service disparities during their longer stay in these placements. Findings from Needell et al. (2004) revealed the median length of stay in kinship care for children to be as follows: African Americans, 854 days; Hispanics, 649 days; Asians, 539 days; and whites, 546 days. Family reunification is also impacted by family structure, especially for children who are members of single-parent families. Harris and Courtney (2003) found the following in their study of children in the California child welfare system:

- Males were slightly less likely to be reunified than females.
- Infants and adolescents were reunified more slowly than children of other ages.
- Children removed from home because of neglect returned home at a slower rate than children removed for other reasons.
- Child health problems slowed the rate of reunification.
- Children in kinship foster homes and foster family homes returned home more slowly than children in other placement types.
- African American children were reunified at a slower rate than other children.

- Children from two-parent families were returned home more quickly than children from single-parent homes, regardless of the gender of the single parent. (423)

It is clear that children of color continue to be disproportionately represented at each key decision point in the child welfare system from the initial call to CPS to their exit from the system. According to Cross (2008),

> The real culprit appears to be our own desire to do good and to protect children from perceived threats and our unwillingness to come to terms with our own fears, deeply ingrained prejudices, and dangerous ignorance of those who are different from us. These factors cumulatively add up to an unintended race or culture bias that pervades the field and exponentially compounds the problem of disproportionality at every decision point in the system. (12)

OPTIMAL GROWTH AND DEVELOPMENT OF CHILDREN

One of the primary goals of child welfare is preservation of the relationship between children and their parents. This relationship between children and their parents impacts the growth and development of all children, regardless of their racial or ethnic background. Child development is also impacted by socioeconomic status. From a life-span perspective human development, including child development, is based on the following premises: (1) development is a lifelong process, (2) development is multidimensional and multidirectional, (3) development is plastic, (4) development has contextual influences, and (5) development is multidisciplinary (Baltes, Smith, & Staudinger 1997; Smith & Baltes 1999). Key stages in development include infancy, toddlerhood, early childhood, middle childhood, adolescence, early adulthood, middle adulthood, and late adulthood.

Children develop physically, cognitively, emotionally, and socially. Every child develops at her or his own pace. However, a child's early relationships play a crucial role in brain development. According to the National Scientific Council on the Developing Child (2007), children who have healthy and stimulating experiences will have "brain architecture" that maximizes its greatest genetic power; however, when children's lives are filled with adversity, their brain architecture is weakened and cannot operate at maximum capacity. Many children of color have numerous adverse experiences once they enter the child welfare system, and these experiences are harmful to their developing brain architecture.

> The child welfare system is typically characterized by cumbersome and protracted decision-making processes that leave young children vulnerable to the adverse impacts of significant stress during the sensitive periods of early brain development. The powerful and far-reaching effects of severely adverse environments and experiences on brain development make it crystal clear that time is not on the side of the abused or neglected child whose physical and emotional custody remains unresolved in a slow-moving bureaucratic process. The basic principles of neuroscience indicate the need for a far greater sense of urgency regarding the prompt resolution of such decisions as when to remove a child from the home, when and where to place a child in foster care, when to terminate parental rights and when to move towards a permanent placement. The window of opportunity for remediation in a child's developing brain architecture is time-sensitive and time-limited.
>
> (National Scientific Council on the Developing Child 2007, 6)

It is very clear that time is of the essence when decisions are made to remove children from their birth families and place them in out-of-home care, especially children of color who continue to enter the child welfare system in disproportionate numbers and remain in the system for extensive periods of time. The brain is especially reactive to environmental influences during early infancy and childhood. Optimal brain development is promoted by nurturing and responding parents and/or caregivers, good stimulation, and positive environmental experiences. Synapses are being produced by the brain during this period of early growth and development, and they need to be stimulated because a pruning process is also occurring. Synapses are "pruned away" during the stages of childhood and adolescence if they do not receive stimulation (Huttenlocher & Dabholkar 1997).

- The architecture of the brain depends on the mutual influences of genetics, environment, and experience.
- Early environment and experiences have an exceptionally strong influence on brain architecture.

- Different mental capacities mature at different stages in a child's development.
- Sensitive periods occur at different ages for different parts of the brain.
- Stimulating early experiences lay the foundation for later learning.
- Impoverished early experience can have severe and long-lasting detrimental effects on later brain capabilities.
- Stressful experiences impact the functioning and architecture of specific neural circuits in an adverse way.
- Brain plasticity continues throughout life. (National Scientific Council on the Developing Child 2007, 1–4)

It is imperative for child welfare professionals at key decision points in the child welfare system to realize that a child's relationship to her or his birth parents and/or caregivers plays a major role in the development of the child's brain architecture, as well as in her or his developmental outcomes across the life span. Loving, sensitive, and nurturing parents or caregivers are essential for children to have optimal growth and development. Birth parents and/or caregivers must be supported in their efforts to provide a safe and nurturing environment for children to grow and develop to their maximize potential.

ECOLOGICAL SYSTEMS THEORY AND ATTACHMENT THEORY

Ecological Systems Theory

Ecology is the science that focuses on the relationships between organisms and their environments. It facilitates taking a holistic view of individuals and their environments as a unit in which neither can be fully understood except in the context of its relationship to the other. The relationship is characterized by continuous reciprocal exchanges in which individuals and their environments influence and shape each other. Human beings try throughout life for the best fit between themselves and their environment.

Bronfenbrenner's ecological systems theory (1979, 1989, 1993) as well as Bronfenbrenner and Evans (2000) view the individual as developing within a system of interrelationships and interconnections that are impacted by five systems or contexts in the environment. According to this ecological model of human development, each child is at the center of these systems or contexts, which can be conceptualized as environments and which influence each other and are ultimately influenced by culture. This model is also referred to as the bio-ecological model.

The five systems or contexts that influence a child's development are as follows. *Microsystem* refers to a pattern of activities, roles, and interpersonal relations experienced by the developing child in a particular setting. *Mesosystem* refers to the interrelations among two or more settings in which the developing child actively participates. *Exosystem* refers to one or more settings that do not involve the developing child as an active participant; however, events occur in these settings that affect the developing child. *Macrosystem* refers to the culture or subculture of the developing child, along with any belief systems, values, and ideologies and the sociopolitical, historical, economic, and environmental forces that impact the developing child's overall well-being. *Chronosystem* refers to changes and transitions in the child's environment throughout her or his life course (Bronfenbrenner 1986; Bronfenbrenner & Evans 2000; Bronfenbrenner & Morris 1998).

It is important to remember that each child of color who enters the child welfare system is at the center of Bronfenbrenner's ecological system (see figure 3.1), interacting directly with individuals in the microsystem and being impacted by other systems in her or his environment. In addition, all of the aforementioned, including the child, are constantly changing as the child grows and develops.

Ecological systems theory can be used to assess the numerous factors that impact children who enter the child welfare system because of child maltreatment. It is imperative to understand the impact of child maltreatment on the growth and development of children. Ecological systems theory shows all the systems or contexts that affect the developing child before and after entry into the child welfare system.

Attachment Theory

Another theory that is significant in working with the disproportionate number of children of color who enter the child welfare system is attachment theory. Attachment theory grew out of ethology, developmental psychology, and psychoanalysis. According to Bowlby (1969, 1977a, 1977b), attachment is an essential process in human ontogeny and impacts development across the life span. It is essential for a child to have a continuous attachment to a primary caregiver because the child's patterns of attachment impact not

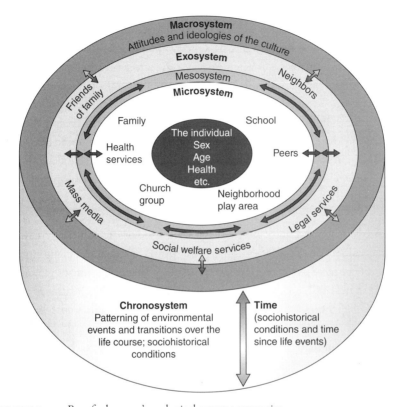

FIGURE 3.1 Bronfenbrenner's ecological systems categories.

Source: J. W. Santrock. (2004). "Bronfenbrenner's Ecological Theory of Development." *Life-Span Development* (p. 55). Boston: McGraw-Hill Higher Education. Permission to Reprint: McGraw-Hill.

only development but also relationships across the life span. Self and object representations begin in childhood and continue throughout adult life. According to Blatt and Lerner (1983), "the development of the representational world into a cohesive and integrated sense of reality initially occurs within the context of the primary caretaking relationship. Eventually this context expands to include significant others" (25). These significant others are part of a "small hierarchy of major caregivers" (Bretherton 1980, 195).

The core of attachment theory is "internal working models" (Bowlby 1973).

In the working model of the world that anyone builds, a key feature is the notion of who his attachment figures are, where they may be found, and how they may be expected to respond. Similarly, in the working model of the self that anyone builds a key feature is his notion of how acceptable or unacceptable he himself is in the eyes of his attachment figures. . . . Confidence that an attachment figure is . . . likely to be responsive can be seen to turn on two variables: (a) whether or not the attachment figure is judged to be the sort of person who in general responds to calls for support and protection; (b) whether or not the self is judged to be the sort of person towards whom . . . the attachment figure is likely to respond in a helpful way. Logically these variables are independent. In practice they are apt to be confounded. As a result, the model of attachment figure and the model of self are likely to develop so as to be complementary and mutually confirming.

(Bowlby 1973, 203–204)

Consequently, the child's internal working models are highly dependent on the caliber of the relationship to the primary caregiver, including the responsiveness of the caregiver to the needs of the child. Although a child can form new relationships during her or his life span, one of the assumptions of attachment theory is that internal working models that begin in the early stage of development tend to be significant as a child grows and develops. "Although these mental representations continue to evolve as individuals develop new relationships throughout their lives, attachment theory assumes that representational models that begin their development early in one's personal history are likely to remain influential" (Harris 2011, 43).

Entry into the child welfare system disrupts the attachment relationship between a child and her or his primary caregiver, usually the child's birth mother, and when this relationship is disrupted and/or lost, the child can experience irreparable harm. Attachment theory can be helpful in understanding the types of attachment that are prevalent in children when they enter the child welfare system. It can also help in understanding children's issues of separation and loss when they experience a disruption in their primary attachment relationship because of placement in out-of-home care as a result of child abuse or neglect.

Ainsworth (1989) discussed the attachment bond as "entailing representation in the internal organization of the individual" (711). The attachment bond is a type of "affectional bond" that is reflective of "the attraction that one individual has for another individual" (Bowlby 1979, 67). According to Ainsworth (1989), the individual is looking for security in her or his attachment bond with another individual. Ainsworth used the Strange Situation technique to study the responses of infants when they were separated from their mothers and their subsequent responses when they were reunited with their mothers. She delineated three types of attachment: "secure," "avoidant," and "ambivalent or resistant" (Ainsworth et al. 1978). Subsequently, Main and Solomon (1986, 1990) discussed the "disorganized/disoriented" type of insecure attachment in their research findings. The attachment research demonstrates the importance of the mother–infant relationship during the first year of life. However, children who enter the child welfare system have experienced some type of child maltreatment, and many of these children have a disorganized/disoriented type of insecure attachment. Family risk factors such as child maltreatment, parental mental illness, and/or parental substance abuse have been linked to an increase in insecure attachment, particularly the disorganized type (Egeland et al. 1991; Lyons-Ruth et al. 1991; Harris 2011).

Main and Goldwyn (1984) developed the Adult Attachment Interview protocol, including a four-category system for classification and scoring; the categories are secure/autonomous, dismissing, preoccupied, and unresolved/disorganized. The aforementioned classifications are important in work with the disproportionate number of children of color entering the child welfare system due to child maltreatment because this process results in the loss of their primary attachment relationship, as well as relationships with other significant family members. Research has also shown a correlation between the attachment classifications of parents and those of children (Main, Kaplan, & Cassidy 1985; Hesse 1999; Riggs & Jacobvitz 2002). These studies show the significance of parental internal working models in forming attachments. Bowlby (1973) stated that one's internal working model is a mental representation that gives one models of the workings, properties, characteristics, and behaviors of attachment figures, the self, others, and the world.

Risks and Resilience for Children Entering the Child Welfare System

There are risk factors associated with entry into the child welfare system and placement in out-of-home care. According to Keyes (2004), "risk factors are causes of undesirable, non-normative outcomes. Put differently, risk factors generate negative change in or persistent (i.e., chronic) poor behavior or functioning" (223). Children who enter the child welfare system experience the loss of a primary caregiver, as well as other members of their family, including siblings; siblings are often separated and placed in separate foster homes. They also experience the loss of their home, school, and neighborhood. For the disproportionate number of children of color entering the child welfare system there is the added risk of multiple foster care placements during their inordinate amount of time in out-of-home placement (Harris & Skyles 2005; Harris & Hackett 2008; Washington State Racial Disproportionality Advisory Committee 2008). Family environmental conditions that are internal (parental substance abuse) or external (parental unemployment) can adversely affect a primary caregiver's or family's ability to provide an environment that is conducive to the optimal growth and development of their at-risk children (Bergen, 1994).

It is a highly traumatic experience for all children who enter the child welfare system—but this is especially true for children of color because many of these children are already high-risk as a result of prior adverse and stressful life events. Furthermore, according to the Substance Abuse and Mental Health Services Administration (2011), children can have problems across their life span if they have a traumatic experience and do not receive any type of treatment or intervention:

- More than 60 percent of youth age seventeen and younger have been exposed to crime, violence, and abuse either directly or indirectly.
- Young children exposed to five or more significant adversities in the first three years of childhood face a 76 percent likelihood of having one or more delays in their cognitive, language, or emotional development.
- As the number of traumatic events experienced during childhood increases, the risk for the following health problems in adulthood increases: depression; alcoholism; drug abuse; suicide attempts; heart and liver disease; pregnancy problems; high stress; uncontrollable anger; and family, financial, and job problems. (1–2)

However, with the appropriate intervention and support resilience can be seen in children when they are faced with a traumatic experience.

A link has been shown between adverse health outcomes in adults and adverse childhood experiences (ACEs)—i.e., physical, sexual, or verbal abuse, as well as family instability, including incarceration, mental illness, and substance abuse—by the Centers for Disease Control and Prevention

(2010). "The high prevalence of ACEs underscores the need for 1) additional efforts at the state and local level to reduce and prevent child maltreatment and associated family dysfunction and 2) further development and dissemination of trauma-focused services to treat stress-related health outcomes associated with ACEs" (Centers for Disease Control and Prevention 2010, 1). Clearly, it is important to focus on resilience for all children who enter the child welfare system. However, a focus on resilience for children of color is important to facilitate better outcomes in light of their past traumatic experiences and the continued disadvantages they will encounter during their long stays in out-of-home care.

Children of color in the child welfare system need to be helped to develop resiliency skills. What is resilience? There are numerous definitions in the literature. Masten and Coatsworth (1998) define resilience as "manifested competence in the context of significant challenges to adaptation or development" (206). Resilience has also been defined by the American Psychological Association as "the ability to adapt well to adversity, trauma, tragedy, threats, or even significant sources of stress" (Pizzolongo & Hunter 2011, 67). Children need protective factors to help them adapt and/or counteract adverse experiences in their lives—to become resilient. Protective factors are highly significant for those children who are at risk for child maltreatment (see table 3.1).

Protective factors can serve as a buffer for children who are at risk for child maltreatment. Sometimes children are at risk but still manage to have positive outcomes when faced with adverse factors in their family and/or environment. When children, even young children, have resilience skills, they react and cope in positive ways (Band & Weisz 1988). However, when children are in an environment that is considered high-risk, protective factors are essential for their physical, social, and emotional survival. Environmental protective factors needed are a stable and close-knit family, including extended family, as well as a strong and viable external system of social support; membership in or linkage to some type of church, faith in a higher source of power, or a sense of spirituality can also serve as a protective factor (Pinkney 1987; Ianni 1989; Wilson 1989; Pearson et al. 1990; Werner 2000). The key to survival for children of color in the child welfare system is the quality of their relationships within and outside their families and the availability of multiple networks of support.

TABLE 3.1   Risk and Protective Factors for Child Maltreatment

	RISK FACTORS	
CHILD RISK FACTORS	FAMILY RISK FACTORS	ENVIRONMENTAL/ COMMUNITY RISK FACTORS
Age	Parental Substance Abuse	High Rates of Crime
Temperament	Parental Mental Illness	High Rates of Unemployment
Physical and/or Developmental Challenges/Illnesses	Social Isolation	Low-Quality Schools
Level of Self-Esteem	Low Socioeconomic Status	Repeated Exposure to Racism, Bias, and Discrimination
Relationship with Primary Caregiver and/or Significant Others	Single Parent with No Social Support System	Lack of Child Care or Low-Quality Child Care
Lack of Social Support	Domestic Violence	Repeated Exposure to Crime/Violence
Poor Peer Relationships	Insecure Parent–Child Attachment	Homelessness
Premature Birth	Parental Stress	Lack of Residential Stability

	PROTECTIVE FACTORS	
CHILD PROTECTIVE FACTORS	FAMILY PROTECTIVE FACTORS	ENVIRONMENTAL/ COMMUNITY PROTECTIVE FACTORS
Good Temperament	Religious Faith or Spirituality	Good Access to Health Care and Social Service Systems
Positive Peer Relationships	Secure Parent–Child Attachment as Well as Stable Parental Relationship	Good Social Connections and Supports in Community
High Intelligence Level	Strong Extended Family Support	Good Schools
Positive Early Social Experiences	Gainfully Employed Parents	Residential Stability with Healthy Communities
Good Developmental History	Good Housing	Middle or High Socioeconomic Status
Good Physical and Mental Health	Consistent Family Rules and Structure	Good Social Capital

The best practice for the disproportionate number of children of color in the child welfare system is for professionals across systems to work from a child- and family-centered frame of reference at each key decision point. Alleviating the problem of the overrepresentation of children of color in the child welfare system does not require development of some type of "magical" program. It requires a paradigm shift from professionals across the board, and that shift means a team approach rather than the current fragmented and turf-based approach.

Many "professionals" are all about exerting their power with each other and especially with clients. Good child welfare practice means working with children and families so they will be empowered to enhance their level of functioning; it does not mean trying to "teach them a lesson" about how much power will be used in a negative way if they fail to do exactly as they are told by their child welfare worker and/or other professionals. Good child welfare practice also means working collaboratively with other professionals, agencies, and organizations in the community to do what is in the best interest of children and their families. For example, at the third key decision point in the child welfare system, when determining whether or not to substantiate an allegation of child abuse or neglect, is a comprehensive assessment of the child completed? The typical modus operandi is to complete some type of risk assessment utilizing a standardized tool—for example, structured team decision making. Of course, it is important to assess for child safety because no child should be in an environment where she or he is subjected to any type of child maltreatment. However, if there are supports within or outside the family that can keep a child and/or sibling group from entry into the child welfare system, it is crucial to do a comprehensive child assessment to identify these supports prior to bringing that child and/or sibling group into the system (see figure 3.2).

Differential Response Systems

The decisions to substantiate an allegation of child abuse and/or neglect and subsequently to remove a child from the care and custody of a birth parent or other family member(s) should be based totally on objective criteria and not based on stereotypes, biases, prejudices, and beliefs about children of color and their racial, ethnic, and/or cultural background; socioeconomic status; or distressed environment. A system of differential

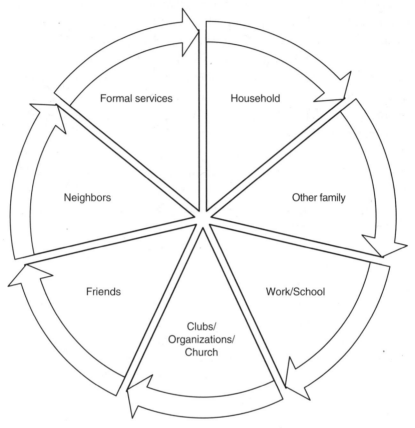

FIGURE 3.2 Social network map.

Source: E. M. Tracy and J. K. Whittaker. (1990). "The Social Network Map: Assessing Social Support in Clinical Practice." *Families in Society: The Journal of Contemporary Social Services, 71*, 461–470. Permission to Reprint: Alliance for Children and Families.

response should be in place for child welfare systems across the country at these key decision points. Yet only twenty-two states in this country have fully or partially implemented some type of differential response.

"Differential response is a CPS practice that allows for more than one method of initial response to reports of child abuse and neglect" (Child Welfare Information Gateway 2008, 3). If a decision is made that a report is not very serious and the family simply warrants further assessment, the family is put on the "assessment track" and given an opportunity to engage in services that are more intense and culturally appropriate (Schene 2001). Differential response is more family-focused and less adversarial. Positive outcomes have been shown for families of color, as well as for white families (Institute of Applied Research 2004).

The following are the basic tenets of differential response systems:

- *Assessment-focused.* The primary focus tends to be on assessing families' strengths and needs. Substantiation of an alleged incident is not the priority.
- *Individualized.* Cases are handled differently depending on families' unique needs and situations.
- *Family-centered.* A strengths-based family engagement approach is used.
- *Community-oriented.* Families on the assessment track are referred to services that fit their needs and issues. This requires the availability and coordination of appropriate and timely community services and presumes a shared responsibility for child protection.
- *Selective.* The alternative response is not employed when the most serious types of maltreatment are alleged—particularly those that are likely to require court intervention, such as sexual abuse or severe harm to a child.
- *Flexible.* The response track can be changed based on ongoing risk and safety considerations. If a family refuses assessment or services, the agency may conduct an investigation or close the case. (Child Welfare Information Gateway 2008, 8)

It greatly benefits children of color if they are assessed prior to making a decision on their entry into the child welfare system. Assessment using a contextual model provides an objective and thorough view that allows analysis of all environmental systems and their reciprocal interactions (see figure 3.3).

Once children of color enter the child welfare system, all work should be directed toward expediting family reunification rather than allowing lengthy stays in the system. Although child welfare systems continue to state their commitment to family reunification, their actions are explicitly contrary to this stated commitment, especially for children of color. These children of color spend longer periods in out-of-home care when compared to white children, they grow up in and age out of the foster care system in substantial numbers, they and their families experience service disparities, they wait an inordinate amount of time for adoption, the services their birth parents receive to facilitate family reunification are lacking or non-existent, and their birth fathers and paternal relatives are not involved in permanency planning.

Child's Name: _____   Date: _____

Social Stage
  (Meeting and greeting the child)
Child's Strengths
  (Child's perspective)
  (Social worker's perspective)
Presenting Problem
  (Clear and concise statement of reason services are being requested for the
  child)
History of Presenting Problem
  (Attempts to solve the problem—self, family, informal, and formal help)
Child's Developmental History
  (Discuss developmental milestones, risk and protective factors—child, family,
  and environmental/community)
Ethnic/Cultural Background
  (Ask the child and family how they identify themselves and do not make
  assumptions based on physical appearance; include any significant extended
  family and/or community support systems)
Religious or Spiritual Beliefs
  (Explore the child's and family's religious and spiritual beliefs, values, and activi-
  ties; identify religious and/or spiritual supports/resources)
Social Supports/Relationships
  (Discuss best friend, peers, persons the child turns to when in need of support,
  qualities that are significant when developing friendships)
Educational History
  (Discuss in detail: Is the child functioning at appropriate grade level? Is the
  child in special education classes?)
Legal History
  (Discuss in detail: Are there custody issues? If so, who has legal custody of the
  child? Are the child and/or family recent immigrants to this country? What
  are the child's feelings regarding current legal/custody status and living
  arrangements? Is the child involved in a case that is currently open in family
  court or juvenile court? Who is the attorney of record?)
Play/Leisure Activities
  (Explore play/leisure activities with the child and family)
Health History
  (Explore past and current status of health, any serious illnesses, hospitalizations,
  etc.)
Client's Role and Social Worker's Role
  (Discuss the role of the child and family, as well as your role in the helping
  process, including informed consent, confidentiality, etc.)
Schedule Next Session
  (Plan date/time for session)

FIGURE 3.3 Child Assessment Format.

One long-standing practice that is definitely not a "best practice" is that of mandating in the service plan that each birth parent in the child welfare system complete a generic parenting course. First of all, it is erroneous to assume that every birth mother or father in the child welfare system needs to complete a generic parenting course. Second, a thorough assessment of parenting skills needs to be made prior to recommending any type of parenting course. Finally, after an objective assessment of parenting skills has been completed and the worker and parent agree that a parenting course is needed prior to family reunification, every parent of color should be referred to a culturally specific or culturally sensitive parenting course. Culturally specific parenting courses include the following: Los Niños Bien Educados, CCICC's Effective Black Parenting Program, and Nurturing Parenting (curriculum materials are available for English, Hispanic, Kreylo, Arab, Hmong, Chinese, and African American families). The Strengthening Families Program is a culturally sensitive parenting program that is not culturally specific; it has proved to be successful with African American, Asian/Pacific Islander, Hispanic, and American Indian families; it has also been translated for work with Chinese, Dutch, French, Russian, Spanish, Portuguese, Swedish, and Thai families. There is also a Strengthening Hawaii's Families Program.

Programs Serving At-Risk Children and Youth

There are a number of programs that are currently serving children and families of color in communities across the country, and for some reason child welfare professionals have been remiss in their utilization of many of these programs. For example, a multitude of churches exist in most high-risk communities that have programs in place for children and families. Yet many child welfare professionals don't bother to explore the communities where they work; consequently, they are clueless as to services that exist outside their sometimes limited referral and/or network system. For example, in Tacoma, Washington, the Greater Christ Temple Church has a child care program for low-income families and a multifaceted youth program that serves over two hundred at-risk youth per week at its Oasis of Hope Center. The First Baptist Church and the Peace Lutheran Church in Tacoma also have numerous programs for at-risk children and youth.

These churches are mentioned because most children and families of color have some type of social support system, including their ties to some type of church or religious organization, when they enter the child welfare system. The church has always been a protective factor in the African American community because of the high level of social support and services that it has provided since slavery. "The church has also provided families with the hope and courage they need to sustain hard times, whether due to limited financial resources or any other form of racially based prejudice and oppression" (Prater 2000, 102). The church has been shown to be a protective factor for African American children and has resulted in documented positive outcomes (Brown & Gary 1991; Hill-Lubin 1991; Zimmerman & Maron 1992; Haight 1998).

Best practice would dictate that child welfare professionals assess for social support whenever children of color and their families enter the child welfare system (see table 3.2 and figure 3.3). The church is a protective factor that can be utilized in a differential response system to keep children of color from entering the system and in permanency planning for the disproportionate number of children of color that have already entered the system.

It is imperative for professionals in the child welfare system to work collaboratively with American Indian Tribes to make sure that services for Indian children are culturally sensitive, as well as culturally appropriate. An example of this type of collaboration is the work that was done by the American Indian Tribes in Washington State and the Children's Administration of the Washington State Department of Social and Health Services. The end result of this work was the Washington State 2012 Indian Child Welfare (ICW) Case Review Tool, which is utilized to evaluate "compliance and quality of practice in meeting the: Federal Indian Child Welfare Act (ICWA); Washington State Indian Child Welfare Act (WSICWA); Children's Administration (CA) ICW policies; Washington State Tribal/ State Agreement and Local Tribal/State agreements" (Federally Recognized Tribes of Washington State & Washington State Department of Social and Health Services, Children's Administration 2012, 2). This evaluative tool is also used to measure the quality of practice, comprehensiveness of service delivery, and cultural competence of case management and other services for American Indian children and their families.

Native American children, youth, and families can receive a range of culturally appropriate services from the Circles of Care program. This federally

TABLE 3.2 Social Network Grid

ID _____

RESPONDENT _____

	AREA OF LIFE	CONCRETE SUPPORT	EMOTIONAL SUPPORT	INFORMATION/ ADVICE	CRITICAL	DIRECTION OF HELP	CLOSENESS	HOW OFTEN SEEN	HOW LONG KNOWN
	1. HOUSEHOLD	1. HARDLY EVER	1. HARDLY EVER	1. HARDLY EVER	1. HARDLY EVER	1. GOES BOTH WAYS	1. NOT VERY CLOSE	0. DOES NOT SEE	1. LESS THAN 1 YEAR
	2. OTHER FAMILY	2. SOMET MES	2. SOMETIMES	2. SOMETIMES	2. SOMETIMES	2. YOU TO THEM	2. SORT OF CLOSE	1. A FEW TIMES A YEAR	2. 1–5 YEARS
	3. WORK/SCHOOL	3. ALMOST ALWAYS	3. ALMOST ALWAYS	3. ALMOST ALWAYS	3. ALMOST ALWAYS	3. THEY TO YOU	3. VERY CLOSE	2. MONTHLY	3. MORE THAN 5 YEARS
	4. ORGANIZATIONS							3. WEEKLY	
	5. OTHER FRIENDS							4. DAILY	
	6. NEIGHBORS								
	7. PROFESSIONALS								
	8. OTHER								

Name #

01
02
03
04
05
06
07
08
09
10
11
12
13
14
15

| 1–6 | 7 | 8 | 9 | 10 | 11 | 12 | 13 | 14 | 15 |

Source: E. M. Tracy and J. K. Whittaker. (1990) "The Social Network Map: Assessing Social Support in Clinical Practice." Families in Society: The Journal of Contemporary Social Services 71, 461–470. Permission to Reprint: Alliance for Children and Families.

funded grant program has been developed and implemented in many tribal and urban Indian communities in this country. This system of care is defined as a coordinated network of community based services and supports that are organized to meet the challenges of children and youth with many needs and their families. In a system of care model, families and youth work in partnership with public and private organizations to design mental health services and supports that are effective, that build on the strengths of individuals and that address each person's cultural and linguistic needs.

(Substance Abuse and Mental Health Services Administration 2010, 1–2)

The following are some of the tribal and urban Indian communities that have implemented Circles of Care: the American Indian Center of Chicago; the Indian Center, Lincoln, Nebraska; the Mashantucket Pequot Tribal Nation; the Standing Rock Sioux Tribe of North Dakota; the Karuk Tribe of California; the Pueblo of San Felipe, New Mexico; and the Crow Creek Tribe of South Dakota. This culturally appropriate program would greatly benefit many of the Native American children who are disproportionately represented in child welfare programs across the country.

Another community service facility with varied programs is the Odessa Brown Children's Clinic in Seattle, Washington. This clinic provides services to a large number of children in the foster care system. It takes a proactive approach in its work with multicultural families to help them discover their voices and where they belong in the world. The clinic was started in 1970 and named in honor of Ms. Odessa Brown, an African American community activist who advocated for quality health care with dignity for children in the central area of Seattle. Ms. Brown and her young children lived in Chicago prior to relocating to the Seattle area. In Chicago she tried to get medical care at a hospital for her health problems but was turned away and denied care because of her race. The mission of the Odessa Brown Children's Clinic is to be "an enduring community partner with a dedication to promoting quality pediatric care, family advocacy, health collaboration, mentoring and education in a culturally relevant context" (Odessa Brown Children's Clinic 2011, 1). Two noteworthy programs at the clinic are Reach Out and Read (ROR) and the Medical-Legal Partnership for Children (MLPC). ROR is a national program developed to increase children's literacy skills; any child who is seen for a well visit at the clinic always leaves the clinic with a new book. Medical providers, social workers, and lawyers work together in the MLPC to address legal problems of patients and families. The program has a full-time attorney who provides free legal services to most families and a training component to teach medical providers and social workers about the legal and advocacy needs of patients and families. The Odessa Brown Children's Clinic provides children and families with a high caliber of comprehensive medical, dental, and mental health services; mentoring; education; and family advocacy in a culturally relevant context.

It is a known fact that extended families in many cultures are ready and willing to be actively involved in making decisions about children who are a significant part of their lives. However, the formalized practice of family group decision making (FGDM) developed as a result of a need to find solutions to the problem of racial disproportionality and disparities in the child welfare system. New Zealand's Children, Young Persons, and Their Families Act mandated the use of FGDM, known there as family group conferencing (FGC), many years ago to deal with institutional racism experienced by the disproportionate number of Maori children in the child welfare system and to facilitate better outcomes for these children (Connolly 2004).

FGDM was implemented in the United States in the early 1990s and is touted as a promising practice to address the pressing problems of disproportionality and disparities in the child welfare system today. Sheets et al. (2009) found that when African American and Hispanic families in Texas participated in FGDM, there was an increase in family reunification, earlier exits from the child welfare system, and more reports of positive experiences by birth parents and extended family members with FGDM than with other child welfare practices. Findings from another study in Texas demonstrated that "32 percent of African American children whose families attended such a conference returned home compared to 14 percent whose families received traditional services" (U.S. Government Accountability Office 2007). FGDM is a practice that is culturally sensitive and congruent with the natural support system that has been prevalent in families of color for many generations.

Merker-Holguin, Nixon, and Burford (2003) analyzed international research on FGDM and reported that the practice provides child safety, it allows a greater percentage of children to stay with their extended family, it results in timely decisions and outcomes, it provides a higher degree of family support and thus improved family functioning, it encourages stability for children as a result of plans, and it protects other family members so family groups are willing to participate in meetings if provided the opportunity.

An exemplary multifamily group program is *FAST* (Families and Schools Together); this evidence- and theory-based program was developed by Dr. Lynn McDonald in 1988 in Madison, Wisconsin. The goals of *FAST* are to increase child well-being, enhance family functioning, prevent the target child from experiencing school failure, increase parental involvement in the child's school, increase social capital, and reduce the stress that parents and children experience from the circumstances of their daily lives (Families and Schools Together n.d.). *FAST* builds protective factors into the child's ecological system by enhancing the child's relationships with other family members, with peers, and with other families, as well as the child's relationships with the school and community.

Twelve to fifteen families participate in a series of eight weekly meetings that are usually held in the evening at a school in the community where the children and families reside. A team of parents and professionals provides activities for the family as a unit, parent and child, parents, peer groups, self-help groups, and the entire group of twelve to fifteen families, utilizing a "fun/play-based approach" (Families and Schools Together n.d., 1). Outcomes for families who have graduated from the eight-week program have been very high—e.g., an 80 percent graduation rate and 50 percent participation in parent-run multifamily meetings for two years after graduation. Parents and teachers reported vast improvements in the home and school functioning of at-risk children who participated in *FAST* for eight weeks. Children of all ages, cultures, and races can participate in *FAST* (Baby *FAST,* Pre-K *FAST,* Kids *FAST,* Middle School *FAST*, and Teen *FAST. FAST* is a most successful program in thirteen countries (Australia, Austria, Canada, England, Germany, Kazakhstan, the Netherlands, Northern Ireland, Russia, Scotland, Tajikistan, the United States (46 states), and Wales.

Finally, it is important to keep in mind that best practice also includes providing services to children and families of color that are culturally relevant. Child welfare professionals must have cultural sensitivity, as well as some level of cultural competence, in their work with children and families of color.

CULTURAL SENSITIVITY AND CULTURAL COMPETENCY

It is imperative for all child welfare professionals to have sensitivity, knowledge, and skills in their work with children of color and their families, who continue to enter and remain in the child welfare system in disproportionate numbers. There is much diversity among the different children of color who are overrepresented in the child welfare system. Diversity is defined by De La Cancela, Jenkins, and Chin (1993) as follows:

> Diversity is the valorization of alternate lifestyles, biculturality, human differences, and uniqueness in individual and group life. Diversity promotes an informed connectedness to one's reference group, self-knowledge, empowering contact with those different from oneself, and an appreciation for the commonalities of our human condition. Diversity also requires an authentic exploration of the client's and practitioner's personal and reference group history. This exploration empowers the therapeutic dyad by providing a meaningful context for understanding present realities, problems of daily living, and available solutions. (6)

There are primary and secondary characteristics that distinguish diversity. Primary characteristics—for example, gender, age, size, and ethnicity—are often visible but can be quite different for varied groups; however, secondary characteristics—for example, socioeconomic status, marital/family status, religion, and education—tend to be invisible and can change (Purnell 2002). Child welfare workers, supervisors, administrators, researchers, and policy makers need to have cultural sensitivity, cultural awareness and self-awareness, and some degree of cultural competency in all facets of work with a diverse group of children of color and their families. There are numerous definitions of cultural competency; however, the following definition seems most appropriate in this discourse regarding racial disproportionality and disparities in the child welfare system:

> Cultural competence comprises behaviors, attitudes, and policies that come together on a continuum that will ensure that a system, agency, program, or individual can function effectively and appropriately in diverse cultural interaction and settings. It ensures an understanding, appreciation, and respect of cultural differences and similarities within, among, and between

groups. Cultural competency is a goal that a system, agency, program or individual continually aspires to achieve.

(U.S. Department of Health and Human Services 2003, 6–7)

One does not attend a conference, workshop, and/or training session and declare herself or himself culturally competent. Cultural competency is a process that takes commitment and work throughout one's life span. No one is expected to know everything there is to know about the many diverse racial, ethnic, and cultural groups that exist in this country today; however, it is crucial to have some level of cultural knowledge, awareness, and competency in order to work effectively with children of color and their families in the context of their culture. Culture is the beliefs, values, and life lessons passed from one generation to another, including language, religion, modes of thinking, and ways of developing and maintaining interpersonal relationships. It is a strength that empowers children and enhances family functioning. It is also a key factor in child welfare practice today.

The child welfare professional's level of cultural competency is significant because it will impact his or her relationships with clients—i.e., children, birth parents, and extended family—and will determine whether or not the professional is able to identify and provide services, interventions, and so on that are culturally relevant to diverse children and families. It is incumbent upon child welfare supervisors and administrators to monitor and evaluate the cultural competence of child welfare workers and other staff that are providing services to children of color and their families. This evaluation should be closely tied to annual performance evaluations for caseworkers and other staff.

According to Cross et al. (1989), cultural competence can be viewed as a developmental process for individuals as well as for organizations/agencies. During this evolving process individuals and organizations are at varied levels of awareness, knowledge, and skills along the Cultural Competency Continuum (see table 3.3). The continuum ranges from cultural proficiency to cultural destructiveness. The six stages along the continuum include (1) cultural destructiveness; (2) cultural incapacity; (3) cultural blindness; (4) cultural pre-competence; (5) cultural competency; and (6) cultural proficiency. An individual or organization/agency should not view the continuum in a linear matter. Individuals or organizations/agencies should always work to increase their level of cultural competence (see table 3.3).

TABLE 3.3   Cultural Competency Continuum

CULTURAL DESTRUCTIVENESS CD	CULTURAL INCAPACITY CI	CULTURAL BLINDNESS CB	CULTURALLY OPEN CO	CULTURALLY COMPETENT CC	CULTURAL PROFICIENCY CP

Cultural Destructiveness	Represents a set of attitudes, practices, and/or policies that is designed to promote the superiority of the dominant culture and that purposefully attempts to eradicate the 'lesser' or 'inferior' culture because it is viewed as 'different' or 'distasteful.'
Cultural Incapacity	Refers to a set of attitudes, practices and/or policies that, while not explicitly promoting the superiority of the dominant culture, adheres, either explicitly or implicitly, to the traditional idea of 'separate but equal' treatment. This naturally breeds segregation and discrimination and eventually institutionalizes such practices. Organizations thus predisposed are therefore incapable of helping ethnic/racial clients or communities.
Cultural Blindness	Refers to a set of attitudes, practices, and/or policies that adheres to the traditional philosophy of being unbiased. Under this paradigm, culture and people are basically all alike, and what works with one culture should therefore work as well with another. The eventual consequence of this belief is to 'make services so ethnocentric as to render them virtually useless to all but the most assimilated people of color.'
Culturally Open	This organization adheres to attitudes, practices, and/or policies that are geared toward learning and receptivity of new ideas and solutions to improve services rendered to one's particular target group. The initiating processes of cultural diversity may begin with the hiring practices of one's staff, staff training in cultural sensitivity, minority representations in the board membership, and so on.
Culturally Competent	These agencies are characterized by a set of attitudes, practices, and/or policies that respects, rather than merely shows receptivity to, different cultures and people. In the process of enhancing their quality of services, such agencies actively seek advice and consultation from clinical/racial communities and actively incorporate such practices into the organization with a sense of commitment.
Cultural Proficiency	A set of attitudes, practices, and/or policies that holds cultural differences and diversity in the highest esteem. Culturally proficient organizations hold a 'proactive' posture regarding cultural differences; their aim is to improve the existing quality of services through active research into cultural issues in preventive and therapeutic approaches that affect the service outcome. They not only engage in the dissemination of such research findings, but also promote improved cultural relations among diverse groups in society through public education and awareness campaigns.
'Cultural'_____	Awareness . . . Sensitivity . . . Competence . . . Appropriateness . . . Relevance . . . Diversity . . . Congruity Multicultural . . . Culturological

Source: Cross, T. L. (1989). *Cultural competency continuum.* Portland, OR: National Indian Child Welfare Association. Reprinted by permission of Terry L. Cross, MSW, Executive Director, National Indian Child Welfare Association.

In working with diverse children and families it is also important for child welfare professionals to have self-awareness. Self-awareness means internal and external knowledge of one's personality traits, attitudes, emotions, biases, preconceived notions, prejudices, history, values, and so on. It is imperative in any type of training for cultural competency to strongly encourage participants to develop self-awareness. Lack of self-awareness will hamper one's efforts to gain the knowledge and skills essential for working effectively with the disproportionate number of children and families of color in the child welfare system. Self-awareness is a powerful connector to one's present as well as to one's past. With a sense of self-awareness child welfare administrators, practitioners, policy makers, and researchers are able to develop and implement plans to work proactively to eliminate disproportionality and disparities in the child welfare system (see the following Self-Assessment Tool).

SOCIAL WORK CULTURAL COMPETENCIES SELF-ASSESSMENT TOOL

This instrument measures your level of cultural competency. Rate yourself on your level of competency on a scale of 1–4: 1 = Definitely; 2 = Likely; 3 = Not very likely; and 4 = Unlikely. Circle the appropriate number.

CULTURAL AWARENESS

1. I am aware of my life experiences as a person related to a culture (e.g., family heritage, household and community events, beliefs, and practices).

Definitely	Likely	Not very likely	Unlikely
1	2	3	4

2. I have contact with individuals, families, and groups of other cultures and ethnicities.

Definitely	Likely	Not very likely	Unlikely
1	2	3	4

3. I am aware of positive and negative experiences with persons and events of other cultures and ethnicities.

Definitely	Likely	Not very likely	Unlikely
1	2	3	4

4. I know how to evaluate the cognitive, affective, and behavioral components of my racism, prejudice, and discrimination.

Definitely	Likely	Not very likely	Unlikely
1	2	3	4

5. I have assessed my involvement with cultural and ethnic people of color in childhood, adolescence, young adulthood, and adulthood.

Definitely	Likely	Not very likely	Unlikely
1	2	3	4

6. I have done or plan to do academic course work, fieldwork, and research on culturally diverse clients and groups.

Definitely	Likely	Not very likely	Unlikely
1	2	3	4

7. I have or plan to have professional employment experiences with culturally diverse clients and programs.

Definitely	Likely	Not very likely	Unlikely
1	2	3	4

8. I have assessed or plan to assess my academic and professional work experiences with cultural diversity and culturally diverse clients.

Definitely	Likely	Not very likely	Unlikely
1	2	3	4

KNOWLEDGE ACQUISITION

9. I understand the following terms: ethnic minority, multiculturalism, diversity, people of color.

Definitely	Likely	Not very likely	Unlikely
1	2	3	4

10. I have a knowledge of demographic profiles of some culturally diverse populations.

Definitely	Likely	Not very likely	Unlikely
1	2	3	4

11. I have developed a critical thinking perspective on cultural diversity.

Definitely	Likely	Not very likely	Unlikely
1	2	3	4

12. I understand the history of oppression and of multicultural social groups.

Definitely	Likely	Not very likely	Unlikely
1	2	3	4

13. I know about the strengths of men, women, and children of color.

Definitely	Likely	Not very likely	Unlikely
1	2	3	4

14. I know about culturally diverse values.

Definitely	Likely	Not very likely	Unlikely
1	2	3	4

15. I know how to apply systems theory and psychosocial theory to multicultural social work.

Definitely	Likely	Not very likely	Unlikely
1	2	3	4

16. I have knowledge of theories of ethnicity, culture, minority identity, and social class.

Definitely	Likely	Not very likely	Unlikely
1	2	3	4

17. I know how to draw on a range of social science theory from cross-cultural psychology, multicultural counseling and therapy, and anthropology.

Definitely	Likely	Not very likely	Unlikely
1	2	3	4

SKILL DEVELOPMENT

18. I understand how to overcome the resistance and lower the communication barriers of a multicultural client.

Definitely	Likely	Not very likely	Unlikely
1	2	3	4

19. I know how to obtain personal and family background information and determine the extent of his or her ethnic/community sense of identity.

Definitely	Likely	Not very likely	Unlikely
1	2	3	4

20. I understand the concepts of ethnic community and practice relationship protocols with a multicultural client.

Definitely	Likely	Not very likely	Unlikely
1	2	3	4

21. I use professional self-disclosure with a multicultural client.

Definitely	Likely	Not very likely	Unlikely
1	2	3	4

22. I have a positive and open communication style and use open-ended listening responses.

Definitely	Likely	Not very likely	Unlikely
1	2	3	4

23. I know how to obtain problem information, facilitate problem area disclosure, and promote problem understanding.

Definitely	Likely	Not very likely	Unlikely
1	2	3	4

24. I view a problem as an unsatisfied want or an unfulfilled need.

Definitely	Likely	Not very likely	Unlikely
1	2	3	4

25. I know how to explain problems on micro, meso, and macro levels.

Definitely	Likely	Not very likely	Unlikely
1	2	3	4

26. I know how to explain problem themes (racism, prejudice, discrimination) and expressions (oppression, powerless, stereotyping, acculturation, and exploitation).

Definitely	Likely	Not very likely	Unlikely
1	2	3	4

27. I know how to find out problem details.

Definitely	Likely	Not very likely	Unlikely
1	2	3	4

28. I know how to assess socioenvironmental stressors, psychoindividual reactions, and cultural strengths.

Definitely	Likely	Not very likely	Unlikely
1	2	3	4

29. I know how to assess the biological, psychological, social, cultural, and spiritual dimensions of a multicultural client.

Definitely	Likely	Not very likely	Unlikely
1	2	3	4

30. I know how to establish joint goals and agreements with the client that are culturally acceptable.

Definitely	Likely	Not very likely	Unlikely
1	2	3	4

31. I know how to formulate micro, meso, and macro intervention strategies that address the cultural and special needs of the client.

Definitely	Likely	Not very likely	Unlikely
1	2	3	4

32. I know how to initiate termination in a way that links the client to an ethnic community resource, reviews significant progress and growth, evaluates goal outcomes, and establishes a follow-up strategy.

Definitely	Likely	Not very likely	Unlikely
1	2	3	4

33. I know how to design a service delivery and agency linkage and culturally effective social service programs in ethnic communities.

Definitely	Likely	Not very likely	Unlikely
1	2	3	4

34. I have been involved in services that have been accessible to the ethnic community.

Definitely	Likely	Not very likely	Unlikely
1	2	3	4

35. I have participated in delivering pragmatic and positive services that meet the tangible needs of the ethnic community.

Definitely	Likely	Not very likely	Unlikely
1	2	3	4

36. I have observed the effectiveness of bilingual/bicultural workers who reflect the ethnic composition of the clientele.

Definitely	Likely	Not very likely	Unlikely
1	2	3	4

37. I have participated in community outreach education and prevention that establish visible services, culturally sensitive programs, and credible staff.

Definitely	Likely	Not very likely	Unlikely
1	2	3	4

38. I have been involved in a service linkage network to related social agencies that ensures rapid referral and program collaboration.

Definitely	Likely	Not very likely	Unlikely
1	2	3	4

39. I have participated as a staff member in fostering a conducive agency setting with a friendly and helpful atmosphere.

Definitely	Likely	Not very likely	Unlikely
1	2	3	4

40. I am involved or plan to be involved with cultural skill development research in areas related to cultural empathy, clinical alliance, goal-obtaining styles, achieving styles, practice skills, and outcome research.

Definitely	Likely	Not very likely	Unlikely
1	2	3	4

INDUCTIVE LEARNING

41. I have participated or plan to participate in a study discussion group with culturally diverse social work educators, practitioners, students, and clients on cultural competency issues, emerging cultural trends, and future directions for multicultural social work.

Definitely	Likely	Not very likely	Unlikely
1	2	3	4

42. I have found or am seeking new journal articles and textbook material about cultural competency and culturally diverse practice.

Definitely	Likely	Not very likely	Unlikely
1	2	3	4

43. I have conducted or plan to conduct inductive research on cultural competency and culturally diverse practice, using survey, oral history, and/or participatory observation research methods.

Definitely	Likely	Not very likely	Unlikely
1	2	3	4

44. I have participated or will participate in the writing of articles and texts on cultural competency and culturally diverse practice.

Definitely	Likely	Not very likely	Unlikely
1	2	3	4

What are your questions and views on cultural competency and cultural competencies?

What are your reactions to this self-assessment instrument?

Please add up your scores on the 44 self-assessment items. Then identify and circle your level of cultural competency on the following list.

Level 1: Definitely (scores 43–95)

Level 2: Likely (scores 96–128)

Level 3: Not Very Likely (scores 129–171)

Level 4: Unlikely (scores 172 and over)

Source: D. Lum. (1999). "Social Work Cultural Competencies Self-Assessment." In *Culturally Competent Practice: A Framework for Growth and Action* (pp. 183–189). Pacific Grove, CA: Brooks/Cole Publishing Company. Permission to Reprint: Cengage Learning/Nelson Education.

Cultural Competency Training

Training for cultural competence is a continuous and lifelong process. The following is an example of a five-day cultural competency training module.

CULTURAL COMPETENCY TRAINING MODULE

Day 1

Introductions

Define Culture and Aspects of Culture

Discuss Meaning and Relevance of Cultural Competency in Child Welfare

Discuss Cultural Competency Continuum—Refer to table 3.3

(Participants will review the continuum and decide where they are on it and why. There are six stages along the continuum (cultural destructiveness; cultural incapacity; cultural blindness; cultural pre-competence; cultural competence; and cultural proficiency).

Measure Participants' Level of Cultural Competency—Refer to Self-Assessment Tool

Video: *Knowing Who You Are* (Casey Family Programs 2005)

(This video explores the importance of race and ethnicity, as well as the importance of integrating racial and ethnic identity in child welfare practice. Racism, white privilege, and diversity are also explored.)

Day 2

Undoing Racism Training

(This session is facilitated by trainers from the People's Institute for Survival and Beyond—a national and international institution of multiracial and antiracism community organizers and educators from New Orleans, LA, http://www.pisab.org/who-we-are.)

Day 3

Continuation of Undoing Racism Training

(This session is facilitated by trainers from the People's Institute for Survival and Beyond.)

Day 4

Discuss the Ethnographic Interview

(An ethnographic interview consists of descriptive and structural questions and allows clients to give "a vivid description of their life experiences" [Westby, Burda, & Mehta 2003, 1].)

Participants Role-Play Ethnographic Interviewing

Example Question from Interviewer: What is your tribal affiliation?

Example Reply from Respondent to Question: Well, I'm affiliated with the Yakima Tribe, the Puyallup Tribe, and the Colville Tribe. When you talk about the cultural end of it, my family feels very strongly about being Native American. But we are not like the stereotype of reservation Native Americans like you see on TV. I went to school here in Tacoma, Washington, and have always lived here. My family is not connected in the stereotypical way.

Interviewer: That is a very interesting way of looking at it. For people you know who think of themselves as Native American, what makes them "not connected"?

Discuss Principles for Identifying Cultural Characteristics of an Individual or a Family—Refer to Sloan (1991)

Day 5

Discuss Microaggressions in Race, Ethnicity, and Sexual Orientation—Refer to Sue (2010)

Measure Level of Cultural Competence—Refer to Self-Assessment Tool

Video: *The Color of Fear* (Wah 1994)

(This video provides a cogent discussion of racism and the state of race relations in America as seen through the eyes of eight North American men.)

Debriefing for Participants Regarding Training

Complete Training Evaluation Forms

The following is a case study of Ms. C and her children, who were involved with the child welfare system for approximately two years prior to family reunification.

Case Study

Ms. C, a twenty-five-year-old, white single mother, was referred for an assessment and psychotherapy to the Department of Psychiatry at a large university in the Midwest by her social worker from a private child welfare agency.

Ms. C had been mandated by the courts to get an assessment and psycho-therapy if she wanted to be reunited with her children. During her intake interview she revealed that she was depressed because her children had been removed from her care and placed in the home of her maternal aunt. She stated that a neighbor called the CPS office because her children had been left home alone for two days. Her children—a nine-year-old daugh-ter and two sons, ages five and three—were removed from her care nine months ago. Ms. C reported a history of drug abuse but is currently receiv-ing outpatient treatment for her substance abuse problem. She informed the intake worker that her goal was to remain drug-free and eventually have her children returned to her care.

Ms. C's case was assigned to a therapist for psychotherapy. At the ini-tial meeting Ms. C was adamant that the only reason she was in this office was "because that Judge Sands told me I had to come here." The therapist informed Ms. C that their sessions were confidential; however, she was a mandated reporter, and if any information was revealed during their ses-sions regarding the abuse and/or neglect of a child or children, she would have to make a report to CPS. Ms. C stated that she understood and knew "all about you mandated reporters." Ms. C was also informed that if she ever stated that she was planning to harm herself or any other individual, the therapist would have to notify the authorities.

The therapist shared information with Ms. C about her educational background and clinical practice experiences, as well as other practice experiences, including her experiences with the child welfare system. Ms. C immediately started to ask questions when the therapist mentioned that she had worked as a social worker, supervisor, and administrator in the child welfare system. At this point the therapist explained to Ms. C that it would be helpful to her if she would be willing to share some information about herself. The therapist further explained to Ms. C that information about her background would be helpful in their work together.

"I don't trust you, and I definitely don't trust the system."

The therapist spent time talking about trust and what both of them needed to do in order to build a therapeutic alliance.

"What do you mean by a therapeutic alliance?" "Never heard anyone use those words with me."

The therapist told Ms. C that a therapeutic alliance meant their working relationship.

"Oh, now I understand."

Patients come to therapy with positive expectations and hopes for the therapeutic relationship, and they come with fears about the consequences of the
relationship and even dread at the possibility of failure for their wishes for
acceptance and growth. This mixture of feelings and attitudes, this expression of patients' selves, constitutes the contextual transference and is present
from the beginning of the therapy. If the contextual transference is positive,
the therapist will experience the patient as trusting, open, collaborative, and
perhaps grateful. In the countertransference to the contextual relationship,
the therapist will feel benignly regarded, positively valued, or simply useful in the positive way that a loved mother feels securely valued most when
taken for granted. The assumption of this willingness and intention to be
helpful will lend something of a rosy glow to the relationship. If the contextual transference contains a predominance of negative elements—fear
of persecution, scorn, or envy—the therapist will find the patient suspi-
cious, untrusting, quick to criticize or express feelings of being criticized, or
spoiling and rejecting of the therapist's efforts. In this negative contextual
situation, the therapist's countertransference will consist of a sense of rejec-
tion and devaluation, frustration and disregard. In reaction, therapists may
wish to be rid of the patients and may feel depressed, hopeless, or angry
much of the time. In the ordinary situation, the contextual transference is
a mixture of positive and negative elements, although there will usually be a
prevailing attitude with noticeable fluctuations.

(Scharff 1992, 54–55)

According to Zetzel (1989), there is a correlation between transference
and the therapeutic alliance. The goal of the therapist here was to establish
a positive therapeutic alliance with Ms. C. Ms. C stated that she had an
older sister who was thirty-one years of age and a younger brother who was
seventeen years of age. She never knew her birth father.

"He left us when I was two years old and never returned." "I was raised by
my alcoholic mother and my stepfather who sexually abused me." "Don't you
ask me about the sexual abuse because I don't want to talk about it now."

The therapist told Ms. C that she did not have to talk about her sexual
abuse today and the decision as to when she talked about it would be left to
her. However, at some point in their work together it would be helpful to
Ms. C to talk about the abuse.

"I like the way you think, lady."

This initial session ended with a plan for the therapist to see Ms. C the next week at the same time and Ms. C and the therapist would develop a treatment plan for Ms. C together. This treatment plan was developed during the next session by the therapist and Ms. C.

Many birth parents do not have an opportunity to actively participate in the permanency planning process for their children. In a subsequent session Ms. C informed her therapist that she was simply given a case plan by her child welfare worker and told that she had to sign the plan. Of course, this is definitely not good child welfare practice. All birth parents must be involved in their case plans from the time their children are removed from their care and placed in the care and custody of the child welfare system until their children are reunified with them, if reunification is in the best interest of the children, or until another permanency goal is reached that is in the best interest of the children. According to Rzepnicki and Stein (1985), the likelihood of family reunification is higher if caseworkers engage the child's birth parents early in the life of the case; negotiate a goal-oriented, time-limited service plan with the parents; and provide services to parents to assist them in their reunification efforts. The therapist realized right away that her role as a psychotherapist would have to include advocacy for this birth mother in the reunification process.

Ms. C spent the next few sessions talking about her children and how much she loved them. She stated that she missed her children but realized that she was not ready to assume the parental role at this time. There was a high level of tension between Ms. C and her aunt because her aunt did not want her to have parent–child visits.

"Judge Sands said I can visit my children as long as I am not high on drugs. I have not used any drugs for the past six months and go to the drug treatment center twice a week. I have a drug counselor and also attend my group meeting every week."

The therapist informed Ms. C that she knew how important it was for birth parents and their children to maintain their relationship when the children are placed in kinship care or foster care. They discussed the importance of Ms. C scheduling a meeting with the child welfare worker to make her aware of the parent–child visitation problem. Ms. C stated that she had a new child welfare worker and had never met her. She also stated that this was her third worker since the placement of her children with their maternal aunt. Frequent change in caseworkers is common in child welfare, and this lack of continuity is not good for children and families. However, even if there is a change in caseworkers, it is important for children to maintain the attachment relationship with birth parents and other family members.

> Regularly scheduled visits are valuable, as a means of helping the child maintain his or her sense of connectedness and identity with the biological family. Even when children cannot live with their biological parents, they continue to belong to them. . . . Regardless of the outcome (of care), their sense of roots and heritage should be theirs to keep. This identity is best preserved when regularly scheduled visits are planned and encouraged.
>
> (Maluccio, Fein, & Olmstead 1986, 164)

Ms. C and the therapist subsequently decided that it would be in her best interest to meet her new child welfare worker and try to develop a positive relationship with her. In the meantime Ms. C continued to come for psychotherapy sessions once per week. Among the issues explored during these sessions were the following: Ms. C's sense of self, her past relationship with the father of her children and other men in her life (including adult attachment issues), her relationship with her mother, her continued relationship with her children, and her relationship with her Aunt Mary, the kinship caregiver. Her relationship with her mother was a negative one because her mother introduced her to drugs, including marijuana and crack cocaine. Ms. C also blamed her mother for not protecting her from being sexually abused by her stepfather when she was eight years of age. Although she told her mother about the sexual abuse the first time it happened, her mother stated, "You are lying about John; he would never do such a thing." Ms. C received psychotherapy for a year to address sexual abuse during her childhood.

Ms. C stated that until her mother stops drinking and using drugs, she will not attempt to have a relationship with her. She also disclosed that once she became a teenager, her older sister revealed that their stepfather had also sexually abused her. Their mother "kicked John out of the house" when her sister revealed that he had also sexually abused her. Ms. C stated that although her mother has repeatedly stated, "I am sorry for not believing you," Ms. C is not "emotionally ready to deal with her mother because I have to get my children back."

Ms. C continued her substance abuse treatment and regular urine analysis because these things were stipulated in her court order. Her case was eventually transferred to a private child welfare agency that had a contract with the Department of Children and Family Services. Once again, she had a new caseworker. However, the new caseworker decided that since she was adhering to her case plan and drug-free, she would be allowed to have supervised visits in the parent–child visitation room at the child welfare agency; parent–child visits were held at the child welfare agency because the relationship between Ms. C and her Aunt Mary were still contentious, to say the least. When Ms. C discussed her relationship with her Aunt Mary, she stated that earlier in her life the two of them had a "real good relationship." However, the relationship fell apart when Ms. C started using drugs and neglecting her children. According to Ms. C, her aunt still believes she is a drug user and a "bad mother." At this point in their work the therapist requested that Ms. C sign a release of information form in order for her to have a conference call with the child welfare worker; the purpose of this call was to request that the child welfare worker have a family conference with Ms. C and her Aunt Mary.

Another recommendation by the therapist was that Ms. C, her children, and her Aunt Mary attend a new program at the Department of Psychiatry for families involved in kinship care. The impetus for this recommendation was that the three children were being caught up in family dynamics and this was unfair to them. Conflictual relationships between family members are not uncommon in kinship care placements. The therapist hoped that Ms. C and her aunt would be able to work on their relationship during sessions in the kinship care program because the family dynamics were hindering the family reunification process. The therapist felt that it was important for Ms. C and her family to have access to as many services as possible to facilitate that process. So many children in kinship care placements and their families, especially children of color and their families, are unaware of available services and supports, fail to receive services and supports, or receive a lower caliber of services than children and families in other types of placements.

Research has shown that children and kinship caregivers do not get the services and supports that they need to help them (Dubowitz 1990; Berrick, Barth, & Needell 1994 Harris & Hackett 2008; Harris & Skyles 2008). However, this case study was the exception and not the rule. The new kinship program included assessments for the family, kinship caregiver, birth parent(s), and children. This eight-week, intensive group treatment program included three different groups (birth parents' group, children's group, and kinship caregivers' group). Problems that were distinct to birth parents, children, and kinship caregivers were addressed in these groups. At the termination of the group there was a celebration, including graduation with certificates for all family members. Ms. C and Aunt Mary were able to greatly improve their relationship by participating in this program. Both of them commented about how beneficial it was to them when birth parents and kinship caregivers had several meetings together. They also expressed positive feelings about having an opportunity to give and receive support from other families in the program. After the eight-week, intensive group program ended, Aunt Mary attended the four-week relative caregiver support/follow-up group, Ms. C attended the four-week birth parent support/follow-up group, and her children attended the four-week support/follow-up group for children.

Ms. C was assisted in her search for employment by her counselor at the substance abuse treatment center; her counselor helped her get a full-time job working as a cook in a local restaurant. She stated that her long-term goal was to return to school and become a registered nurse. She had already graduated from high school and attended a community college for a year and a half.

After several court hearings Ms. C was finally able to have unsupervised visits with her children at her small apartment. She was informed by her child welfare worker that she needed to get a larger apartment or a house before her children could be returned home. Her anxiety increased about trying to locate affordable housing in such a large city. Her child welfare worker suggested that she would help in the search for affordable housing, and the DCFS caseworker stated that Ms. C would be given a furniture voucher once she was able to find "suitable housing." Ms. C's application for Section 8 housing was approved; her current landlord told her that he had a three-bedroom apartment in another housing complex that he would rent to her because he accepted Section 8 tenants. Once Ms. C moved to the three-bedroom apartment, she was allowed to keep her children overnight.

Eventually her children were allowed to spend the weekends with her at her new apartment. Ms. C's child welfare worker and the DCFS caseworker informed Ms. C that they would be recommending "return home" at the next court hearing. Ms. C and her children were attending family therapy sessions with another therapist at the Department of Psychiatry who was working to address issues of separation and loss, as well as issues that might surface once the family achieved its permanency goal of family reunification. The case plan stipulated that Ms. C and her children would continue family therapy for six months after family reunification. Ms. C was highly successful in achieving her individual therapy goals, including work focused on her trauma as a result of childhood sexual abuse. Therefore, psychotherapy was terminated at the end of two years. The therapist submitted a final report to the court concurring with the recommendation of family reunification for Ms. C and her children.

Ms. C and her children were finally reunited after a two-year placement of the children in kinship care. Ms. C continued to attend an outpatient substance abuse group at the drug treatment center. This case was subsequently closed by the DCFS office. Ms. C married a man that she met at her church. The two of them continue to provide a loving and nurturing home for her two sons; her older son is enrolled in a community college, and her younger son will graduate from high school next year. Ms. C's daughter has graduated from college and teaches elementary school in another state.

This reunification was successful because Ms. C, a young white birth mother, and her children, as well as the kinship caregiver, received support and services before and after family reunification. It is imperative to remember that family reunification is a process that requires strong supportive relationships among the birth parents, children, kinship caregiver, child welfare caseworker, and other services providers. Family reunification is an emotional as well as a physical process. Children who are reunified with their birth parents after placement in kinship care are less likely to reenter the child welfare system than children placed in traditional foster care (Courtney & Needell 1997; Conway & Hutson 2007; Harris & Skyles 2005, 2008; Harris & Hackett 2008).

Would there have been a different outcome in this case if the children, birth mother, and kinship caregiver had been African American, Native American, or some race other than white? Studies have demonstrated differences in services received by children and families based on race (Jeter 1963; Fanshel 1981; Olsen 1982; Katz et al. 1986; Maluccio & Fein 1989; Courtney et al. 1996; Harris & Hackett 2008). It is imperative to remember that race, culture, and ethnicity do matter at all key decision points in the child welfare system from the point of entry to the point of exit.

REFERENCES

Ainsworth, M. D. S. (1989). Attachments beyond infancy. *American Psychologist, 44*, 709–716.

Ainsworth, M. D. S., Blehar, M. C., Waters, E., & Wall, S. (1978). *Patterns of attachment: A psychological study of the Strange Situation*. Hillsdale, NJ: Erlbaum.

Baltes, P. B., Smith, J., & Staudinger, U. M. (1997). Life-span theory in developmental psychology. In R. M. Lerner (Ed.), *Handbook of child psychology: Theoretical models of human development* (5th ed., Vol. 1, pp. 1029–1143). New York, NY: Wiley.

Band, E. B., & Weisz, J. R. (1988). How to feel better when it feels bad: Children's perspectives on coping with everyday stress. *Developmental Psychology, 24*, 247–253.

Bergen, D. (1994). *Assessment methods for infants and toddlers: Transdisciplinary team approaches*. New York, NY: Teachers College Press, Columbia University.

Berrick, J. D., Barth, R. P., & Needell, B. (1994). A comparison of kinship foster homes and family foster homes: Implications for kinship care as family preservation. *Children and Youth Services Review, 16*(1/2), 33–63.

Blatt, S. J., & Lerner, H. (1983). The psychological assessment of object representation. *Journal of Personality Assessment, 47*, 7–28.

Bowlby, J. (1969). *Attachment and loss: Attachment* (Vol. 1). New York, NY: Basic Books.

Bowlby, J. (1973). *Attachment and loss: Separation* (Vol. 2). New York, NY: Basic Books.

Bowlby, J. (1977a). The making and breaking of affectional bonds. *British Journal of Psychiatry, 130*, 201–210.

Bowlby, J. (1977b). The making and breaking of affectional bonds. *British Journal of Psychiatry, 130*, 421–431.

Bowlby, J. (1979). *The making and breaking of affectional bonds*. London, England: Tavistock.

Bowser, B. P., & Jones, T. (2004). *Understanding the over-representation of African Americans in the child welfare system: San Francisco*. Hayward, CA: Urban Institute.

Bretherton, I. (1980). Young children in stressful situations: The supporting role of attachment figures and unfamiliar caregivers. In G. V. Coelho & P. I. Ahmed (Eds.), *Uprooting and development* (pp. 179–210). New York, NY: Plenum Press.

Bronfenbrenner, U. (1979). *The ecology of human development: Experiments by nature and design*. Cambridge, MA: Harvard University Press.

Bronfenbrenner, U. (1986). Ecology of the family as a context for human development: Research perspectives. *Developmental Psychology, 22*, 723–742.

Bronfenbrenner, U. (1989). Ecological systems theory. In R. Vasta (Ed.), *Annals of child development* (Vol. 6, pp. 187–251). Greenwich, CT: JAI Press.

Bronfenbrenner, U. (1993). The ecology of cognitive development: Research models and fugitive findings. In R. H. Wozniak & K. W. Fischer (Eds.), *Development in context* (pp. 3–44). Hillsdale, NJ: Erlbaum.

Bronfenbrenner, U., & Evans, G. W. (2000). Developmental science in the 21st century: Emerging questions, theoretical models, research designs and empirical findings. *Social Development, 9*(1), 115–125.

Bronfenbrenner, U., & Morris, P. A. (1998). The ecology of developmental processes. In R. M. Lerner (Ed.), *Handbook of child psychology: Theoretical models of human development* (Vol. 1, pp. 535–584). New York, NY: Wiley.

Brown, D. R., & Gary, L. E. (1991). Religious socialization and educational attainment among African Americans: An empirical assessment. *Journal of Negro Education, 3*, 411–426.

Cahn, K., & Harris, M. S. (2005). Where have all the children gone? A review of the literature on factors contributing to disproportionality: Five key child welfare decision points. *Protecting Children, 20*(1), 4–14.

Caliber Associates. (2003). *Children of color in the child welfare system: Perspectives from the child welfare community*. Washington, DC: U.S. Department of Health and Human Services.

Casey Family Programs. (Producer). (2005). *Knowing who you are* [DVD]. Available from http://www.casey.org

Centers for Disease Control and Prevention. (2010, December 17). Adverse childhood experiences reported by adults—five states, 2009. *Morbidity and Mortality Weekly Report (MMWR)*, pp. 1–5.

Chand, A. (2000). The over-representation of black children in the child protection system: Possible causes, consequences and solutions. *Child and Family Social Work, 5*, 67–77.

Child Welfare Information Gateway. (2008). *Differential response to reports of child abuse and neglect*. Washington, DC: U.S. Department of Health and Human Services.

Church, W. T. (2006). From start to finish: The duration of Hispanic children in out-of-home placements. *Children and Youth Services Review, 28*, 1007–1023.

Church, W. T., Gross, E. R., & Baldwin, J. (2005). Maybe ignorance is not always bliss: The disparate treatment of Hispanics within the child welfare system. *Children and Youth Services Review, 27*(12), 1279–1292.

Close, M. M. (1983). Child welfare and people of color: Denial of equal access. *Social Work Research and Abstracts, 19*(4), 13–20.

Connolly, M. (2004). *Fifteen years of family group conferencing: Coordinators talk about their experiences in Aotearoa, New Zealand.* Unpublished research report, University of Canterbury, Christchurch, New Zealand.

Conway, T., & Hutson, R. Q. (2007). *Is kinship care good for kids?* Washington, DC: Center for Law and Social Policy.

Courtney, M. E., Barth, R. P., Berrick, J. D., Brooks, D., & Parks, L. (1996). Race and child welfare services: Past research and future directions. *Child Welfare, 75*(2), 99–137.

Courtney, M. E., & Needell, B. (1997). Kinship care: Rights and responsibilities, services, and standards. In J. D. Berrick, R. Barth, & N. Gilbert (Eds.),*Child welfare research review* (Vol. 2, pp. 193–219). New York, NY: Columbia University Press.

Cross, T. L. (2008). Disproportionality in child welfare. *Child Welfare, 87*(2), 11–20.

De La Cancela, V., Jenkins, Y. M., & Chin, J. L. (1993). Diversity in psychotherapy: Examination of racial, ethnic, gender, and political issues. In J. L. Chin, V. De La Cancela, & Y. M. Jenkins (Eds.), *Diversity in psychotherapy: The politics of race, ethnicity, and gender* (pp. 5–15). Westport, CT: Praeger.

Dubowitz, H. (1990). *The physical and mental health and educational status of children placed with relatives: Final report.* Baltimore: University of Maryland.

Edwards, L. (2011). *Court improvement in child abuse and neglect cases: A historical perspective.* Seattle, WA: National CASA Association.

Egeland, B., Erickson, M., Butcher, J., & Ben-Porath, Y. S. (1991). MMPI-2 profiles of women at risk for child abuse. *Journal of Personality Assessment, 57,* 254–263.

Families and Schools Together. (n.d.). *Building relationships for children's mental health.* Madison, WI: Author.

Fanshel, D. (1981). Decision-making under uncertainty: Foster care for abused and neglected children? *American Journal of Public Health, 71*(7), 685–686.

Federally Recognized Tribes of Washington State & Washington State Department of Social and Health Services, Children's Administration. (2012). *Washington State 2012 Indian Child Welfare Care Review Tool.* Olympia, WA: Author.

Haight, W. L. (1998). "Gathering the spirit" at First Baptist Church: Spirituality as a protective factor in the lives of African American children. *Social Work, 43*(3), 213–221.

Harris, M. S. (2011). Adult attachment typology in a sample of high-risk mothers. *Smith College Studies in Social Work, 81*(1), 41–61.

Harris, M. S., & Courtney, M. E. (2003). The interaction of race, ethnicity, and family structure with respect to the timing of family reunification. *Children and Youth Services Review, 25*(5/6), 409–429.

Harris, M. S., & Hackett, W. (2008). Decision points in child welfare: An action research model to address disproportionality. *Children and Youth Services Review, 30*(2), 199–215.

Harris, M. S., & Skyles, A. (2005). Working with African American children and families in the child welfare system. In K. L. Barrett & W. H. George (Eds.), *Race, culture, psychology, and law* (pp. 91–103). Thousand Oaks, CA: Sage.

Harris, M. S., & Skyles, A. (2008). Kinship care for African American children: Disproportionate and disadvantageous. *Journal of Family Issues, 29*(8), 1013–1030.

Hesse, E. (1999). The adult attachment interview: Historical and current perspectives. In J. Cassidy & P. R. Shaver (Eds.), *Handbook of attachment: Theory, research, and clinical applications* (pp. 395–433). New York, NY: Guilford Press.

Hill, R. (2001). *Disproportionality of minorities in child welfare: Synthesis of research findings*. Washington, DC: Westat.

Hill-Lubin, M. A. (1991). The African American grandmother in autobiographical works by Frederick Douglass, Langston Hughes, and Maya Angelou. *International Journal of Aging and Human Development, 33*, 173–185.

Hines, A. M., Lemon, K., & Wyatt, P. (2004). Factors related to the disproportionate involvement of children of color in the child welfare system: A review and emerging themes. *Children and Youth Services Review, 26*, 507–527.

Horne, A., Travis, T., Miller, N. B., & Simmons, D. (2009). *Court reform and American Indian and Alaskan Native children: Increasing protections and improving outcomes*. Reno, NV: National Council of Juvenile and Family Court Judges.

Huttenlocher, P. R., & Dabholkar, A. S. (1997). Regional differences in synaptogenesis in the human cerebral cortex. *Journal of Comparative Neurology, 387*, 167–178.

Iannelli, V. (2010). *Child abuse statistics*. Retrieved from http://pediatricsabout .com/od/childabuse/a/05_abuse_stats.htm

Ianni, F. A. J. (1989). *The search for structure*. New York, NY: Free Press.

Institute of Applied Research. (2004). *Minnesota alternative response evaluation: Select interim evaluation findings*. Retrieved from http://www.iarstl.org

Jeter, H. (1963). *Children, problems and services in child welfare programs*. Washington, DC: U.S. Department of Health, Education and Welfare.

Johnson, E. P., Clark, S., Donald, M., Pedersen, R., & Pichott, C. (2007). Racial disparity in Minnesota child protection system. *Child Welfare, 86*(4), 5–20.

Johnson, W. E., Jr., & Bryant, V. D. (2004). Unwed African American fathers' participation in child welfare permanency planning: Caseworkers' perspectives. In J. E. Everett, S. P. Chipungu, & B. R. Leashore (Eds.), *Child welfare revisited: An Africentric perspective* (pp. 169–191). New Brunswick, NJ: Rutgers University Press.

Jones, W. G. (2006). *Working with the courts* (p. 4). Washington, DC: Office of Child Abuse and Neglect, Children's Bureau.

Katz, M., Hampton, R., Newberger, E. H., & Bowles, R. T. (1986). Returning children home: Clinical decision making in child abuse and neglect. *American Journal of Orthopsychiatry, 56*(2), 253–262.

Keyes, C. L. M. (2004). Risk and resilience in human development: An introduction. *Research in Human Development, 1*(4), 223–227.

King County Coalition on Racial Disproportionality. (2004). *Racial disproportionality in the child welfare system in King County, Washington*. Seattle, WA: Author.

Lemon, K., D'Andrade, A., & Austin, M. (2005). *Understanding and addressing disproportionality in the front end of the child welfare system*. Berkeley, CA: Bay Area Social Services Consortium.

Lyons-Ruth, K., Repacholi, B., McLeod, S., & Silva, E. (1991). Disorganized attachment behavior in infancy: Short-term stability, maternal and infant correlates. *Development and Psychopathology, 3*, 397–412.

Main, M., & Goldwyn, R. (1984). *Adult attachment scoring and classification system*. Unpublished manuscript, University of California at Berkeley.

Main, M., Kaplan, N., & Cassidy, J. (1985). Security in infancy, childhood and adulthood: A move to the level of representation. In I. Bretherton & E. Waters (Eds.), Growing points of attachment theory and research. *Monographs of the Society for Research in Child Development, 50*(1–2, Serial No. 209), 66–106.

Main, M., & Solomon, J. (1986). Discovery of a new, insecure-disorganized/disoriented attachment pattern. In T. B. Brazelton & M. Yogman (Eds.), *Affective development in infancy* (pp. 95–124). Norwood, NJ: Ablex.

Main, M., & Solomon, J. (1990). Procedures for identifying infants as disorganized/disoriented during the Ainsworth Strange Situation. In M. T. Greenberg, D. Cicchetti, & E. M. Cummings (Eds.), *Attachment in the preschool years: Theory, research, and intervention* (pp. 121–160). Chicago, IL: University of Chicago Press.

Maluccio, A., & Fein, E. (1989). An examination of long-term foster care for children and youth. In J. Hudson & B. Galaway (Eds.), *The state as parent* (pp. 387–400). Dordrecht, The Netherlands: Kluwer Academic.

Maluccio, A., Fein, E., & Olmstead, K. (1986). Working with children. In *Permanency planning for children: Concepts and methods* (pp. 156–169). New York, NY: Tavistock.

Masten, A. S., & Coatsworth, J. D. (1998). The development of competence in favorable and unfavorable environments: Lessons from research on successful children. *American Psychologist, 53*(2), 205–220.

Merkel-Holguin, L., Nixon, P., & Burford, G. (2003). Learning with families: A synopsis of FGDM research and evaluation in child welfare. *Protecting Children, 18*(1 & 2), 2–11.

National Council of Juvenile and Family Court Judges. (2011). *Courts catalyzing change.* Reno, NV: Author.

National Criminal Justice Reference Service. (2013). *Drug courts* (p.1). Washington, DC: U. S. Department of Justice.

National Scientific Council on the Developing Child. (2007). *The timing and quality of early experiences combine to shape brain architecture: Working paper no. 5.* Retrieved from http://www.developingchild.harvard.edu

Needell, B., Webster, D., Curraco-Alamin, S., Armijo, M., Lee, S., Lery, B., . . . Kim, H. (2004). *Child welfare services reports for California.* Retrieved from http://cssr.berkeley.edu/CWSCMSreports/

Odessa Brown Children's Clinic. (2011). *Our mission.* Seattle, WA: Author.

Office of Children & Families in Courts. (2009). *Court improvement project.* Harrisburg, PA: Author.

Olsen, L. (1982). Services for minority children in out-of-home care. *Social Services Review, 56,* 572–585.

Pearson, J., Hunter, A., Ensminger, M. E., & Kellam, S. G. (1990). Black grandmothers in multi-generational households: Diversity in family structure and parenting involvement in the Woodlawn community. *Child Development, 61,* 434–442.

The People's Institute for Survival and Beyond. (2011). *Who we are: Our mission and history.* Retrieved from http://www.pisab.org/who-we-are

Pinkney, A. (1987). *Black Americans* (3rd ed.). New York, NY: Prentice Hall.

Pizzolongo, P. J., & Hunter, A. (2011, March). I am safe and secure: Promoting resilience in young children. *Young Children,* 67–69.

Prater, G. (2000). Child welfare and African-American families. In N. A. Cohen (Ed.), *Child welfare: A multicultural focus* (2nd ed., pp. 87–115). Needham Heights, MA: Allyn & Bacon.

Purnell, L. (2002). The Purnell model for cultural competence. *Journal of Transcultural Nursing, 13*(3), 193–196.

Riggs, S. A., & Jacobvitz, D. (2002). Expectant parents' representations of early attachment relationships: Associations with mental health and family history. *Journal of Consulting and Clinical Psychology, 70*, 195–204.

Rivaux, S. L., James, J., Wittenstrom, K., Baumann, D., Sheets, J., Henry, J., & Jeffries, V. (2008). The intersection of race, poverty and risk: Understanding the decision to provide services to clients and to remove children. *Child Welfare, 87*(2), 151–168.

Rzepnicki, T., & Stein, T. J. (1985). Permanency planning for children in foster care: A review of projects. *Children and Youth Services Review, 7*(2–3), 95–108.

Scharff, D. E. (1992). Contextual and focused transference and countertransference. In *Redefining the object and reclaiming the self* (pp. 29–65). Northvale, NJ: Jason Aronson.

Schene, P. (2001). Meeting each family's needs: Using differential response in reports of child abuse and neglect. *Best Practice Next Practice, 2*(1), 1–24.

Sheets, J., Wittenstrom, K., Fong, R., James, J., Tecci, M., Baumann, D. J., & Rodriguez, C. (2009). Evidence-based practice in family group decision-making for Anglo, African American and Hispanic families. *Children and Youth Services Review, 31*(11), 1187–1191.

Sloan, M. B. (1991). Principles for identifying cultural characteristics of an individual or family. In *Children, culture, and ethnicity* (pp. 79–81). New York, NY: Garland.

Smith, J., & Baltes, P. B. (1999). Life-span perspectives on development. In M. H. Bornstein & M. E. Lamb (Eds.), *Developmental psychology: An advanced textbook* (4th ed., pp. 275–311). Mahwah, NJ: Erlbaum.

Substance Abuse and Mental Health Services Administration. (2010, November/December). Circles of care. *SAMHSA News, 18*(6), 1–2.

Substance Abuse and Mental Health Services Administration. (2011). *Building resilience in children and youth dealing with trauma*. Rockville, MD: Author.

Sue, D. W. (2010). *Microagressions in everyday life: Race, gender, and sexual orientation*. New York, NY: Wiley.

Tracy, E. M., & Whittaker, J. K. (1990). The social network map: Assessing social support in clinical practice. *Families in Society: The Journal of Contemporary Social Services, 71*, 461–740.

U. S. Children's Bureau. (2006). *Working with the courts in child protection user manual series* (#9). Washington, DC: Author.

U.S. Department of Health and Human Services. (1997). *National study of protective, preventive, and reunification services delivered to children and families.* Washington, DC: Children's Bureau.

U.S. Department of Health and Human Services. (2003). *Definitions in the compendium of cultural competence initiatives in health care.* Retrieved from http://bhpr.hrsa.gov/diversity/culcomp.htm

U.S. Government Accountability Office. (2007). *African American children in foster care: Additional HHS assistance needed to help states reduce the proportion in care.* Retrieved from http://www.gao.gov/new.items/d07816.pdf

Verhovek, S. H. (1995, August 30). Mother scolded by judge for speaking Spanish. *New York Times.* Retrieved from http://www.nytimes.com/

Wah, L. M. (Director). (1994). *The color of fear* [DVD]. Available from Stir Fry Productions, 1904 Virginia Street, Berkeley, CA 94709.

Washington State Racial Disproportionality Advisory Committee. (2008). *Racial disproportionality in Washington State.* Olympia, WA: Author.

Werner, E. E. (2000). Protective factors and individual resilience. In M. Shonkoff & S. J. Meisels (Eds.), *Handbook of early childhood intervention* (2nd ed., pp. 113–134) New York, NY: Cambridge University Press.

Wessler, S. F. (2011, November 30). Georgia couple fights to regain custody of kids. *Colorlines News for Action* (p. 1).

Westby, C., Burda, A., & Mehta, Z. (2003, April 29). *Asking the right questions in the right way: Strategies for ethnographic interviewing.* Retrieved from http://www.asha.org/about/publications/reader-online/archives/2003/q2/f030429b.htm

Wilson, M. N. (1989). Child development in the context of the black extended family. *American Psychologist, 44,* 380–385.

Zetzel, E. (1989). Therapeutic alliance in the analysis of hysteria. In *The capacity for emotional growth* (pp. 182–196). New York, NY: International Universities Press.

Zimmerman, M. A., & Maron, K. I. (1992). Life-style and substance use among male African American urban adolescents: A cluster analytic approach. *American Journal of Community Psychology, 20,* 121–138.

4

Child Welfare System Change

THIS CHAPTER WILL CRITIQUE the child welfare system and provide proactive steps that can be taken to address institutional racism, disproportionality, and disparities in any child welfare organization/agency whose goal is equitable treatment for all children and families. A measurement instrument will be included to assess disproportionality in child welfare organizations/agencies. The chapter will conclude with narrative interviews with individuals who discuss their experiences with the child welfare system. Interviewees include a birth mother, a birth father, a former foster parent and kinship caregiver, a former juvenile court judge, an executive director of a private child welfare agency and adoptive mother, an adoptive mother, a female alumnus of the foster care system, and a male alumnus of the foster care system.

HISTORY OF CHILD WELFARE IN UNITED STATES

The child welfare system is a human service organization that has existed for decades; evolution of this organization has been predicated on the ever-changing attitudes and beliefs regarding the government's role in protecting and caring for children who experience child abuse and/or neglect. It is imperative to reflect on the history of the child welfare system in order to provide a context for change in the current child welfare system. According to Lewis, Packard, and Lewis (2007), the goals of human service organizations are always focused on making life better for the populations they serve. Although the stated goals of the child welfare system are focused on improving the lives of children and families involved in the system, children of color do not receive equitable services to improve their lives once they enter the child welfare system.

> Child welfare, in its broader and ideal sense, should be concerned with the general welfare of all children. This has never really been true of the child welfare endeavors in this country. Like other American social welfare endeavors, child welfare efforts have been predicated on the belief that institutionalized services need be extended to only a small segment of the population, because individuals can ordinarily be expected to perform the functions of these services for themselves. In the case of children, the American society expects that children's fundamental needs for survival, sustenance, and socialization will be met through functions performed by their parents. Only when their parents fail them—and it is expected that not many parents will so fail—does it become necessary for society, through special institutionalized services, to assume responsibility for meeting these needs. This narrow concept of child welfare is the system's definition, its historical basis, and its major failure.
>
> (Billingsley & Giovannoni 1972, 4)

In the 1700s children whose birth parents could not provide care for them and orphans served as indentured servants for families. Almshouses were prevalent in large cities in the 1800s; many children, including some African American children, lived in almshouses. The first orphanages were also established in the early 1800s, but policy prohibited African American children from living in these orphanages prior to the Civil War. In 1836 Anna Shotwell and Martha Murray established the Association for the Benefit of Colored Orphans in New York; the purpose of this orphanage was to save African American children from the "real dangers" that were prevalent in the almshouse.

> One chilly spring day when Miss Anna Shotwell and her step-niece, Miss Martha Murray, were walking along Cherry Street, near where the base of the Brooklyn Bridge now stands, they saw two miserable looking little Negro children huddling on the steps of a dilapidated house. Inquiries revealed that the children were orphans, being kept—"cared for" were scarcely the proper words to describe their state—by a woman in the neighborhood. The

woman was too poor herself to continue this help for long, and it seemed that the next step for the little waifs was the Almshouse. There were, at that time, three orphanages in New York City for white children, as well as the Long Island Farms, a public institution for white orphans. But for the Negro orphan there was only the public Almshouse. The discrimination against those unfortunate children was a matter of great concern to Miss Shotwell and Miss Murray. Being Quakers, they shared strong feelings of that group that all men, women and children were equal and should have equal rights in society. Nor was it enough for them simply to deplore this situation. They wanted to do something about it. Emptying their purses, they instructed the woman to keep the two children for a few days until some plan could be made for their future care. . . .

When the two women returned to Cherry Street a few days later, they found not two, but six orphans. That the number of their charges could triple in a few days made Miss Shotwell and Miss Murray realize that their personal benevolence was not going to be equal to the problem. At this point the idea of an asylum for Negro children came into being, and work to bring it into effect was started.

(Leonard 1956, as cited in Billingsley & Giovannoni 1972, 27–28)

It is apparent that a disparity in services has existed for African American children since the beginning of the child welfare system in this country. "In one sense it might be said that until 1865 slavery was the major child welfare institution for Black children in this country, since that social institution had under its mantel the largest number of Black children" (Billingsley & Giovannoni 1972, 23).

However, African American children are not alone when tracing the history of the U.S. child welfare system and the racist, discriminatory, and disparate practices that have been used with children of color from the beginning of the system to the present time. Native American children have also been the victims of discriminatory and biased practices when involved in the child welfare system. "As part of the assimilation campaign promulgated by the federal government, beginning in the late 1800s, it became U.S. social policy to remove Native American children from their families and communities and educate them in distant boarding schools. In these schools, children were forbidden to speak their languages, practice their religions, or practice any of their cultural traditions.

Rather than helping, at times services have been destructive" (Weaver 2005, 12). Boarding schools had a most deleterious effect on Native American children and families.

The concern about the long-term impact on their well-being for children growing up in orphanages prompted private agencies to begin placing orphans with foster families. Children placed in foster homes worked for their foster families and remained in placement until they were adults; the foster families did not receive any type of board payment for children in foster care (Billingsley & Giovannoni 1972). A foster home study or background check was completed prior to placement of children with these foster families.

Charles Loring Brace founded the Children's Aid Society in New York in 1853 and initiated a formalized system of foster care placements that were family-focused. By the early 1900s the first state laws were enacted for the prevention of child abuse and neglect. The first White House Conference on the Care of Dependent Children was held in 1909, and the U.S. Children's Bureau was established in 1912. Today all states have enacted laws not only prohibiting child abuse and neglect but also mandating its reporting, investigation, and treatment. The policies and procedures for reporting allegations of child abuse and neglect to child protective services (CPS) are found in these reporting laws.

It is important to note that the first juvenile court was established in 1899 in Illinois. According to Flicker (1982), "The most significant fact about the history of juvenile justice is that it evolved simultaneously with the child welfare system. Most of its defects and its virtues derive from that fact" (29). Juvenile courts have jurisdiction over juvenile delinquency cases, and most juvenile courts also adjudicate child welfare cases that involve child abuse, neglect, and dependency. In some states juvenile courts are known as family courts and have jurisdiction over adoption, legal guardianship, emancipation, establishment of paternity, child custody, child support, and parent–child visitation.

INSTITUTIONAL RACISM AND THE CHILD WELFARE SYSTEM

The stated commitment of the child welfare system to family preservation and prevention of placement of children in out-of-home care unless the children are unsafe and at risk continues. However, this commitment seems an anomaly when one examines the facts and figures regarding the disproportionately large numbers of children of color who continue to be removed from the care of their birth parents and placed in out-of-home care; these children experience much difficulty exiting the child welfare system and being reunified with their birth families. "African American/ Black children continue to be the most overrepresented racial group in the United States [in foster care]. . . . Native American children are overrepresented in foster care at a rate of 2.2 times their rate in the general population" (Padilla & Summers 2011, 7–8). Unfortunately institutional racism continues to prevail in the child welfare system and must be addressed if the child welfare system is indeed truly committed to preserving families and eradicating the problem of racial disproportionality. The child welfare system should be focused on family preservation for all children and not just white children, who enter the system in smaller numbers and have early exits from the system.

It is time for the child welfare system to seriously examine any and all racist practices that have existed in this system for decades and to end any institutional and individual racism that continues to be perpetuated from the point of entry to the point of exit. According to Miller and Garran (2008), "*Institutional racism* indicates systemic, durable racism that is embedded in institutions, organizations, laws, customs, and social practices" (29). Billingsley and Giovannoni (1972) explored three types of white institutional racism in their groundbreaking work regarding black children and the child welfare system: (1) negative view of black people; (b) exclusion of black people from development, participation, and control of institutions that impact the lives of black people; and (c) exclusion of black people from services and supports. There is a link among institutional racism, sexism, and classism; this type of racism is prevalent toward poor families that are headed by women of color (Hill 2004). Many of these poor women of color and their children are involved in the child welfare system. However, findings from prior studies show that poverty and substance abuse are not explanations for the racial disparities experienced by children and families of color that are involved in the child welfare system (McRoy 2004). "'It's no coincidence that the community of color, particularly African Americans and Native Americans, are overrepresented,' said Raymond Reyes, associate vice president for diversity at Gonzaga University. 'It's symptomatic of the historical legacy of racism in this country'" (Graman 2007, 3). Institutional racism of any type is wrong—and certainly not in the best interest of any child in the child welfare system.

Miller and Garran (2008) further note that "Individual and institutional racism coexist side by side and also are interactive; they potentiate one another" (30). Therefore, it is prudent for individual racism to be examined within any child welfare organization/agency. Racial bias in decision making was reported by individuals (caseworkers, child welfare supervisors, judicial officers) who participated in focus groups in Oregon as well as in Washington State (King County Coalition on Racial Disproportionality 2004; Harris & Hackett 2008; Miller et al. 2010). "The real culprit appears to be our own [white social workers'] desire to do good and to protect children from perceived threats and our unwillingness to come to terms with our fears, deeply ingrained prejudices, and ignorance of those who are different from us" (Cross 2008, 11). It is not an easy task for some white social workers and other professionals in the child welfare system to work with children and families of color because their backgrounds and life experiences have been confined to the white world of power and privilege. They come to work in the child welfare system with an entirely different worldview than that of the children and families of color involved in the system. They also come with their own biases, stereotypes, and prejudices about children and families of color that often impact the decisions they make regarding children and families of color. This type of decision making is indeed problematic for children and families of color, as well as for the child welfare worker.

Child welfare workers, regardless of their background and sometimes limited experiences with children and families of color, must value and respect the many faces of diversity and recognize the significance of culture in their work. Otherwise, they will be prone to engage in cultural racism. "Cultural racism is the overarching umbrella under which both individual and institutional racism flourish. It is composed of a worldview that contains a powerful belief: the superiority of one group's cultural heritage over another" (Sue 2010, 141). Cultural racism or any other type of racism is inherently wrong and unacceptable in work with children and families of color in the child welfare system.

DIVERSITY AND CULTURAL COMPETENCE IN THE CHILD WELFARE SYSTEM

All children in the child welfare system, especially the disproportionate number of children of color in the system, would greatly benefit from a system that is committed to diversity and cultural competence and that embraces rather than negates the role of culture in the daily lives of children and families in the system.

A culturally competent agency is one that emphasizes the strengths inherent in all cultures, respects cultural differences, and effectively incorporates cultural knowledge into service provision. The goal of equal and nondiscriminatory services is included in cultural competence, but true cultural competence goes further to ensure that service provision is responsive to the cultural needs of clients. Cultural competence also involves working in partnership with natural, informal support and networks within communities, such as neighborhood centers; religious institutions; day care programs; cultural arts; music and after school programs; and extended family networks. A commitment to cultural competence is most likely to pervade agency practice if it begins with a formal statement at the highest administrative level. In addition to providing services that respect cultural considerations, administrators can help to ensure culturally competent practice by promoting staff diversity and providing worker training that teaches respect for cultural considerations and imparts cultural knowledge. The assessment and treatment modalities that are taught and utilized by the agency should define what is "normal" in the context of the client's culture. Workers can also be helped to develop cross-cultural communication skills, and the agency should provide bilingual services when appropriate. Periodically, agency administrators should formally assess the progress of the agency as a whole in reaching its goals to provide culturally competent services, delivered by a diverse and culturally aware work force. In the final analysis, a culturally competent child welfare agency is one which: (1) values diversity through acceptance and respect for cultural difference, (2) has the capacity for self-assessment of cultural competence, (3) is attentive to the dynamics of cultural interaction, (4) has an institutionalized base of cultural knowledge and resources, and (5) has adapted its service resources to meet the needs of children and families from all racial and ethnic backgrounds.

(American Humane Association 1994, 1–2)

Cultural competence is significant at all key decision points in the child welfare system, including (1) the initial allegation/report of child abuse and/or neglect, (2) referral of the allegation/report to CPS for investigation, (3) substantiation of the allegation/report, (4) entry of the child into the system, (5) the juvenile or family court process, and (6) exit of the child from the system. Child welfare organizations/agencies can examine their level of cultural competence by utilizing the Cultural Competency Continuum (see table 3.3) (Cross et al. 1989).

It is also important for the child welfare system to thoroughly assess individual, systemic, and societal factors that continue to perpetuate service disparities for African American, Latino, Native American, Asian American, and Pacific Islander children involved in the system. The National Association of Public Child Welfare Administrators developed the Disproportionality Diagnostic Tool (American Public Human Services Association 2008) to assist child welfare agencies in examining disproportionality in their respective jurisdictions and granted permission for inclusion of the tool and instructions in this book. A description of the tool and instructions for its use follow.

DISPROPORTIONALITY DIAGNOSTIC TOOL: DESCRIPTION

Background

The National Association of Public Child Welfare Administrators (NAPCWA) has made the issue of disproportionate representation of children of color in the child welfare system one of its highest priorities. We recognize and acknowledge that disproportionate representation and the disparate treatment of certain cohorts of children exist in child welfare agencies across the country. The over-representation of these cohorts negatively impacts child and family outcomes. We recognize that helping agencies address such an issue deeply embedded in their organizations would not only reduce disproportionate representation over time, but improve outcomes for all children as critical practices of child welfare are assessed and improved.

When an agency is faced with the reality of disproportionality and disparity in its system, it can be difficult to know where to start interventions. Agencies need specific, accurate data and data trends on children involved in the system at all decision points. Agencies also need to examine their own strengths and weaknesses in their performance of service delivery to children and families. As a result, NAPCWA has focused on developing materials and tools to help members assess their current performance and that of their communities under a more systematic and systemic approach. Our most recent effort is the development of the Disproportionality Diagnostic Tool created to help you examine disproportionality in your child welfare agency's jurisdiction.

Purpose of Diagnostic

The Disproportionality Diagnostic Tool helps users examine societal, system, and individual factors that may be contributing to disparate treatment of certain groups of children (e.g., African American or Native American Indian children). It provides a preliminary broad assessment from which a user can consider a more robust analysis of the root causes of disparate treatment that children of color tend to face. The tool will be followed by written guidance to help users understand what their assessment results mean and will include reflective questions that child welfare agency personnel can consider as they develop a plan of change and move to take corrective action within their agencies.

Keep in mind that the tool is meant to contribute to the understanding of baseline data about the existence of disproportionality in a particular jurisdiction and related directly to disproportionate representation—it is not a general agency diagnostic.

DISPROPORTIONALITY DIAGNOSTIC TOOL: INSTRUCTIONS

Limitations of the Diagnostic

The Disproportionality Diagnostic Tool was designed to be a thoughtful, initial approach to examining the pervasive issue of disproportionality in child welfare systems in communities. With this in mind it is important to note that the tool is not designed to gather all the information needed to understand all the nuances of disproportionality in an agency. Rather it helps agencies identify gaps in their systems, get ideas about where improvements may be needed, and also highlight agency strengths that could mitigate against disproportionate representation. Please also keep in mind that the tool is being presented at this time in a 1.0 version and will be periodically improved.

Diagnostic Model: DAPIM

A committee of NAPCWA members and subject matter experts devoted significant time and energy to designing the diagnostic instrument as a necessary starting point in this continuous improvement effort. The diagnostic tool parallels DAPIM, a proven model used by APHSA in its consulting practice. Under the DAPIM model, an agency Defines what the issue is; Assesses its current and desired state; Plans both rapid and long-term improvements; Implements those plans in detail; and Monitors plan progress and impact for ongoing adjustment. The diagnostic tool addresses the first two elements of the DAPIM model: Defining the issue and Assessing the current state of your agency and community.

Design of the Diagnostic Tool

The tool is designed as a two-dimensional matrix. The first dimension consists of 11 identified domains:

1. Strategy
2. Culture
3. Policy
4. Legal System
5. Training and Education
6. Communication
7. Resources
8. Practices
9. Economic Issues
10. Data Collection
11. Personnel and Community

Each domain was chosen because of its significant point of leverage within a system. Designers of the tool hypothesized that choices child welfare agencies make in the context of these domains could be contributing to disproportionate representation and equally that positive changes in these same areas could materially impact dispro-portionate representation. A definition of the 11 domains can be found at the begin-ning of each section in the diagnostic.

The second dimension has been labeled Spheres of Influence to examine the interconnected layers directly influencing child welfare service delivery: Society, System, and Individual. In fact, child welfare agencies exist within a society of individuals that struggle with institutional and systemic racism. For instance, case-workers, supervisors, and administrators come into child welfare agencies with their own outlooks, approaches, and stereotypes. It is important then to under-stand how the 11 domains operate at the three levels of influence on service deliv-ery as a whole. Looking at the 11 domains as they relate to each sphere of influence can help agency personnel identify what is clearly in the realm of the child welfare system and where the agency can play a role. The three spheres of influence are defined below:

Society—includes community agencies; local, state and federal government; major institutions such as education, churches, and banking; and the culture and val-ues of society. It is important to recognize that disproportionality in the child welfare system reflects institutional and systemic racism at the societal level. While child welfare agencies cannot expect to single-handedly overcome bias in society, [they] can be expected to play an active role in reducing disparities through an equitable service delivery approach for families. To positively impact society, child welfare agencies can weigh in on public policies, participate [in] community collaborations, raise awareness of issues, and coordinate preventive resources for families at risk of being separated.

Example: A child welfare agency can work with universities and colleges to pro-vide input on [a] cultural competence curriculum for students enrolled in social work programs.

System—Though policies and practices in child welfare are unlikely to be explicitly biased, there is reason to examine and revisit long-standing approaches to service. Child welfare agencies have the ability to reduce disparities by implementing cultur-ally sensitive standards, policies, regulations, training, and supervision.

Example: The agency adds culturally relevant intake questions, specific to a large number of minority children in the community, to its foster care placement procedures and monitors whether the addition has improved equity for children entering foster care.

Individual—can be a caseworker, supervisor, or administrator that works in the child welfare system and enters with his or her own outlooks and approaches, reflective of his or her family, community, and society at large. The role of the child welfare agency is to reduce the impact of any potential individual bias by concentrating on enhancing and improving individual skills, knowledge, and competencies.

Example: The agency includes a "cultural competence" component to agency-trainings and also evaluated this component on individual performance reviews.

Completing the Diagnostic: User Instructions

The tool is designed to be flexible to the needs of your agency. The number of options showing how to complete the tool is outlined below. Keep in mind that the more inclusive your input is, the richer your results and feedback.

Option 1: You may initially decide as an agency lead to make the first attempt at addressing the issue by completing the diagnostic on your own.

Option 2: To obtain a more collective assessment, you may instead start the diagnostic process by seeking the input of other agency personnel, including professionals from senior and middle management, as well as child welfare workers at the frontline.

Option 3: You may also complete the tool by seeking the input of other agency personnel and also relevant, external stakeholders in the community (e.g., a pediatrician or school teacher for input as mandated reporters).

Each section has a series of questions on each of the 11 domains. You will be required to respond with one of the following answers: Y, S, N, or UK for Yes, Sometimes, No, or Unknown, respectively. Use the following guide to select an answer:

Y = if the question asked *occurs* in your community, agency or among individuals

S = if the question asked *sometimes occurs* or is somewhat true in your community, agency, or among individuals

N = if the question asked *does not occur* in your community, agency, or among individuals

UK = if you do not know whether the question asked does or does not occur in your community, agency, or among individuals

Mark the appropriate box to the right of the question by filling in the box. For instance:

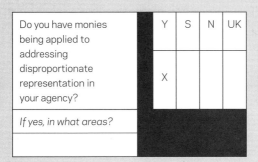

Do you have monies being applied to addressing disproportionate representation in your agency?	Y	S	N	UK
	X			
If yes, in what areas?				

Please also answer any corresponding open-ended, follow-up question in italics that may apply to your agency (i.e., questions beginning with *"If yes"* or *"if no"*). There is an unlimited amount of room to respond to the italicized question by typing the answer in the provided box. In answering the follow-up question, you may be required to retrieve information from your own data reports or synthesize agency information, e.g., your SACWIS system. If you respond to the primary question with No, Sometimes, or Unknown, the italicized follow-up question may not be applicable to you but afterwards can be used to help guide your thinking about concrete steps your agency can take to address disparities.

Follow-Up Guidance

Guidance on how to make sense of your agency's data will follow after completing the entire diagnostic and will include reflective questions that your agency can use to guide a continuous improvement process. This process will address the last three elements of the DAPIM model: Planning for improvements, Implementing the plan, and Monitoring the plan's progress.

Source: "Disproportionality Diagnostic Tool Description." (2008). Permission to Reprint: The American Public Human Services Association.

NAPCWA DISPROPORTIONATE REPRESENTATION: AGENCY DIAGNOSTIC

AGENCY STRATEGY

Strategy: Strategy refers to specific, thoughtful efforts focused on addressing disproportionate representation. Strategy carries out the vision, values, goals, and priorities that guide the work of the community's governing agency.

SOCIETY LEVEL STRATEGY

Does your agency's governing body address the issue of disproportionality in a strategic plan?	Y		N	UK
If yes, in what ways; e.g. listed in values?				
Does your agency's strategic plan address issues of diversity in the values, mission, and goals?	Y		N	UK
If yes, in what ways; e.g. listed in values?				
Is disproportionality addressed explicitly in documents other than your strategic plan?	Y	S	N	UK
If yes, in what documents; e.g. policy manual?				
Do you have stated outcomes or goals that address the specific needs of ethnic and racial minorities (e.g. reduce the length of stay for African-American children in care)?	Y		N	UK
If yes, identify those outcomes.				
Do you have a plan for achieving specific stated outcomes or goals for racial and ethnic minorities?	Y		N	UK
Have you gathered data to determine the specific ethnic and racial populations in your jurisdiction (e.g.: demographic patterns, rates of poverty, educational levels, infant mortality)?	Y		N	UK
If yes, what were the data sources and/or tools used?				
Have you gathered data on the ethnic and racial breakdown of children being referred by specific groups of mandated reporters, including teachers, medical professionals, and others?	Y	S	N	UK
If yes, what were the data sources and/or tools used?				
If yes, what actions were taken as the result of the data gathered?				

INDIVIDUAL LEVEL STRATEGY

	Y	S	N	UK
Does your staff demonstrate that they have internalized the values, mission, and goals related to diversity and disproportionality?				
If yes, identify the evidence of this internalization (e.g.; in actions, behaviors, and/or decisions).				
Is cultural competency explicitly addressed in individual staff evaluations?				
If yes, how is cultural competency measured?				

NAPCWA DISPROPORTIONATE REPRESENTATION: AGENCY DIAGNOSTIC

AGENCY CULTURE

Culture: Culture refers to the attitudes, values, experiences, and beliefs of both the organization and the community it is in.

SOCIETY LEVEL STRATEGY

	Y	S	N	UK
Are you aware of key events in your community's history related to ethnic and racial disparity (e.g., redlining, riots, and high profile court cases)?				
If yes, what are they?				
Has the community actively addressed these issues?	Y		N	UK
If yes, what were the outcomes?				
Has the community conducted studies or polls related to racial and ethnic relations?	Y	S	N	UK
If yes, what were the major findings?				

SYSTEM LEVEL STRATEGY

	Y	S	N	UK
Do you have a diversity committee or other kinds of purposeful forums to discuss issues of fairness and equity regarding practice and policy?				
If yes, does your diversity committee have a clear and articulated vision, mission, and goals?				
If yes, which of the committee's goals have been achieved?				
Does the agency have staff that represents the community being served?	Y	S	N	UK
If not, why? What steps have been taken to recruit a more representative staff?				

Are agency policies, protocols, and practices developed with input from staff of diverse backgrounds?		Y	S	N	UK
If yes, how do staff participate?					
Has the system developed mechanisms to gather feedback from staff regarding their concerns about bias in policy as well as behaviors and/or decisions of colleagues?		Y	S	N	UK
If yes, what actions have been taken based on feedback?					

INDIVIDUAL LEVEL STRATEGY

Do most staff communicate with one another during formal and informal conversations using culturally sensitive language?		Y	S	N	UK
Do most staff encourage one another to be culturally sensitive?		Y	S	N	UK
If yes, in what ways does staff do this? (e.g.; do staff actively discourage culturally insensitive language?)					

NAPCWA DISPROPORTIONATE REPRESENTATION: AGENCY DIAGNOSTIC

AGENCY POLICY

Policy: Policy refers to both legislation and agency policy and regulations on child welfare, ranging from federal policy, to office memos on particular issues.

SOCIETY LEVEL STRATEGY

Are there specific references to disproportionality or other racial and ethnic issues in state human services policy?		Y	S	N	UK
If yes, in what policy?					
Are there specific references to disproportionality or other racial and ethnic issues in other local or state agency policy? (e.g., education, juvenile justice)		Y	S	N	UK
If yes, in which agency's policy?					
Do other [agencies'] policies affect your reports of maltreatment, acceptance of referrals, investigations, substantiations, placements, exits, and re-entries?		Y	S	N	UK
If yes, which decision points have been affected?		Y	S	N	UK

SYSTEM LEVEL STRATEGY

Have you evaluated agency specific policies vis-à-vis their effect on outcomes for families and children of diverse ethnic and racial backgrounds? (e.g., placement rates)	Y	S	N	UK
If yes, what policies were changed?				
Are staff made aware of MEPA and ICWA requirements?	Y	S	N	UK
If yes, what is the mechanism and frequency of making staff aware of MEPA and ICWA requirements?				

INDIVIDUAL LEVEL STRATEGY

Does staff consistently apply policies related to disproportionality?	Y	S	N	UK
If yes, in what ways?				
If yes, how do you track that staff are consistently applying these policies?				

NAPCWA DISPROPORTIONATE REPRESENTATION: AGENCY DIAGNOSTIC

AGENCY WORK WITHIN LEGAL SYSTEM

Legal System: The legal system includes courts, law enforcement, attorneys, and other people associated directly with enforcing the law. This includes child welfare workers interaction with and understanding of the legal system.

SOCIETY LEVEL STRATEGY

Has law enforcement made any public effort to address disproportionality in their system?	Y	S	N	UK
If yes, how has law enforcement done this?				
Have the courts made any public effort to address disproportionality in their system?	Y	S	N	UK
If yes, how have the courts done this?				
Do judges, court appointed attorneys, and/or law enforcement officials receive training related to effectively working with ethnic and racial minorities (e.g. training to examine individual biases and stereotypes and how these may affect their decision-making)?	Y	S	N	UK
If yes, what training is provided?				
Are there efforts to ensure that judges, court appointed attorneys, and law enforcement professionals reflect the ethnic and racial composition of the communities in which they work?	Y	S	N	UK
If yes, what are those efforts?				

SYSTEM LEVEL STRATEGY

Do families of all ethnicities and races have access to legal representation?		Y	S	N	UK
Do families of all ethnicities and races have culturally sensitive and culturally competent legal representation?		Y	S	N	UK
If yes, please describe how families receive culturally competent legal representation.					

INDIVIDUAL LEVEL STRATEGY

Is there a mechanism in place to ensure that staff can articulate the legal process to their families in a culturally competent manner?		Y	S	N	UK
If yes, please describe these mechanisms.					
Does the language used in court reports and other written documents reflect cultural competence and sensitivity?		Y	S	N	K

NAPCWA DISPROPORTIONATE REPRESENTATION: AGENCY DIAGNOSTIC

AGENCY TRAINING AND EDUCATION

Training and Education: Training and education are the formal activities used to engage and instruct anyone associated with child welfare. This could include activities ranging from formal, required child welfare training, to mandated reporter training, to informal, voluntary community education programs, or even "teachable moments" such as newspaper interviews.

SOCIETY LEVEL STRATEGY

Do mandated reporters receive training on working with families of various racial/ethnic backgrounds?		Y	S	N	UK
If yes, what kinds of training are available?					
Is the issue of disproportionality included in community education programs?		Y	S	N	UK
If yes, how is it specifically included?					

SYSTEM LEVEL STRATEGY

Is cultural competency training included in the agency's strategic plan?		Y	S	N	UK
Are the trainers aware of the issue and extent of disproportionate representation?		Y	S	N	UK
Does the agency include the broader system (courts, attorneys, CASAs, etc.) in its trainings on cultural competency?		Y	S	N	UK

If yes, how does the agency do this?				
Is cultural competence training provided to staff at all levels of the organization?	Y	S	N	UK

INDIVIDUAL LEVEL STRATEGY

Does the staff receive information about disproportionality issues of the organization?	Y	S	N	UK
Have you evaluated whether practice related to disproportionality outcomes is impacted by the training staff receive?				
If yes, what were the findings?				

NAPCWA DISPROPORTIONATE REPRESENTATION: AGENCY DIAGNOSTIC

AGENCY COMMUNICATION

Communication: Communication is the formal or informal discussion around disproportionality. This exchange of ideas can involve agency interaction with mass media and the community all the way down to a worker's ability to interact with other staff and people outside of the agency.

SOCIETY LEVEL STRATEGY

Has the mass media outlet covered issues related to disproportionality in the community?	Y	S	N	UK
If yes, how has the public responded to the media coverage?				
Have you communicated with key community stakeholders (faith based groups, schools, etc.) about disproportionality?	Y	S	N	UK
If yes, what were their responses?				

SYSTEM LEVEL STRATEGY

Do you have a communication plan to create value for your work on disproportionality?	Y	S	N	UK
Do you have a specific strategy to communicate with key community stakeholders and agency staff?	Y	S	N	UK
If yes, what are the principal components of the communication plan?				
Does agency staff demonstrate a clear understanding of disproportionality?	Y	S	N	UK
If yes, what evidence do you have of this understanding?				
Do you regularly communicate with your staff about disproportionality?	Y	S	N	UK
If yes, what is the response of the staff to this communication?				

Is staff encouraged to communicate about the agency's goals related to disproportionality to people outside the agency?	Y	S	N	UK
If yes, in what ways are they encouraged?				

NAPCWA DISPROPORTIONATE REPRESENTATION: AGENCY DIAGNOSTIC

AGENCY RESOURCES

Resources: Resources are the facilities, services, and supports available to clients. In addition to general availability, there are many factors that can limit families' access to important resources crucial to their success.

SOCIETY LEVEL STRATEGY

Do clients know the physical location of community services (including social services, mental health services, physical health services, and child care)?	Y	S	N	UK
Are human services readily available to communities of diverse ethnic and racial populations (including social services, mental health services, physical health services, and child care)?	Y	S	N	UK
Is public transportation available in all neighborhoods including areas of high racial or ethnic minority concentration?	Y	S	N	UK
Does public transportation go to the places families in need must get to (including social services, mental health facilities, physical health services, etc.)?	Y	S	N	UK
Are adequate emergency services, hospitals, schools, faith based institutions, and other necessary or beneficial services available to communities of diverse ethnic and racial populations?	Y	S	N	UK

SYSTEM LEVEL STRATEGY

Do you have a comprehensive plan (e.g., foreign language services, assistance with reading comprehension, etc.) to ensure that parents of all races and ethnicities have access to necessary resources?	Y	S	N	UK
If yes, will this plan enable parents to complete a treatment plan?				
Has your agency worked to develop needed services in communities where children are at risk of being removed or have been removed?	Y	S	N	UK
Has your agency developed a resource directory for staff and families that assists in locating providers who are culturally competent, geographically diverse, etc.?				

INDIVIDUAL LEVEL STRATEGY

	Y	S	N	UK
Does staff use available resources (e.g., mentoring programs)?				
Does staff assess the adequacy of available resources?				
If yes, how is this assessment used to improve resources?				

NAPCWA DISPROPORTIONATE REPRESENTATION: AGENCY DIAGNOSTIC

AGENCY PRACTICES

Practice: Practices are any of the deliberate ways of interacting with families involved with the child welfare agency.

SOCIETY LEVEL STRATEGY

	Y	S	N	UK
Are community organizations aware of agency practices and/or protocols that impact disproportionality?	Y	S	N	UK
Are there community partnerships that support agency practices and/or protocols that impact disproportionality?	Y	S	N	UK
If yes, who are these partners?				
Do community organizations understand how their practices and/or protocols impact disproportionality?	Y	S	N	UK
If yes, how is this demonstrated in their work with children and families?				

SYSTEM LEVEL STRATEGY

	Y	S	N	UK
Do you evaluate whether and to what extent agency practices impact disproportionality?	Y	S	N	UK
If yes, what were your major findings (e.g., foster care is used before placement with relatives)?				
Do you have a plan for introducing new practices specific to outcomes with minority families?	Y	S	N	UK
If yes, how are new practices determined?				
Do you have families involved in decision making (e.g., Family Group Decision Making or Team-decision making)?	Y	S	N	UK
Are resource families from diverse backgrounds and neighborhoods actively recruited?	Y	S	N	UK
If yes, how have your community partners been engaged in these efforts?	Y	S	N	UK
Have you evaluated the success of resource family recruitment and retention efforts?	Y	S	N	UK
If yes, what were your major findings?				

		Y	S	N	UK
Are agency practices equitably administered, particularly among ethnic and racial minority populations?		Y	S	N	UK
If yes, what evidence supports this?					
Do you monitor consequences imposed on racially and ethnically diverse families for non-compliance with their case plans?		Y	S	N	UK
If yes, what are the major findings? (e.g., minority and ethnic populations are frequently in non-compliance)					

INDIVIDUAL LEVEL STRATEGY

		Y	S	N	UK
Does staff employ the practice orientation of your agency (e.g., strengths based assessment)?		Y	S	N	UK
If yes, how are you assured of this?					
Can staff describe their decision making processes in a culturally competent manner?		Y	S	N	UK
Does staff consistently ask families for their ethnic or racial identity?		Y	S	N	UK
If yes, how is this documented?					
Does staff engage racially and ethnically diverse fathers (both absent and involved fathers) in cases involving their children?		Y	S	N	UK
If yes, what evidence supports this?					

NAPCWA DISPROPORTIONATE REPRESENTATION: AGENCY DIAGNOSTIC

AGENCY AND ECONOMIC ISSUES

Economic Issues: Economic issues are those matters directly affecting the finances of families in your jurisdiction. The issues may be an ongoing condition or a one-time event. Economic issues can include anything from bank practices such as redlining to child welfare worker coordination with economic service workers.

SOCIETY LEVEL STRATEGY

		Y	S	N	UK
Has money been made available to the community to address disproportionality in any system (education, social services, juvenile justice, etc.)?		Y	S	N	UK
If yes, by whom and for what purpose?					
Are there financial resources, traditional and non-traditional, available to diverse community populations for specific outreach programs such as foster care recruitment and retention or transition services?		Y	S	N	UK
Are there any measures by the community or state to discourage discriminatory financial practices (e.g. redlining)?		Y	S	N	UK
If yes, what are they and how have they been addressed?					

SYSTEM LEVEL STRATEGY

Do you know the socio-economic makeup of all the communities in your jurisdiction?	Y	S	N	UK
Do you have specific monies being applied to address disproportionate representation in your agency?	Y	S	N	UK
If yes, in what areas?				
Have you identified additional funding streams that have the potential to be used in this area?	Y	S	N	UK
If yes, what are they?				
Does the agency have collaborations with other departments such as Community Development, Housing Authority, or Workforce Development that could influence economic development in at-risk communities?	Y	S	N	UK
If yes, what is the nature of the collaboration?	Y	S	N	UK
Has the agency promoted Earned Income Tax Credit (EITC) to assist clients economically?	Y	S	N	UK
Does the agency link child welfare and managed case plans and case management?	Y	S	N	UK

INDIVIDUAL LEVEL STRATEGY

Are positive attitudes towards different socio-economic classes reflected in practice (placement decisions, worker visits)?	Y	S	N	UK
If yes, how do you track this information?				
Are workers coordinating case plans with TANF/Workforce service workers?	Y	S	N	UK
If yes, how do you coordinate?				

NAPCWA DISPROPORTIONATE REPRESENTATION: AGENCY DIAGNOSTIC

AGENCY AND DATA COLLECTION

Data Collection: Data Collection refers specifically to computerized data collection methods and how the data entered is used.

SOCIETY LEVEL STRATEGY

Is community level data available (demographics, key issues) and easily accessible?	Y	S	N	UK
If yes, what is the source of this data?				
What would improve the accessibility of the data?				

	Y	S	N	UK
Do you have the appropriate technology for staff to enter the data needed by the organization?				
Do you have practices and/or protocols in place to collect and analyze data to ensure that outcomes related to disproportionality are met?				

INDIVIDUAL LEVEL STRATEGY

	Y	S	N	UK
Does staff enter data?	Y	S	N	UK
If yes, what practices and/or protocols do you have in place to monitor this?				
Does staff enter timely data?	Y	S	N	UK
If yes, what practices and/or protocols do you have in place to monitor this?				
Does staff have access to summary data about their own performance (i.e., can they see a racial and ethnic breakdown of decisions they have made across decision points)?				
If yes, how do they use this information to improve performance?				

NAPCWA DISPROPORTIONATE REPRESENTATION: AGENCY DIAGNOSTIC

AGENCY PERSONNEL AND THE COMMUNITY

Personnel: Personnel refers to child welfare staff with knowledge about agency services, policies, practices, protocols. Personnel have intimate knowledge of the community it serves and engages leaders of the community.

SOCIETY LEVEL STRATEGY

	Y	S	N	UK
Have you identified specific people or agencies in the community who can be used as resources?	Y	S	N	UK
If yes, list the specific people or agencies in the community who can be used as resources.				

SYSTEM LEVEL STRATEGY

	Y	S	N	UK
Do you know the demographics of your staff? (e.g., ethnic, racial, religious, geographic, socio-economic breakdown)	Y	S	N	UK
If yes, what are they?				
Does your agency have specific policies on the recruitment and retention of diverse staff?	Y	S	N	UK

If yes, what are they?					
Have you identified specific, relevant skills that would make your staff and organization more culturally competent?		Y	S	N	UK
If yes, what are they?					
Is staff at all levels in your agency held accountable for providing culturally competent services?		Y	S	N	UK
If yes, describe how all staff is held accountable.					

INDIVIDUAL LEVEL

Are there staff who are "champions" and "influencers" that can be models for culturally competent casework?		Y	S	N	UK

Source: "Disproportionality Diagnostic Tool Description." (2008). Permission to Reprint: The American Public Human Services Association.

After a child welfare organization/agency has collected baseline data regarding children of color at key decision points in its system and completed the Disproportionality Diagnostic Tool, it will be ready to take the actions required to address disparities in the system. This significant step will inevitably require changes in the organization/agency. First of all, an organization/agency must decide if its goal is to become a multicultural organization or an antiracism organization. There is a difference between the two types of organizations.

A multicultural organization values all consumers and employees while responding to the varying cultures that are part of the human mosaic. It respects all cultures and asserts that none should be privileged or marginalized. An anti-racism organization goes beyond this and acknowledges the destructive power of racism in society, which it attempts to ameliorate. An anti-racism organization certainly includes a commitment to multiculturalism but goes beyond this to examine power and inequities in privilege in addition to building cultural responsiveness and competency. We use the term "anti-racism" rather than "anti-racist." The former implies a commitment to dismantling racism, which has dimensions that are institutional and social as well as attitudinal and behavioral.

(Miller & Garran 2008, 210)

If a child welfare organization/agency is truly serious about ameliorating racial disproportionality and disparity, it should engage in a planning process to become an antiracism organization. This process will include a change in the organization's mission, as well as in its vision statements. This process must include changes in any racist policies and practices that involve agency staff, as well as in any racist policies that impact service delivery to children and families served by the organization/agency. According to Miller and Garran (2008), there are two questions that warrant consideration: "Do the policies continue racial inequities, whether intentional or not, and do these policies do anything to dismantle racism?" (212). Changes in a child welfare organization/agency must also include changes in the allocation of resources. It is an exercise in futility to embark on this type of organizational change without the necessary resources. Both social capital and fiscal resources are essential for an organization to change from its current status quo to an antiracism organization. In all likelihood there will be many individuals within the organization that will be resistant to this type of organizational change/ transformation. "Each organization has a set of stakeholders—people who have a vested interest in maintaining the status quo. Interests may range from job security to fear of the uncertainty that results from the process of change" (Gibelman & Furman 2008, 196). An administrator or leader of any child welfare organization/agency must publicly sanction the change and continuously demonstrate support of and commitment to the change in order for institutional and individual racism not to continue to prevail as part of the culture of the organization/agency. Data must be routinely collected, analyzed, and disseminated about the racial disproportionality and disparities change process, including changes in racist policies and practices in the organization/agency. The next section of this chapter will focus on interviews from several individuals who have been involved in varied facets of the child welfare system. These individuals will share their personal and/or professional experiences with the child welfare system.

INTERVIEWS

We now turn our attention to several individuals who have been involved in the child welfare system. Interviews were conducted with the following individuals: a birth mother, a birth father, a former foster parent and kinship caregiver, a former juvenile court judge, an executive director of a private child welfare agency and adoptive mother, an adoptive mother, a female alumnus of the foster care system, and a male alumnus of the foster care system.

BIRTH MOTHER

This African American woman is the mother of ten children. She has been married and divorced three times. She is forty-nine years old.

DR. H When did you get involved with the Department of Child and Family Services?

MS. K I became involved with my first three children. I was . . . like . . . the issue was I was, um, at the birth of my third child. I was tested positive for co . . . cocaine (takes a deep breath) and so did my child. And CPS came to my life and placed my children with my parents and left me in their home.

DR. H Did they provide any services for you?

MS. K Yeah they offered me services. Because I was raised, um . . . very spoiled, I didn't adhere to a lot of them and my kids were with my parents and I basically did partial services. . . . I – b*** s****** . . . it partways that I was never taught to be responsible for my behaviors growing up.

DR. H Did your parents become foster parents for your children (Ms. K interrupts, "No." Then Dr. H continues to ask the rest of the question.) or did they just raise your kids because they were their grandchildren?

MS. K They didn't raise my children.

DR. H Okay.

MS. K During the time my kids were with my parents I had shared some language I learned in treatment; my mother . . . parents were enabling me. The social worker wondered why I wasn't in compliance. And I used that word, and then my mother asked for respite care to open up a restaurant . . . two restaurants since she needed time to get those opened. Two weeks just to concentrate on the restaurants. Then when the time came to get them back, they said, "No," because she's enabling me. And they didn't report to it and give her back the children; and that was a crazy reason but, um . . . instead of making me leave the home, you know, which is a smarter thing. (Dr. H interjects, "Right.") So my children are placed with this abusive family; I found out later that they were very abusive. My children were sexually, physically and . . . and (Dr. H interjects, "And how old were your children, Ms. K?" Ms. K. finishes her sentence.) and mentally abused.

DR. H   What were the ages of your children?

MS. K   They were one and two when it began. When I lost my parental rights, they were two, three, and four years old. And I had given birth to another one and they came and took him when he was six months old. When they discovered him they pulled him into the termination, which I felt was kind of illegal and I wish I could've done something because I was in partial compliance by the time they did it; and I wish I had pursued that.

DR. H   Did you have any legal advice?

MS. K   At least for the fourth one, my attorney at the termination hearing he forgot to file my papers. I saw him a year later. He said, "Oh," about almost a year later, he said, "Oh I'm sorry I forgot to file it on time." And he tried some other jack-legged thing which didn't work.

DR. H   And so that's four kids. . . .

MS. K   Gone.

DR. H   Four kids that are known in the system.

MS. K   Terminated . . . (stutters) . . . and . . . I believe it just said it was too little too late. And had I been educated about my rights, I could have done something. By the time I did know, I guess it was too late. It was just too (stutters) late to do anything.

DR. H   K, where was your social worker?

MS. K   Umm . . . the, ah, I didn't trust the social worker because usually whenever I said anything, it would be used kind of twisted against me and so there was no relationship there and they lied to me many times, and would say one thing and then it . . . another thing would occur. Basically, even particularly after several years, there was no relationship with my social worker, even in my second case, when I got my life together. I got married and had three other children; after that, um, I found out that my first three children were in a foster home by that time. I signed my rights to my fourth child over to the dad which saved him from that misery, that terrible pain. I didn't know at the time, but because I gave him the child to him and his family he was protected from that pain. But . . . um, when I found my three . . . first three children were being molested and . . . um, abused by another aunt . . . and, ah . . . the parents were on crack and alcohol and had all kinds of kids being removed by CPS out their home, but they didn't take mine or their own.

DR. H   And this home was a licensed . . . (Ms. K finishes this sentence along with Dr. H.) foster home?

MS. K   All the way, they did . . . they did child abuse. They abused children from here, Washington to Nevada, before their license was pulled in Nevada. And the whole time my daughter was sexually assaulted by the father and when she told the mother at six; then she beat her and made her the scapegoat of the family until she left home at fifteen.

DR. H   I'm so sorry because no child should ever be sexually, physically, or emotionally abused.

MS. K   Me too. . . . I'm sorry that I failed to protect my children. That's what I did, from not only my issues but for allowing them to enter the system and be abused. It was more . . . to me; the state did not serve my children in that capacity they should have. They should have figured out that it was best to keep my kids with my family. My parents had no issues; they should have gave my kids to my family and got me out of my family's home. That would have been a better fit than a great adoptive home.

DR. H   And, you know, and I know that family is supposed to be considered first before placement with nonrelatives i.e., strangers. (Ms. K agrees, stating "Um.")

MS. K   Right! And particularly one who is having issues with children . . . other children being removed for sexual abuse allegations. Anyway, I found that out and I . . . instead of. . . . You know, I was smoking weed the whole time so I wasn't all the way clean. So I consumed . . . I didn't react to that news in a smart way. I was pregnant with my third child in that marriage and I took a hit because I was so devastated by that news and then I . . . being an addict, that's what I (stutters momentarily) went to, to kill the pain and went into immediate pre-labor. The first hit I don't even have to . . . feel (chuckles) the hit at all. But, um, then CPS got involved. I called, um; I was in there. I held the baby. CPS didn't get involved for some reason. I didn't know why, but I was concerned about my children being taken care of because the father he was right behind me and the parents, his parents who we lived with were both elderly and one was on oxygen. So I feared for my children's well-being; so I called Catholic Community Services asking for assistance while I'm in the hospital holding my child and had a maternity case manager worker. Three . . . workers came in and started working with me and, um, got me a treatment bed for me to go to after the child is delivered. And, um, so I got a pass to go home from the hospital to get my kids to Catholic Community Services, sign them over to them so they can care for them until my child was born. CPS came with them and they lied and said, "If you sign over custody, we're going to return them to you when you come out the hospital." And I . . . soon as I gave birth, they . . . they put a . . . (stutters) . . . hold on my children.

DR. H   They took your kids?

MS. K   Um, and so I went straight to in-patient treatment from there and, um, and got my kids back.

DR. H   How long were you in in-patient treatment?

MS. K   Until my kids came home. . . . I was in treatment for a year, six months in inpatient and six months in outpatient in Spokane. During that time the state didn't really monitor the father. So while I'm being monitored heavily, complying in progress and treatment, he was in compliance as well but using; he was high the whole time. And when I got back, um . . . before I got back, the worker had told me, if he or I, cause I lost four before, if he or I relapsed I'm going to lose my babies, and she said there was no option. I couldn't control him and it was a lot of stress for me when I got back, so he's using. I couldn't tell her because she already told me that if he's using or me, either one is using, we're gonna lose our kids. And I already lost kids before. So I didn't understand I had rights . . . that I really wouldn't lost them (Dr. H interjects, "Right.") so I held it for four months when I got back. And I kept peeing for him, UAing [urine analysis] for him and would come home from work. I got a job; I had a car. I would come home, and people were in my house, getting high around my kids. And I just . . . about four months into that, one day I woke up and the car was gone, and I went out and I found him and . . . I don't know how it happened, I just asked for a hit. I didn't curse him out this time. I didn't hit him. I just asked for a hit and that's what caused me to lose my kids . . . and I lost those kids. They came and got those children and then me . . . ah. . . .

DR. H   That's three more kids?

MS. K   That's three more!!

DR. H   That's right, right; these are you and your husband's three kids.

MS. K   Yeah, and so I didn't go to court for that termination. And, ahh, then I had . . . after that my life consisted of self-mutilating myself to punish myself for losing my children. And also I was simultaneously . . . not coping. I was not coping to feel that pain. And I was very intelligent. I was always in very high IQs.

DR. H   Yes, these days you seem very smart.

MS. K   Oh, I learned how to sell it. And from, ah . . . wholesale. I mean buy wholesale or just front from big buyers; dealers just manipulated my way higher up in the drug world. And I became a very large drug dealer and all I did . . . my life consisted of buying more drugs and selling more drugs, to pay for my sustenance; you know, my apartment and my, you know, cigarettes and all of that including whatever clothes and, um, the rest was just to get high. And . . . ah, and I just started not to work anymore, but it was just that bad. I was involuntarily committed to a mental hospital twice. Um . . . so, um, then I had my ninth child and I was, um . . . I was trying to do the services, but it was just that they were not what I wanted. To me, the services available were not commensurate to my culture or commensurate to education.

DR. H They weren't culturally sensitive.

MS. K They were not significant to my issues. Because I went to a parenting class (stutters) and engaged with all my might. And I never had parenting issues. None of my issues were ever parenting. They never had anything to do about parenting concerns. But they just gave me any old parenting class, which I took. And I and my husband engaged very thoughtfully. I was clean and then nine days later got the most horrible report from this white woman who obviously was not reporting about me; because of how bad it was it could not have been me. Because I am polite; I am smart. I (pauses momentarily) was catching on. I was not regurgi . . . I mean not regurgitating. I was reiterating, ahh, the tools I'm learning. I'm asking questions; I'm more heavily involved than any parent in that class and I got the worst review. Like some person . . . like she had no idea who I was and the . . . the experience that I encountered was different from her experience.

DR. H And you were in one of these generic parenting classes.

MS. K Right.

DR. H You were not in . . .

MS. K A case specific . . .

DR. H . . . in a parenting class that was case specific or culturally specific.

MS. K . . . specific to me or my wishes.

DR. H Oh! You were not in a parenting class that was developed for African American parents.

MS. K No. No and I was raised white, so I can definitely fit into that (Dr. H interjects, "Right") mold. So I had no issues with the. . . . But it was just the issue with this white woman misjudging . . . jus . . . just totally lying on me basically. That's all I can put . . . basically say (Dr. H interrupts asking, "Do you think that she . . . ") I was very open to feedback.

DR. H . . . stereotyped you?

MS. K Yes and didn't take into account for what I was doing, and just kept some. It was so insane I thought that was the twilight zone when I was listening to the report. It's like this cannot be said, because first of all, I was up in there all those months and they should have been teaching me if I was in error and giving feedback . . .

DR. H Right.

MS. K . . . and asking questions and giving more feedback; so I'm thinking I'm on . . . right on. You've never said at any point, during the whole time, "you're incorrect." And, of course, because I've never had a parenting issue, throughout all my cases, I never had any parenting issues but issues with my lifestyle choices and addiction.

DR. H Are you saying that everything resulted from the addiction?

MS. K Yeah, so, um, then my tenth child I, I mean my nine . . . no, that was my eighth child . . . then my ninth, tenth child I was incarcerated. It . . . no, that child was born clean. My eighth child was born clean. I feel that they should have placed him in the home with me. I was doing required services and everything; but they removed him, so that was another thing I'm trying to change now in the systems. I have been speaking a lot against it. When mothers are already engaged, there is a high chance that they're gonna keep a child with them. They're gonna keep doing what they're doing to keep their child.

DR. H Of course, most mothers who have a child removed from their care will comply with service requirements.

MS. K They're already started before you get involved. And so that was the start for me and then struggling with the addicted husband and not a lot of services around men; you know, the male part. Everyone is watching me but no one's checking him.

DR. H Children are motivators for moms to do better.

MS. K Yeah. So, um, and then so I failed in that one, my eighth child because, because I was co-dependent and the state didn't diligently provide. . . . I feel . . .

DR. H You didn't get the services that you needed.

MS. K . . . the stakes were high and no, I didn't get the services nor did my husband.

DR. H The system failed both of you by not providing services.

MS. K Actually, the father, right, um . . .

DR. H How old was this baby when he was placed in foster care?

MS. K . . . But, um, okay, so the second set were . . . the first set was zero, one, and two, and then the newborn. Right the first four. (Dr. H, "Right.") The second set was one and two. They were one and two when I was pregnant with the . . . so zero, one, and two again and the same pattern, zero, one, and two. And, um, my eighth child was born and was taken at birth. And my ninth child, when I was in . . . I was in Purdy. And I was . . . programming, doing excellent and applied for the baby program. They even put me over there; the prison wanted me to have my child there. But the state would not let them.

DR. H Why?

MS. K They had to agree because the state has part in their decision making. (Dr. H agrees, "Right.") The state comes in gives priority; the state has to decide yes or no. So the state said, "No." And, um, ah, and, ah . . . so then that was . . . I got a lot of PPD; you know, post-partum depression. (Dr. H agrees, "Right.") And then I didn't know where my baby was for three months and then it had a couple of visits before I got out. When I got out I didn't have adequate housing because I had to go back home. I had no place to live, back then you got $40 gate money and a prison garb to get out; that's what I was released with and I lasted about three months without adequate help. My brother had my mother's house; my mother was blind and bedridden by then. He had turned her house into a dope house. And that's where I was released. So, umm, I didn't check in with the department and didn't have no way to talk . . . to discuss that. And the dynamics or the environment, you know, caused me to lose that one too. And then, ah, so I just . . . lived a life. I escalated my dealings and my drug use.

DR. H And this is your ninth child gone into the child welfare system.

MS. K Yes, gone. And after that it was . . . I was going to leave a message; you know, just literally gone. I was voluntary committed and just literally dived all into the drug world and, um, didn't actually start getting that . . . it wasn't working anymore. It was getting hard, the pain. I would literally wake up in the middle of the night, "OW!" from a pain over losing my kids; my husband knew. He wouldn't say anything; he would just hug me. Because he knew after we loss that child . . . what I was going through.

DR. H It was emotional pain.

MS. K YEAH! But it would physically hurt me. I would be in dead-sleep, coma-tose from crack . . . being up for four days and would wake up from that. POW! Just jump in the bed, "OW!" And then I would go into psychoses . . . for . . . um, on the street farm, in between dealings. I would lose myself into, on purpose, to mental illness. Because it was, I made my . . . I made my drugs . . . my drugs would roll, but I'm not smoking it (laughs momentarily) and I'm stressing everybody out around me which felt . . . misery wants everybody else miserable right? (Dr. H agrees, "Right.") And, um, my . . . it would be my kids. My kids would be my trigger. I . . . shh . . . I'd be like, "Shh, do you hear that?" And they'd be like (whispering in a childlike voice), "Mommy," oh, it was awful, ooh, it was horrible. So I got into some, you know, from drug-induced psychosis over the pain, grief, sorrow, and loss. And, um, it was a lot of systemic barriers that precluded me; mainly, um, just the cultural divide of just . . . I would try to be honest and they took it somewhere else and misconstrued it. And, um, didn't understand it. I mean . . .

DR. H   It sounds like you got no support.

MS. K   No support, no services, they ordered me services, but the services were not commensurate to my needs . . . it was . . . particularly I didn't trust the services anymore; particularly after I engaged with all my heart, asked questions, asked for feedback, and got the most horrible review.

DR. H   And you had lost nine children to the system. That's a tremendous loss for any mother.

MS. K   Mm, yeah, and then on my tenth child I was like, ah . . . like again. I was the largest drug dealer in Tacoma; we had the FBI, C.I.A.; everybody was coming at me. It was crazy; it was insane. I started doing income tax and other paper scams. Remember Capitol 1?

DR. H   How did you learn how to do all of these criminal acts?

MS. K   I had the gifts. Remember Capitol 1 started giving anybody loans with ID and Social Security cards?

DR. H   Yes.

MS. K   I used to go in the streets, pick up every addict I can find, and load them in the car. I would have one person . . . I would be doing one person's tax evasion on a cell phone. I would have one person on this payphone, and I would have one person take the optical in his eye and take the other person in and I did this all day long and they are getting $500 to $1,000 loans each. I give them three crack boxes. I said, "All you need is a Social Security card and ID." I can give you three credit cards, come in with me, sit in the car, don't think, don't ask questions and I did this all day long. I would be taking in thousands of dollars in a day and then I would get all these apartment complexes with thrifts. I made up taxes for these W-2 forms getting rapid returns in two days from, ah . . . H&R Block and each one came up to $3,033 and every two days I would be getting $3,033; I got caught on that one because someone told on me. But they didn't come looking for me; I had a car. The FBI car would sit in this big old complex that I was at every day. Every one of the neighbors didn't even get out of their cars; these people had my name on their car on their door. So I did a lot of that to kill the pain. I was, um . . . so I was out there and I was, um, bout five months along; so I was pregnant. No, no I found out I was pregnant. I starting calling out to God. I said "Oh my God, I'm pregnant again and I can't. . . . I'm horribly deep in now. I'm never going to stop because I'm never going to run out, right?" I was . . . I was talking to God and I said, "God I can't stop, but you can change

me." And then I started changing, even on the street I would start apologiz-
ing to people because I was so scary. I was so mentally ill, emotionally ill, not
mentally but emotionally ill and hurt. I hated myself so much I think I became,
spirit demons too. Men were afraid of me; they would literally not fight me and
I would fight men. I was so strong when you want to fight me I would go to the
ledge, that ledge right there. (Dr. H said, "Yes.")

I would go over there and I'd be like hold on a minute and I'd go do some
push-ups with two hands on my fingertips and then do one hand and then
say, "Let's go," and they'd go (makes a callusing noise), "Somebody get her." So
that's how my life was. It was just insane, but any ways I had my tenth child,
God, five months late. On March 23, 2004, my prayers were answered in the
form of an arrest. I was wanted on a warrant. I was on escape for bail jumping.
I escaped a bail jumping warrant, and I got caught in a drug den with a large
quantity of drugs and they were Officer L and I ended up painting a mural. I
still have this mural in my room and I drew an angel with Officer L with his
vest and gun and angel wings because that's the day God set me free. So I went
to jail looking at eight years in prison. I'm now looking at five abbreviated
to six to eight months minimum because I already had eight points, and by
statute our citizen guiding laws state that because of the eight points and the
felony that I already had against me, I was automatically given eight months,
right? That's my minimum, but the prosecutor wants to get the five-year
enhancement period on the escape; so they were gonna give me 180 months;
so I'm there in jail again. I'm pregnant again. I'm looking at all this time in jail
and about a week later I give my life to the Lord and started reading the Bible.
About less than a month in I saw a picture that said, "I had to go to prison."
They had it on the news when I got out of prison. It was, um, Isaiah 55:50-8
and it said something like, "if you turn from your ways and return to your
God he will have mercy and God will hear you" and I'm like, "Oh my God!"
And I just started. . . . The governor can pardon a murderer and the president
can pardon in a . . . this. That was my exact thinking. God can pardon me and
I'm ready to go to prison; so I'm telling everybody, "Oh my God, look I'm not
going to prison." I am telling other people in the cell who are going to prison
and they like, "Girl, get out of my face"; so about a month into it was when I
found out my future. About a couple of weeks later, my lawyer pulls me aside
and he's all excited he's been working trying to get me out or get me a lower
sentence and he goes "K, I got you down to 40 months plea, sign here and give
me 43 months." I'm like, "T, 43 months? First of all, I'm going to lose this baby

because then the baby program is not going to keep me, right? They are going to let me have it and second of all, T, God is gone get me out, right?" So he's like (scuffs) right? Then I got into the tank.

DR. H   Did he think you were mentally ill?

MS. K   He sent the mental health to see me (laughingly). I got into the tank; mental health pulled me out, right? Yeah, he called mental health and, ah, I told them that he called mental health and I got mental health services, but I would not sign that plea. I told him, "T, God is gonna get me out, be encouraged." I'm encouraging him to believe. He's all depressed and stressed, right? So all the time in that tank all I did was to leave the whole tank to Christ, the whole entire tank except for one Wicca. The other Wicca let me pray for her; the other Wicca told me that she's the only one who talks about God that she respects, right? Two white supremacists start taking me in their room and kissing me and loving me; the whole others are saints. That's all I did; people were coming and I'd have a commissary. I would be giving people commissaries and it kept growing. I swear to God that chest grew and I'm, oh . . . and I'm giving them, you know, love gifts and then this one girl says, "K, come here." This is all I did, three months in jail, and she says, "Come upstairs," you can go upstairs and downstairs. (Dr. H said, "Right.") I go upstairs and she says, "look." I say, "What?" She says, "Everyone is doing Bible studies, K, and I got an A." "K, I got a hundred percent" and that's all I did for three months . . . my court papers. People were calling my lawyers asking, "When's my pretrial? What are we gonna do? What's my strategy?" Hmm, I pulled all my energy into pulling up God's book and started learning about Him. I stop cursing. You know me; I was a terror. I wouldn't hurt anybody, but you hit me, it's over, right? (Dr. H said, "Right.") Girls would come and say, "Daannana," and I would say, "I'm so sorry, please forgive me" and they'd be like, "What is wrong with you?" and I started changing and, ahh, then on the day of my court hearing, he came back saying to me that the prosecutors got made. We came back like a month. Two months later he said, "They have withdrawn the plea, they're going to go for the high end, 108 months; that's nine years and you're going to lose. I'm so sorry. Because there is no way you are going to fight them, you've got a large credit debt, drugs, bail, and one escape charge." I had been arrested over forty-nine times and this is my fiftieth time being arrested. So July 1, 2004, that's when I told him, "Be encouraged God is going to do it, right?" (Dr. H says, "Right, and he thought you were out of your mind."). Right, so then, ah, um, July 1, 2004, before I go to court, I'm shackled in here seven months pregnant with my arms ried. I go downstairs and I wait to go into the court for my trial to lose, right? He comes out the courtroom like this with a pen and paper shaking like he just took a blast right? He said, "K! Sign here, they're p . . . . (pause) you today; zero to twelve months stipulated sentence, whatever that means, the prosecutor can tell B from chocolate what that means later." But that day, not only did God squash the prosecutor's brain that were made and were going to go on the high end; he literally squashed their brains that morning. Right, because he's just shaking. He just surprised him, "Here, sign this," right? He just did it that morning at the midnight hour. He had to squash the judge's brain too because that is illegal. (Dr. H says, "Right.") So! So, ah, I go back to my cell right? And everybody who did not listen said, "K, K, K, how did you do this? What are you going to do?" Yeah, "Just go talk to Jesus." We started the songs. The Lord let me out and I went to Swedish Hospital. Ah, by then this other great counselor, mental health counselor who also happened to be a maternity case manager too, she got me a treatment bed at Swedish just in case I got out. I kept telling her, "God is going to do it," but she just said, "Let me do it." Well, I didn't know on the backseat this guy had . . . but she's already making things move like. . . . She didn't believe T when he told her, "It's not going to happen. Give up!" She did it anyways; then I got out; she was there and came got me out. And then would love on me and all that and then a week later had I not been there, the doctor would not have been able to come and test the heart rate. A little something, they test you all day long because its treatment and you can't even do drugs, right? (Dr. H, "Right because you were hospitalized."). So another doctor came back and he was like, "I'm just feeling funny about this; take her to the other Swedish and they got me down there and within five minutes they rolled me in to have a C-section. She would've died and maybe me too because you know how they do when you are in jail. I would not have known that something was wrong. I could have been dead from my labor. But if you go into labor in jail, it's not nice because they gotta, "Hold on, call control first. Control got to send for the nurse." People like me would have had their baby right there in about five minutes in that jail cell.

DR. H   But that's so inhumane.

MS. K   It is so gross. You know, they're going to have to change that shackling law. You know that right? (Dr. H said, "Yes.") I was all over the legislators, in the House. This lady said, "Tell me your story." I felt so horrible. I didn't remember the birth of my child. I do not remember my child coming out because that guard was in there too.

DR. H   But was the baby okay?

MS. K   It was a boy. He was perfect. I was in jail/prison so long.

DR. H   I am pleased to hear that your baby was okay.

MS. K   But I'm saying the guard was in there too. Why was the guard there while my lady's parts were open? Why was the male guard in there? (Dr. H said, "I assume it was a policy of the prison that a guard had to be with you.") Mm, yup, with all my goods being seen. (Dr. H said, "Why didn't the prison superintendent send a female guard with you?")

MS. K   I don't know.

DR. H   Is your son okay at this time?

MS. K   Oh yeah! He lives with. . . . I found him.

DR. H   He's the one you're parenting, right?

MS. K   No, I have . . . I get my twelve-year-old, my eighth child every weekend. I was getting my eleven-year-old too who was my ninth child when I was in prison. (Dr. H says, "Right.") Well, she moved to Oregon now. Because she's really insecure; she makes these long phone calls about why she moved to Oregon and how she didn't. . . . You know all this; but her insecurities are about me. She is a heavyset woman, like 500 pounds; she's not raising my child right at all. He didn't brush his teeth. It just makes me so mad to have someone just like trailer trash raise him. She has him looking like he just came out a Goodwill dump truck. I try to give him as much as I can when I see him. When I give him stuff . . . like, she doesn't take care of it.

She says, "I don't know"; she's really good. I didn't see him as much as my other child; we were not bonded. Because she is so big she might die anytime. I explained to him if anything ever happens, I want you to come home and he said, "I might go with my aunty." She and I haven't got that bond and she isn't giving me that bond; so he can feel comfortable to love me too. (Dr. H said, "Right.") Whereas the other mother is just all open. You know what I am saying? (Dr. H says, "Yes, I know exactly what you are saying.") I have him all the time and she knows that if anything happens to her he's coming to me. Yes, and he already knows.

DR. H   But foster parents are supposed to support birth parents.

MS. K   Yup, yup, I only have the one that does, and then, ah, the other . . . the white ones are okay . . . ah, so then, ah . . . okay. Keep it line, right? (Dr. H says, "Right.") So, ah . . . I had my tenth child, okay, had her and I'm in Seattle right? She came in healthy, perfect, and wonderful. I had been clean for like seven to eight months because I was in jail; you know treatment. I was in jail four months. No, it was March, April, May, June, and July. Five months when I had her, so I was only clean four months; but she was healthy, perfect and, ah . . . no, nothing was wrong with her. And then, ah . . . when I was there at the hospital, you know, I had a flag on my name, right? So guess who came to see me? The African American Union came and asked, "Everything okay, you gonna keep your baby (mockingly in a childish voice)?" I never had heard of such a thing. I thought they said something in Greek. She said, "Ump ump what? Do you want to keep your baby?" You never hear that in Pierce County, ever?! (Dr. H says, "No."). So I never heard that. So I was like, "Yeah!" She said, "Well we'll go to see him, right?" And I already had that set up, wrote my plan blah . . . blah; so she let me go through this crazy place, Ginger's House, and basically no one should ever go there; it is crazy. (Dr. H asks, "It is?") Yes, so I went there, two weeks later with her and left there two weeks later because they're crazy and I had a C-section, right? (Dr. H says, "Yes, you stated earlier that you had a C-section.") The second day they wanted me to do the car wash. (Dr. H says, "Oh my goodness.") Girl please, there wasn't even sleeping all day long; you got a wake-up program. I was on ordered bed rest for two weeks and they wouldn't follow the doctor's orders.

DR. H Did you call your social worker?

MS. K They wouldn't let me call her. They wouldn't let me call nobody until I said, "I'm out of here, right." So when I said I'm leaving and they tried to hold my baby, then they called her in. She said, "Nobody is holding her baby." Then they let me talk to her. I told her what happened. She worked at OAACS.

DR. H That was the only program developed to primarily serve African American children and families, although they also served children and families from other racial, cultural, and ethnic backgrounds. That program was the voice for many African American children and families involved in the child welfare system in Washington State. It was the only program that made a concerted effort to return kids home and work with birth mothers, work with birth fathers, and work with kinship caregivers and it had to be closed.

MS. K Did they get that back?

DR. H No.

MS. K That's crazy. But anyways that's . . . I was . . . they kicked me out and made me go on the porch. I mean wait on the street; so I put on a plastic bag in my hand and my baby in the other hand. I was on the corner, with no money, trying to go to Tacoma from Seattle and called their dad. What happened was he was using when I went in, right? A week before, this is all God, a week before

I aborted treatment, he was still using because we were dealers, right. We lived right next to our neighbors who were making and using crack. He said, "God I have a baby now and I need to quit this stuff. I need you to help. I need you to deliver me." He said, "God said if you flush it down the toilet I'll set you free," right? He hops the vine up; that was his treatment and flushed it down the toilet and he has not ever used since. I told him, "Man you should have given that to me" (jokingly). He said, "God didn't say to give it to you, God said 'flush it down the toilet.'" (Laughs hysterically.)

DR. H   But that's wonderful! It sounds like he had a reality check and wake-up call.

MS. K   Isn't that something? So he had sent for me. He told the cab driver to come get me. I called the cab driver because the Greyhound bus wouldn't let me take the plastic bag on the Greyhound bus, and he had to call the cab people to tell them that he'll pay for the cab when it got there. I got home and so I was doing well. I enrolled in college classes because I pretty much knew God was gonna get me out because he said it right? So I was preparing to go to college when I got out. So while he was in doing the AD classes I was enrolled in college classes. I was said to my teacher, "Teacher can you bring me something harder?" College stuff, she would bring me Algebra one day and Advanced Algebra, Geometry, and Trigs the next day. She's bringing it all back to me, including Advanced English and I'm taking it in my cell getting ready for college.

I got out and enrolled in college and entered at college level; school started January 5. This is October, right. So I needed to get a job now because I need a car. Back then on welfare you only got $349 because I had done these drug things. You couldn't get welfare for me then; it changed the next year. But that year, I could get no welfare for me except for my daughter and I needed to go to work and get a car so I can start school in January and be more comfortable. I contacted the maternity case manager and told her that I was going to church, and singing in the choir. I went to DOC [Department of Corrections] when I . . . as soon as I departed treatment. I went to DOC. I didn't even go home first, went to DOC and said I need treatment. I'm scared because I had the baby in this hand. I'm a long-time addict . . . uh, "You won't let me out without treatment on my own, right?" So I went to DOC and I had a warrant and I didn't know it because they wouldn't let me call the DOC while I was in there, right? But I left messages before I went and they said they thought that and they didn't take me to jail. And I said, "I can't leave here without treatment," and I ran out of my doses. I had no more dosage treatment, but they gave me other treatment anyway. And I was in in-patient. I studied as an in-patient; they said,

"We give you out-patient." So I take out-patient treatment. I started out-patient the next Monday, got home Friday, and went to Office of Probation Monday. I asked for five days a week; they said, "No, we'll give you three." So I did it three months later starting from July. I left in August, September, and October. Two months later I got all this stuff set up; I did everything in two months on my own. I had no attorney. The case manager was not coming to my home every week; no home nurse coming over to my home every week. A case worker and three different people came to my home every week.

DR. H Did these people come from the Office of African American Children's Services?

MS. K No! I had moved to Tacoma, she said she was going to transfer me.

DR. H Okay.

MS. K I called her on my phone trying to keep my baby; she said, "Let that baby go." And I said, "Let me call you back when I get out of here." She said, "Call me when you get to Tacoma," right? So I called her and she said, "We'll transfer your case; keep doing what you're doing," right? Because I told her I set up everything. I'm just . . . I'm cool. I'm thinking my case is up there waiting for it to get down here; soon as I said, "I need daycare and the seat" and the maternity case manager lady call CFWS; that's not CPS. So I called CFWS; she gave me the number and I took the number from her. I called and I said, "I'm K; I'm a single mom" . . . single then because we're not married . . . "and I'm trying to find daycare for my child; so I could go to work." They said, "Okay Ms. K." About an hour or two later my old social worker who was the supervisor, the one who told me that Kenny's daddy had relapsed, said, "Both of you are going to lose the kids." She said, "K, you got another baby? Where are you at?" Right? I'm like calm down. I gave her my address and I said, "Come on by." She sent a CFW and CPS worker to my house. They investigated; I showed them all the documentation and my UAs for the last . . . from August until ah . . .

DR. H Do you mean from July?

MS. K From two months and two days and three times, I had all of them. I had copies of people I was working with; my probation officer's number. So I told them to call him. I'm in perfect compliance with my probation. I gave them my church pastor's name. They investigated all that information. I had a great job. They saw my home; it was immaculate. They saw my baby; she was perfect. I said, "Here's the doctor's name; call him." I had records of all appointments and shots, everything; so they said, "Great job; find the daycare we'll pay for it." They left my home, right? The next day the police came to my home. They were so heartbroken, the two workers. The supervisor and the people who had been my caseworkers didn't care; they said, "Take the baby, make those women take that baby against." This decision was against the recommendation of the two workers who had been to my home. So, um, so . . . I was shaken up. I was like, "Oh my God," devastated right?

DR. H Right, I can certainly understand why you were devastated.

MS. K This is re-traumatized and I figured surely they're going to argue my case in the court. They are going to send me to court and the judge is going give these people a piece of his mind, right?

DR. H Right.

MS. K So I bring the record of the agency. I was under the maternity caseworker. My probation officer wrote me a letter, and my pastor wrote me a letter saying, "I'm faithful; I'm going to church almost every day," right? And then she comes and brings all that and they would not give my baby. My stomach was upset. And I found later after my first degree that that was an illegal removal. I could have sued them because the matrix says imminent harm. There has to be a history of imminent harm to the child and there was no imminent harm. I had done no harm to my baby. I had every protection factor in the freaking world there!

DR. H And they still took your child?

MS. K Took it, but, you know, in hindsight, I think of Isaac when he laid his son down and was about to stab him, but the Lord had the ram, right? I had to sacrifice my being able to breast-feed my child and all that; that was the Lord allowing them. They couldn't touch me; I was full. I was covered under his wings. I was so saved under warmth. I'm telling you, liberal people can save lives and I was serious about it. The church van was picking up folks in crack allies and all that; so, I knew God had to let them do that. And I remember leaving the 72 and they kept my baby. I said, "Lord I'm mad." I'm cool with Him. I said, "Lord, I don't trust you. I don't know how I'm going to tell anybody to proclaim your name right now because about I don't trust you; but I am not going nowhere because you hold the word of the liar." That's what I said, "I am not going nowhere because I'm not going there again." I . . . so I went through it and if I hadn't done that . . . at my dismissal they had a party They shut the courtroom down . . . Judge L, who's a hard ass, shut the courtroom down and said, "Can you start helping parents in Pierce County?" Had I not done that dependency for no reason at all, then I wouldn't be doing the great work that

God planned for me. I would not be doing God's great work that I'm doing today if I hadn't done that. So, I had to go through that so I could take that one. Okay, God orchestrated that one; he didn't orchestrate it because it was meant for evil. He turned it out for good because he already knew you take whatever you want to, but he had got a plan behind it.

DR. H Think of all the parents you've helped.

MS. K I know it's crazy, hundreds literally, and yup so, it was really tough during that one, but I just kept focusing. People say, "Where's your baby at?" I say, "Long-term day care." Those are the ones who don't really care; you know people be acting nosy. I leave them with that one and I (laughs momentarily) . . .

DR. H Right.

MS. K So that's how I did. I started studying; my first quarter I started flunking because my post-traumatic stress syndrome was untreated. I didn't know and I would be going to the wrong classes. My midterms I got two Ds and C. So I talked to someone. So, I am glad I had the Lord. One of the ladies, a teacher, I told her what's going on; she said, "Talk to the counselors." And then she made me do my case. She made me write a letter. She made me do all kinds of stuff for these babies right (laughs). Because I wouldn't look at no pictures. The police had all my pictures, but I didn't know they were all gone. She had all my kids' pictures; she had saved them because I couldn't at the time. Someone had kids in a dope house and they were willing to let me pay $50 for a clean and sober person in their life to watch them. I'm out of here; you're not going to be doing that around my kids. So, I had a lot of pain, but the counseling helped me with the post-traumatic stress. Counseling helped me and by the end of that quarter I got two B's and an A. From then on I got straight A's and from then on by the Glory of our God. Yup, I remember all through my life I got Evergreen A's because my grades went right to the top.

DR. H I remember when you graduated from college. And then you got your job in King County.

MS. K No, first I started after dismissal. I started helping in Pierce County; then I joined B, who was the first veteran parent. Both of us started meeting with the parents at court hearings; we would get $25 slices here and there.

DR. H I know her because she is a strong advocate for birth mothers.

MS. K Yeah, she's phenomenal too and we started getting. We get $25. We started getting $25 slices and we were doing this phenomenal work way above what we were being paid. We got that program up and running. For three years I worked in that program. I continued my education. I got my AA, BA, and Masters in, like I said, five and half years.

DR. H   Right.

MS. K   At the end of my bachelor's degree program, I was waiting to start my master's program. That fall, I got hired at King County and before then I was in Girl Scouts, which is amazing. I had a lot of jobs that where I was filling in. Every job I ever had they only hire people who were filling in. I thought, "Girl Scouts for real come on."

DR. H   But they hired you.

MS. K   And, ah . . . (laughs momentarily) I was hired by the Washington State Senate and King County Superior Court. Isn't that something?

DR. H   That's wonderful. I think you're a phenomenal woman who has overcome many adversities in her life.

MS. K   It is all Him, cause He is just looking for vessels just like me to do this work. I tell everybody that's behind me that these parents are doing amazing things; the ones that we're touching.

DR. H   Right.

MS. K   Because we put that in them, God wants a vessel just like you that didn't have anything going for her so that he can show up. All you got to do is wake up every morning and say, "God here I am and what are we gonna do now?" (Laughs joyously.) That's all you got to do; that's all I do.

DR. H   But He always has a plan for you and everyone else.

MS. K   But you got to acknowledge Him and invite Him to have and give you that plan.

DR. H   But some people don't.

MS. K   Right, that's what we tell them, "Get up; this is so simple." There is a dad who has been pushing, Africa American fathers; you might want to interview him too, the state did him so dirty, girl.

DR. H   I actually do want to interview him.

MS. K   This talk has made me have a flash about him. Judge C has a flash on this state by this black man.

DR. H   I do want to interview him or some other African American father.

MS. K   Yeah, you got to. He's a black man, African American. He is in King County. He is just working hard to get his baby back. It is so ridiculous, girl, the services they didn't have for him. This African American man, everywhere he went, you know, people were intimidated by him because he is a big black man. This ape . . . ah. . . . They just lost their minds, and did not want to hear what he had to say. Every time somebody talked to him they required him to do more things. This boy was doing what he was told to do in spite of his 500, no, 400 pounds, and right? He was getting on a bus, sometimes walking to get to every service and he's doing twenty times more services than they're asking him. He's repeating services on top of that; he's doing twenty thousand AA meetings. He's on work force; all that, so that there's nothing they can do to him, right?

DR. H Right.

MS. K But give his baby back to him. They said he was getting high, girl. Now, I'm an addict, right? As an addict you going to miss at least one appointment.

DR. H Right.

MS. K You're not going to do the extra. You are not going to do twenty extra groups on top of the ones you were supposed to do; it's impossible. It is not go and get it. You cannot get high and make all your appointments; it's impossible.

DR. H I know; I know that it is impossible.

MS. K So they fought him and tried to terminate his rights all the way to the end. Just until recently, in Judge C's statement she had the flash. But anyway I think you hit me in remission. But yeah, what I have seen is from working in it is that the main problem is the disproportionate number of service providers. I mean the disparate, nonculturally competent service providers and cookie cutter people who approach families from the wrong perspective. They are not validating that families have their own kinds of safety net.

DR. H They also have their own support systems.

MS. K Right and the ways they interact with their child are not going be the way you think; it's still not unsafe because it's different. Their difference is seen as unsafe.

DR. H Difference does not mean it's bad.

MS. K Yup, or it's unsafe, right?

DR. H Right, difference does not mean that you are putting your child at risk of harm.

MS. K So, yeah.

DR. H Is there anything else that you want to tell my readers?

MS. K No, I think that was an earful.

DR. H I agree; thank you very much for talking to me.

BIRTH FATHER

This is an interview with a forty-eight-year-old birth father of nine children. Four of his children are living at home. He is a married black man who is a facilitator for the Father Engagement Program. He has an associate degree. He is a strong advocate for birth fathers. He formerly worked in sales and as a forklift driver.

DR. H   How did you get involved with Father Engagement?

MR. B   Well, I got involved . . . um, my kids were removed back in probably 2004 or 2005, and, ah, through my worker I tried to put my family together. It became part of my vocation I guess, as I learned how to navigate these systems.

DR. H   Is it hard to navigate the various systems when you want to reunify with your family?

MR. B   In many cases it's almost impossible.

DR. H   Did you feel that you were treated differently because you were a male as opposed to a female? And I ask you that because it's been my experience that the child welfare system and other systems seem to favor mothers more than fathers.

MR. B   I think, ah . . . the answer is yeah. You know, I was treated differently, but I can't say I was treated differently just because I was a male. I was also a male criminal, black, broke . . . um . . . ah, uneducated when it came to things that were systematic. Um . . . and definitely under-resourced when it came to what I needed to have to do and what the department wanted me to do.

DR. H   Let's back up a little bit. When you became involved with the department and your children were removed from your care, I assume that you were seeing a social worker or a child welfare worker.

MR. B   Well they were not removed from me; they were removed from their mother.

DR. H   They were removed from their mom, okay.

MR. B   So what I wanted to be was their father. I wanted to be their father.

DR. H   How did you find out that they became the wards of the state?

MR. B   Well they didn't become wards so . . .

DR. H   Okay, so tell me what happened?

MR. B   So my wife now, who wasn't my wife then, was at a shelter and, you know, went somewhere and started smoking crack, and left my kids with the elder daughter and you know the shelter turned them all of them in basically.

DR. H   The child welfare system considers that abandonment when parents leave their kids.

MR. B   Ha! Ha! Yeah. And go smoke crack. Yeah, that's the bad news. Um, I was locked up. I wasn't in any better shape, but what I was trying to convey to them was that, um . . . she had a crack problem and they were basically saying that I was a monster. I wasn't denying the fact that I was a monster. What I'm saying is . . . you know, I might be a monster, but I wanted them to know that I'm still their dad.

DR. H   Why did they call you a monster?

MR. B   They didn't give me the term. I created that term.

DR. H   Right, you created it. Why did you feel that you should be called a monster?

MR. B   My whole life, my whole life span was that of a monster. I was a drug addict, a drug dealer, um . . . a criminal enterprise; everything I did was monstrous. It wasn't like I had a kind of . . . a gentlemanly approach to anything. Um, but I think that the biggest thing of concern to them was that I'd beat her and so that they had a case. I was definitely a monster when it came to women. So, um . . . as I was explaining to them, I agree to everything you say about me, but is there some help? Because I'm still their father and what I want to be is their dad. So, I asked for help.

DR. H   And I think that's the positive thing, the fact that you asked for help. I think that's strength.

MR. B   I didn't get it.

DR. H   And I think that's a travesty.

MR. B   There we go.

DR. H   Because if you say that you battered your wife, well, she wasn't your wife, but the mother of your children and people batter for a reason; it's typically for control. But also sometimes men who batter have been physically abused during childhood and/or adolescence or witnessed domestic violence. There are many reasons why men batter their wives; men who are batterers do need help because it is unacceptable for any man to batter his wife or partner. Now, did you get any help for this problem?

MR. B   No, I didn't get any help.

DR. H   And I want to ask you another question. During this time did you still have your parental rights?

MR. B   Oh yeah, yeah, I never lost my parental rights. Um, what the department . . . their position was that my wife needed to separate from me and stay far away from. We had a no contact order for many years and I didn't feel that the department was interested in preserving my family. I feel that they had made a decision, you know, based on whatever criteria that they use, but the end result was that this family was to be split up. And I didn't think that was right. I didn't think that was right because, you know, that's not what I felt in my heart.

DR. H Not only is that not right, but that is not good social work or good child welfare practice. The first goal for all families should be family reunification.

MR. B Should be, so we say reunification or children reunified.

DR. H I'm talking about children reunifying with their birth parents. Family reunification means returning children to the care of their birth parents whenever possible; family reunification should always be the first permanency planning goal.

MR. B They didn't have a problem with that. The thing is if you reunify my children with their mother, then you still wouldn't have a complete family and you still would be reunifying them with a mother who still had a drug problem. What I was trying to get them to understand was that in order for us to be a family, the head of that family was the one that understood what the problem was. So if you were gonna put that piece of the family together, but cut off the head then that really wasn't gonna be a family reunification.

DR. H Right, the family is mom, dad, and children.

MR. B There we go.

DR. H And if mom and dad have a problem or problems, then services should be put into place to alleviate the problems; that's good child practice.

MR. B Okay.

DR. H And I know good child welfare practice is not always implemented.

MR. B And I'd go a step further and say that good child welfare practice is rarely implemented if we're talking about the criteria we just talked about. Because in our reality, um . . . I very rarely see families reunified. I do see children reunified with mother or father. That's fine because, you know, you can't get a family together.

DR. H Right, sometimes dad might be present and he's willing and able to be the primary caregiver for the children and he should not be denied the opportunity to be the sole parent when it is in the best interest of the children. However, sometimes it's mom; sometimes it's mom and dad and that's the best of all worlds if children have a mother and a dad who are willing to step up and are able to parent them. The child welfare system should be putting services into place to make that happen; you know and I know that does not happen and that's why I'm writing this book.

MR. B. Correct.

DR. H Do you think that race played a part in these decisions?

MR. B I think that race played a part in it; ah . . . my wife is Native American and white. I'm black and Native American. Um, when it gets right down to it I think that . . . I can't say from . . . I just think that incompetence is incompetence and that the department isn't good at family reunification. Not saying that they can't give a child into the arms of the parent, but when it comes to preserving the family as a unit, some of the damage that is done is irreversible. I don't think that the department takes enough responsibility in that. You know, for them, child safety is first and foremost and that's great; but for a child to be healthy and for a child to be well rounded you don't just place it with one or the other if there's a possibility that the whole unit can be mended.

DR. H I agree with you.

MR. B So, so when it comes to racial I think yeah . . . it would definitely be racial, but I think I mean how do you say . . . um, to the department? How do you say to the department that your incompetence is . . . um, also racial because the same thing that they do incompetently with black families they do with white families.

DR. H I think an issue here is what do we mean by family? I do talk about the meaning of family in my book. And I think it is incumbent upon social workers to ask, "What does family mean to you?" Because what I'm hearing you say is that to you family means you, your wife, and your children. It doesn't mean that to everybody and so I think that there isn't a cookie cutter mold that can be used in working with families and children of color; each family is different and they need to be respected and valued for their differences. But I'm coming from a different perspective and I know that when I am talking to people. I'm coming from a perspective that I know works. Long before I became a researcher and an educator, I was a social work practitioner. I've actually worked in foster care and in adoptions. I'm not saying anything to you today that I didn't practice twenty-five years ago; it worked and I reunified families. I know that it can be done. I think that what happened was that you made your voice known and apparently it was ignored.

MR. B Right, my wife went to services. You know, on the surface, she got herself clean. You know, I mean the classes that she was supposed to go to, she did.

She maintained a job; she got a house, but she still was an alcoholic. A lot of the decisions and choices that were being made were still putting my kids in jeopardy. What I know now that I didn't know then was that while I was trying to get the department for looking at my wife for her incompetence, what I should've been doing was looking at myself for my incompetence because I was expecting my wife to do a job that was designed for me to do. So it would be like me trying to do Bill Gates's job; I'm not qualified to do his job. Once I started realizing that at that time I was pointing a finger, I got tired of basically saying, "You guys are looking at this all wrong." Meaning just, you know, that the department was looking at this all wrong. What I started doing then was saying, "Fine let me put myself in the game." So I took a domestic violence course. I took an anger management course. I went to intensive in-patient treatment. I got off of DOC. I no longer got arrested.

DR. H   How did you find these services?

MR. B   Really, um, well, DOC, you know, you don't find that service; they find you. Um, it took me thirty years to get off of the Department of Corrections. So, that was a whole . . . you know, that was a skill set in itself that nobody talked about. They assumed that everybody who gets on Department of Corrections eventually someday . . . you know, they'll get off of it or they'll learn how get off of it. What they don't understand is that we don't know how to get off of the Department of Corrections; that's a whole different institution that we've never even . . .

DR. H   It's a very different system than the child welfare system.

MR. B   Exactly, and that's one that if you're a part of it is going to be hard to do anything within child welfare and many of these fathers once the kids are removed, you know, they start looking at a lot of these fathers that have been incarcerated or are incarcerated now. You got a whole different skill set before you can even deal with child welfare. So for me, I figured that out. It was difficult for me to say, "Hey my kids, I need to be in my kid's life." If I was gonna be arrested every 60 days or so for a probation violation, I had to learn that skill set. I had to learn how not to violate my Department of Corrections probation rules. One of those violations by the way was I married my wife, in violation of the no contact order. That was a big no, no! But the reason why I did that one was to honestly institute God's covenant into my life.

DR. H   Okay, I understand what you are saying.

MR. B   And so, I had to just go ahead and throw caution to the wind and say, "If we were gonna be a family, we're gonna do it God's way." You know, a husband and wife . . . um, I was going to take care of my household.

DR. H   And so religion is important to you.

MR. B   Oh, absolutely, without it none of this would've come about. I mean . . . I probably would have stayed who I was and I know she would have stayed who she was. But the thing that I needed to learn then is department etiquette, terminology. One of the biggest obstacles, you know, is being in compliance by completing services. You know, these services to me just sounded like the white man putting his foot on my neck again. You know, my Department of Corrections officer telling me to pee in a cup. Um, all of these things sounded familiar and really were making me angry. Because these were my kids and you're talking to me like a parole officer and these were my kids and so I had to understand that and really get help.

DR. H   Did anybody, and when I say anybody I'm talking about the social worker or child welfare worker, sit down with you and explain to you we need to work with you and develop your service plan? We need to write this plan together. This is what I mean when I talk about being in compliance. You have to go court; you have to let the judge know that you're getting services.

MR. B   First of all, there are no conversations with the social worker; the social worker feared me. Everybody feared me; so, you know, everything was in a cryptic. You know, they tell my wife what to say; you know, they'd deal with my wife.

DR. H   They did not interact with you.

MR. B   And then, you know, not me. And then it was always . . . was always pretty clear to me that I wasn't really welcome.

DR. H   But you're the dad. You're part of the family.

MR. B   Yeah I'm the dad, but I'm a bad dad. And so, you know, there's a difference between being a dad and being a bad dad. You know, it's interesting because who's making the determination on who's a good dad or bad dad? And as a social worker, as long as . . . my understanding is that shouldn't even be a judgment that they're making.

DR. H   Social workers are supposed to be nonjudgmental; we are supposed to accept people as they are in their lives. It's our responsibility if you're not where you want to be or where you think you should be in terms of parenting then we have a responsibility to sit down with you and say, "These are the things that we think you need to do in order to be able to parent your kids; this is where you go to learn how to do these things."

MR. B   In order for me to understand that, you have to talk to me.

DR. H   You have to talk to parents including fathers, of course!

MR. B   So if you're a Caucasian social worker and you look on my file and you see that I beat white women, and you look at me to the left and I look back at you to the left, now we have a problem.

DR. H   Right, because your social worker is not communicating with you.

MR. B   Right, so that was always my history with the department. We didn't communicate well; we didn't play well with each other. Now I can say this, the department is changing.

DR. H   It is and a lot of it has to do with who works at the department and the legislation that was passed in terms of racial disproportionality. The committee that I cochair . . . we're kind of like an advisory watchdog for the department. It shouldn't have to be that way, but it is. And the department has to answer to us; at our meetings we want to know what they're doing for families and how they're doing it, especially what they are doing for children of color and their families.

MR. B   So when I first got involved with them again there were no services; the only thing you could possibly get as a father was a parenting class and a domestic violence class. Oh, you could get drug treatment.

DR. H   Yes, they seem to feel that everybody needs a generic parenting class. Not every parent needs a parenting class. I strongly feel that parenting should be culturally specific. There should not be just some generic parenting class for every parent that is involved in the child welfare system.

MR. B   I thought it was kind of weird that I'm learning about little Johnny, but my son's name is A. . . . I'm learning about little Mary, but my daughter's name is D. . . . And I'm sorry, but, you know, when you go and you tell D it's timeout, you need to go into the corner, D is going to look at you like you're crazy. That's just the way that she's cut; she doesn't know anything about timeout, timeout? What are we talking about here? But I learned that if I was going to understand the department I was going to have to understand what they were using, the medicine that they were using so to speak, and whether I liked it or not or agreed with it or not wasn't the issue. In order for me to be in compliance and to understand the language and know what they meant, I was going to have to pick up on this stuff. I still, you know, teach people to do this to this day.

DR. H   There's a way to navigate the system and you have to learn how to navigate the system. If you're an outsider you have to learn it; you might not like it, but you have to think of the larger goal and your goal was to reunify with your family.

MR. B That being said . . . um, it's also like brainwashing; when you want something very . . . very bad and somebody is in control of it and the only way to get it is to do what they say to do. If I do that it's called manipulation. It's called coercion; it's called strong arming, but when the department does it, it's called good practice. All I'm saying is a lot of this stuff's damaging.

DR. H And I don't think it is good practice; it is not good social work practice or good child welfare practice.

MR. B So, one of the things I was left with at the end was kids who knew that they had done wrong would say something like . . . like my daughter in kindergarten, no this must've been in second grade. You know, she had acted up and knew she was going to be in trouble. She knew that she had to go to school and get good grades. She knew what she was supposed to do, so they said that they were going to call her dad and she said, "No, don't call my dad because my dad will beat me." The child has maybe gotten a whipping twice in her life. She's fourteen now and she says that and, you know, they said, "Tell us more." So, she goes on to talk about he beats me and they're like well how does he beat you and she says, you know, he beats me with a belt and they said, "How many times has he beat you?" "You know, five or six times." And they say, "Well, how big is the belt?" And so by time she's done telling this story about getting these beatings, what she failed to tell them was that she wasn't even the one getting the beatings. It was her brother getting the whipping and these weren't beatings. The guy had gotten a spanking and that was probably two years before that time, maybe a year before that time. The other thing she failed to tell them is that he never does it. He says he's going do it, but he never does it. So anyways, CPS showed up at my house, and as soon as they do, my daughter breaks down. She's boohooing because I invite them into my house and we have a conversation. She's just boohooing . . . just like, "Why are you crying?" and she's like, "Because I don't want to go." And they're like, "Who said that you're going?" She said, "My daddy." I didn't say anything. She says, "But no, they're coming to take me and you're going to let them." I said, "I should . . . huh?" and she goes, "No." I say, "Now, why don't you tell the people in all reality what is going on?" And she goes on to tell them that she didn't want to get in trouble and so, you know, she knew that was what they wanted to hear, but she didn't know that it was going to come to all of this, but now that it came to all of this, you know, they're surprised. Well, this is something she's learned; this is . . . she has been through the system and she's learned a few tricks. You know, this is residual stuff; you know, with the department being in your life that it is kind of hard to get out them of your life. It is kind of hard to wash out your family stuff. One other thing that I can think of is my son who is now fifteen years old. He has this whole demeanor with his mom; it's disrespectful and my wife says, "You know, he learned it from you; you know, the way you used to treat people." And my son says, "No I didn't learn it from him. I learned it from watching the way they used to talk to my dad." Meaning all social workers were women, and so when they were talking to me and he would be seeing these things, it was irking him on the inside. He started getting this animosity towards women that he never spoke about. It just started coming out later.

DR. H Well children are always observing; they're listening, even when people think that they're not. Is he in counseling?

MR. B Nah, he's . . . ah. One thing about both of my kids is that they let you know by their behavior when counseling is definitely what's needed. And so far, you know, they're holding down their grades and he's a sophomore in high school and he's playing football. So far so good and I've asked him, "Man, do you need counseling because if that's what you need, that's what you need." And another residual is once you've been in counseling or you've been in the department or have had any kind of counseling, as soon as you're done with it, you don't want no more. So you may need it, you just won't do it because you just . . . you know, you just don't want anything to do with it.

DR. H But I think that speaks to being referred to the wrong counselor. I think that . . . and this is not to say that every person of color needs to go to a counselor who is a person of color, but people need to have choices. And sometimes people go to counseling and it's not the right counselor. They need to be referred to feel empowered to say, "This is not working. I need to another counselor." Counselors should do ongoing evaluations with their clients about treatment. I say that because I have a psychotherapy practice. I see children and families and I say to families, "We have to decide if this is a good fit. I have to feel like I can work with you and you have to feel like you can trust me to work with you; otherwise, it's a waste of time." So, you learned how to negotiate these systems and got your family back together. How long did that take?

MR. B Yeah, well about three years. So my family we were together, but it was a typhoon. Number one, I still had a no contact order. The case was still open; the dependency was still open. My wife was in out-patient and I was in in-patient. The problem was I married and when I married her I threw muck into the whole thing. They were telling her that she needed to be away from me, but now she's my wife. DOC said I was out of mind because part of my stipulation clearly said I was to stay away from her and I married her. When I married her it put a big monkey wrench on everything and the only reason why I married her was because God told me that he already gave me a wife and that wife is her. Now, I'm wise enough to understand that although he gave me a wife, it didn't necessarily mean that I was supposed to marry her at that particular time. I may have jumped the gun and in so doing I brought everything to a head. And so a couple of things happened. I had to get an advocate to fight for me to get my no contact order rescinded and that came in the form of Union Gospel Mission, the legal team. They were able to get a temporary stay in the no contact order so that we could live together and raise our family, provided that we were both in compliance. My requirement was that I attend and complete a domestic violence course, anger management, and intensive drug treatment; the intensive drug treatment came in because in 2003 I had a heart attack from a drug overdose.

DR. H I'm sorry to hear that you had a heart attack.

MR. B Thank you. But it was that drug overdose that changed my whole life around and made me even think about the father that I'm supposed to be to my kids or marry A.

DR. H It was probably like a wake-up call.

MR. B More than a wake-up call, yeah, massive heart attacks will definitely change any person if you listen close enough. So, getting the no contact order rescinded with conditions put the focus on me squarely. That in order for this to happen, I had to stay in compliance and do exactly what it was I had to do. That meant I had to get employed; um, again, I had to do the drug and alcohol treatment, the domestic violence. I hadn't had a license since 1978 and one of the first victories that I won was getting my driver's license.

DR. H That's independence.

MR. B That doesn't sound like a really huge thing, until you've been suspended since 1978 and that one win it was victory after victory. When I knew that this family belonged together, not in bits and pieces, not with the kids with me or their mother, was when I got baptized. And when I got baptized and came out of the water the pool was sitting up six feet and my son who was about six years old jumps up and says, "I want to be baptized too," and his little sister who apparently can talk says, "Me too." My wife who wasn't my wife yet, we were just together, said, "If they are then we should." Then her older daughter and her future husband and so on and so forth, like thirteen people got baptized. And I said, "Okay." So, I'm going forward with this. And so that gave me the strength, not necessarily to take on the department but to definitely be strong and with-stand what they were saying.

DR. H   It gave you the strength to do what you needed to do for your family.

MR. B   Umm, correct, correct. Had I not known that or had that strength it would've been easy for me to just concede that department knew what was best for my kids; that they should just be with their mom and I should just go off and start a new family. And that's what some of us do in the black community. I got five baby mamas; um, so these kids definitely weren't my first set. And I'd be remiss if I didn't include this part in it. This wasn't the first time that kids were removed from me; my first kids, my daughter is thirty and my son is now twenty-five. And you know the kids got removed then. You know, I got arrested and the mother got busted turning tricks to cops. Um, I remember I knew nothing about family preservation.

DR. H   I think we can go right down into that little basement to finish your inter-view. There is too much noise in here.

MR. B   Umm, so to follow up, if I would've known about family preservation then I would've tried harder to get those kids out of the system.

DR. H   Okay.

MR. B   And what I did was . . . I just basically let the mom deal with it and I went and got another baby mama. And that was a pattern. I think that child welfare needs to understand that I personally wouldn't point a finger at them. Some-body has a dirty job and somebody has to do it. I think that, you know, they're trying to do it the best they can. I don't know, but they have to look deeper, especially when it comes to black families. We have way more mitigating cir-cumstances that they're not even putting into calculations when they're talking about removing our kids. I also think that they're putting a lot of stipulations on our kinship caregivers, people that we can put our kids with when we're struggling.

DR. H   You are talking about extended families.

MR. B   Right, extended families, you know, grandma may have only one leg, but if she can still walk she knows exactly where every kid is at.

DR. H   Well, most grandparents, aunts, uncles, if they know that a family member is about to get involved with the system, they will step up to the plate. And the age of the grandparent doesn't really matter in black families; they are willing to take those grandkids into their home.

MR. B   Absolutely, absolutely. . . . I think that if we don't factor that kind of thing in we're coming up with different types of minority kids.

DR. H I think the key here is putting in whatever services that grandmother or other relative needs in order to keep those kids in the family.

MR. B Yes, absolutely, I would agree. So, I guess for me after I got my act together it was then just a matter of maintaining that year after year after year.

DR. H Okay, how long have you all been together?

MR. B Um, my wife and I have been together it will be twenty years in January 2013.

DR. H That's wonderful. It is, and I think that it's wonderful that you are helping other dads.

MR. B That is a good thing.

DR. H Because the child welfare system . . . in fact, all of these systems, they're complicated, including the court system. What can you tell me about the court system?

MR. B (Chuckles briefly; he says, "Um.")

DR. H How difficult was it to navigate the court system?

MR. B It's the biggest one. As big as child welfare is, it's nothing compared to the criminal system. It's just, ah . . . I guess I'm going to approach it from a black man's perspective.

DR. H Okay, because there are a lot of black men who are involved with the criminal justice system.

MR. B Yeah, so I'm looking at it from a black man's perspective and a black father's perspective. When we're young and we start indulging in criminal activity we don't see thirty years down the line. We don't see what our position in life is going to be; we don't see that. So when we are in the juvenile system and they tell us that we take this felony. You know, we're gonna be back by summer time. We don't look at that and see it as a problem thirty years from now. So we sign it and we take our first felony. They tell us it was a juvenile offense and it can be expunged. You know, it can be wiped away; you won't have a problem. They don't give us any tools to make sure that we don't commit another crime. Because the moment you commit the other crime, you can only get one of them expunged, so . . .

DR. H This means you've got a criminal record.

MR. B You've got a record. Even if you . . . whichever one you've got expunged that felony will stay in place once you catch another charge after that. Nobody is really explaining that to us. Not to mention that if that's close enough to your eighteenth birthday and you continue with the pattern that you are doing, you know, at sixteen, that's just when you get your first adult criminal charge. You're going to look as if you did. You know, I need to take this plea. I'll be back by summer. You are signing it; now it's official.

DR. H And you're an adult.

MR. B It's official, those charges are from your juvenile record. There are charges as an adult, they are all one. The criminal record is plain to see, and now your criminal record goes back. In my case it went all the way back to 1976. So in 1976, the last thing I was thinking was that I was going to buy a home for somebody. I was going to live in a nice lofty neighborhood with some cart cages around me and perhaps buy a boat. I never thought about it. Well, here I am and the decisions that I made in 1976 are impacting me right now today. That being said means that we are missing out on a whole line of education as black men in our community pertaining to the criminal system and fatherhood. If you can't maintain freedom you can't maintain consistency when it comes to finances. When that can't happen you can't possibly take care of children and when you can't take care of children, more than likely the relationship is going to dissolve. Family preservation involves a strong covenant. When you're away long periods of time being locked up, then actually it's going to be a downfall for your family.

DR. H That is absolutely right.

MR. B So for the last fifty or sixty years we as a black people have been in these systems and nobody is teaching us about the impact that it's going to have on us. Nobody is teaching about the criminal system and the impact that it's going to have on us rearing children and taking care of our families. Then is it any wonder that there's so little family unity today?

DR. H Because in listening to your story, reading the literature, and even talking to women who are incarcerated this criminal activity and subsequent imprisonment have a lifelong impact on men and women, not just some six-month impact.

MR. B Right, it has a lifelong impact. And what I'm finding is that it is not a lifelong impact just on you; it's a lifelong impact on your kids and probably their kids.

DR. H It has an intergenerational impact.

MR. B Absolutely, I have a twenty-five-year-old, the first ones that I told you about. They were the first kids that were removed; he's now doing ten years in an Oregon prison. My first child, his older sister, she's now battling an opium addiction. So, those decisions that I was making back in 1976 when I had my first kids, this was what I was teaching them; this is what they saw. He won't be having any kids at least for another ten years. She already has one son and he is without his mom because, you know, she's on drugs right now. Now, he's being raised by his grandmother. She was the first mother that I had a child with in the first place. Our kids were removed. So here it is now the second generation is off doing their thing and now the third generation is now being raised by the people who started it first.

DR. H   And so these behaviors have repeated themselves and they're impacting the current family members and will impact future generations. And so what I'm hearing you say is that we need to stop the pattern.

MR. B   Correct, and one of the ways we can stop the pattern when it comes to child welfare is child welfare needs to stop thinking that the two are the same; ah . . . European American and African American families. These are troubles that they have; these problems that they have. African Americans, these are problems that we have and if we don't start becoming specific in dealing with them then I think you're doing both of them a disservice.

DR. H   I think that we need to never forget that American Indian families are different. Latino families are different. African American families are different. European American families are different. They're all different and they need to be worked with and talked to in ways that are culturally and ethnically specific. And within these groups of people there are differences. For example, if you identify as a black or African American man it doesn't mean that you are the same as every other black or African American man.

MR. B   That is correct. Um, honestly I think that probably covers everything except I guess I'll give this one to you. It's been my catch phrase for about six years now. Um, when it comes to fathers throughout every system how important is the dad?

DR. H   I think that dads are very important. I think that for too long, the courts, the child welfare system, the education system, the medical system, and the juvenile justice system have forgotten and/or ignored dads. Every child has a father. I feel that it's the responsibility of the child welfare system to find dads and try to get them involved in their children's lives because it makes a difference. It makes a difference to girls and it makes a difference to boys.

MR. B   I'm done; thank you very much.

DR. H   Thank you, thank you.

FORMER FOSTER PARENT AND KINSHIP CAREGIVER

Ms. T is a thirty-seven-year-old African American woman who was a foster parent and a kinship caregiver for over ten years. She is a social worker who has a Master of Social Work degree and many years of experience in the social work profession. She is divorced and the mother of one teenage son.

DR. H   I would like for us to start by having you tell me how you became involved with the child welfare system.

MS. T   Okay. I first became involved with the child welfare system in 1993. Um . . . at that time I was approached by a social worker, Jim K, about two siblings of mine (my sister and my brother). At the time, they were three and one years old.

DR. H   Okay.

MS. T   I was asked to see if I can take them in as a relative placement.

DR. H   Okay. And did you go through the licensing process?

MS. T   Yes, ma'am. First I took them in and I was a temporary placement; not a foster care placement at first. And then I went through the process to become a relative placement. I had to do the physical, the licensing and all that good stuff and I had to talk to my husband.

DR. H   Okay. And so you became a licensed kinship care provider?

MS. T   Yes, ma'am.

DR. H   For your sister and brother?

MS. T   Yes, ma'am.

DR. H   Okay. And how long did you keep them?

MS. T   I had my sister for . . . right before . . . until January of 1995. I had her just a couple of months before I had my son.

DR. H   Okay.

MS. T   And I ended up finding her dad about six to eight months prior in Tennessee. And talked to the social worker and got permission. They . . . his mother, which would have been my sister's grandmother, went through the process to be a kinship caregiver for my sister.

DR. H   Okay.

MS. T   So I transported her down there after all that was approved by the social worker.

DR. H   And did the social worker help you to locate your sister's birth father? Or did you do that on your own?

MS. T   I did that on my own.

DR. H   And what can you tell me about your brother?

MS. T   My brother, I had him until 1998. And he stayed with me until then.

DR. H   That's a long time.

MS. T   Yes, that is a long time.

DR. H   And what would you say your experiences were with the Department of Social and Health Services? Did you get the services that you needed?

MS. T   Uh . . . no, ma'am. Being a relative placement, I was restricted from a lot of services. I was restricted from the stipend at the time that they would normally pay a foster parent or somebody like that because I made too much money. My husband and I made too much money. So we didn't qualify for that. We did get medical services for a period of time. The services were really inconsistent; we didn't get a lot of services. The main services that we were able to get . . . I was able to get child care through DSHS and medical through DSHS. I wasn't able to get food stamps because, as a household, we made too much and, thus, we were unable to get the family stipend as relative caregivers.

DR. H   But I'm looking at . . . and maybe I'm looking at this wrong . . . being a relative care provider, what does your income have to do with these children? From my perspective, these children are additional members of your household. Yes, they are your family and you love them, but their expenses are also a drain on your finances.

MS. T   Yes, ma'am, it was. I think at the time I was so young; when they moved in with me I had just barely turned eighteen. So when they came in, I didn't really understand the process and I had a new social worker that was non-English-speaking. So I think that it was easier for them to say well, "She doesn't know the system and I don't really know the system so let her take care of them."

DR. H   But what I'm also hearing is confirmation of a finding in research done on kinship care. This finding states that kinship care providers receive a poor quality of services and also receive fewer services than traditional foster parents.

MS. T   Yes, ma'am. And I did not realize that until after I got foster kids, after my siblings left. And then I saw the differences in services.

DR. H   How long after your siblings left your home did you decide to become a traditional foster parent?

MS. T   It was about . . . maybe a year or two. What I noticed is that my son didn't like being an only child. So having him start to grow up with my brother at the time, which would have been his uncle, and then having him leave, he didn't really like that. So I went through the process to still do temporary placement or foster care placement.

DR. H   Okay. And how long did you do foster care placement?

MS. T   I did that until 2007.

DR. H   When did you get your first foster children . . . well children in foster care?

MS. T   Are you talking about children other than my siblings?

DR. H   Right, I am talking about nonrelative children.

MS. T   My first kid was 1999 I believe, if my memory serves me right.

DR. H   Was it one child?

MS. T   Yes, ma'am . . . no, ma'am; it was two boys.

DR. H   Okay, were they siblings?

MS. T   Yes, ma'am.

DR. H   And did you get the services that they needed?

MS. T   Yes. By then I knew a little more about the system. I worked for the state by then and kind of knew what I should have got prior.

DR. H   And so I'm hearing you say that in order for foster parents to be successful, they need to know how to navigate the system?

MS. T   Yes, ma'am, that's huge. That's very imperative to be successful, to get what you need and to get what your kids need. In order for them to be successful in the placement there are certain services that are essential.

DR. H   I'm wondering, because I know that when anybody becomes a licensed foster parent, regardless of whether they are a kinship foster parent or a traditional foster parent, they are required to attend foster parent training classes/sessions.

MS. T   Yes, ma'am.

DR. H   I guess you would say there are preparatory classes for foster care or kinship care. They don't talk about services and how to navigate the system in these classes?

MS. T   The classes are very limited; it's a basic overview and it just says what your rights are and it says . . . they stress, over and over, that every household is different. So it leads you to believe that, yes, they offer medical, child care, a stipend, and all of these services, but they may not be for you or for you and your kids. So, it's not very clear that . . . it's not presented that we have these services and all you need to do is contact us; that's not the way it's presented. It was presented: you may qualify. As people raise their hands and ask questions, you know, it's like, you may qualify or you may not . . . so it wasn't very consistent. And that's only in the first training that you get that overview. The trainings, thereafter, are very specific in behavioral content and they're optional type courses.

DR. H   But what I'm hearing, and please correct me if I'm wrong, is that there do not seem to be objective criteria when it comes to service or services that families receive.

MS. T   Yes, ma'am.

DR. H   By virtue of that fact that you become a licensed foster parent, it doesn't necessarily equate to: these are the array of services that you are going to receive?

MS. T   Exactly, yes.

DR. H   Do you think that race enters into this picture? Or that race is insignificant?

MS. T   I think race is very significant in determining who gets services, who knows who, and how to get those services, how to obtain those services. I don't think that information is readily available to anyone who may walk in off the street and/or someone of minority descent. I think that it's hard for a minority to navigate the system because your views and perspectives are different than the majority of the workers that you encounter. Therefore, it makes it hard to try to advocate for yourself and the kids placed in your home.

DR. H   I'm also hearing that it sounds like people who are working in child welfare including social workers, child welfare workers, and CPS workers need to have some type of cultural awareness, some cultural competence and cultural sensitivity, as it relates to different racial, ethnic, or cultural groups.

MS. T   Yes, ma'am.

DR. H   People parent differently; they define family differently on the basis of their racial, ethnic, or cultural background.

MS. T   Right.

DR. H   And if workers are not sensitive to these various factors, then children and families end up not getting the services that they need.

MS. T   Exactly, that's correct. And you see, it needs to be more than the two hundred dollar training that we got as foster parents because we got a cultural awareness class shortly after becoming a foster parent, but it was only two hours, very basic; if you are African American and you have a white child placed in your home, there are many things you need to be prepared for prior to placement of that white child in your home.

DR. H   But as social workers, we both know that cultural competence, cultural sensitivity, cultural awareness are lifelong trainings and not a one-time training session.

MS. T   Exactly.

DR. H   We can't go to a two-hour workshop and say we are culturally competent.

MS. T   Right.

DR. H   It just doesn't work that way.

MS. T   Exactly.

DR. H   And it doesn't matter what your racial, ethnic, or cultural background is; cultural competence is something that you have to continuously work on.

MS. T   Yes, ma'am, that's true.

DR. H   Now, are there experiences that you had in child welfare that you feel would be helpful to readers of this book? I am referring to experiences that you feel should not be repeated. And when I say that, I'm talking about experiences that you feel were negative and damaging to children in your care that really need to be rectified. Are there some things that you feel the system should not be doing? Or that they could improve on?

MS. T   Yes.

DR. H   It would be helpful if you would share some of those things with the readers.

MS. T   Yes, I can do that. There have been a number of different issues I've had being an African American social worker, as well as a foster parent, dealing with other social workers, who weren't as culturally sensitive as they needed to be. And like I stated before, most of them were European American social workers who were coming into my household, who were bringing kids, visiting kids, working with kids. And so some of the things that I found really distasteful and offensive were, for example, when I had my two boys in '98, the social worker would come in and have a problem with the way the boys communicated with each other in the household. And she insinuated, as if I spoke to the kids that way; that's why they spoke so loud and aggressively to one another. And that was really disrespectful because I hadn't had the kids but for a few weeks. And it was assumed that . . . you know, "How do you talk to the kids, is that how you talk to the kids?" And I had nothing to do with their conversation; it was a two-way conversation that had nothing to do with me. But the conversation from the social worker was that I somehow taught them to speak to each other that way. And that was really disrespectful I felt. And I did talk to the social worker about that.

DR. H   Well, as you know, some African Americans speak loud.

MS. T   Yes, ma'am, they do.

DR. H   I've been in places, in homes with large families, where people were excited, and their talking was very loud. They were not talking loud in an aggressive or offensive way, but this loud tone was just the way they talked.

MS. T   And that's true, but I think that if the social workers would have knowledge of the fact that's the way some families talk, I think she would have approached me differently; I think her interaction with me would have been different. Instead of assuming that I yell at my kids like that, she would have approached me in a nonaccusatory way; after all, I hadn't had them long enough to teach them those behaviors.

DR. H   Right, I'm sure that was hurtful.

MS. T   Yes, it was very hurtful. Um, and I like to deal with those things because I've had a number of occurrences with social workers, um, so I always want to deal with those things and ask them what's your training and background around, you know, kids and African Americans and working with other families that are not like the Western culture.

DR. H   And I feel that, especially in child welfare, if you're going to work in the system you need to have some education, some knowledge, and cultural awareness about different families because the largest percentage of children in the child welfare system are children of color.

MS. T   Yes, ma'am.

DR. H   And there is not a book that you can read that's going to make you, for example, culturally competent; but there are some basic things that you need to know about families.

MS. T   Yes.

DR. H   For example, you need to know about family systems and family dynamics, if you are going to work with kids and families in the child welfare system. I strongly believe that this type of knowledge is highly essential.

MS. T   I agree. And I think that the other big issue for me was with my social workers; we needed to build an alliance for these kids and we can't do that if you have some issues that you haven't resolved or you're not used to working with children of color and foster parents of color. And so you don't respect them in the same way as white children and white foster parents; you don't communicate to them in a respectful manner.

DR. H   And I think that gets at self-awareness . . .

MS. T   Yes.

DR. H   . . . and being able to say, "I really don't know about these families, but I'm willing to learn about them . . ."

MS. T   Yes.

DR. H   . . . "I really don't like African Americans but because I have to work with them . . ."

MS. T   Yes.

DR. H   ... "I'm going to treat them respectfully and I'm going to learn something about the African American culture."

MS. T   Yes.

DR. H   We all have biases; we all have prejudices. Your background does not matter, but we have to admit that we have biases and prejudices and learn to deal with them.

MS. T   Yes, ma'am. And I did have a couple of social workers . . . who, after noticing a pattern of the way they communicated with me, I did address those issues and say, you know, "Do you have a problem with African Americans? Do you have a problem with African American females? Because I feel like there's some tension in these relationships." And I did have a few that did admit it and they said, "Yeah. What I know of you all," you know, um, "I don't really care for it." And, um, I've had a few admit it and, say, agree that they needed some help to accomplish something.

DR. H   But just using the expression "What I know of you all . . . " is based on some type of stereotype about African American women.

MS. T   Yes, ma'am.

DR. H   That, in and of itself, says to me that you're lumping all African American women together.

MS. T   Exactly.

DR. H   And there are differences within any group of people.

MS. T   Right.

DR. H   There are differences within African American families.

MS. T   Right. Well, and some of the things that the social workers have told me over the years are that they didn't feel that they were adequately trained, did not have enough practical training, in working with different populations and so that's why it was hard for them to come to my home or any other African American home and work with us because they didn't feel like they had been trained adequately enough to be able to go out and work with these minority children and families and such.

DR. H   Did you find as a social worker and as a foster parent that people you have encountered in your work including colleagues were open to asking questions when they didn't know? Or were they more apt to make assumptions and generalizations regarding people of color?

MS. T   I didn't find a lot of question asking; um, I think I had a really good social worker towards the end of my career in foster care and she was big on asking questions. But my earlier years in foster care, um, there were more assumptions than questions.

DR. H I am not working in child welfare at this time, but I have worked in child welfare in the past and always asked many questions. I always asked questions if families were doing something and I didn't understand why they were doing it. I would ask, "What does that mean? Why do you do that?" and I didn't encounter problems working with families. Even with families in which English was their second language.

MS. T Yes, I understand where you are coming from.

DR. H We managed to communicate with each other.

MS. T Exactly, yes. And that's important. I think it goes back to the awareness you were talking about earlier. When you are aware of your issues, yourself, and your biases, then you are able to recognize those things and try to ask the questions because you realize you don't have the knowledge about that other culture. And so, you utilize questions, you know, in a way that you gain information that you need to work with that family . . . and you know you will be able to help and communicate with that family.

DR. H Now, you were a foster mom for many years.

MS. T Yes, ma'am.

DR. H In addition to the issues we've talked about, are there some other issues that you would like to discuss at this time?

MS. T Yes, there are several that come to mind. Um, another incident was, um, I just had some, um, children. . . . I'm African American. I had some children that were European American. Uh, a family composed of three siblings. Um . . . and I wasn't asked, I was told that, um, "I'm probably not Catholic, but I need to make sure these children go to a Catholic church. And so, um, this was earlier in my career, um, when I didn't have all the knowledge I needed to know that I can make some choices here. Um, so I took these kids to Catholic church every Sunday, um, and one of them, the oldest boy, um, the ten-year-old, he asked me one day . . . he said, um, he said, um, "Why do you take us to this kind of church?' and I said, "Oh, isn't this your church?" And he goes, "No," and I said, "What kind of church do you go to?" Come to find out, he was Seventh Day Adventist and not Catholic, but the social worker had me taking him to a Catholic church, um, based on what she thought he had grown up as. And so when I asked her about it, I said, "I talked to D, and D is saying 'Why are you taking me to this kind of church every Sunday?'" I went to this Catholic church because for my kids, you know, I'm trying to respect their culture. And so one

Sunday we would go to my church and the next Sunday we would go to their church and the next Sunday my church; and so we would alternate. And so that way, they'd get their time in at their church. But I had no knowledge that these kids were not Catholic. I was exposing them and myself to a religion that these kids had not known or experienced before being placed in my home.

DR. H   But I think that gets to the importance of doing a thorough and comprehensive assessment.

MS. T   Yes, ma'am.

DR. H   Religion and spirituality should be a part of any comprehensive assessment. It gets back to the importance of asking questions. Did she ever think to ask the children what was their religious affiliation?

MS. T   Right. Well her excuse was, when I asked her about it, the thing was she saw D with a cross around his neck, so she thought that that meant he was Catholic. And she said she's Catholic and she wears a cross around her neck. So to her it was Rosemary—I think is the name of the cross that they wear. And so that's the false assumption that she drew.

DR. H   Did she think that the cross that D wore around his neck was a rosary?

MS. T   Yes, ma'am, that is what she thought it was.

DR. H   I mean, I'm Catholic and I do have a rosary upstairs in my jewelry box. I don't wear it around my neck. No, I don't, but I take it to mass and often hold it when I am praying at home.

MS. T   Right, but he had on a cross and she assumed that he was Catholic like her. And that was what she gave me. So, um, after we got it sorted out, of course, you know, I began taking him to the church that he needed to go to; what he was used to going to.

DR. H   I'm listening to you and I think a lot of what you are saying is reflective of the fact that you are a graduate-level social worker. You have a strong knowledge base about social work, families, and people. I'm thinking about all of the kinship care providers and foster parents who don't have your knowledge, background, and experiences nor do they know the appropriate questions to ask. They are trying to be good parents to the children in their homes. They are not getting the services that they need; they are blundering through the child welfare system because they do not know how to navigate the system; consequently, they find it difficult and frustrating too when dealing with the system.

MS. T   Yes. It is difficult getting calls returned, and getting your questions answered and all that. I mean, if you call in and say that you want to know something about a kid—for example, can I cut this kid's hair? You know, you may not get a call back for a month or two. And this kid is going to visits with their hair down their back or big afros because it's hard to navigate the system and get a call back. And the social workers' standpoint is that they have communication.

DR. H So, there's a lack of response?

MS. T Yes, ma'am. There's a lack of response.

DR. H This lack of response is definitely not a good thing for any foster parent and/or relative caregiver to experience.

MS. T No.

DR. H Again, do you think that race plays a part in whether or not you get a response back in an hour, as opposed to a couple of days?

MS. T I believe so and this is why I say it: um, when I joined the Washington State Foster Association, I began going to meetings with other foster parents, of other ethnicities, and finding out that my white peers, in the foster care system, were receiving services. I mean, um, Wild Wave tickets, going and taking kids there and to other places, having uniforms purchased for their foster children, etc. I had been working in the foster care system for over ten years; I had never known the state to pay for all of these services. I had always paid out of my pocket. And so I go to these meetings and I was like, well, how did you guys get all this? And if you're a part of the right clique, um; and most African Americans joining the system are not part of the clique; we don't know about services that are available for children in our care; we're not given that information, we're not hearing them say, "Hey! You want to come over and, you know, join our club?" and I noticed in that room that there was about 90 percent white people. There were about forty . . . forty people at the meeting. And we met every first Tuesday at Sizzlers. I saw that once I started going to the meetings and started providing names to my social workers who were less culturally sensitive, I started getting a better response. And so, it was kinda weird, you know, "Oh! I talked to so-and-so, and she said I should be getting this for my kid." And then all of a sudden I could get a call back, or I could get them to come out and respond but, otherwise, it was like I was in this fog, by myself, you know, trying to navigate through the system; get answers, get whatever . . .

DR. H I think of how many foster parents and kinship care providers, especially those of color who are still in a "fog" as they try to navigate the child welfare system.

MS. T Yes.

DR. H Am I correct in thinking that you are no longer a foster parent?

MS. T Yes, ma'am. And before I left foster care, um, I was asked to be a foster care mentor. Because part of program, when they were trying to retain foster parents in the state of Washington a few years ago, was to hire mentors; to help people go through the licensure process; to have a mentor, you know, by their side. And I did get the chance to . . . mentor some African American foster parents; it was no problem, but I was always asked to mentor African Americans and had no problem with that; however, I just found it kind of ironic. Why couldn't I, you know, mentor someone . . . someone white?

DR. H   Right, I certainly see your point.

MS. T   Um, but I did it. And, um, I did, I worked with families that wanted to give back . . . one family in particular; she had been in foster care years ago and had lots of problems; she didn't feel like she was getting the help she needed. She had some kids that were level two and level three. And she felt like, she just was all alone in the situation and, um, and in talking to her I found out that she had been where I was; where you have no services, no help; supervisors won't call you back; workers won't call you back. You go up to the office, they have you waiting there all day and it was one of those things where she felt completely isolated, to the point where she had to let the kids go. And I could totally relate to her; I've been in that situation several times. And so it was nice to mentor her through the process because she had some basic knowledge about the foster care system.

DR. H   Right.

MS. T   And so basically, I was trying to get her through the licensing process and let her know: these are the services, these are the people you need to be connected with because if they know you're a part of the Washington Foster Care Association, there is better training, there's better . . . there's more training, there's, um, more research, and there are people you can contact if the state doesn't respond.

DR. H   Yeah.

MS. T   There are all kinds of stuff that, when you live in your bubble as a foster parent, you don't have access to that kind of stuff.

DR. H   It sounds like the Washington State Foster Parent Association is a great support network.

MS. T   Yes, it is a very great support network. You go to your meetings once a month; you know, the first Tuesday of every month, and you share stories, and you find out that you are not the only one having problems with the social worker, or that there may be a certain set of social workers that you have the same problem with. Or somebody who you might have thought, um, you know, neglected only you or didn't return your calls, you know this worker had a pattern of nonresponse to other foster parents.

DR. H   Right.

MS. T   Or the worker didn't . . . or neglected to give you all of the information. That was a huge piece of foster parents' issues; former foster parents and/or social workers would not give you all of the information about a child. So you find out later, after you take the kids to the doctor, you know, oh, this child is HIV positive. Well, nobody told you. And that is information that's supposed to be shared with the foster parent before they take them in the home . . . or this child has been sexually abused . . . it's in the records from the past doctor, but nobody shared that information prior to placing a child in your home; the social worker's goal was to get you to take the child in your home and give as little information about the child's background as possible, you know.

DR. H   But the medical information that you mentioned is important information . . .

MS. T   It is.

DR. H   . . . because, um, being sexually abused children exhibit certain behavior patterns . . .

MS. T   Yes, information about any child who has been sexually abused needs to be shared with the prospective foster parent prior to foster care placement; there are behavioral and emotional characteristics that are common in children who have been sexually abused. Consequently, it is the responsibility of a social worker to provide comprehensive psychosocial and medical information to foster parents.

DR. H   . . . and your work with that particular child will be entirely different . . .

MS. T   Yes.

DR. H   . . . than your work with a child who has never experienced sexual abuse . . .

MS. T   Yes . . . and it makes you vulnerable.

DR. H   . . . and the way this child is possibly going to behave towards other children . . .

MS. T   Right.

DR. H   . . . who are in the home is also a factor in foster home placement of children who have been sexually abused.

MS. T   Right. And so going to those meetings allowed you to understand that, "Oh, this service worker has a history of not giving you all the information so you could take the kid." And then you get the kid and then you slowly find out all these things, you know. Or, you know, for example, my, my first . . . second set of kids: probably nineteen . . . uh . . . in the military . . . two-thousand . . . ninety-nine—two thousand, my next set of kids, um, had been kicked out of

four foster homes in the month prior to me getting them. I had no knowledge
of those four foster homes. I had been told that they were . . . they had been in
a receiving home too long and that they needed to move ASAP. So I took them
in that same day, even though I didn't want to. I . . . you know, I went ahead and
did it. And then as I got them in the house and started talking to them . . . and
they were telling me they were here-there and I called the social worker to verify
it and she was like, "Oh, yeah, they were kicked out of there and they were . . .
oh, I got their file mixed up with somebody else." And so, I'm like, okay, what
did they do? And so, you know, and then you're getting the behavioral problem
and then you're starting to know. And . . . and that's really compromising—it
can put you in a compromising situation and the kids because these kids had a
dual diagnosis. I had no knowledge of that when I took these kids in. Um, they
had also . . . had a history of touching other people. And that puts you in a complicated situation, especially when my own son is in the house . . .

DR. H   Right.

MS. T   . . . and then these kids also had behavioral—they were level two and level
three kids, sexually, um, sexually . . . um, I forget the name of it . . . there's, uh . . .
sexually behavioral kids . . . or . . . there's a name for it. But they were level two and
level three kids and that meant that their risk was high . . . for engaging in behaviors that had been done to them. And so, not having that knowledge when those
kids moved in . . . I mean, it really put me in a situation. And I had to redo and
refigure out how I was going to respond to these kids and their needs . . .

DR. H   Right.

MS. T   . . . um, and getting them services, you know, counseling services and stuff
like that is really difficult because . . .

DR. H   Yes, especially with them being sexually aggressive towards other children.

MS. T   . . . yes, knowing that you have to work every day, you need to put them in
child care, but you can't put them in child care because they might start touching other people's private parts; you know this type of behavior will be problematic in any type of child-care center. And then they get kicked out of general
care and off the school bus. And then social workers don't want to respond
because they know that you're calling in to have them taken back into the system, so they just choose not to respond, you know. So it's really difficult.

DR. H   Did you keep them a long time?

MS. T   Yes, ma'am, I did. Um, I was able to . . . you know, work with those kids and
I actually received a couple of letters from the state, in regards to those kids,
because those kids did a three-sixty. And what . . . what I found happened with

those kids is that they had gotten into a pattern of moving from home to home. And so . . . it was like they were waiting for me to tell them that they could no longer stay in my home. They would do something just so they could go to the next home.

DR. H Having worked in the child welfare as an administrator, supervisor, and social worker, I know that children will repeatedly test foster parents, especially when they have had multiple moves.

MS. T Yes.

DR. H This testing is common when children are placed in a new home.

MS. T Yes.

DR. H They will sometimes do very aggressive things to see if they are going to be able to continue living in their new foster home.

MS. T Yes.

DR. H Do they really want me here?

MS. T Yes.

DR. H Or am I going to be packed up and moved again?

MS. T Yes. And I saw that early on with my kids after the honeymoon phase was over. I saw that early on, especially with the youngest boy. Um, a lot of anger, a lot of bitter resentment, um, very defiant, um, and I saw that as a challenge to be able to make a difference, and to do what I needed to be a good foster parent to him as well as his siblings. And, uh, and so I did, I took those kids and, I tell ya, a lot of sleepless nights . . . it was a lot of work but . . . um . . .

DR. H Well sure.

MS. T . . . those kids . . . every time they did something, my motto was to say, "I love you, and you are not going anywhere. Unless you are going home to your mom, you're not going anywhere." So, they were doing it like, "Yeah, yeah!" and they would flip over TVs, tear up stuff, write on the walls, pee, touch my son's privates, you know . . . I was writing incident reports all the time. And, um, but my thing was not to give up on them because I felt the pain that the little one felt . . .

DR. H Right.

MS. T . . . you know, just being moved from place to place to place, and not feeling like he belonged anywhere, you know.

DR. H Right, I am sure this little boy had never experienced any sense of stability in his young life.

MS. T Yes. And those two . . . they were a part of eight siblings that were split up into about four different foster homes. So it was really important for me to try to keep those two together, although the state was thinking about, you know, separating them because they were such a handful. So, there was lots of work with those kids but, you know, in the end they . . . I kept them until they were adopted out and . . .

DR. H   Oh, that is why . . .

MS. T   . . . I'm still in contact with them.

DR. H   Are you?

MS. T   Yes and they're doing really good . . . yes.

DR. H   But I'm sure that you made a difference . . .

MS. T   Yes . . . yes.

DR. H   . . . in their lives.

MS. T   Some of the stories they tell me, I'm kind of embarrassed of (ha ha). I'm like, "I said that to you?" (Ha ha) I'm like, "Whoa!" Um, but some of the stuff they told me, you know, I'm really proud it stuck with them.

DR. H   Right.

MS. T   We went over and over. And, um, and they still call me Mama T and it's, uh, a lot of my kids do. And so, um, even though it's hard on them, they, you know, they still remember, they will say, "Remember when you told me how important it was to learn to read; you know, I've learned how to read," and, you know, "And you said all I have to do is keep trying and I was going to learn how to read?" Then I was like, "Yeah." And he was like, "I know how to read and I'm a superstar reader." You know, and the littlest one was . . .

DR. H   That must make you feel good.

MS. T   It does . . . it does . . . it does . . . because he was in the fourth grade and didn't know how to read. I mean, he couldn't read a three-letter word. And it was hard for him, um, and he kept telling me . . . we had so many behavioral problems. I was constantly off work, um, going over to the school. And I worked at a penitentiary then. So it was hard, I mean; there was stress on my job when I had to leave my job to have to run to the school and handle something. But he'd get frustrated and have these explosive attacks; uh, he had RAD and ADD and he was a handful but a sweet kid just looking for love. And I tell you, I killed him with love. And he just . . . he blossomed . . . he just blossomed. And we studied and worked on his reading. I think it always helped because I was always in school with my kids and so I'd work and go to school and we spent a lot of time in the library. And I told him, "Just start off small." We'd start off small with little words, you know, we had Phonics on tape; we had the little ABC DVDs; we had it all. And we were like, "Okay." And we sat out blocks of times, um, and we worked it out. Because when each . . . when a different family comes in my home, I have a set base house rule that we have . . .

DR. H Okay.

MS. T . . . and then we sit down as a family, within the first week, and come up with family, household rules . . .

DR. H Okay.

MS. T . . . and we all agree on it. And we sign and we post it.

DR. H It's important to have rules and structure . . .

MS. T It is.

DR. H . . . when you are raising kids.

MS. T Yes, one of the things that the kids wanted as a rule was to have study time—a set study time. They really didn't want to be behind in school, missing a lot of school, or changing schools. So that was huge for them.

DR. H I'm sure the kids wanted that rule because it hurts kids when they are in a classroom and they're not working at the same grade level as other kids in their class.

MS. T Yes . . . yes, ma'am.

DR. H Kids can be cruel to other kids.

MS. T Yes, ma'am, really cruel. And so these boys had more street knowledge than a grown person had. But when it came to book stuff, they . . . they were lacking. Um, and so it was really nice when they wanted to implement that study time; I was excited. So I took advantage of it and . . . we learned how to cook, and we read ingredients, and we tried to make it fun so we could bring them up to par in their classroom in order for them to not always have to be pulled out and, you know, have these explosive outbursts.

DR. H But just think of what a difference you made in their lives.

MS. T I know . . . I know . . . I look at it now and I see their Facebook posting and they call me and want to come by and I'm like, wow! You know, yeah . . . it makes you feel good because you're fighting the system . . .

DR. H Yes, you are fighting the system to make a difference in the lives of children placed in your home.

MS. T . . . and you're fighting against the odds that . . . you know, you don't really know what you're getting when they drop those kids off . . .

DR. H Right.

MS. T . . . and, um, to be able to take them in and, you know, to love them and, you know, give them something, you know, nuggets to live on.

DR. H The nuggets were ones that they never had in their lives before coming into your home.

MS. T Yes. I mean, it's an awesome feeling; taking them on experiences that they've never had before. You know, taking them to Disney World, hiking, camping, and, you know, very inexpensive things, but it means a lot to them . . .

DR. H Right.

MS. T . . . that we're out together. We're out roasting marshmallows at night.

DR. H And they are part of a family.

MS. T Yes, yes, they are always a part of a family. So it was a very rewarding experience for me and for them.

DR. H Are there other things that you want to tell the readers?

MS. T Yes, I think, um, cultural sensitivity training is a huge piece of social work dynamics. It doesn't matter what the ethnic or cultural background is of the child you receive in your home. I think it's important for social workers not to make assumptions based on their own past experiences but to really ask questions and to get to know that child as an individual or that family as an individual. Um, because I found it really hard to deal with social workers; they wanted to do textbook social work. And textbook social work doesn't work for everybody . . .

DR. H No, it does not because every child and every family are different.

MS. T . . . and it didn't work for most of the kids that I had in my home. So, it was really difficult to work with the social workers that didn't have the experience . . . the practical experience of working with these folks.

DR. H You know, textbooks provide information.

MS. T Yes.

DR. H Experience and practice vary and can be different. You know, we can read things in books, but when we get out and actually have to interact with children and families, this interaction is one of our most valuable learning experiences.

MS. T Yes, and so I found that really important; you know, another thing that I found really offensive happened in 2002. I received a set of kids from the Lakewood Police Department. They were brought to my door with the social worker. And it's a long story how I ended up getting them. It was supposed to be a seventy-two-hour hold because this mom had always dropped off her kids, and come back. She'd go on a drug binge and come back. So . . . so I knew this officer and so he'd frequent my house at night for seventy-two-hour holds. And so I ended up with these kids and it lasted longer than the seventy-two-hour hold. Um, one of my encounters . . . one of my first encounters with the social worker after the initial visit was when she came out to see and meet them and . . . the interaction was limited to her coming out and doing a welfare check on the kids; the thirty-day track; she accused me of not being racially sensitive to my foster daughter at the time. And she didn't have the words to say what she meant; she spoke all around the issue, "Aren't you ethnically, aren't you culturally, aren't you . . . ," you know, never said "Are you black? Are you African American?" And she used to . . . never just come out and said it. She spoke all around the issue. And what she was basically getting at was that she felt my hair was always in corn rows and my foster daughter's hair was very thin and very wiry; it was all over her head. But because she was a mixed race child, the social worker thought that I should have her hair braided all neat like mine instead of having it all frizzy in ponytails all over her head. Her words were really offensive. Because she said, you know, "Why don't you have her," you know, "J's hair braided like yours?" you know, "Aren't you culturally . . . " you know, so the first assumption was that all black people know how to braid. I don't know how to braid.

DR. H . . . or . . . so . . . but black people wear their hair braided.

MS. T She didn't have her hair in braids, yes. So those were . . . that was the first two assumptions that, you know . . . that she got. And then, um, the way she kept digging at me as if I'm lying to her, um.

DR. H Did she ever ask J, your foster daughter, do you like the way your hair is styled?

MS. T No, she did not. What she did . . . she tried to prove a point to me, after our conversation, the kids were outside playing while we spoke and they usually go and see the kids in their room or somewhere private, you know . . .

DR. H Right.

MS. T . . . and so what she did was . . . she wanted to prove a point to me, I think. Um, and so she called J in from outside and asked her to come in and, you know, I explained to her, "J doesn't like her hair braided, J is very tender head," you know; every time you touched her head she cries. You know, um, J . . . um . . . you know, she had been through enough trauma with the, the life that she had when the police brought her to my door, you know, and having to go through all of that made no sense to me. So I explained all of these things to her and she still proceeded to, you know, call J in and say that J would look nice with her hair braided like mine. She called J in; she got, uh, uh, a comb. And she started to comb J's hair and twisted it into, you know, a little braid. All while J is squeezing, and turning, and crying, "Mama T and . . . " and I'm sitting there . . .

I let it go on for a couple of seconds and then I said, "Isn't that emotional abuse, isn't that physical abuse? She's crying. She's calling me, crying and you're still braiding her hair."

And she's trying to talk J into, you know, saying, "Oh wait honey, be still," you know, "I'm just going to braid your hair and you're going to just look so cute." J was not interested in that at all.

DR. H   But cute ... to whom?

MS. T   Right, exactly. Because I thought she was cute with her ponytails, you know. And so I found it very offensive and, um, you know, we had an extensive talk. I definitely filed an incident report and went to the supervisor at the state office. And I did, later, get an apology. Um, but, um, you know, I feel like there needs to be more practical training before you let these social workers go out there into foster homes.

DR. H   But then again, this speaks to individual differences...

MS. T   Yes.

DR. H   ... within a culture.

MS. T   Yes, within a culture.

DR. H   Every black or African American girl or woman and even girls and women who are here from Africa...

MS. T   Right.

DR. H   ... does not want her hair braided.

MS. T   Right. And the other thing is . . . is, you know, in the classification, you know, um, you know, the mixed kids, um, they have a different grade of hair and it's just like, you know, a white person's hair. Just because society gave them that label, that they are black, um, it doesn't mean, um, for J, she wasn't black. If you asked J what she was, she could name it off. I mean, that little girl was as smart as a whip. "I'm Anglo-Saxon, I'm European, I'm Indian," I think I was surprised that she knew her ethnic origins. So don't call her black because she will break it down to you what she is and she could tell you a quarter of this, a third of that . . . I mean, she knew her historical background. But the social worker addressed her as African American. And she was not African American; the social worker did not understand her ethnic background.

DR. H   But again, it is putting a label on an individual based on physical characteristics.

MS. T   Yes.

DR. H   And many times the labels are false.

MS. T   Yes, exactly.

DR. H   It is important to ask people how they identify themselves.

MS. T   Right, because it is wrong to make assumptions about any person.

DR. H   The people that I know will readily tell you who they are . . .

MS. T   Yes, yes.

DR. H   . . . and how they would want to be identified.

MS. T   Yes, yes. Um, but that's not the experience in the field. And so it's hard when you get these social workers, um, and I think the biggest problem with DSHS is because, I think, a lot of my social work friends were slipping Sure, Casey Family Programs or some of the other private agencies tend to hire experienced social workers. But I noticed with the state agency, I think because they have that contract for CWTAP (Child Welfare Training Alliance Program), they bring on/hire kids fresh out of school; they don't necessarily have the hands-on field experience they need to adequately work with people that don't look like them. And it doesn't matter who it is, what race, what culture, they just don't have it and I think some will admit it, and some will say, "I have an MSW and so I'm right." And until you pull out your MSW, and you say, "I also have an MSW; you're not right." When you do that, you can get them to back down and work with you. But for other foster parents, who may not have that education . . .

DR. H   Right.

MS. T   . . . or they may not be in that position, and maybe of a different racial or ethnic background, it would be harder for them . . .

DR. H   Right.

MS. T   . . . and then we lose foster parents and we have all of these kids still coming in the system that don't look like the people that are coming out to their homes to visit them, you know. And so it's been difficult, you know. And so there have been a lot of things to deal with as a foster parent.

You know, even with the guardian ad litem, I always advocated that we need more guardians ad litem that look like our kids, i.e., children of color, especially African American. Um, some of our kids I've had in my home have asked, "Who's that lady?" I've had a couple that ask, "Who is this white lady that just wanna come in and take me out, and I don't know who she is." They don't introduce themselves, you know. I mean, besides a one-day visit, these kids have no knowledge of who these people are and they are allowed to come in the home and just take these kids out.

There are many problems that point to racial disparities in the services that are received by children of color and their families in the child welfare system that definitely need to be addressed.

DR. H   Well, I appreciate you talking to me. Is there anything else that you haven't said that you'd like to say?

MS. T   No, I think, you know, really, you know, my thing would be to . . . if there's going to continue to be a CWTAP (Child Welfare Training and Advancement Program) for MSW students at schools of social work I'd like to see some ongoing training on culture sensitivity, culture awareness, cultural competency for social workers because with the disproportionality of children of color in the child welfare system and the disproportionate number of social workers in the system, it is very difficult for the social workers who lack cultural awareness and cultural sensitivity to interact with foster parents and/or kids who identify as people of color. And if you're not culturally competent or not able to put aside your stuff and/or just have the experience to communicate effectively with another race without offending them then you're not going to get far. I've had a few social workers that have offended me and I was done with them; I was done communicating. You say what you need to say, allow them to visit with the kids, and get out of my house . . . that's all I'm thinking about. So, to be able to give them some ongoing cultural training experiences would be helpful. Um, in terms of getting them better prepared to work in these households, you know. I think that we can all use it. I mean I love to learn about other cultures and how to interact with people in these cultures.

DR. H   And so do I because I value and respect individuals from all cultures.

MS. T   Yes, so I think it would be great. I think it would be a great suggestion and I'd like to see it implemented.

DR. H   Well, thank you for sharing your experiences.

MS. T   Thank you.

DR. H   (Silence)

MS. T   Oh yes . . . I forgot to tell you about another incident, um . . . experience I had with another foster care system and some relatives . . . a relative placement. Um, in . . . um, a few years back, um, before I got out of foster care, um, I had a set of kids in my household. And I received a call from the state or . . . uh, no . . . I received a call first from my sister saying that, um, she might need me to take her kids because they had been, you know, um, were in foster care placement . . .

DR. H   Okay.

MS. T   . . . um, so I contacted the state because I was already licensed . . .

DR. H   I understand why you wanted to have your sister's children placed in your home.

MS. T   . . . and tried to go through the process to get them in relative placement because . . .

DR. H Right.

MS. T . . . allegedly, relative placement is first but that's not the reality.

DR. H Well that's what the federal law says but . . .

MS. T That's not what happens.

DR. H . . . okay, but the federal law stipulates that if there are viable relatives . . .

MS. T Right.

DR. H . . . children should be placed with relatives. And social workers should try and locate relatives and assess their homes prior to placing children in nonrelative placements.

MS. T Right, so maybe I wasn't viable because I had kids at the time.

DR. H But your home was licensed, right?

MS. T I was licensed. I was licensed for five kids and I only had two at the time. Three of my nieces and nephews needed to be placed. So, technically, I could have been able to take these kids . . . but I wasn't allowed.

DR. H Why?

MS. T I went through the process, and they said that I had my hands full and that, um, they had found suitable placement in the respite care they were in; they were just going to leave them there. And I fought against it for a while. Um, and then, by the time you get responses, try to go to these hearings, it's already months into it and the kids are there. So I had kids placed in my home already and, so, I sort of just let it go because I wasn't getting anywhere with the state at all. Um, consequently, about . . . I don't even think it was a year later; I received a call from the state asking me if I would like to take my nieces and nephews.

DR. H Are you talking about the same nieces and nephews that you wanted to take earlier? At the time that you were told, you're hands were full . . .

MS. T Yes.

DR. H . . . and you were not allowed to have them placed in your home by the child welfare system.

MS. T Yes, ma'am.

DR. H What happened in a year's time to make them change their mode of thinking?

MS. T There was a new social worker and I wanted to know the same thing; that was my first question. I still have the same kids . . . the two boys that I had when I tried to get them a year ago. So now you're calling me because of what? At that point, they explained to me that the home that the children had been in, um, the girls ended up being molested by the foster father of the home.

DR. H Oh, I'm so sorry to hear that the children were sexually abused.

MS. T   Yes, it was very disgusting, very hurtful. Um, it just tore me up because I was open, willing, and available to take them.

DR. H   Right.

MS. T   Um, and for the state to tell me, um, that I couldn't have them because I already had kids and, um, you know, they knew I was not overloaded. They didn't ask me if I was overloaded, but they had already suggested that "Oh, you have your hands full already." Um, and so . . .

DR. H   But you weren't at maximum capacity . . .

MS. T   . . . No, ma'am, I wasn't.

DR. H   . . . in terms of licensure?

MS. T   Right. Right, and so it was interesting to receive that call and I was just traumatized. I said, what services will come with them because now they've been molested; they were removed from my sister's house, went to the home that you guys said was better than my home; my home is the same home that you want them to come to now. Nothing has changed, I still live at the same address, but now I'm fit enough to take them . . . after they've gone there and been molested? Um, we had some conversations about that placement, and the state didn't want to own up to anything. Uh, they wanted to say that they needed to consult with their legal department anytime you wanted to ask them a tough question about their . . . about their reasoning for placing them there and having the girls in that predicament. Um, and so it was . . . it was, um . . . being African American, um, working with African American and Hispanic kids, uh, being placed in this white home, having this incident happen; it was difficult. I sort of felt at that time the state had already let me down. Um, this was my third potential relative placement at this time. Um, and they had already sorta let me down and didn't want to take responsibility for their decision about the placement of my sister's children. I didn't want to take on what they had already made a mess of. Um, and so . . .

DR. H   I can certainly understand your decision.

MS. T   . . . I let them find a placement on their own. Um, as a result, luckily, the girls were able to go with another sibling that was already in care and they adopted the girls and they moved to Florida. And so, the girls are, currently, doing very well.

DR. H   That's good to hear.

MS. T   Yes, and so it was difficult, you know, to have to go through that. I had another incident with a relative placement in 1997. It was my nephew from another sister. And he was placed in my home, and they brought him to my home. He was placed in my home from the hospital. Um, he . . . the date that they gave me for his birthday was wrong. He didn't have a birth certificate or a card. It was very interesting how this whole ordeal played out. He came to my home; they dropped him off with just a bottle and a couple of things from the hospital. So I ran out, got all this stuff for the little guy. Um, I was working at the time so the next couple of days after I had him home, I enrolled him in daycare; I went through the entire application process. And one day I left work to go and pick him up . . . I was still working out at the prison . . . I left work to go pick him up and he was gone; he wasn't at the daycare. And so I called the social worker . . . and so I said, "Um, I was told that you signed my nephew out of daycare," and I was going on and on to her.

And she's like, "Ya, let me call you back. I'm in the middle of something." And I'm like, "Well, wait a minute. This child is in my care, I have a guardianship order; he's in my care and he's missing." To me, I thought it was a crisis . . .

DR. H   Right, I certainly would have thought that a missing child was a crisis.

MS. T   . . . you know, this is my nephew, you know. Um, and so it was interesting because what . . . even though I had only had him a couple of weeks . . . I don't even think it was a couple of weeks . . . I think it was about a week . . . yeah, it was about a week . . . it wasn't a couple of weeks. . . . It was about a week . . . um, they had come up with this plan that I didn't agree with. And a part of the plan was that he was allowed to see his mother. Um, even though they took him away from her, they were placing him with family so that they didn't have to worry about visitations. So I would do the visitation, and she would be able to nurse him and bond with him and all of those things. And I didn't really agree with it . . . and not because I didn't want him to bond with his mother. I just felt like it would be very confusing for this infant to go to a new home from the hospital, have his mother involved, and daycare involved. I just thought that it would be a lot, in terms of attachment . . .

DR. H   Right, especially because it was a newly born infant.

MS. T   . . . and so I went with what the state said, of course. Um, and we did it that way. Well . . . fast forward . . . once I got in touch with the social worker, you know, because I'm devastated, I'm frantic, I don't know what's going on.

DR. H   He's gone!

MS. T   I don't know what's going on; he's gone from the daycare, I dropped him off before I went to work, I come back . . . he's gone. So when the social worker . . . had finally called me back, she and her supervisor said they didn't know I worked full-time when they placed him in my home. They . . . they said . . . they didn't know he was going to be in daycare ten hours a day, um, and they didn't want that for him. Um, and then they proceeded to say that I allowed my sister to see him at church when, that Sunday before, um, when he wasn't supposed to have a visit that Sunday. And there was like all of these random things that were really weird. And I'm sitting on the phone, I'm stressed out because I'm thinking, where's my nephew? I just got everything ready: new crib, new playpen, all of this stuff and this baby's gone. And this social worker, on the phone, insensitively, telling me all of these things that don't make sense to me. And I said, um, "I've been a foster parent for a number of years. How do you not know I work? You know; I've never been a stay-at-home foster parent, you know, so . . . you have a record about me; I've been licensed with the state since 1993; there are no secrets about me." There were a number of things that came about through the investigation; the social worker was consequently fired, um, because a number of things that she said were very inappropriate in terms of race; for example, she said that my nephew was a Cuban baby. Somehow she labeled him a Cuban baby; she gave me the wrong date for his birthday and this . . . this was a stickler for the state. They had already placed him, but this is what I found out down the road. She gave me the wrong birthday. A child who is an infant can't be enrolled in daycare until he or she is about five weeks old. This child was four weeks old. So I had enrolled a four-week-old into daycare based on the information that the social worker gave me . . .

DR. H   Right, you enrolled him in daycare on the basis of inaccurate information.

MS. T   . . . that was all that I had to go off of. There was no birth certificate, Social Security card . . . nothing. Um, the stuff that she said about the Cuban baby, uh, and me being black, and asking me questions about who my sister sleeps with, uh, all that stuff the supervisor found was not relevant to my nephew's placement; you know that those were things that she should not have been asking. Um, because at the time I was not a relative placement, I was a foster care placement. So those were questions that if she had placed him with another foster parent, she would not have been asking. And like the supervisor said, it doesn't matter who she slept with, you know. Um, and where did she get the Cuban from? She said that it was from the baby's hair and how pale he was; and so she made up her own race, made up her own . . . um, and so, like I said, she was fired, but consequently, I ached for a long time . . . my heart just ached because I had this child and had started to become attached to him. I tried to get him back, but by then he had already become attached with a foster parent in another home. And it's one of those things you really have to figure out. Was I going to be selfish and take him because I could as a relative? Or was I going to allow him to be successful in a home where there is a stay-at-home person who could be there for him. I wasn't in a position to be a stay-at-home relative foster caregiver. So yes . . . I've had quite a number of experiences that I felt were racially inappropriate and I think it goes back to what I said about practical experience in the field. So . . . that's it.

DR. H   Thank you very much for taking the time to share so many insightful experiences.

MS. T   Thank you.

JUDGE X

This is an interview with a judge who has been a judicial officer for many years and has heard criminal cases, family cases, juvenile court cases, etc. He also has many years of experience with the child welfare system, the court system, including drug court, and the mental health system.

JUDGE X   One of the first things I'd mentioned is that working on child welfare judicial cases is without a doubt the most difficult rotation that we have. Um, you're required to learn about and deal with all sorts of family dynamics with adolescent and childhood development issues as well as a number of esoteric legal issues and federal and state legal issues, all of which guide the child welfare system. So it's the most difficult assignment that judges have. I believe.

DR. H   And I know that in law school there are no courses on child development . . . family dynamics . . .

JUDGE X   (Interrupts) There is nothing to prepare you; in fact the story I tell young lawyers is when I first became a judge, I was anticipating what would be the first case I actually tried. What would it be? And I thought it might be a murder case, it might be a robbery, or it might be a theft. And, of course, the very first case that I was assigned was termination of parental rights. And I have to tell you I was in shock. I was . . .

DR. H   (Interrupts) I'm sure.

JUDGE X   . . . you mean, you mean remove the kids from the parents? And it's just not—you know you forget that's an important part of this job. And, and so it hit me straight away, um, and it's just a very difficult assignment.

DR. H   Well, you're making decisions that are gonna change lives.

JUDGE X   Yes. Now I think the other thing that is difficult about it is that you are dealing with parents and family members at probably the most vulnerable time in that family's existence. Imagine having a child removed from your care for whatever reason. Um, the child is in trauma. It's got to be traumatic for the parents as well; not understanding whatever kind of parental deficiencies they are dealing with. And so you're dealing with the family at a very critical moment. And yet it's a time where you have to be able to show respect and have some understanding as a judicial officer to deal in an evenhanded way with this family notwithstanding the fact that the reasons that they're appearing in front of you may be, um, just really awful. I mean involving things like abuse and neglect. But notwithstanding those allegations, you still have to deal with these people with respect. The goal is hopefully either reunification or some other type of permanence and stability for the children. So it just makes it really tough. I found it, I believe minority kids have maybe a tougher time because there is a pattern of disproportionality that surfaces that's evident from my practice; um, it's evidenced by a couple of things. By the achievement gap and the academic setting and you see the same disproportionality and the rates of young minority kids being incarcerated in the juvenile justice system. And you see the same type of disproportionality in the child welfare system in terms of, um, permanence, adoption, um, number of relative placements, um, foster care placements, the, the fact that, um, relative placements aren't as aggressively, in my view, pursued with minority families.

DR. H   And they should be.

JUDGE X   And they should be.

DR. H   Because federal law stipulates that . . .

JUDGE X   (Interrupts) You have to.

DR. H   . . . relatives should be considered the first choice . . .

JUDGE X   (Interrupts) The first, the first choice, yeah . . .

DR. H   . . . in terms of placement unless there is something in that relative's background or in the home . . .

JUDGE X   (Interrupts) . . . that stands in the way.

DR. H   . . . that is going to put a child at risk.

JUDGE X   And unfortunately I think what happens is sometimes a lack of what, you know, this old term, cultural competence or not understanding the strengths of relatives particularly in minority families makes them look less attractive. When, in fact, those are probably, um the least disruptive placements for kids . . .

DR. H (Interrupts) I agree.

JUDGE X . . . and so, yeah . . .

DR. H (Interrupts) Because a lot of times especially if it's a European American caseworker who is accessing, for example, an African American family, sometimes they come in looking at these families from a deficit perspective, rather than a strengths . . .

JUDGE X . . . strengths . . .

DR. H . . . perspective.

JUDGE X Yeah, yeah, and you know that's what happens, um, I had, um, a family, I, um. It's not often, but periodically families are successful and work hard and are reunited and those are really, um, those are good outcomes from my perspective. They're difficult, but they're good. But you have to understand when people have really turned the corner, um, when they're truly motivated, um, what their strengths are, what kind of support systems they have. Um, and it's never easy and I know every time I return kids to a family, I, there's some degree of trepidation. Is this gonna work? What is gonna happen? But I've been actually pretty successful when I've seen some of families do really well.

DR. H It's very rewarding, especially when children are reunited with their families.

JUDGE X It really is.

DR. H It's been years since I've been a child welfare practitioner.

JUDGE X Yeah.

DR. H But in Chicago, as administrator . . .

JUDGE X (Interrupts) Yeah.

DR. H . . . that was the goal. I worked for a private child welfare agency and, of course, we had more resources.

JUDGE X Right.

DR. H But anyone that I hired always knew that we were about families and keeping families together.

JUDGE X Yes.

DR. H When we are returning kids home, families need services . . .

JUDGE X Yeah.

DR. H . . . We have to put all the services into place . . .

JUDGE X (Interrupts) Right.

DR. H . . . to return these kids to their families.

JUDGE X Yes.

DR. H And it takes work.

JUDGE X And, you know, and I think that's an important point because we have to be able as a judicial officer to be objective about what are identified as their parental deficiencies. But I also want to be able to appreciate what are the strengths? And as you said, you know, being strengths-based makes a difference. And, um, so, um, you know, as difficult as it has been, it's also been some of the most rewarding work that I've been involved in. And, um, if you can help families heal and if you can reunite kids with their biological parents, it, it really is worth it. I mean it's difficult.

DR. H I agree with you. I'm wondering if you would talk a little bit about (pause) bias against birth fathers because it's been my experience as a researcher and also as a practitioner . . .

JUDGE X (Interrupts) Um, um.

DR. H . . . to notice that some judges are very reluctant to pursue placements with dads and with the parental side of the family.

JUDGE X Well, it's interesting because in Washington, in divorce or dissolution cases, there's no longer any presumption that kids would be placed with the mother. The presumption is joint or shared custody. And I believe it's because the legislature intended for fathers, biological fathers, to have the same parental rights as the mother would have. But this hasn't quite transferred over into the child welfare system yet. And there still is a bias, and it may be because we don't tend to traditionally think of men as nurturers. Um, possibly because of developmental issues and, um, and I think occasionally the courts may not look at the child's developmental age and ability and assess that, um, relative to who is in the best position to care for the child. And so, um, so the presumption is that, unfortunately, and I think it's an incorrect presumption, that the biological mother or the maternal grandparents or families are preferred placements and I think that's the question of training. I think it will take (Dr. H interrupts: "I agree, I agree.") a lot of change in our mindset to do that. And I think training is needed for social workers, judicial officers and guardians ad litem.

DR. H Well I teach my students, and I'm only one professor, that children have a mother and a dad. And I still believe in what's in the best interest of the child.

JUDGE X Right.

DR. H And if dad's (Judge X interrupts: "Right.") going to be a better parent (Judge X interrupts: "Right.") then this is where the child needs to be placed.

JUDGE X And I've seen a lot of cases where mom may have a drug addiction or co-occurring drug and mental health disorder and the dad may be doing okay.

Um, you know there may be situations where an out-of-home placement can be avoided if the father was actually sought after and reasonable efforts were made to place the child with the father. I don't think that we always make those types of reasonable efforts to involve the father.

DR. H   Do you think that social workers, child welfare workers do a good job or a poor job in locating fathers?

JUDGE X   Um, I think overall the, the, the, the social workers I've dealt with did their job and did a pretty good job in engaging fathers. Uh, I'm not sure how, you know, procedurally, how they go about their searches in whether they're thorough enough. I will tell you this though; I have noticed that some dads, well, a lot of the social workers in our county are females. I think the overwhelming majority. Um, and sometime there is a tension between the social worker and the dad. I've seen that happen a lot. And the dad feels like the kids have been taken away, and he's been disrespected, and the social worker maybe has not started services as quickly as they should have or whatever. Um, but the best social workers are the ones who are willing to engage the dad and deal with them straight up. And, um, I will tell fathers at review hearings that, you know, if you want to be a player, if you want your kids back, you're gonna need to cooperate with this social worker. Um, and I've told them on many occasions that this is the social worker who's able to reunite kids with their families. So you want to work with this one. Um, so it takes some cajoling on both sides to get them to start to work collaboratively toward this goal of reunification. But there is a tension there, which is really hard to break.

DR. H   I agree with that. Um (Judge X interrupts: "There's some tension."), but I think that dads should be given the same message (Judge X interrupts: "Oh, yeah.") that moms are given (Judge X interrupts: "Now, I agree."); they should be given the same message and the same services.

JUDGE X   In the same . . . and I had another one. You know, I had, I had a guy who was across the mountain, and he, I could tell he really loved his son, and his wife really had the problems. But he just had not been the most stable person and hadn't, um, been in the kid's life as much as the mom had before she just blew off on drugs and her mental health issues. Um, and this guy would come across from eastern Washington every other weekend and the visits were regular; he was always on time, and was really dedicated. And we worked out an arrangement, um, that just involved him, and helped him move ahead and, um, corrected deficiencies that he had and that turned out to be just another really, I think, real big success. The child did well and had a great relationship with his father; mother hasn't been seen. Um, but I imagined that this young child is a lot more emotionally stable knowing that he has this good relationship (Dr. H interrupts: "Right.") with his father. It makes all the (Dr. H interrupts: "It does make a difference.") difference in the world. Yeah, yeah, so, um, that's a tough one but yeah.

DR. H   I'm wondering have you noticed in your work any service disparities when it comes to relatives or families of color.

JUDGE X   Um (long pause), there are some services disparities throughout the system which makes it, I think, at times more difficult for some low-income people and minority people. Um (pause), and let me see what would be the best example I could give. Um, well one example that is a different sort of example is the following: here, if you are a gang member you can get in drug court. Um, and the Tacoma Police Department and the Lakewood Police Department have lists of supposed gang members and their affiliates. The problem is those lists only deal with Crips and Bloods. So if you're a Hell's Angel, if you're part of the Gambino Organized Crime Family, if you're really a gang member, you can get in drug court. But if you're a minority, a young parent who use to be involved or whose girlfriend or boyfriend or family member was involved with a gang you can't get in drug court. So that's an example of a disparity that's based on supposedly a facially neutral policy that has a desperate impact on minority people.

DR. H   And you know and I know that the largest number of children who come into the child welfare system come in because of substance abuse issues of their parents.

JUDGE X   Substance abuse. Exactly.

DR. H   For my readers . . .

JUDGE X   (Interrupts) Yeah, uh, hum.

DR. H   Will you explain what drug court is for my readers?

JUDGE X   Drug court is an alternative to incarceration that allows an individual to go through treatment, and basically they check in, in drug court once a week or if they graduate they get to a higher level. It could be once a month. And, um, it's a way to help them overcome their addiction which as you indicated is often for a lot of parents the reason that they're before the child welfare system. And so, um, that's basically drug court in a nutshell. We have a special drug court for child welfare cases called Family Dependency Drug Court. At one point it was called Meth Family Court because a lot of the users were on methamphetamines. Um, and meth, you know, if you go back to it, that's kind of another historical disparity because, um, I don't have statistics, but I can tell you anecdotally that, you know, a lot of the substance abuse you see here in Pierce County when we started the meth drug court, it was, I believe, more difficult for minority parents who might have had a heroin addiction or a cocaine addiction or if they were doing something other than methamphetamines. And sometimes, um, at least in the early 2000s methamphetamine was more the drug of choice. Again, this is just anecdotal; predominantly white addicts were using methamphetamines and I thought there were a lot of black people and Hispanics who were doing, you know, crack, coke, and heroin. And so we didn't really have a program for them, we had a program . . .

DR. H (Interrupts) Right.

JUDGE X . . . primarily for folks who were doing meth who were predominantly white and that's not to suggest, I mean, that no blacks were doing meth because I know plenty of black defendants who come before me for use of methamphetamines. But at the time we started that family drug court to help defendant families, it was really targeted toward the methamphetamine population.

DR. H It means that if they couldn't get into drug court . . .

JUDGE X (Interrupts) It meant a harder time.

DR. H . . . the time clock in terms of parental rights was still ticking . . .

JUDGE X (Interrupts) Was ticking, yeah. . . . And with, and with the family drug court, the family dependency drug court, um, we have review hearings every three months. There were no six-month reviews. It was all three-month reviews and it was a fast track. And it was anecdote information that folks had higher success rates and reunification and quicker reunification which meant less time to care for the kids.

All those things, um, and again you know what's difficult is, is that a lot of these policies we put in place are what I would call facially neutral; they're not designed to hurt anybody. But people just don't think ahead enough and aren't conscious or culturally conscious enough to understand, um, that this is where the disproportionality starts to become evident because of these little facially neutral policies. Anyway, um, let's see.

DR. H What do you think we can do? And when I say we, I'm talking about these systems, the child welfare system and the family court system, to make things equitable for all children and families.

JUDGE X Well, in my opinion the government is not a good parent.

DR. H I agree with you.

JUDGE X (Laughs)

DR. H I'm writing about policies in my book.

JUDGE X Yeah.

DR. H And although a lot of them have been on the book for years I think that a lot of them need to be revisited and changed.

JUDGE X Yeah, I, I, um, what I would like to see is more, um, engagement by child welfare officials with those communities, um, particularly communities of color to engage them and involve them in the child welfare process. And more efforts to try and find placements that are close to kids' homes. Um, and trying to implement those decisions like the *Braam* decisions. That we're not going to let minority kids continue to experience disparities; and, you know, and *Braam* kind of showed us where the disparities were in the child welfare system in this state.

DR. H Right, right.

JUDGE X Minority kids had more foster placements. I mean bombing out more? Why don't we put them closer to home? Why don't we place them closer to relatives? Why don't we start to use indigenous types of resources?

DR. H And why don't we put services in the homes? And keep children in their homes if possible.

JUDGE X Yeah.

DR. H Every case that comes in doesn't necessarily have to result . . .

JUDGE X (Interrupts) In removal.

DR. H . . . What's wrong with family preservation?

JUDGE X Yep, these things I believe are more cost efficient and are less likely to cause trauma because when you remove kids from their parents they are traumatized, even for short periods of times. So if you can avoid removal and keep kids home, you can do it at low cost. And I think as you indicated, it's much more cost efficient; the child welfare cost skyrocketed right now and we're not as effective as we could be. So I think engaging the communities is important. I've seen some models in King County which were interesting; they had sort of a hub home and there were other foster homes around it. And they did respite for each other; they kind of supported each other. So there have been a number of different models that engage the community more and I think that's what we really need to look at.

DR. H And communities of color are basically interested in their kids.

JUDGE X Oh, they are. I meet regularly with the ministerial alliance here and we have a number of campaigns trying to recruit CASAs and guardians ad litem and, and, um (pause). . . . But I'm not sure that we have the expertise at the local level to reach out. I think we have commitment of our current assistant secretary for the DSHS Children's Administration; I know Denise Revels

Robinson and we've had dinner and she's been at my house. And so I know she's committed to that kind of reaching out. Um, but it's hard, you know, when you're at . . .

DR. H (Interrupts) It is; it is very hard.

JUDGE X . . . the top of a big institution to try to ripple change out; it is really difficult.

DR. H It is and people are resistant to change.

JUDGE X They're resistant, I know.

DR. H They will often say, "Well, this is the way we do it here."

JUDGE X And, Doctor, I'll tell you I was, um, I was like the assistant to the secretary with the Department of Mental Health in Tennessee, long before I became a lawyer. And so the secretary and I did a tour of one of the developmental centers like F . . . but, um, a big state hospital for people with developmental disabilities. And so we're walking down the hall and I see this kid D. And D is the kid that my wife and I had done respite for. He was big, and he's intimidating looking, but he's not. He just looks intimidating and he's developmentally disabled. Anyway, I'm walking and I'm like the number two. I'm just walking; the number two guy in the Department of Mental Health and here's this kid I've done respite for and he's just beat up. Somebody has beaten him up. And, uh, the point was that even if you have that kind of power, like I had at that point, it's hard to ripple it down through institutions and to frontline workers that you know will say, "We don't do it like that anymore." You don't have to be abusive; we can be more progressive, but it's hard to make that kind of change. That's the point.

DR. H That it takes time. Thank you very much for talking to me.

JUDGE X You are welcome.

EXECUTIVE DIRECTOR OF PRIVATE CHILD WELFARE AGENCY AND ADOPTIVE MOTHER

Mrs. F is a sixty-two-year-old African American woman. She is happily married and the proud mother of sixteen children. She is the executive director of a private child welfare agency that focuses on providing a high caliber of services to children and families.

DR. H How many children do you have?

MRS. F (Pause) Are you talking about biological children?

DR. H Yes, I am talking about biological children.

MRS. F Well, we were talking about being politically correct.

DR. H Right.

MRS. F Well, this is not politically correct. But, um, it's a family thing, that, um, I have sixteen children.

DR. H Okay.

MRS. F I don't mind saying how many, you know, of those are adopted because of this book.

DR. H Right, I want you to tell me that.

MRS. F Right, yeah.

DR. H I know that they are your family.

MRS. F They are all together. They are all mine.

DR. H That's right.

MRS. F So I have sixteen legal children (laughs).

DR. H That's what family is about.

MRS. F And that's family. Yeah, um, this is kinda going off a little bit just to give you a background on why I put it that way. (Sigh.) Um, there was a time when I introduced people to my children, you know her. You know they, how many, you know, are your children? Well, how many? You know what I am saying?

DR. H Well, all of them are yours.

MRS. F Yes. Um, and I had one of my daughters and that is, um, adoptive. Well, that adoptive one come up to me and say, "Mom, um, from now on I can just be an F." And it just. . . . When she said, I was like she is F. But I knew what she was saying.

DR. H Right.

MRS. F Our family has changed, our whole, um, whenever people approach us. So, um, let me know if you need to know how many are biological for a specific reason and I will tell you. But other than that, I have sixteen children. (Laughing afterward.)

DR. H Oh, okay. I think it's more important, since this book is focusing on child welfare and the child welfare system. (Mrs. F interjects: "Uh-huh.") I think it would be relevant for you to tell me when and why you and your husband became involved with the child welfare system. And I know that we have talked about the two of you being foster parents (Mrs. F interjects: "Yes.") at one point and time in your lives. Why don't we start with that?

MRS. F Okay, alright. So, um (short pause), I was very young, and, um, I think I had I don't know how many children at the time, maybe five or six children. I don't know. And, um, we were at church, you know my pastor (Dr. H interjects:

"Right."), but at the time we were not pastoring. We were at our home church where I grew up in the Lord. And this young girl who is the same age or maybe a little older as mine as one of my sons, um, came and she would always sit next to me. At the time her mom and dad weren't in the picture so to speak. (Dr. H interjects: "Okay.") She was raised by her grandmother, and grandmother went to the same church. And she would always sit with me and people would always comment how much she looked like me and is that really your daughter, and that type of thing. (Dr. H interjects: "Right.") And she just really loved it. And just a real sweetheart. And one day at this time, she was thirteen, and she came sat by me, and, um, she took my hand and said, "Mama F, I'm pregnant." (Mrs. F chuckles.) Everything just dropped out of me. (Dr. H interjects: "Oh, sure.") And so, you know, I was happy we were in church because I didn't have to face her because I didn't want my face to tell. I just kept on holding her and, um, I said, "We'll talk after church." And I think during offering time I just couldn't hold anymore and I pulled her out and said what I can do for you and how can I help you through this. And we've talked and I just let her know that I was there for her. Slowly, she stopped coming to church and, um, she had the baby. Her grandmother, who is the baby's great-grandmother, began to take care of the child, and, um, the young girl started really hitting the streets a lot and really lost contact with her. I figured I would only see her once a month maybe. Um, I wanted to help her grandmother because she was suffering also, um. Here she was a great-grandmother with a husband that has cancer, no supports around her. You know. (Dr. H interjects: "Right.") So, every weekend I would always go and pick up the baby and sometimes after school, you know, me and the kids would go over and take her to the park or something like that to give her grandmother a break.

DR. H   And I'm sure her grandmother appreciated the respite.

MRS. F   Oh, yah. DSHS stepped in and, um, told her that she would need to, because of everything was on her at the time, her husband was dying. Um, she would need to find family to take care of the child or they would have to put her in foster care. And, um, the family is large, but there was no one that would be able to take her. And so, um, and she asked me how I felt about it, but it was actually my best friend who was her daughter-in-law that asked me what about you. I would love to, that would be fine. What does that mean and we didn't know anything about the foster care system. So, um, I talked with her and then a worker called and she says would you be willing and we have her I say a third of her life anyways, you know. The baby knew us and we were connected with family. We would be able to keep the family connections and all that was important. Um, I said okay and we went over and picked her up. I didn't know anything about the foster care system as she started going through this whole paperwork. You know, all of these home studies and everything, autobiographies process. Went through the process and we became her parents. And that's how we got into the system.

DR. H   Was it a long process?

MRS. F   It was a long process for us because now that I understand the process, I was very protective of my information. Um, they asked a question on the autobiography and I talk about this when I'm doing classes. How did your parents discipline you? And the idea is "How did they discipline you?" . . . you probably discipline the kind of same way. And my answer was, very well. And that's how my whole autobiography was, you know. And so because of that it was lengthened. I didn't know why and no one really explained to me the why.

DR. H   That was going to be my next question. Did anyone sit down with you and go over the process? Did anyone explain the reason why information about the way you were disciplined by your parents was important?

MRS. F   No. No, never went through any of that. I was totally, um, I didn't understand the foster care system. I didn't understand what I was getting into. I just wanted to be a person to open our home and hearts to . . .

DR. H   This baby who needed you.

MRS. F   . . . this child and assist this family in going through this process. I didn't know that it was all of this legal stuff. You know.

DR. H   And I think that as a social worker, I understand that there must be rules, policies, and regulations. But at the same time I strongly feel that social workers and child welfare workers have a responsibility to explain the process to families.

MRS. F   I agree.

DR. H   I'm an educated woman and I've never been a foster parent. And certainly if I walked into an agency and I wanted to be a foster parent, I would need the process explained to me. I know what's involved in it, having been an administrator at a private child welfare agency. However, being a child welfare administrator is entirely different than being a foster parent.

MRS. F   Right.

DR. H   But again, I've never been personally involved with the child welfare system.

MRS. F   And then for me coming from where I came from, the African American community, regardless I mean there's a lot of other things in my DNA, but that's what I hold on to. And being surrounded there, my grandmother I know that she was not a "legal foster parent." There were always children at our home, always. And they were always cousin so and so. You know.

DR. H But that's one of the strengths of the African American community.

MRS. F And that's all I wanted to do.

DR. H We take care of our own.

MRS. F Right.

DR. H And when I say our own, it doesn't necessarily have to be blood kin . . .

MRS. F Right, exactly.

DR. H . . . to be taken in by a family.

MRS. F And so this is all knew. You know. I saw it with my family. I saw it with my mom, and dad, and grandparents. I saw it with aunts, and uncles. That if someone needed, it could the next-door neighbor, it could be someone at church, or it could be someone they specifically just met.

DR. H Sounds like my grandparents.

MRS. F And if the need was there, someway there is going to be. . .might not be a bed, but it would be a cot someplace, you know, or roll up something.

DR. H As I reflect back, hmm, on my career and childhood, I realize that my grandmother was practicing social work and didn't have a title.

MRS. F All I wanted to do and that I knew, all of these papers, um, it didn't match what I was trying to do for me. Um, I was blessed to have in the middle of the process or I guess towards the end another licensor stepped in. I don't know why. It might have been because I don't was standoffish to the process. I mean, I am sure we were two of those people whose family goes through the process that was a headache to the system. I am sure we were because we were always fighting, "Why, well, why?" because I am not going to give that information. No, you can't have that information; you know (laughs), you can't have a copy of my Social Security number. (Dr. H interjects, "Well, I think some information is very personal and not needed for foster home licensure.") My Social Security number, what for? I just want to take care of the child, and so this other licensor stepped in and she was a gem, a gem and, um, she proceeded with the licensing and, um, she literally wrote down the steps; actually you will see that same paper, well I made it prettier, um, at my agency. We use that same thing. I mean it was very important to me that families really know about the process. We have it blown up really big and we take them through the steps.

DR. H Well, I think that you need to tell my readers all about your agency. I know all about it.

MRS. F Well, um, One Church One Child, Washington State, is a nationwide African American organization that recruits African American families for African American children that are in the foster care system, um, primarily for adoption. In Washington State, we began breaking away from that, and, um, we began recruiting for foster care and adoption. We were the first One Church One Child to also recruit for foster care families.

DR. H I think that's wonderful. I'm familiar with One Church One Child because I lived in Chicago for many years. I actually knew Father Clements and went to his church, Holy Angels, several times.

MRS. F Ooh, ooh. He is still with us. We wanted to start this program and in 1988 we began One Church One Child of Washington State. And in 1998, we decided to become a placement agency because we saw that families that we were recruiting were slipping through our fingers. We were recruiting for all agencies, but the state agencies would let them slip through their fingers because at that time, I don't know what it is now. (Dr. H interjects, "Right.") We don't refer families to them. We license them ourselves but at that time (Dr. H interjects, "And that's a good thing.") . . . what we would do is the class, then the application to the agency. Sometimes I would go into the workers' cubicles and see applications piled up on their floor. I'm talking about at least a foot high or maybe higher, piles, piles of applications and packets, and, um, files and just, you know, all sorts of paperwork. I could see why they were slipping through our fingers, and sometimes they were not responded to in a timely manner and this is why we started our agency because . . .

DR. H It means that children were waiting for families.

MRS. F . . . Exactly, exactly. And this is why we started One Church One Child at our agency. The — part is the placement agency, so now we are licensed and the only African American placement agency in Washington State. Um, with a focus on African American children; um, we do not discriminate; we do not show a difference or anything like that. We've had white families, Indian families, — families, Asian families, — families. Um, we've placed children of all races and ethnic backgrounds that I can think of right down to children from Somalia. Um, but our focus, our focus is always is our children, our African American children. (Dr. H interjects: "Because . . . ?") There is no other agency that has that focus.

DR. H You and I know that African American children are disproportionately represented (Mrs. F interjects: "Absolutely.") in the child welfare system. Although there are services out there, there are also many families that need services. African American children come into the system in large numbers and they continue to stay in the system. I think it is wonderful that you and your husband started this agency and you have continued to be proactive in terms of finding families for these children.

MRS. F It is not easy because, we had. . . . When we started out I had nothing but my Garfield High School graduation certificate; that was my education. I was a mom; I was serious about our children, period. Um, I wanted to do something; actually it goes back to my first placement when she became legally free, well, um, her mom came to me and, you know, said, "Mama G, I think they are going to probably take her away from you and put her in a home that will adopt, and I want you to adopt her." I said, "Well, you are not using names right." (Dr. H interjects, "No.") I said sure. But the problem is that I don't know anything about adoption, and is this what you want? And she said, "I want her with you, period." And we had a family meeting, and the whole family, everyone; of course there wasn't anyone that didn't say no. And two years later, she's been with us for two years. So we began the adoption process and after we adopted her, after it was finalized, then I called my licensor and I said I wanted to do my exit interview to turn in my license and she said, "Oh okay." She came out to do the interview and she said, "So why is that you want to turn in your license?" And I said that I've adopted and, you know, that there is no need for me to have the license anymore. We kept on talking; as we talked, she would put down a child's picture on the dining table; we just kept on talking and she never said anything about the pictures. We kept on talking (Dr. H interjects, "Right."), and she would put down another picture after a while. We talked about the moon, space, church, my plant, or anything, then she would put down another picture. There were about five pictures that were put down; finally, I said, her name was G and, um, I said "G, what is this? (Laughs. What are these?" So she said, "Oh, well, you are saying that there is no need, but I just want you to see some of the faces of children that need you and where are they going to be when you turn your license" and she went just like this, you know . . . and I was like, huh, needless to say. I was a foster parent for twenty years after that conversation. Because of that . . .

DR. H Approximately how many children did you parent?

MRS. F . . . because we had the agency we were very careful not to, um, we didn't want lots of children. Plus, I had the agency, and so I didn't want to just be a foster parent that took in a lot of foster children. I was not able to parent every child who needed a home, but I was able instead to use my impetus to recruit families. (Dr. H interjects, "Okay.") The children, all of the children that came into our lives as foster children, um, came in because I could not find a placement; they were the harder to place, they were runners, sexually active, drug users, promiscuous, ones that would not stay in school, um; usually they had a combination of three or four of those problems.

DR. H   The children who came into your life, and eventually into your family, are the children that you and your husband adopted . . . right?

MRS. F   Yes, all of the children that we've adopted have been hard to place children not because of their African American ancestry. I mean they were not hard to place because of their ethnic background. Our children are hard to place (Dr. H interjects, "Right.") because of the other things. I'm trying to think, but I believe all of them, there might have been one I can think of real quick, um, were born drug and alcohol affected, and they all had multiple problems in some area.

DR. H   But I think even in my experience, of course I haven't parented any children placed in foster care. However, working in child welfare, if a child is born with drugs and/or alcohol in his/her system and placed with a parent or parents who can really love and support him/her and get the services the child needs the child is going to thrive.

MRS. F   I believe that. I believe that wholeheartedly because of my experiences, both positive and negative, with our very first child; the one that came . . . she was, um, drug and alcohol affected but with high alcohol affects; the other children we had were also drug and alcohol affected but more highly drug affected. She was highly alcohol affected. I could cry just thinking about her. I did not get the supports I needed. I know now from being in the system so long that the supports were there; the supports were given to others. I did not get those supports because I did not understand what were my rights, what were the child's rights, and even through school I did not get it.

DR. H   Do you think that race impacted the quantity and quality of the services you received?

MRS. F   Yes, absolutely it does. Um, skipping around, I am also on a CPT (Child Protective Team) or I used to be; you sit on a team and when the families come in, they more or less fight for the children and you listen to them; you listen to the social worker, you listen to all of this, and then we make some decision about, you know, when the child should return home, and what other services are needed. I remember time and time again people saying, "That's the grandmother, you know, but, you know, the apple doesn't fall far from the tree."

These types of things were said about African American families and I never heard that, never, never heard that said when a white family came in.

DR. H But that in and of itself is discriminatory. (Mrs. F interjects, "I can call them on it as long as I am there.") This type of statement is clearly a prejudgment of people based on their racial/ethnic background.

MRS. F And so when I look at my children, and, um, particularly that child, when workers have that kind of discriminatory belief and/or attitude, I know that I have to be a strong advocate for my children; they might not even know that they have it, you know.

DR. H I think that is really important to have self-awareness. And I talk about this in the practice section of my book; it's really important for social workers and child welfare workers to have some self-awareness, as well as cultural awareness and sensitivity, especially if you are going to work with children and families of color (Mrs. F interjects, "Right."), and it is not to say that as people of color we don't have biases or prejudices. But anyone who is going to be in the social work profession, I strongly feel needs to have some self-awareness or you can't effectively do this work.

MRS. F You know, it's one thing to have a bias. I believe that there is not one person on this earth that does not have a bias. (Dr. H interjects, "I agree.") It is just impossible. And even people different from me are biased sometimes to the point of prejudice. My whole thing is come in my face and be prejudiced, but just know that you are and acknowledge it and be aware of it. Because then you can do something about it; you can't do anything with something you don't acknowledge that you have.

DR. H I teach my students that we all have biases and prejudices, but you can't allow them to interfere when you are working in any facet of social work. You have to leave them at the door because as social workers, we are cannot judge people; we're supposed to be nonjudgmental. And if you allow those biases and prejudices to enter in your professional work, you are not going to be objective; everybody needs to be treated the same.

MRS. F I totally agree. It's harder, I think . . . I know it was harder for me in my younger days when I was going through this stuff, not understanding and not knowing how to fight this type of thing. Um, I wanted to get us to why we began One Church One Child community services because every step of the way, um, it's not that we are better than the state, but we can give our families better services than the state can give them. And I don't mind saying that. Um, I know that. I look at things like kinship . . . when we first started out in 1988, our whole thing was kinship. Then, fifteen years later, all of the sudden, it's like kinship, kinship, kinship; you know, it's a big deal thing . . . only they called it fictive kin. I told them, "Don't say fictive kin because fictive means pretend and my relationship with my aunts and uncles, and cousins who are not blood is stronger than some of my relationships with my blood aunts, uncles, and cousins and these are not fictive and these are not pretend relationships, these are real. I am a real person, you know, I am flesh and blood. I am not plastic."

DR. H   I feel the same way about terminology. I remember this training in the early nineties. I was at a conference and a woman from the Child Welfare League of America had given a presentation on kinship care; she was talking about grandparents and she referred to them as foster parents and she talked about foster grandchildren. I raised my hand and I said, "You know, I think that's a horrible misnomer because one's grandmother is one's grandmother; one's grandchild is one's grandchild. There nothing foster about it; it's real." The presenter acknowledged that what I had said made perfect sense.

MRS. F   I believe that, of course.

DR. H   I think a lot of the terminology that we use for children and families has negative connotations. For example, I don't even like the term foster child. (Mrs. F interjects, "It's better to say a child in care." Laughs.) I tell my students, in this class if you are writing a paper, you will have to say "a child in foster care, not a foster child; this is a child just like any other child" (Mrs. F interjects, "Yes, it is.") and it is not the child's fault that she/he is in the system. Do you think that in the child welfare system we have institutional racism?

MRS. F   Yes . . . (laughs) yes! I know we do and the sad thing is that we keep going around in circles around it; you know and I know that we do. You are an educator and researcher; but my take on it is that sometimes, somewhere along the lines, you know . . . I've been doing this since 1988 and you have probably been doing this work before that time and others before that, but we're doing the same thing. When do we get to the point where we say, "Yes it is now and what do we do about it now, to get rid of it and stop it now." You know, I'm like (laughs) . . .

DR. H   Well, I'm saying that in my book, but I'm just one person. But I'm hoping that this book will be read and not only utilized by people in the child welfare, but by professors who are preparing young people to go and work in child welfare. I think that we are never going to eradicate this problem until we call it what it is and acknowledge that it exists in the child welfare system as well as in other systems. My book is on racial disproportionality and disparities in the child welfare system; in my mind racial disproportionality is simply a politically correct term that is used for racism in the child welfare system. It is what is it and it's been in existence since the child welfare system started because the child welfare system was not started to serve children of color. And that in and of itself is a racist act.

MRS. F   Absolutely, absolutely.

DR. H   What else would you like to tell me that you think might be helpful to readers of this book?

MRS. F   (Pause) I don't know; we've . . . and I apologize; we've jumped around so much that I am wondering what was left out. (Dr. H interjects, "I think what you've said makes sense.") I think it is really important to call it what it is; um, racism and I think we need to stop being afraid of . . . and when I say, "We," I am not talking about we African Americans, we people in the child welfare system; all of us are afraid of hurting people's feelings or try to say things just the right way or, you know, this type of thing. Um, all of the trainings that we go to, all of these different projects and everything, sometimes it gets so heavy on me that I feel like I can't breathe, and I'm just cut by a different piece of leather and I want to roll up my sleeves and I just want to do what is right. I just want to see outcomes. (Dr. H interjects, "You know, I want to do the work [laugh], and, you know, we've worked together in the past and we are working together now; you know that I've resigned from certain committees because I felt these committees were not serious about working on and trying to eradicate this problem.") And unless you can have a conversation about it, you cannot resolve the issue. I think that is a thing that I would really like to see hit in your book. I think I say it a lot with my mouth because, um, I'm not . . . and when I say I am not educated, I'm talking about, um, I don't have a PhD. I, um, I am not putting down the education that I have. Sometimes I just put it out there. I look at people that can act it like you; I look at people that act it and I learn from you. I learn that you don't always have to open your mouth and that sometimes a closed mouth says more. And so, I know this is way off, but this is my time to give you your kudos, oh, okay. (Dr. H interjects, "Thank you, I know . . . And I learned the way I act from my maternal grandmother.") I just want you to know that I've learned that and I've watched you. There are three people and I won't name them, but you are one of them that I have watched and I've grown through watching each one of you; I have learned to speak when I have something to say that is going to hit it hard. Even in the transition design committee I learned that; I am sticking it out, but I'm opening my mouth at the right times, at the right times which is hard and a learning process for me (laughs).

DR. H It is a learning process. It's hard, but what you'll find is that when you do open your mouth it has some impact.

MRS. F I'm saying that's what I'm learning; and so I want you to know that it came from listening and watching you.

DR. H Well, thank you.

MRS. F Yeah, um.

DR. H I try to teach that to my students but unfortunately some of them even as they graduate with their MSW, they don't get it. But I've had some to come back and say, "I've finally learned what you were trying to teach me. I put my foot in the mouth in the wrong place." (Mrs. F interjects, "Right, right.") It can have a negative impact. Sometimes you don't realize the negative implications until after you have mistakenly opened your mouth and made a statement. (Mrs. F interjects, "You taught me without even saying it.") Yes! What you're trying to say is that you don't reach your goals when you speak before you think.

MRS. F Right, right . . . how come we do that . . . um, I don't know. I think the only other thing that would be is that not only is my organization important, but other African American organizations, agencies, groups, or work groups, whatever also have an importance in our community and in the child welfare system. My colleague CG and I started a group called the Association of African American Service Providers and it's now incorporated. We are moving forward with a small group. We started because I began seeing that I was called to the table constantly if there was a work group going. You know . . . was looking around and I am thinking, is there no one but me? You know . . . is there really nobody but me in this whole world?

DR. H I feel that way.

MRS. F Oh, I know, I know you must have the same thoughts. What I started doing these last three years whenever I get called, I would send somebody else from my office like C or E or I would take somebody else over with me because I wanted to make a statement, you know, that I am not going to be here forever. In fact I am on my way to retirement. I can mentor those individuals and bring them in. Otherwise, this system is going to be under water.

DR. H Who was serving on all of these boards and committees before I relocated to Washington State?

MRS. F Nobody, not us. . . . But not us . . .

DR. H I am not going to be here for the rest of my life. (Mrs. F interjects, "We are not there.") Another thing that I say to these committees is that they are not about me or me being at the table and that doesn't mean that's me; it is the African American community. I look at some of the groups; some of the groups that are not headed by people of color; but these groups are trying to speak for me and other people of color; they don't speak for me; you cannot speak for me. You can't. I can speak for myself. (Mrs. F interjects, "No.") I need to be at the table, and if I am not at the table then your work group or committee doesn't represent me or mean anything to me. Because the thing that is missing is our lived experiences and there is no book, no degree that can compensate for that.

MRS. F   Right, right, so . . . that's another big, big, thing that I think our agency did a lot to bring to the forefront. Tiny, tiny, agency, very small agency, um, yet it's been around since 1988. Next year, we will be celebrating twenty-five years.

DR. H   I think that's wonderful; that's wonderful. I don't know if you readily know the answer to my next question. Appropriately how many children have families because of your agency?

MRS. F   I don't know the number, but it's in the thousands, because of what we did . . . even before we were recruiting. When you think of it we did classes; that's all we did. We recruited, did classes, and help fill out applications and send them on their way. Um, I do have the figures for how many we have that are self-licensed, but that is a very small number. You know, we say small, but one thing that I wanted to make sure is that we were personable, make sure that if you picked up the cell and you called my office and you pushed my extension, my cell would ring. If I am not at the office, my cell is on twenty-four hours of the day. I am on and every one of the families knows that. Every one of the families can get hold of absolutely anyone in the agency either because they have their direct cell number or because they call the office number. There is also a worker and all the families know his direct number. His office line does not ring to his cell phone number because they don't need to because they can dial his cell number directly. In fact, families can reach all of our workers. All of our workers and also the front desk people can be reached 24/7 at our agency. This is another thing that I don't believe is available at any other agency maybe in the world (laughs) that other agencies will do something like that for their families.

DR. H   I tend to agree with you because I think some agencies that I've called just to confirm the time for a meeting and I get a machine. (Mrs. F interjects, "You, well, you might get a machine with us.") But I don't get the call back from these agencies; apparently someone always responds to calls to your agency.

MRS. F   You'll get the call back; you'll get the call back.

DR. H   I can deal with the machines, but my issue is that it's unprofessional not to return calls.

MRS. F   I agree. You know, when I was going. . . . That's why we started our agency. There was so many things that I felt needed to be done for our families. Things that I would liked to have seen done for me; returning phone calls was one. If I had a problem between 9:00 and 4:30, then I probably could get somebody; but that's not the problem. But between 9:00 and 4:30, my children are in school and I'm probably not going to have a problem. You know (laughs). . .

DR. H   Well, you know, in the child welfare system, a crisis can occur at any time.

MRS. F   Crises usually occur after hours. Crises usually do not occur between 9:00 and 5:00. Crises occur when the child gets home and is out running or playing and hurt themselves or over the weekend when the office is closed. Crises occur after 5:00 and on weekend; that's when you cannot get anybody at the office. I wanted to change that, at least for the little pot of families we had. So our families can get us; our families can call any of our workers by their cell phone number. Um, I've had a worker that was literally out of the country and then called me because somebody had called him and he didn't want to let them know he was out of the country because he didn't want to put them on hold until he returned; he called me and then I called some others and we went to see about it. You know, he was there to talk them through it until we arrived to handle the situation. He said, "Don't worry, we will handle this," and we were there like in an hour.

DR. H   I am sure for the families this type of immediate response has made a tremendous difference to families served by your agency (Mrs. F interjects, "I know it has.") to know that they can call their worker.

MRS. F   We call them family workers. We don't call them social workers; they are family workers. (Dr. H interjects, "Well, they are providing services to children and families . . . right?") Right, they are the M family workers, and then that was one thing; then kinship was another thing. Helping them fill out the applications was important; we help them fill out the applications, you know. Just all of this is like a one-stop shop; you know, always being there for our families. I think it is so important. I see now where agencies and the state agency, the DSHS, the Children's Administration, is really making big strides testing unified home studies; they are now doing these. I have mixed emotions about these home studies. Um, I don't hold that back and I think anybody that I have come in contact with knows that. First of all, we've been doing unified home studies since 1998. We've always done foster care/

adoption unified home studies; that's what's been done at our agency. And, um, we are not the only one; most private agencies do unified home studies. It's just the state agency that didn't. These studies are a new thing for them. You know, its unified homes, big deal, and they want you to go through this training and all of this. And, um, but it's comical because I think we've been doing unified home studies for over twenty-five years. We've been doing them and now you're just caught on, kudos to you.

DR. H   It's really amazing to me, but I guess it's because I never worked in child welfare for a state agency. My work has always been with private agencies, and there is a definite difference in the quality of services that the children receive.

MRS. F   Yes, absolutely. I'm going to give this. . . . It is a much shorter packet of M, our agency. I will give you some information that is much shorter. I know that our time is up, but thank you so much for talking to me. Dr. H, if you wanted this interview to continue even over the phone, I would be glad to. I feel like I did not do the interview justice because of our short time; you know, if I have left any holes and you need to fill the holes, give me a call.

DR. H   Thank you, I'll call if I think of anything that you did not discuss; however, I think that you provided a wealth of information for my readers.

ADOPTIVE MOTHER

This is the interview of a forty-two-year-old African American/Caucasian mother of three biological sons who is a divorced, single parent. She recently adopted her three-year-old niece, who was four in December 2012. She is a college graduate with a Bachelor of Arts Degree in Social Welfare (BASW).

DR. H   How long has your niece been with you?

MS. B   Just now . . . four months.

DR. H   Did you adopt her through a private agency or the state agency?

MS. B   It was through the state agency.

DR. H   When did you first become involved with the state agency?

MS. B   I am part of the maternal family. O will be four in December 2012, and her brother S will be two in August 2012. They were in foster care together. It was looking as though they were originally going to be adopted by their foster parents. This did not work out, their misfortune. I came to find out that if I wasn't able to adopt both of them together I could not adopt singularly. Being the single mother of three boys this was not an option for me. Then, shortly after a few months passed I learned that her brother was going to be returned back home to his biological father.

DR. H   Okay, that was a good thing.

MS. B   Yes, that left O that was to be adopted by the foster family she was residing with at that point for almost a year.

DR. H   But she has family of her own.

MS. B   Yes.

DR. H   And I am wondering why the social worker didn't pursue adoption by a family member rather than what I consider a stranger foster family.

MS. B   I asked that same question myself. Even though I made myself available in the very beginning I was never contacted outright to adopt O but I was pretty much told that she was in a good place and that she had adjusted and that she had already come so far in the family that she was living with.

DR. H   But federal law states that maternal relatives and/or paternal relatives should be the first option for any child who comes into the state foster care system.

MS. B   Yes, yes, that is true. And I think that had I not had a background in social work and been someone not knowledgeable about the law and the system and the way things work, and having a support system that I could fall back on, that would have been the end of the case. She would have been adopted outside of the family. This being the only one out of all five children that would have ended up being adopted outside the family. Another reason that I was adamant about adopting her.

DR. H   And it is important to keep children with their family.

MS. B   Yes, and I wanted . . . never wanted O to ask the question of "Why my family never came for me?" I believe that, you know, that a lot of our children that are adopted out must always wonder that there is family that is available. Um, and I wanted to step forward and make sure that I did everything I could to adopt her and bring her home so that she would know not only her family but our family history, the culture that we come from. She would know both sides because we are biracial. She was going to be adopted by a white family. Um, and I wanted her to be able to know growing up as a biracial child some of the things that you are going to encounter which are very different than someone just of a white background, someone of just an African American background. It is very difficult for them to understand what we have gone through.

DR. H   You are right.

MS. B   I also wanted to make sure that O had contact with her mother. Her biological mother is my stepsister. She has multiple aunts, uncles, grandparents.

DR. H   All the research that is done with children who exit the foster care system demonstrates that these children go and find their birth families. It is interesting to me as a social worker because social workers will say when they are doing a diligent search for families that they can't find parents. "We can't find his mom; we can't find his dad. We're terminating parental rights." Yet, when these children age out of the system they go and seek out their birth families.

MS. B   Yes, yes.

DR. H   Well, why don't you share with me the process involved in adopting your niece? Was it an easy process?

MS. B   It was not an easy process. I wish I could say that it was. As I said earlier, having the background in social work definitely helped me to be able to navigate through the system because it was never made easy for me. I was basically kept being put on hold, not even knowing when there were court dates, happening to hear from it through my stepsister and appearing at the court dates to kind of get an idea of even what was going on, where she was at with things and found that it just seemed that they were fast tracking her to the adoption with her foster parents. So, someone who didn't have that knowledge would never know that they could appear at these court hearings, that they had a right to be privy of what is going on in this case.

DR. H   Right, you are absolutely right. Do you feel that race or institutional racism played a part in how O's case was dealt with and in how you as a relative were treated throughout this process?

MS. B   That could be some of it, but I think that most of it was the social worker who was handling the case at that time was very new to the profession and I think was probably under a lot of pressure and had a lot of other cases that she's handling. It was just easier to please the foster family. It just made it a smoother system for her to just continue on to let O stay in this home that she has been in and to tie up the ends by completing the adoption. Whereas, when I presented I presented an additional amount of work that was going to have to take place. With that starting out as the background check and, you know, them coming to your home and doing a home study; there were multiple steps that needed to be taken that she had already taken with the foster family.

DR. H   But you are family to O.

MS. B   Right and the sad thing is she did not see that as a benefit. That is what would have hurt O had I not been someone who was very determined that I was going to adopt my niece.

DR. H   For me what I am hearing is a problem in terms of social workers. This is one particular social worker, but it makes me wonder how many other cases are being handled this way. What it says to me is if you are going to do child welfare work then you need to learn that families come first.

MS. B   Yeah.

DR. H   You need to learn how to engage with families. It is not about making your tasks easier. It is about doing what's best for the child. In the long run it is best for children to be with their families if at all possible.

MS. B   Yeah.

DR. H   That speaks volumes about what we are teaching in schools of social work to future social workers who are going to do child welfare work.

MS. B   Yeah.

DR. H   Are we not teaching them about families and the significance of families?

MS. B   You know, it was something that really worried me that someone in my profession would not have grasped the importance of family and that there is so much value in keeping family together and even the odds that you can keep the biological parent connected to the child.

DR. H   Right, because adoptions sometimes are usually closed. Although sometimes foster parents say they are going to keep the birth parent involved, in reality in the majority of cases this does not happen. I don't know if it is fear or insecurity, but they don't want birth parents involved once that adoption is finalized.

MS. B   Yes, yes, I agree. That does seem to be that . . . that tends to be the case. And I am sure in this situation that would have definitely been the case from some of the comments that the foster parent had made about my sister and those types of things. Even though she was mentioning at the time that I would be able to come in and still have a relationship, I just never felt that I could not bank on that; that I needed to do everything I could to pursue adoption of O.

DR. H   Throughout this process did your sister make her wishes known that she wanted O placed with you?

MS. B   Yes, it was always my sister's choice to have O come and live with me. Her three older daughters that I mentioned earlier were adopted by their paternal grandparents and this was after their biological mother's rights were terminated. She had O shortly after those rights were terminated. I had talked with her that O would be taken from her care as well. So, she had always said from the beginning that if that happened she wanted O to come to me. She was able to get O back into the home and then lost custody again. And then at that point she knew that she didn't want her rights to be terminated. Because with her attorney that she was working with it would be better for her to relinquish her rights and O would come to me. "If I relinquish my rights it has to be that O is going to live with my sister."

DR. H Why were her older girls placed in the child welfare system?

MS. B So, their mother suffers from . . . she has some developmental challenges.

DR. H Okay.

MS. B There was some neglect and also domestic violence. And I think making a decision to stay in those relationships was therefore not protecting the children.

DR. H Right, I understand.

MS. B So, the children were taken from the home. And they did more than a year of counseling and different trainings for my sister to go to and they just were not seeing what they wanted out of her. So, her rights were terminated.

DR. H Is O in counseling or speech therapy?

MS. B She is currently in speech therapy. They said that when she came into foster care she was probably a year behind in her speech and when I got her in the home she was communicating, but there were a lot of words you could not understand. And then there was also not yet at three she still was not making four- or five-word sentences and just a lot of one-word commands.

DR. H Right.

MS. B But in these four short months her vocabulary has definitely expanded.

DR. H Oh, that's wonderful.

MS. B Yes, and we have gotten past the frustration of her not being able to communicate with you.

DR. H Right.

MS. B Helping her to either learn new words or show us in a way and from there we are able to teach her how to say that back in its form.

DR. H I think that is wonderful. Well, what are some of the challenges that you encountered on this road to getting this adoption finalized?

MS. B Dr. H, I have to say that the biggest challenge for us was . . . ah, it just really felt the initial social worker had a lot of control over how this could have gone. She delayed a lot of things to where more time had gone by where she was left in that foster home and able to continue that bonding relationship there and not able to begin a relationship in the possible home that she was going to be adopted in.

DR. H Right, right.

MS. B It was also very difficult to maneuver through the system and kind of understand and I felt that there were a lot of stereotypes about how family was perceived when they are coming forward to adopt a child.

DR. H Can you give me some examples?

MS. B Yes, I began a weekly visit with O after going to visits with her mother. They began visits in my home which would be for about an hour and a half once a week.

DR. H Okay.

MS. B We were very limited to be in the house for that time. So, I asked at one of the visits if we couldn't have permission to go to the zoo or the park, taking her outside of just that home visit.

DR. H Right.

MS. B They said, "You have to have a car seat." Which . . . I was very much aware of. I asked, "Does she not have a car seat? Could you provide one?" And it was immediately . . . I found out in some of the transcribed papers that were given to the adoption social worker that I was seeking money for O because I asked for a car seat. And when I was told that I had to provide my own car seat. Even though at this point I had not . . . you know . . . there were . . .

DR. H You were still having visits.

MS. B We were just beginning our visits and nothing had been started on the application for adoption. I didn't know if I was going to have her in my care. It was really looking as though she would be turned over to the adoption family. So, I just felt that, you know, it being a state law that parents have to have a car seat for their child, that O would have been provided one because she is given benefits by the state. She would've had a car seat.

DR. H Well, she also is in foster care.

MS. B Exactly.

DR. H It is my understanding that the Children's Administration keeps a supply of car seats in the regional office for use when transporting kids.

MS. B What I also found out after asking this question because she also told me that I could not share the car seat that the foster mom had that I had to have my own. And again I think that this was just another thing that she was throwing up, an obstacle, something that she was trying to throw in the way to deter me from my decision to adopt O. It wasn't so much about the means of getting a car seat. I found a way to get a car seat, but I just felt that the state should have provided her a car seat.

DR. H Especially since they have car seats.

MS. B   Yes, what I found out from the adoption social worker once she had taken this over and she saw this write-up, she asked me, "What is the big deal about the car seat?" She said that you were seeking money for this. I said, "All I was asking was, Where the car seat is for O? O should have had her own car seat; when she came into foster care she is a ward of the state. She should have had her own car seat." "I can't believe they did not give you a car seat. We have a budget specifically for these things."

DR. H   That's what I was talking about.

MS. B   You should never been required because she was not in your care. I did purchase the car seat. And I was told by the social worker after I kept pushing the issue that there was not a specific law about me sharing the car seat with the foster parent, but that she just did not think that it was a good idea. That just told me it was her own (laughs).

DR. H   This almost sounds like social worker bias.

MS. B   It was her own bias that she had. And then there were the difficulties with turning and gathering all the paperwork and learning what was required of me to be able to adopt her.

DR. H   Did she sit down and explain what would be needed in terms of documentation?

MS. B   I never heard from her, never heard from her. She never offered to sit down with me or to have a meeting. If it wasn't for me just looking for other routes . . . my sister's lawyer had hired a social worker to come in and actually do an adoptive home study because we were not getting anywhere with the state. Out of her own funds she paid for the social worker to come in. And she did an adoptive home study of me. She sat down and explained what the process was and what I would need to do. And then they also had a legal aide who went out and found out what it was I needed to do class-wise, so what training needed to take place. I had a twenty-seven-hour course I needed to sit through just as if I was becoming, applying to be a foster parent.

DR. H   Because I think the state requires . . . I think it's called "From Foster to Adopt." You actually have to serve as the child's foster parent, even if you are a relative prior to moving into adoption.

MS. B   And so, they called and found out when the class was; the class was the day that they called. It just had started.

DR. H   Why is everything always last minute?

MS. B   Because I didn't have a social worker who was willing to work with me to make sure I had that information. That was not her goal. So, it wasn't something that she put anything into.

DR. H   You are a professional person who works full-time.

MS. B   Yes, she knew that. Yes, I think that she was hoping that I would just become so engrossed in my life and see that this was too much work. She was not getting anywhere and I would not follow through.

DR. H   Obviously, she did not plan on you following through.

MS. B   I just had to find other avenues to get what it was that I needed. We even had to contact the state to find out why is it that things are not moving? And why is it that we are not having visits? It took calling someone who was above this social worker's supervisor to actually get the ball rolling.

DR. H   I remember when I talked with you. Tell us what happened.

MS. B   So very frustrating, not knowing when courts dates were, and the court dates that I did find out about, going and there really being no mention of my wanting to adopt O. And when it was mentioned it was more of a "Well we really don't know if she will be able to; you know, she stepped up before, but nothing ever happened." So, I was written off. And never did they come back and revisit and want to sit down and figure out why O was not adopted the first time she was put into foster care.

DR. H   You stated that what was presented to you was adopt O and her brother.

MS. B   Yes.

DR. H   Not one child, but two. I understand that because state law says if at all possible siblings should be placed together. I understand that, but you also made it very clear in your own personal family and circumstances that you could not adopt two children.

MS. B   I knew that it would not be fair to those children. The ages that they were and my work schedule and I also have three older boys.

DR. H   Right.

MS. B   So, when I was told that, it was devastating to me and it was really something that I had to really be honest with myself. You know, could I really do this? And I'm walking away from both of them is what it felt like to me. And it was very hard for me to even tell her at the time that I just can't possibly take both of them. But on the other end of it I knew that it was the best thing for me to do.

DR. H   Right.

MS. B   But then after that they never called me to tell me that . . .

DR. H   O was going to be in the system and placed for adoption as a single child.

MS. B   No, I was never told that; only I had found it out through her mother who had called and said that "S is going to go home, her younger brother is going to go home with his father." I said, "That means they are splitting them; so that means that O will be up for adoption." And then I called the social worker back and told her, "If she's going to be up and then I want to adopt her." The attorney had to also write a letter to them to tell them to stop any type of proceedings that you are trying to do for adoption of O by the foster parents; we have someone who is very seriously looking to adopt O but she never got back to me with any paperwork, never took it upon herself, you know, to explain what this process would be like and never got me the classes that needed to be taken, none of that. She knew all of that early on.

DR. H It appears that you had to advocate for yourself and have others advocate for you.

MS. B Oh, yeah, yeah, it was very much the attorney and her assistants who they also did their own home study; it was just kind of a walk-through of the home. Mind you still at this time, this social worker had never been to my home. It wasn't until I contacted the state upper leadership who actually got some fire behind her. It was her and the guardian ad litem who came to my home to do what they called a home study. And if they were there all of ten minutes I would be surprised.

DR. H Well, one cannot do a home study in ten minutes.

MS. B (Laughs) They both walked through the home; let me explain where things were. I was actually opening doors and explaining which room was . . . belonged to which person in the home, where O was going to be set up and was explaining we were in the process of getting a bed pulled out of the garage that had been my older son's bed when he was a young boy.

DR. H Right.

MS. B And the comment that I got from the social worker was "All you need is a mattress; as long as they have a place to lay their head."

DR. H A mattress, what kind of statement is that for a social worker to make when discussing sleeping arrangements for a young child?

MS. B I didn't have to have a bed or a frame. As long as they had a place to lay their head that was all they cared about. I thought wow! I said, "She will not have to lie on the floor. I will be seeing to it that she has a bed." They didn't. . . . They never looked for anything to see if it was safe and toddler-proof. They noted that it was very clean and O should be fine there and they were out of the door. And I still did not really hear from her after that point just to make sure we were continuing. We increased our visits; we were having overnight visits at this time. She would contact us if there was something that the foster parent needed and she was sort of the in-between person. She ended up turning that over to us ourselves. We just worked together to find out the best way to meet up.

DR. H   How active was the juvenile court judge in this case?

MS. B   And, once I was presented even though it was presented in the light of not being a trusted . . . trusted individual to follow through on this adoption, he saw otherwise. He read my letters of recommendation; saw that I had gainful employment for more than 20 plus years, and that I had raised three boys.

DR. H   Well, you are a good mom.

MS. B   Thank you, that I had did due diligence on my own, and had brought forth background checks from individuals who were going to be in the care of O, that I had gone through measures to make sure that my home was ready for O and he was one, I can remember him saying when she said, "Well, when I called her and told her that if she could not adopt both of them that this was not going to happen." He said, "I actually admire her for not jumping the gun and saying I'll take them. They are my niece and nephew; I'll take them." He said that "This tells me that she's got a head on her shoulders and she really thought this through. It must not have been an easy decision for her. I want this case fast tracked for dual." They still had not gotten the mother's rights terminated and where they were with the father's rights.

DR. H   And that is in federal law that they do concurrent planning and work with parents, but also try to pursue another permanency goal.

MS. B   He wanted to see O in my home within the next few months. The transition had better start taking place. Because as I was telling him I just felt like every time we would come back to court there was another continuance and still that was another month that O was there or two months. Just seeing her one hour a week was just not enough.

DR. H   Right.

MS. B   He agreed. He agreed that we should be looking at this case as being an adoption and that we should start building this relationship and everything we should have in place for this foster home to adoption.

DR. H   And children can attach. Just because a child has been in a foster home does not mean that the child cannot attach to someone else, especially a child as young as O.

MS. B   Right and so she was just three years old when we were moving into the transition. That was commonly shared with me. "She is really bonded with this foster family and we just don't know how well she will bond with you. It can be really difficult when you have to move a child more than one time. She has now had three placements." Those three placements being her placement from birth she was taken and put into foster care; she was returned to her mom and then she was returned to foster care and then had still been staying in that same foster home. They said, "Oh, you create a fourth move; she probably would not bond with you because of that." Because prior to her being in foster care she and I had not really seen each other, maybe once or twice when she was born.

DR. H   Right.

MS. B   When she got her back I got to see her at a family gathering that we had. So they said, "You don't have any close relationship with her; it is not like you saw her all the time. You were not like a caretaker for her. You just are merely related to her and actually you are related through marriage." So, I really thought that I had to defend my relationship with my sister. I lived in the home with my stepsister.

DR. H   Right.

MS. B   And I actually helped to raise them as children, her and her sisters. So, I have a very close relationship with all of them. They look to me for guidance as their big sister. So, it was very difficult for someone from the outside to say that this wasn't family and that we did not want to do anything possible to keep our family together.

DR. H   Well, O's mom voiced her opinion.

MS. B   Yes.

DR. H   She stated where she wanted her child to live.

MS. B   Exactly, that should have said it all, but unfortunately I felt they did not have much respect for her mother. They didn't take anything that she said seriously.

DR. H   That is very sad; it is very troubling to me because she is her birth mom.

MS. B   She is her birth mom.

DR. H   How did this case move along after it was fast tracked?

MS. B   We were really on a fast track. It was turned over to the adoption side of the house and it was just really like night and day. I got a new social worker who was very experienced in the field. She has been doing this for sixteen years. Contacted me right away, the first thing she wanted to do was come to my home, make an appointment for us to sit down and to look at all the paperwork. She had questions herself. She would review the case and saw the notes from the other social worker. Something is just not matching up for me. I reading what she had written in the notes and I see the recommendations from some very qualified folks who say this child needs to be moving forward.

DR. H I had questions. Certainly, I was not working with you as a social worker, but I had lots of questions.

MS. B Right, but I thought, you know, that this is what a social worker should be doing. They should be asking the questions. I do not feel comfortable with this child being here or if someone else has brought up something I need to do due diligence. I need to find out what is really going on. So once she met with me she wanted to know from my own mouth what had happened, why things had taken so long. She questioned it herself. She read what the judge had written. She said, "It seems really odd that only one person that has said anything negative out of everything that was presented in this case." So, she was excited to move things forward. There was not once that I did not know what the process was going to be. I was given every piece of paperwork that was needed. I was always told in advance when the court case was. If I needed to be there or if I didn't; she was always respectful of the fact that I had to work. If there was a court case that I didn't need to be there for or couldn't be there, she either sent me the information or called me or even sent me an e-mail. She was very open and transparent about where we were with the case. Any time I had questions she was right there to answer them quickly, even worked on Sundays.

DR. H It sounds to me like a social worker who is engaging in what I call good child welfare practice and she was doing what was in the best interest of the child.

MS. B She was at all points.

DR. H Where was the guardian ad litem in this process?

MS. B She was there, but I felt that was only making business because this is what I have to do. I would always hear from her a day or two before court.

DR. H But the guardian ad litem is supposed to be an advocate for the child and doing what is in the child's best interest.

MS. B Yeah, yeah, she was also holding up this case. She has worked O's older sisters through that whole case. She and my sister had a history. They did not get along. It came down to where they were trying to get me to keep O in the home that she was in . . . in the foster care home. She called me one day and said, "I am really struggling." I said, "I find that really difficult. I am going to ask you something outright, what are you struggling with? Is your hesitancy because of the feelings that you harbor towards my sister? And you can't get over what happened with the first case and see what is in the best interest with O." At first she did not know what to say. "I appreciate you asking the question. No, it does not have anything to do with that. I struggle with the fact that O is doing so well. I have never seen her do this well with a family and she is now beginning to speak and these types of things." And I said, "And you don't feel that she can get there here in my home in my care? Do you not feel that her being able to have a relationship with her mother, her being able to have a relationship with her cousins, aunts, uncles, grandmas, be in a home where she would be loved by family that she would not be able to flourish in this home?" She couldn't say no to it.

DR. H Right.

MS. B She said, "I'm really glad that I called you and we had this conversation because I was really on the fence. I didn't know if I should go to court and recommend you for placement or if I should stick with where O is where I have seen her bond and where I have seen her flourish." So she came to the home. We were having a visit. She was amazed. She said, "Just in that short time I can tell just in that time she is bonding with you." I said, "Yeah."

DR. H Well, you are her relative.

MS. B So at that point she went to the court and had made the decision. She was also one that I believe had held this up. From that point on she was there. I have to meet with you before I go to court. She has only been to the daycare once.

DR. H Does she like her daycare?

MS. B She loves her daycare. She has made friends which is something she did not have before.

DR. H That's wonderful; that's wonderful.

MS. B She is talking so much more now that she has been in daycare. Also, learning some social skills. When I received her in the home she did not say her name. She recognized her name but did not say it. So, she has learned to say her name. She also didn't understand hello and good-bye. She would always hold her head down when someone would say hello or good-bye. Prompting her to say hello or good-bye you wouldn't get anything out of her. From the time she has been in daycare which was February when I got her, so four months; she has exhibited behaviors that the other children are doing. Saying good-bye to the parents; they know whose parents are who. She runs to me; I am almost afraid that she is going to knock me over.

DR. H. She is glad to see you.

MS. B She is so glad to see me and she jumps into my arms. With my children I was always say, "And how was your day?" For the first couple of days it would be she and I in the car she would not say a word. No, even to answer a yes or no question she wouldn't. There was just no conversation, no excitement. I thought, oh my God, does she not like her daycare? That was not the case at all. I just think she needed to feel . . .

DR. H I think that she was probably still adjusting.

MS. B She was . . . she was. Now, she gets in the car and I ask, "Did you have a good day?" She says, "Yes, I had a good day."

DR. H That's remarkable. For me that means she is in the right place.

MS. B Oh, thank you, thank you.

DR. H Is there anything else you want to tell me?

MS. B No, I think that is everything.

DR. H Thank so much.

MS. B You are welcome.

FEMALE FOSTER CARE ALUMNUS

This twenty-six-year-old young woman identified herself as Caucasian but stated, "We have a little bit of Native American in our family." Mrs. T entered the foster care system when she was in middle school. She has been happily married for three years and has been in a relationship with her husband for almost seven years. She graduated from a Master of Social Work Program in June 2013. She is the proud mother of three children. Her six-month-old baby boy accompanied her to the interview. Not only was Mrs. T placed in foster care when she was entering the preadolescent stage of her development, but she also was separated from her siblings who were placed in foster care.

DR. H As you know, I'm interviewing you for my book. Because I want to bring some voices to this, my book. I am very happy to get a chance to see your baby.

MRS. T My baby just turned six months old today.

DR. H Oh! How exciting. Is he sitting up?

MRS. T He's sitting up; he just started crawling a little bit; he can scoot a little bit. And now he can get on all fours, but then he doesn't know what to do after that.

DR. H Okay, let's start by having you tell me about your ethnic background.

MRS. T Um, I am Caucasian. We have a little bit of Native American in my family. Um, I guess when I was going through the system, they told us not to mark that down because you'd have to through the tribal stuff.

DR. H Right and now, you should. You know, for kids coming into the system, they can mark it down, which is good. I think that we should celebrate our heritage, whatever it is.

MRS. T Yeah, okay.

DR. H Tell me, what age were you when you became involved in the foster care system?

MRS. T It was about seventh or eighth grade.

DR. H Okay; and what brought you into the system?

MRS. T My parents started doing drugs. Well when I . . . my mom first met my dad, they were at a community college in Y, and my mom had me when she was seventeen. So they were kind of in a little bit of trouble up until I was like in third grade. Then they straightened out for a few years.

DR. H Okay. They were young.

MRS. T Yeah. Yeah. And then they straightened out for a few years and then starting about seventh grade my dad lost his job at Microsoft. And when I was a baby, he did a lot of cocaine and then he went through rehab. So then when he lost his job at Microsoft, they both started doing methamphetamine.

DR. H And that drug is very common in this part of the country.

MRS. T Yeah. Yeah and so that's when it kind of started; I think they started up again when I was like in seventh grade, but things didn't really start to get . . .

DR. H Are you an only child?

MRS. T I have three younger sisters that are both my mom's also and my dad has a . . . a son that's about a year younger than me.

DR. H And did all of your siblings come into the system too?

MRS. T My little brother that's just a year younger lived with his mom the whole time, so he wasn't involved.

DR. H Okay.

MRS. T But my younger sisters were, but they lived with a family friend in the Tri-Cities. We lived here.

DR. H That means you were separated. Siblings are often separated once they enter the child welfare system.

MRS. T Yeah, we were.

DR. H This type of separation is not good for kids.

MRS. T No, it is not.

DR. H We know it's best, when children come into the system as a sibling group, to keep them together.

MRS. T Um . . . I can see that. Sometimes I still think of my sisters as like seven and eight years old because that's when we went in the system. It's sometimes hard for me to believe that one is twenty-two and one is about to turn twenty-one.

DR. H I'm sure! I'm sure. Are you all connected?

MRS. T Um, yeah, my one sister, the middle sister is about to graduate from C. W., yeah, at the end of June. She's going to be a history teacher. And then my history teacher, kind of; she finally just found a job. But it's been tough for her. She's the one that's always in trouble.

DR. H Is she?

MRS. T Yeah.

DR. H But I think it's a positive thing that she's got a job.

MRS. T Yeah.

DR. H That's good because work is important to most people. Work can impact how an individual feels about her/himself. I think that will be a good thing for her to be a teacher. And she's got the two of you as role models. (Mrs. T laughs.) Well tell me a little bit about what it was like being in the foster care system.

MRS. T Um, I think I had kind of a unique experience because when my parents started getting in a lot of trouble, I had a friend in high school that asked me if I wanted to start going to her church. So I started going to her church and going to bible study; I had a bible study teacher. And she kind of knew what was happening

DR. H What was going on?

MRS. T I went to . . . I lived with my friend for like two months and that did not work. (Laughs momentarily) Living with your like best friend in high school didn't work out. And then I lived with my grandma for like a month, but the state didn't want to place me with my grandma.

DR. H Why?

MRS. T Things my grandpa did when he was younger.

DR. H Okay.

MRS. T Yeah, he had a couple of criminal history things from when he was like twenty-two or something.

DR. H Okay. Oh my goodness!

MRS. T (Laughs) Yeah.

DR. H I am sure that, you know, those types of issues come up today with some kinship caregivers. One of the things that's being done is they're actually reviewing these types of cases on a case-by-case basis because what somebody did twenty years ago is sometimes no longer an issue when assessing for child safety and best interest of the child. Sometimes it really doesn't have a bearing on whether they can be a good parent twenty years later, especially when a child already has a strong emotional relationship with a kinship caregiver such as a grandmother or some other relative.

MRS. T Yeah, I'd agree with that. And so since it wasn't working out with my friends, my bible teachers said I could come live with them and then the state was trying to make it so I couldn't live them either until they became foster parents. So they had to go through all the . . .

DR. H They had to go through the licensing process in order to become foster parents.

MRS. T . . . rigamarole. Yeah, and that was like a yearlong process while I was there.

DR. H Oh my goodness! However, the licensing process for foster parents sometimes takes an inordinate amount of time, especially if the foster home study is being done by a social worker from a public child welfare agency.

MRS. T And I remember, they went through a private agency. I remember they had to do certain things, like put up the laundry soap when people would come to check out their house and stuff. I'm like sixteen years old; you don't have to keep the laundry soap put away.

DR. H Well to me those were kind of artificial measures. I can certainly understand putting up laundry soap and other household items if you had been an infant or toddler. However, you were a teenager and certainly not going to do anything dangerous with laundry soap? What did those things have to do with being a good parent?

MRS. T Yeah.

DR. H Frankly, there are many other more important factors that are part of a foster home study.

MRS. T Yeah, so I . . . I got lucky with being with my foster family that I got.

DR. H Did the private agency finally approve this family?

MRS. T Yeah, they did. Um, and I lived with them all through high school. I had an opportunity to go live back with my parents and my sisters. Move back with them, but I just did not want to go back to my parents.

DR. H You chose to stay with your foster parents.

MRS. T Yeah.

DR. H Did they adopt you or did they continue to be your foster parents?

MRS. T They were just my foster parents. I think they got guardianship.

DR. H Okay. A lot of foster parents prefer to become a child's legal guardian rather than go through the adoption process. And a lot of relatives also decide to become legal guardians rather than adoptive parents. I know that a lot of relatives that I worked with in child welfare preferred to become legal guardians for relatives in their care; they stated that they did not feel right adopting a relative because they were already blood relatives of the children in their care.

MRS. T   Yeah, that makes a lot of sense.

DR. H   Well, what kind of things did you and your foster parents do together?

MRS. T   Um, well, I moved in November of my sophomore year. And my freshman year was just kind of just bouncing around; I did not get good grades that year at all. And then they, they were trying to have kids for awhile and she ended up getting pregnant like a month after I started living there.

DR. H   Oh my goodness! That kind of thing often happens to some couples when they adopt after trying for years to have a biological child.

MRS. T   Right, they finally. . . . You are finally just relaxed about it. So she had a baby like at the end of August, my first year of living there. So a lot of the time was like preparing for the baby.

DR. H   You and your foster parents were getting the baby's room ready, and also getting the family ready for a new addition.

MRS. T   Yeah, and it was my sixteenth birthday; they actually took me to Disneyland because I . . .

DR. H   Oh, that was nice.

MRS. T   Yeah, I had never been anywhere before. Um, it's just kind of a lot of adjusting still. We still . . . she still had a lot of the bible study for the church. And I then went on, you know, some trips with the church.

DR. H   Okay, so what I'm hearing is that religion was important to them and to you.

MRS. T   Yeah, definitely.

DR. H   And I think that was good.

MRS. T   Yeah and it was hard because my parents aren't religious at all. And I think that's one of the main reasons why I gravitated . . .

DR. H   Was religion one of the reasons that you gravitated toward this family?

MRS. T   Yeah.

DR. H   Are your children being brought up in the church?

MRS. T   He's not right now.

DR. H   Okay.

MRS. T   Maybe, when he gets a little older.

DR. H   Right.

MRS. T   I haven't found a new church since I went to SPU. And some things kind of turned me off at SPU. It was kind of tough going to a religious school because I felt like my family was not accepted because they weren't religious in many ways. So I was kind of struggling with that and now that I have my own child, I definitely want him brought up in the church and now it's just a matter of . . .

DR. H   It is just a matter of finding the right church.

MRS. T (Laughing) Yeah, and getting back on my feet after having a baby.

DR. H Right, and sometimes it helps to just visit churches. Visits help you to actually examine their doctrine, get a feel for the congregation and see if it feels right for you.

MRS. T Right.

DR. H There are a lot of interdenominational churches that welcome anyone. And their doctrines are not strict; you know, some traditional churches are very strict in terms of their doctrines.

MRS. T Yeah.

DR. H Some of them do things that I think a church should do. I think churches should be warm and welcoming to anybody. And that's one of the things I like about my church (Mrs. T chuckles momentarily); they welcome anybody, homeless, poor, etc. But I know that certain churches are very different. You know, religion is supposed to be about helping people, reaching out to the less fortunate, and embracing anyone without any kind of discriminatory practices.

MRS. T Yeah, I agree.

DR. H Well, who encouraged you to go on to college?

MRS. T Um, it's probably my foster family. I kind of. . . . My parents never graduated college, but they were pretty adamant about us going, even when they were in trouble (laughs).

DR. H Right, well most parents want their children to have a better life than the life they had when they were growing up. No matter what they're doing they want their children to excel and do well. And I think that's a positive quality in your parents.

MRS. T Yeah, I'd agree. So it's kind of instilled in us since . . .

DR. H You were little.

MRS. T Yeah.

DR. H That is a good thing because education is extremely important.

MRS. T Yeah, and then I didn't really have the means or the know-how until I was in foster care.

DR. H Okay, I certainly understand what you are saying.

MRS. T My foster mom helped me figure out how to apply, how to get scholarships and those kinds of kind of things.

DR. H And did the foster care system help?

MRS. T They . . . yeah, I got a lot of help from Triage for Kids; they had like . . . a coaching to college mentor type of . . .

DR. H Was that the agency that monitored your foster home?

MRS. T   Ah, no, it was Olive Crest.

DR. H   Okay, I'm familiar with them. I'm actually on their advisory board.

MRS. T   Oh, yeah?

DR. H   Yes.

MRS. T   Yeah, they were the ones; the social worker, she was wonderful; it was just that there were tons of referrals that they had to monitor.

DR. H   Okay. And do you think that these rules were more state regulations than private agency regulations?

MRS. T   Um, they could've been. I'm not sure. It seems that a lot of the rules were geared to whether or not you were going to be long-term foster parents and have kids coming in and out. Not necessarily geared to being foster parents one time. They were becoming foster parents so that I could stay there. It wasn't individualized; it was more about the . . .

DR. H   It seems that the process was more about adhering to the general policies and procedures for licensing any foster home.

MRS. T   Yeah.

DR. H   Okay. What else do you remember about the system?

MRS. T   Um, I did not have a good experience with anyone from CPS or DSHS.

DR. H   Okay, please tell me about your experiences.

MRS. T   Um, my, the very first caseworker told my grandma that at this point since I was already like fourteen or fifteen, there was no reason for her to be doing all this work anyways because I would end up just like my parents.

DR. H   That was a very insensitive thing to say about you. In fact, it was quite a most judgmental statement.

MRS. T   Yeah.

DR. H   It was a very discouraging statement for a social worker to make to you and your grandma.

MRS. T   Yeah, and the second social worker would come to ask . . . just ask for my parents. I had not seen my parents. I did not know where my parents were for about year. And so she would come over every couple of weeks only to ask grandma about my parents. She insisted that I knew where my parents were. And after that my foster mom told her that was like . . . that's enough. Like because she did not act like a social worker, but she was actually a social worker. She graduated from the Seattle campus.

DR. H   Unfortunately, there are some individuals who have a Master of Social Work degree but are clueless about how to be a social worker and how to engage with children, adolescents, and families.

MRS. T   And she's like . . . that's not okay for her to be asking you all the time about your parents. And so she had a friend that was working for DSHS at the time and so she became my case manager.

DR. H   Okay. And was she a good case manager?

MRS. T   Yeah, she was.

DR. H   What do you think was this social worker's motive in continuously asking you about your parents? Was she trying to develop a plan to terminate their rights?

MRS. T   That could've been it. I think also they wanted my parents to be doing their drug analysis treatment stuff that they were supposed to be doing. And I think it was because my sisters were living with my dad's mom in Tri-Cities.

DR. H   Okay, it never ceases to amaze me when I hear of these types of experiences.

MRS. T   So I don't know if they were trying to . . .

DR. H   You don't know if the plan was to return your sisters to your parent's home.

MRS. T   Yeah, but I didn't see them for about a year. I'm not sure really where they were.

DR. H   That must have been hard, not knowing where they were or what was happening to them.

MRS. T   Yeah, it was. I'm glad I had my grandma . . . my grandma was still around the whole time.

DR. H   And I think it is wonderful that you were able to maintain a relationship with her.

MRS. T   Yeah.

DR. H   Because for children whether they're in foster care or not, it's important to have family connections and it's especially important for children in foster care because they lose so much.

MRS. T   Yeah. Yeah, she was, I mean . . . I remember . . . I'd always call her to pick me up from my friend's house. So she'd pick me every evening and I wasn't allowed to spend the night there. She would take me back at like 8 or 9 at night like every single day. I was tired of living at my friend's house. And then we always had Sunday dinner with my grandma and we still do.

DR. H   Oh! I think that's wonderful.

MRS. T   Yeah, so it's been a little rough because my mom is actually with my grandma right now.

DR. H   Is she?

MRS. T   Yeah.

DR. H   Is she clean and sober?

MRS. T   I think for the most part. She's not doing any like street drugs that I know about.

DR. H   Right, I hope that she is drug-free.

MRS. T   But she still drinks every once in a while and I think that she has a problem with prescription drugs.

DR. H   That's sad.

MRS. T   Yeah, so it's been tough not wanting your mom around your child, you know.

DR. H   Of course, however, you have to do what is best for your child.

MRS. T   And since my mom lives with my grandma, I don't feel like I have a good relationship with my grandma anymore because I don't necessarily like or want to be around my mom.

DR. H   Right, and yeah it's really hard. I know this from my own work experience, for grandmas to tell their children, whether it's the daughter or a son, that you can't live here or you can't come because you're using drugs is a hard thing to do. I think it's because they love them, but at the same time they're enabling them to continue to allow them to live or visit their home when they are actively using drugs and/or alcohol. And I don't think that most grandparents see it that way. It's their child and they often say, "I don't want my child out on the streets." But you have to do what's best for your children. And I hope for your mom that maybe having grandchildren will motivate her to clean up her act.

MRS. T   I keep hoping so. Um, but she's better the past year than she's been in a long time. But she's not like well enough that I feel comfortable.

DR. H   Right, and I'm thinking if you want your children to have a relationship with your grandma, she can come to your house without your mom; she sounds like a wonderful person from what you have told me.

MRS. T   (Chuckles) Yeah she definitely is.

DR. H   Is there anything else that you want to tell me about foster care? I think it's remarkable that you're studying to become a social worker. What do you think the foster care system can do to make life better for all children?

MRS. T   I think the main thing, and I'm not sure if it's for every agency, but they need to stop labeling children in foster care. It seems like you're labeled as a foster child and so you are; you're a criminal whether or not you've done anything just because your parents have messed up. And anywhere you go, whether it's, even in the system that's supposed to be working for you . . . you're criminal.

And outside of that, you're labeled kind of as a criminal. I remember, um, in Texas where they had the guy that was marrying all the girls.

DR. H Right, I remember hearing about those girls.

MRS. T And they put all of them in foster care and there was like this whole huge media thing.

DR. H I remember seeing that big story on one of the national news networks about the man and those girls.

MRS. T They were saying that they would end up awful because they were in foster care. And I was thinking that I was in foster care at one time in my life. I actually got a scholarship with Orphan Foundation of America and they were very involved in advocating for foster children and I remember the lady who was in charge of the scholarship I got; she like wrote them this long letter about how, you know, sometimes foster care is better and that the labels given because children are in the foster care system are going to influence them to act badly.

DR. H I don't agree about labeling because I do not think that children in the foster care system should be labeled. I'm not working in the child welfare system now, but when I did, I always told my workers be careful about the language that you use. And in this agency we do not say "foster child." We say, "A child in foster care or a girl in foster care or a boy in foster care"; we don't say "foster child" because that has a very negative connotation in this country. And we don't want to label children. We don't want to make children feel bad about themselves. Why did you decide to become a social worker?

MRS. T Um, well, I worked for Triage for Kids all through my undergrad. I actually was in pre-med my first two years of college and, um, I did fine I just. . . . When my grandpa was really sick I went and visited him during his dialysis.

DR. H Okay.

MRS. T And I almost passed out. It was yeah. . . . That's . . . and I didn't like being in the hospital at all and I kept going with pre-med for like another six months. And then I decided to do something else and I just did English literature. Because I just decided to do something that I wanted to do and then I worked at Triage that whole time and then after that they extended my work study so that I could work there.

DR. H Tell us a little bit about them. What do they do?

MRS. T Ah, they are. . . . They kind of give the supplemental services to foster youth; they have tutoring, or coaching to college; they also have educational advocates who are basically kind of like lawyers for kids in the system to . . .

DR. H I think that's wonderful.

MRS. T Yeah, to make sure they can stay at the same school. Because I think they say that every time you switch a school you are like three months behind the other kids who aren't switching.

DR. H See, that's . . . that's hard for children, not only academically but emotionally because these children have already suffered a lot. And to leave your school and leave your friends that's another trauma for them.

MRS. T Yeah, definitely it's hard. And so I worked in the tutoring department my first year and that was where I would test the kids before and after they entered the program. I think they had to do that for their United Way grant that they had and then they decided to contract that out so I worked at their warehouse; they called it Triage Wearhouse, but its W-e-a-r and it's like a clothing store with new and used clothes for foster kids. And they come like a couple of times a year to pick out their outfits and stuff.

DR. H That's nice.

MRS. T Yeah, so I worked there for like four or five years and then they didn't have money for my position anymore and my student loans were about to come up or they were due. So I got a receptionist job at a granite and marble company and I actually worked there just until I had my baby.

DR. H Okay.

MRS. T Um, and I was the inside sales manager for about a year before I stopped working there. And I didn't really think about going back to school until I started getting very frustrated with my sales job.

DR. H Okay, I can certainly understand your frustration.

MRS. T Because you'd have people call and they'd be like, "This green tile isn't the green tile I ordered. I need this color green to match my sink." And I'm like there are the kids that don't have food. You know, there are elderly people that are being abused, like honestly I don't care about your green tiles.

DR. H Right, I understand because dealing with the public can be difficult.

MRS. T But I have to pretend that I do.

DR. H Right, because people can be insensitive when they're dealing with sales people.

MRS. T Yeah, yeah, so then I remembered how great some parts of being in foster care were, and how awful other parts were. So then I decided to go back and get my Masters in Social Work since I'd looked online for new jobs and half the jobs would say you needed a Master in Social Work. So, everyone I would see said, "It will be good."

DR. H Right, one can never have too much education.

MRS. T Or it would be meaningful.

DR. H And do you plan to work in child welfare?

MRS. T For the most part, I don't want to work for like CPS or anything.

DR. H Right, there are many other areas of child welfare.

MRS. T So, I would probably like to work for a private agency.

DR. H And that's good child welfare work; private agencies tend to have highly trained and skilled social workers and it's not to say there are not some good social workers with the state agency. But by and large children can get a higher caliber of services and children get individual attention. Social workers at private agencies have smaller caseloads. I'm speaking from professional experience.

MRS. T Yeah, yeah ... because technically I had my social worker at the state level and my social worker at Olive Crest. And my social worker from Olive Crest was always there, always helping whereas the state one would not come by for a couple weeks.

DR. H My first job after I got my MSW was at a private agency, the Children's Home Society of Florida. I had approximately fifteen cases. I did foster care and adoptions. I could give every child individual attention.

MRS. T Yeah.

DR. H And it makes a difference. Anything else you want to tell me?

MRS. T Hmm ...

DR. H Do you think that race entered into the treatment or the services you received?

MRS. T It probably did with me not knowing. For instance, I might have received more services or more attention just for being white. Um, or going into Tree House, I don't ... I wouldn't say any of them are racist, but they might have stereotypes where I walk in as a white kid getting services and then a family of African Americans might come in and they might not get as great a service just because of the color of their skin. And I never thought of that until I had that diversity class.

DR. H And it has been shown in research that there are service disparities on the basis of race.

MRS. T Yeah, because I would say there was a far greater number of ethnic diversity in my ... like when I would go for the independent living skills programs. I would be like one of the only white people. And that could be just from starting out at the beginning where they were taken from their home quicker than I was. It was. . . . We were probably living at my house for about a year that they could've taken us out at any point. We didn't have heat, we didn't have water for a while, sometimes we would have water, sometimes we didn't; we didn't have electricity. My dad and his friend, who I'm pretty sure were high at the time, built this weird shed in the back to put a generator back there, so that we could have a couple of electric cords and like we didn't have garbage service and things like that, and that was probably my entire freshman year of high school.

DR. H   And the child welfare system still allowed you to stay at home with your parents.

MRS. T   Yeah, until my parents got kicked out of the house at the end of my freshman year; that's basically when we became homeless technically; that is when they finally took us out. Which they probably they could've just kept us in our house because we were white and you know that deep down, that they were, you know, a little bit racist about it. Whereas I feel like they're really quick to take kids of color out of their house.

DR. H   It's true, it's true, research has shown including some of my research that children of color are removed at a higher number, they remain in the system longer, and it's harder for them to exit of the system once they get in, and these things are prevalent at every decision point in the child welfare system.

MRS. T   Yeah, I believe it. I think it's, you know, bad on the other end too. I feel like we should've been taken out a lot sooner and I think it just needs to be an equal playing field.

DR. H   I agree with you because I feel that you and your siblings living in the conditions that you described were at risk of harm. I mean, what if that cord had caught fire and the house had burned down? I mean that's a risk.

MRS. T   My, I can't eat pancakes to this day because that's all that I could make for my sisters and I for like that entire year, and there was a Jack in the Box down the street so I can't eat Jack in the Box. And like we had a social worker come and interview me at the school and I didn't lie, I told her what was going on but it was . . .

DR. H   She still left you there.

MRS. T   Yeah.

DR. H   And it sounds like you were the person who was parenting your sisters.

MRS. T   Yeah, I think that's one of the things I'm thankful for my foster mom for was that she would always . . . I would start doing something like some kind of . . . taking care of something and she would be like, "This is your time to be a child and to think about yourself." Or I'd be worried about what my parents were doing and she be like, "They're adults, they can take care of themselves. You worry about yourself and just yourself." So that's been tough learning that.

DR. H   Right, I am sure it was a hard lesson after being thrust into the parental role as a child.

MRS. T   But I have been grateful for that kind of lesson in my life.

DR. H   Yet you had a right to your childhood.

MRS. T   Yeah, so there I was . . . I'm very thankful to her for giving me a chance to at least have a little bit of fun.

DR. H   Are you still in contact with her?

MRS. T   Hmm, she actually is . . . I'm going to the NASW conference on Saturday, and my husband is going to be out of town for his state bowling tournament, so she's actually watching my son both days.

DR. H   Oh! I think that's wonderful.

MRS. T   Yeah, and she. . . . Her kids are both eight and ten now, so they are still young. They live in Auburn and so it's a little tough sometimes to drive.

DR. H   Right. But I think it's good that you still maintain a relationship with her.

MRS. T   Yeah.

DR. H   I am sure that is means a lot that the two of you are still close.

MRS. T   Yeah, we get along pretty good. She's only like ten years older than me so it was probably tough. I can imagine it being tough for her before, having a teenager before a kid. I can't imagine.

DR. H   But from what you've described to me, you were not a teenager who was a behavior problem.

MRS. T   No, I wasn't.

DR. H   You were not sneaking out of the house or engaging in some other inappropriate behavior (both laugh).

MRS. T   No. I probably should have given her a little test . . .

DR. H   Are you referring to a test such as talking back and not listening? I bet you obeyed the house rules whatever they were.

MRS. T   Yeah, I did.

DR. H   Is there anything else you would like to say?

MRS. T   I don't think so.

DR. H   Well, thank you so much for talking to me.

MRS. T   Thanks for interviewing me.

DR. H   It was my pleasure.

MALE FOSTER CARE ALUMNUS

This is an interview of a twenty-two-year-old young man who grew up in the foster care system. He identifies as white and Vietnamese. He is currently enrolled in a graduate social work program. He is a very intelligent young man who is kind, sensitive, and caring.

DR. H   Why don't we start by having you tell me a little bit about your background?

MR. T   Um, I was born in Pierce County. My mom was sixteen when I was born; my biological mother was sixteen. She moved to Pierce County with her family. My grandfather and grandmother had moved around the world. They were active duty and I think they were like civilians though . . .

DR. H   Okay.

MR. T   And I don't know too much of the history. I know that they moved here via Vietnam; my grandmother is from Vietnam, my mother (DR. H: "Okay.") is half Vietnamese and I'm a quarter Vietnamese; um, and my father is an American; they met during the Vietnam War.

DR. H   Okay.

MR. T   And, um, they met via Saudi Arabia or somewhere.

DR. H   Okay.

MR. T   And they ended up in Tacoma, ah, in the Tacoma area.

DR. H   Okay. And what is his background?

MR. T   You know, I don't know. It's interesting. I still have communication with my biological mother today and every so often I ask her. I try to find, get information on what my background is. But she has no idea either; um, so my grandfather is deceased; I can't ask him. My grandmother doesn't really know either. Actually, all my grandmother knows is he is white and to her that was really good. Um, there is a lot of internalized racism within my biological family. Um, so mom had me at when she was sixteen; we lived in P . . . . for a little bit and then ended up moving up to the S . . . . P . . . . area and that's where I spent my younger years until the end of grade school. And then I moved to Tacoma, probably the middle of my sixth grade year. And I was with my mom for about six months. And then my brother, my biological brother, he got . . . um, he had a really bad accident; A really, really, bad accident. He, um . . . was playing with fire . . .

DR. H   Oh my!

MR. T   Yeah, he was playing fire and hair spray and he caught himself on fire.

DR. H Oh my goodness!

MR. T Yeah, he was playing with fire and hair spray and he caught himself on fire.

DR. H Oh my goodness, how old was he?

MR. T He was born in '92 so that would make him twenty today; I think, nineteen or twenty. I haven't seen him since then. Um, so, he'd burned himself badly from his groin area until up to his neck and it was third-degree burns. He ended up in the burn unit at H . . . . Um, and from very early in my life, from the time I was about four or five, J, my brother . . .

Okay, yeah, so he, um, and I were like the. . . . We had different fathers; they were just like fathers; they were not involved in our lives whatsoever. But when I was about five or six, my mom got married to this guy who, um, for the next several years was going to be our stepfather and ultimately our abuser. He was extremely physically violent, very emotionally violent, very spiritually violent and just not a great person. Like he did really awful stuff and it never really came to the surface. Like no one really knew about it. My grandparents knew about it, but culturally it just wasn't appropriate to talk about it.

DR. H It was a family secret because no one talked about what was done by your stepfather.

MR. T To talk about it, to leave your partner it wasn't appropriate. My mom has . . . now being educated (chuckles) and having a grounded foot in like social theory, my mom has depended on other people and has really poor attachment relationships herself. So this relationship was a place of stability for her and it was really this decision between my kids and stability. And she ultimately chose stability at the consequence of her kids being harmed. So to get back to Jason, he went into H . . . . and that's when the abuse began to surface. Because, um, I think I can't remember clearly, but medical staff would notice that, um, Jason would flinch like when . . .

DR. H Would he flinch when they touched him?

MR. T Yes, he would flinch when they touched him; like he wouldn't want men to touch him. He was really scared of men; he just displayed behavior that caused staff to question why is he detached? He responded worse to some things psychologically, worse than the treatment for the burns. Um, and that caused a lot of questions. So social services got involved in the case. Ultimately what happened is that through Jason talking about it, there was a lot of abuse in the home. You know, it's hard to reflect on it because I have blocked out a lot of that period of my life. I have little snippets of where I can remember like why I went into foster care, but it's not really clear to me. Like, I can't see it. I can see like screen shots. I see screen shots of it and that's it. Even my first few years of life in foster care, there are kind of little tidbits that I can remember. I really had a talent for like dissociating during that time in my life.

DR. H   And I'm sure a lot of the dissociative behavior is because you were so traumatized.

MR. T   Yeah, yeah, looking back on it today and looking at some, at not issues, but challenges that I have today. I don't look at them as issues but challenges with relationships. I understand why and I see how natural it is for someone who had my experiences to have some of the challenges that I face in developing relationships with people. Um, so what I do remember is there are things that I remember vividly and things I don't remember at all. I do remember that I was very close with my biological mother. I had a really . . . I had this admiration of her that I can't describe and, um, today I can't understand the admiration but at ten years old I admired her. I just admired her so much. I thought she was the most beautiful person in the world. I thought that I wanted to be just like her when I grow up, and I don't know why I wanted to be like her, but I just love my mother. Um, but I always wondered like . . . I love you so much so why aren't you doing anything to keep me safe? Um, there is this vivid moment that I remember when I . . . that I consider my entry into foster care system and it's actually at the building that we were talking about earlier.

DR. H   Okay.

MR. T   Where, um, they said, "You know J is going into foster care; we're going to take him into custody. We don't find you fit to take care of your other kids either." By this time, her and her husband had split; they'd divorced for reasons not related to the abuse. It was just . . . I think it was more like she found someone she was interested in; there was just too much stress going on with the medical stuff, so they split. But they said, "You're not able to protect your kids from abuse." And, um, so I went into foster care too. My mom's two kids that she had with this husband of hers did not go into foster care because he had already taken custody before they could, so they live with him. I haven't seen them in about twelve or fifteen years now either. Um . . .

DR. H   And how old were you when you went into foster care?

MR. T   Ten, ten or eleven roughly, I can't quite remember. Sixth grade for me, that's what I remember the most. I was at that point of my education. Um, so I went into foster care and the vivid moment of entry that I remember is they said, "We need to take custody of T . . . ," and there wasn't this battle really. I think she had accepted that was the reality that I was going into care and it was so simple. I got in the car; my belongings were in garbage bags and she drove me to the DSHS office and walked me into the lobby. She shed some tears and left. I was dropped off and I sat in that waiting room for what felt like hours and hours.

DR. H Nobody came out to talk to you? No one came to explain what the place was or why you're here?

MR. T No (chuckles momentarily), um, no, I didn't even meet a social worker that day. I met a case aide. A case aide that drove me to a foster home and that was my entry into the foster care system. As I sat in waiting room and went to my first of many homes. Um, my introduction was a one-night stay in one house with six other kids; I moved to another home. I was there for maybe a week. Again this was before there was a little bit stricter regulations on how many kids can be in one home. My experience was that there were always many kids and they were respite homes.

DR. H And when you were moving around, did you change schools?

MR. T I changed schools every single year up until I was a freshman in college. Um, granted I started college while I was still in foster care. I started college when I was sixteen; so there's good, there's good and bad to it, and some was by choice too because, um, we'll get to it. So I mean the first few years in foster care were really not traumatic but were melancholic and depressing.

DR. H Were you and your brother placed in the same foster home?

MR. T No, I don't even know where my brother is. I haven't seen him in as many years I've been in foster care.

DR. H I'm asking because as you know good child welfare practice states when siblings come into care, the social worker should try and place the children together. And if you are going to separate them, contact should be maintained via sibling visits.

MR. T No, I think that it was a bit more complicated since it was a medical adoption for J. He was adopted before he was even discharged from the hospital. They had found a family for him that was skilled with taking care of him I think and I can't say for sure because like I said, my memory is not the best, but I feel like J went into foster care first. That's the way that it started out; that is how it was pitched to my mother. She was not medically capable of handling his injuries. There would be a therapeutic foster home that would be able to take care of him, but then the abuse stuff came up and that really made it cement. It made it legal like this has to happen and then it became that a foster family wanted to adopt him. It was really expedited with J. I mean he, um . . . yeah, I think it went straight to adoption. That's when the adoptive parents had more of a right to say like we're going to change his last name. We don't want any visitation rights. So that is less the child welfare system I think, as opposed to the adoptive parent's rights. Um, for me, I went into foster care and there was always talk of reunification. I don't know in hindsight whether or not that would've been a good thing. I know that's the goal, but I don't know if that's the best.

DR. H   Did you have any visitation with your mom?

MR. T   I did. I did, yeah, I mean over time they got very lenient. I mean the first few years in foster care, I was in and out of homes, um, quicker than I could imagine. I think the longest I was in a home, which is pretty long, was eight months and that was with someone that I was really close with, but I was about twelve and I was trying to figure out my identity. Um, I was trying to figure out why do I like guys and it didn't make sense to me. I was really struggling with it and I kind of brought it up subtly with this foster mom that I had and I didn't really get any support from her. I didn't get yelled at or anything like that, but the next day when I came home from school I was replaced. I was removed from that home. I was placed in another home. So, less than twenty-four hours after disclosing that I was struggling with my identity I placed in another home. Um, so I can't help but think that had something to do with it.

DR. H   Were the foster parents in this new home more sensitive to you, your needs and your feelings?

MR. T   I shut down at that point. I remember after moving out of her home that I felt like everything . . . I already felt like everything . . . my, ahh, foundation had been pulled out from underneath me. And at that point I felt like there was nothing under me anymore. I (sighs) . . . this I remember vividly too. I locked myself in that house. I thought maybe if I starved myself maybe someone will hear me. I refused to eat and it was about two weeks later that finally the foster parents said something to the social worker and I got put in counseling. I got labeled with a bipolar disorder diagnosis. I was put on lithium. I was overmedicated. I was considered antisocial and unable to form attachments. And, of course, I'm unable to form attachments. How can you expect that not to be the case? It was such a punitive experience.

DR. H   And I'm looking at and listening to all the loss you've experienced.

MR. T   I had never . . . yeah, I mean . . . I had lost . . . not having anything. I went from having nothing to having nothing. I, um, I think about it now. I know I'm almost done with my graduate degree. I have done so much work in child welfare around LGBT kids and I look at my experience. When I talk to foster parents and I ask them, "Do you want to reject a kid that's already been rejected time and time again?" And I look at my experience and I'm like, that's what these parents did or the system did. They rejected a kid that's already rejected; they took from a kid who had nothing. Um, and there was really no voice for me at that time; there was no voice. So, I moved from that home. I moved to a few homes. Those weren't negative experiences because I was just so withdrawn. I didn't talk about anything. And then I got another move to this home in Tacoma that, um, ended up becoming my permanent home, but it started out from my perspective I think after talking with my foster mom A about my experience and how bleak I saw myself and how bleak I saw my future. She remembered; she mentioned to me that on my second day there, I came out into the living room and, um, my voice was shaking. I asked if I could take a shower. And, um, she had never been asked permission to take a shower before and like she just, she said her heart broke at that point. She had no idea if she could provide for me like what she thought I was going to need. Because she saw that I was pretty damaged, and pretty broke and pretty like lost and didn't have like a sense of self, but she didn't give up. I don't think she did anything that she sees as being really extraordinary either. She said, "Yes, you can take a shower and you never have to ask that again." Um, over time, I think that her personality and her involvement in my life allowed me to open up a little bit more. Eventually, I decided to have that same conversation with her that I had with other people. This was like the middle of my middle school years (age thirteen and fourteen) when this was getting really strong and really confusing. I already had told this girl in my school and she had told my entire class. Granted this was also when A had been encouraging me academically; she saw that I was brilliant. She was an educator and my sister lived with us too, my foster sister. She was also an educator and they saw talents in me that no one else had ever pointed out before and they really encouraged me to do something. I started excelling in school. I was never . . . not good in school, but I never excelled. They found that I missed almost my entire sixth grade because of this mess. I bounced around. I probably went to school like three weeks out of the year and was supposed to be held back, but the school let me move ahead. Which (laughing) today I question because any kid that misses the entire sixth grade year shouldn't be going on to the seventh grade.

DR. H But let's face it, you are smart.

MR. T Right, but looking back on that, I'm like, should we be moving kids on that quickly? But that's a whole other videotape (chuckles jokingly). But during that year, I excelled in that grade. I consider the fact that I didn't go to sixth grade at all and I just went straight to seventh and like excelled with flying colors in a highly capable program. I skipped the sixth grade, that's how I look at it. Um, so, she was really good about challenging me and pointing out my strengths and really like rewarding me when I did things well and not being punitive when I didn't do things well.

DR. H Right, but I think pointing out and rewarding you when you did things well was the road to making you feel good about yourself.

MR. T Yeah, so like I said I was in this highly capable class and in a school with the highly capable kids. I don't know why they called them the basement kids at my school. At my middle school we had six periods and five of our periods, every class, even PE, except for your elective, which I was in choir, um, every class was with the same teacher. So you spent five periods a day with the same teacher, the same classmates and in the same room. So, you were pretty ostracized from the rest of the school.

DR. H Right, you and the other kids had a tight schedule.

MR. T And, um, I came out to this one girl kind of haphazardly. I think that I was just thinking that we were close and that I was making a friend. She told the whole class (chuckles). So, I mean I was in this one class where everybody I . . . there's no one else. I don't have any other friends outside of that class. And that was miserable (chuckles); that sucked. I was in seventh grade and barely figuring myself out and now everybody knew my secret. And it was at that point that I felt close enough to A but still so nervous when I told her. I told her, but I added a little caveat on to the end of it this time that I didn't tell my last foster mom. I told her, you know, "I don't like girls," and that's what I said to her. "You know, I like guys. But I would do anything in the world to change it. I would do anything. If I could take a pill, I would take it." And I remember defending it. Like, "I wish I could change it but what do I do?" And she looked at me and said, "There's absolutely no way you can change something about yourself that you were born as. And you would be a fool I think to think you can change that." And I had never heard anyone say that before. I had never heard anyone say that it was okay; that it was just normal. And that what I was experiencing was not like an illness.

DR. H Right, it is not an illness. It is not a bad thing. It's who you are.

MR. T Right, I had never heard that before. And today, talking to A, ten years later, nine years later, she had no idea what she was talking about is what she tells me. She had never met a gay person before, other than people in her childhood. But she had never met a gay child as he was coming out and she had no idea whether it was a choice or not. But what she tells me today or in the present is that she knew what I needed to hear at that time. And she said what I needed to hear; so, she knew what she needed to do. She went and got herself educated on what she could do to better understand this population so she can better serve this kid. And the results were amazing and absolutely exemplary. Like she paused for a second before saying something that could be harmful and said what I needed to hear and then went and did her work before, um.

DR. H But I think that speaks volumes for her as a person.

MR. T Yeah, yeah, it does. She will never take credit for doing anything exceptional though because for her what she did is supposed to be the norm. Like for her, what she did is what she would call karmically correct. I come from a biological mom, but she's my mom. I call her my mom, but she's my foster mother, she is.

DR. H Well, I see her as your mom.

MR. T Oh, absolutely, she's my mother.

DR. H She did what any good mother would do; that's what mothers do. There are no perfect mothers. I don't know if you have read any of Winnicott's work. He talks about a "good enough mother." And that means that the mother is there for the child emotionally and physically. Not perfect, but you're there. And she was there for you and she gave you what she needed.

MR. T Yeah, yeah, I think that there's a lot of qualitative experience that she's had. She's African American; she's an older woman. Today, she's eighty-three; so, when she was raising me she was in her seventies. Um she's a Buddhist, um, a reformed southern Baptist, and, um, for her that's a lot of identity right there. That's a lot of identity right there and she's probably had plenty of people question her identity as an African American. And you would look at her on Sunday and she's coming home in her like nicest church clothes and people come up to her in the grocery store and people come up to her and very friendly are like "You're just coming home from church, such a good Christian woman," and she'd be like, " No, I'm a Buddhist." And the faces she would get; she knows what it's like. Um, so I think that had a lot to do with it. And another reason why she said it was incorrect for her to chastise me was because she was without any understanding herself. So she went out and did something I think more people need to do and she understood that she did not understand better and she ended up becoming a crusader for gay kids in the foster care system. She doesn't realize today, but she's in publication after publication and her name when it comes to child welfare leaders that work on LGBTQ work she's the poster child for what foster parents are suppose to be like and I don't think she ever knew this because she's too humble.

DR. H   She sounds like somebody I would like to meet.

MR. T   Ah, my God, she's an amazing woman and she'll never know because she's too humble. Um, but the thing is that you can't go to a conference where there's . . . whether it's the entire conference that's on LBGT foster kids or it's a workshop on LBGT foster kids . . . where our story is not used because there were good things about the system that I was in and negative things. So, when it came to planning my particular arrangements, social work was never really involved. There was supposed to be a home visit or what not. I think I saw my social worker once every six months about two days before a court hearing and I remember this one time I was probably fifteen. A and I got into this huge argument, your teenager/mom argument. It was two days before a court hearing and the social worker is frantically getting informa- tion over the phone on how I'd been doing for the last six months. A . . . you know, was upset and venting. "He's been so bad, not bad; no, that's not right. We've been fighting lately; he's been a little argumentative. He's kind of disobeying me at times." You know what, our court review said that I've been irritable, not respecting house rules; that I have no respect for A. . . . And I have really low appreciation of her and the type of home she provides for me. We got that review back; we never went to a court review because we were so solid and stable for us. The social worker never came around to talk to us to begin with; we were flabbergasted. We had an argument like any normal family and then that was what was used to paint a picture of me for the last six months.

DR. H   Did the social worker recommend removal?

MR. T   I don't even remember if he recommended removal. I think he said, "We will reassess the situation at the next court hearing." I meant that's how involved social work was in my life. I don't know if it's a blessing or not because I know that at the beginning of my stay with A . . . it was not intended that I spend six or seven months. It was supposed to be a short-term stay until I could reunify with my mom, but I think that we were so low maintenance. She was so low key because honestly she was so involved with me that she didn't need any extra help. Like she didn't see me as a problem child; she saw me as a. . . . She didn't see me as something to fix either.

DR. H   Right, she simply saw you as a child.

MR. T   Um, so they just eventually turned out to be uninvolved because everything was just . . .

DR. H   Did they provide any kinds of services?

MR. T   Um, you know, we would call once a year to like banter about, you know, getting the vouchers to get clothing and what not, but other than that not really.

DR. H   And was she a foster parent for the state or a private agency?

MR. T   She was a foster parent for a private agency, but I was a state child who did bed loan with this private agency. So, they paid the agency for the bed. I was considered . . . because I got all those labels attached to me earlier on when I first entered foster care as being unable to attach. I was considered a behavioral challenge or a child with behavioral issues, so I had to go to a therapeutic foster home.

DR. H   You were a special needs child.

MR. T   I was a special needs child and the special needs child right here with, um, just not even. I mean nothing that I think about that what A did is. . . . It is if you were to say it about a normal family that's not in foster care, it would not be considered odd. It would just be normal, but with every level of attention that I got from her, with the words of encouragement, the accepting environment, um, this problem child, this behavioral child started college at sixteen. I graduated at nineteen with a Bachelor's in Social Work with a 3.917 GPA. Um, I'm about to finish my MSW at twenty-two after taking two years off of work. I mean off to go work in the workforce. And I'm now in a semi-administrative position at the university . . . ; I mean that's what this problem child did by simply having a solid foundation for once.

DR. H   And you've got me here pushing you to get your PhD.

MR. T   And that's what my future holds. It's like I have all these options ahead of me. I do my day job, but I realize my experience. Unfortunately A has a point when she says what I do shouldn't be exceptional; she has a point; it is exceptional. She doesn't recognize it, but it's exceptional and that's sad. That's absolutely sad that it's exceptional because we have a disproportionate number of youth who are of color in the child welfare system. We have a disproportionate number of youth in the system who are LGBT and the problem is that youth who are in the system who are of color and youth who are in the system who are LGBT, and especially, youth who are in the system who are of color, youth who are LGBT oftentimes have experienced more abuse, more neglect and have been pushed out of homes time and time again or have been kicked out of their own biological homes because of their identity. So, what's happening is there is this cycle that's reinforcing all these negative ideas about who they are as people and what we see is a 3 percent rate obtaining any education past high school. Um, an abysmal number of foster youth are obtaining their high school education.

DR. H   Right, I'm going to ask you, T, . . . did they talk to you about a college education for you? Granted she's an educator and you were going to college because she encouraged you to go. But your social worker or child welfare worker did they talk to you about the Chafee Act and the fact that there might be funds for college? Did anybody bring that up?

MR. T   You know, they would bring up things like independent living skills which I never went to because I mean. . . . Granted I started college really young and A encouraged me. She asked me, "Do you want to get a part-time job?" If you feel like you want a job it is okay. I said, I was sixteen and taking three classes and three classes only in college; you are in class from 8:00 in the morning until 4:00 in the afternoon. She's like, "If you want a part-time job, why not?" So I got a part-time job and ended up becoming a manager in that company while I was still in college and living at home. I learned how to manage money pretty quickly. So, the thought about going and sitting and learning how to write a check and managing a debit account . . . I'm like . . . I think ILS services are great for foster kids and I'm not saying that we shouldn't implement them, but the problem with the foster care system is that we, it's a one-size-fits-all approach.

DR. H   There needs to be work on a case-by-case basis because every child is different.

MR. T   Yeah, I don't think that we look at it that way. So, no, we didn't talk a whole lot about it. Um, where a lot of resources came in for me is A helped me to get involved with this youth center in Tacoma when I was fourteen. It's called Oasis and it's a drop-in.

DR. H   I'm familiar with them.

MR. T   Yeah, a drop-in center for gay, gay youth, and they also recognized that I was going to be somebody. Like I was going to be somebody one day and they knew that I was going to be educated. They were really helping me identify any type of resources that I could get. They helped me identify the PRIDE Foundation, which has paid for my undergrad education and some of my graduate education. It's an LGBT foundation that the Greater Business Association identified.

DR. H   I've heard of them.

MR. T   Yeah, so, um, I now sit on the board with them and get to give back, that is amazing. Um, but they did help me identify the Chafee Act and the College

Success Foundation. I became a Governor's Scholar, which is a scholarship for foster kids. I did get, I think, the passport to college, which is a Chafee; it's under the Chafee Act.

DR. H   Right, but again, these are resources that you were made aware of outside of the child welfare system.

MR. T   Um, and I had to bring it up to my social worker because they had to initiate the paperwork. The problem is I don't know if anybody thought that I would go to college. I don't know if anybody ever considered it.

DR. H   Do you think that they stereotyped you and put you into the mode of "this is a foster child?"

MR. T   Yeah, I think that they put into the mode of this a foster kid associated with this program. My foster mom worked for a program that served some of the most damaged kids, some of the most behaviorally challenging kids, and I think no one expects any of those kids to let alone graduate high school.

DR. H   Do you think race entered into decisions that were made about you?

MR. T   You know, I don't know. I never really . . . I don't think race was ever addressed with me which I think can be just as damaging if it's used as a weapon against you. I was always curious like what it meant to be. . . . Like I . . . like I was talking with you earlier off the record, how I have no idea what my ethnicity is other than my Vietnamese background, which is a minimal part of me too. Like, I'm mostly Caucasian, but I don't know much about that background. Um, so, I mean I always have questions about it; but there's never like resources provided on how could I identify these things about me and it was just kind of ignored. Um, I don't think it was ever addressed what the experience is like living in a multiracial foster home. Not that it was problematic or anything, but I find it curious now to reflect on how at least I was never involved in any conversations about it or what the experience was like. It was wonderful for me, but I just question now like maybe for kids who struggle themselves with their identity and they're trying to figure it out.

DR. H   And many kids struggle with trying to determine their identity, especially biracial and multiracial kids.

MR. T   Yeah, like what type of questions are being asked? And what kinds of conversations are being asked? I wonder that. A and I was talking about it at times and for her it just wasn't that big a deal. Like she said I mean people at times would wonder what our relationship is and that was kind of her take on it.

DR. H   Are you the only child at home?

MR. T   Yeah, A only took one child at a time. Um, so I was an only kid in the home. Oh, so once I had learned about all these potential resources at home. Oh and I mean a blatant example of how sure or how unlikely the system thought that I would actually go to college is I remember it was again one of those six-month court review reports where they were reporting how I was doing; it was one of the earlier ones right after I had just moved in with A. And I had just seen a movie about it. It was like a motion picture about this woman who goes to law school and she just ends up really good at it. It's called *Legally Blonde;* it was a comedy. And I loved it; I loved it.

DR. H   Oh yeah, it's with Reese Witherspoon. I've seen that movie.

MR. T   Yeah, it's with Reese Witherspoon. And I just loved it and I told my social worker that I wanted to be a lawyer and that I wanted to go to Harvard Law School. And he wrote in my court summary that T states that he has goals to become a lawyer and to go to Harvard Law School and something along the lines with that it's a lofty goal and that while it is unlikely, it should be encouraged. And at the time like kind of just mincing words about what he thought. Um, I don't think anybody thought that I was going to college (laughs jokingly). I don't think that; so when we brought that to them. . . . I mean the social worker changed once I turned sixteen. She initiated the paperwork, but it was really up to me to do the work that I needed to do. I filled out the applications; she signed the applications confirming that I was a ward of the state, but I'm the one who really did my research to find out everything. I almost missed out on a big scholarship had I not done a little bit more research I would not have known about. Granted being a foster kid I did get a free bachelor's education. It was covered completely through scholarships for being a foster kid and for being an LGBT leader. Um, but yeah, that was more the work of the community resources that were outside of the child welfare system; community resources staff connected me with those resources. And they were really big advocates for making sure that I got an education.

DR. H   What do you think the child welfare system can do for children of color? What do you think the child welfare system can do for lesbian, bisexual, and transgender kids to make life better for them when they come into the system?

MR. T   Um, I think that's a complex question. I think that there are a lot of systems. There are a lot of systems and a lot of ideas and challenges that interact with one another that make it difficult. Um, but I think that ultimately one thing that I've always thought it's the adults that need to do the work, not the kids that need to do the work. And I think that it starts at the organizational level. I think that with the people that we employ we need to be certain that they're culturally competent to provide care for kids who have experienced the types of things foster kids have experienced and realize that alone without the intersection of race, gender, and sexual orientation. The traumatic experiences of foster kids are enough to cause behavioral issues or to cause a kid to withdraw. Um, first of all, we need to just understand that and I think we go into this field with a good heart, but I think a lot of people (sighs) don't understand when they go into social work the strain that it might put on their personal ethics and personal values, and to understand that this is a professional field where your personal values can do harm.

DR. H Personal values have to be left at the door when one enters workplace. It is imperative to maintain boundaries between our personal and professional values.

MR. T And that's what I mean, personal values certainly have to be left at the door because A is an example. She had no idea what to do, but she knew that didn't matter because I wasn't there to hear her opinion.

DR. H And she became a foster parent by choice, which in my book means that she had a responsibility to you. She agreed to take you into her home and what that means for me is that whatever that child needs you're supposed to step up to the plate. If it involves you going to trainings, if involves you reading a book, if it involves you calling your social worker every day, you do it. If it involves you advocating for the child or children in your home, you do it. And I feel very strongly, T, about social workers and people who are in child welfare. If they don't know something they have a responsibility to be proactive and do whatever is necessary to learn about it; that's a responsibility of a professional social worker.

MR. T Yeah, I agree completely. Um, there's things I won't do in my field of work unless I get training on it first; because I wouldn't feel competent enough to provide the service. I consider myself someone who can walk into almost any situation and not have my jaw drop. I consider myself someone who has a somewhat fair exposure to adversity and to diversity, but I still feel like that if there's a group that I'm going to be working with exclusively or providing services to that I don't have a good grasp on, it's not in their best interest for me to serve them until I make this disclaimer that I need to do this work myself.

DR. H And I think that it's ethically wrong if you don't have the knowledge and the skills to even attempt to serve any group that you know that you're not qualified to serve and if you're not willing to get the education and to develop the skills, then the ethical thing to do is to refer that person or group to another professional or agency who has the necessary training to provide the service.

MR. T   Elsewhere, so I think that one big thing and this is not little like this is not something that can occur overnight that needs to occur is that agencies, organizations, and government systems that serve these youth need to have some sort of credentialed way of certifying that employees are culturally competent to apply their services to work with these disadvantaged youth. It's one thing to say, "I know how to work with children in the child welfare system," but that's like saying, "I know how to work with children." There's no one type of child or children.

DR. H   No, every child is different; even children who come from the same family are different.

MR. T   Right, we have to understand that a heterosexual person cannot understand the difference in worldview that a queer kid is going to have growing up without getting some sort of education on it. A white person is not going to have any understanding of a nonwhite person without some sort of education; even at that point it's still theoretical.

DR. H   I completely agree.

MR. T   Yeah, so I think that we need to be a little bit more cognizant about that. And recognize that it's not the foster parents' fault or the social worker's fault, but training needs to start from the top down. And I think we need to implement ways, just like with a social work education; there's competencies you have to hit. I think that agencies need to meet these competencies.

DR. H   Right, I talk about the Council on Social Work Education Competencies and Practice Behaviors in my book. I'm also doing a whole section around cultural competency because it's important; it really is highly significant in this type of work.

MR. T   Yeah, I think that if a foster agency is going to place a gay kid and that they are going to be taking responsibility for doing that they need to make sure that the language that they use at the organizational level is correct; the way that they treat their employees, the way that their employees interact with each other affirms that these people are welcome in our organization. You create a culture not just among your employees but also among the families that you have working for you. You have the power to influence who provides services for you. If a foster agency is out there who is known in the community as providing exceptional services to LGBT kids, people are also going to be more compelled to work with these agencies that are more competent to provide services to these youth. So, I think that being more public about cultural competency, doing more training around it would be a benefit to these kids. It's a really big systems issue. That's what I mean when I say it's a systems issue is that it's so complicated. It's things that we know work that need to come together and actually be applied.

DR. H I agree, you know, it's nice to talk about them, but we have to be proactive and put them into action.

MR. T And there's an abundance of resources for education; it's just we need to do it. First of all, we have to recognize that there is an issue (laughs joyously).

DR. H I agree; you're preaching to the choir here.

MR. T I know we have to recognize that there's an issue. We can put out as many publications as we want about racial disproportionality or about the negative outcomes of queer foster kids, but unless we implement prevention programs and educational programs, we're not changing those statistics. I mean doing educational programs on the statistics is not going to change anything either (laughs).

DR. H No, it isn't. No, systems have to change including the child welfare system.

MR. T Yeah, we have to talk about why the statistics exist. We shouldn't just talk about the stats, like we can all throw out stats about how many kids end up homeless one night of the year after they turn eighteen. We can all talk about these as professionals, but can we talk about what we can do to change that? Like it's not all about just providing resources, I mean resources are essential, but I mean we also need to talk about what type of conversations start with these kids when they're eleven or twelve? What type of messages are they receiving about self-sufficiency, about the ability to take care of yourself, that you're not broken? And that you are okay and that you can make good decisions. And I think that the more positive messages that are being delivered from a young age that's what separates kids who are successful I think from kids who are grow up in broken homes and kids who grow up in foster care that are not successful.

DR. H Yes, and I think that every child has a right to an education. And when I say education I mean that every child should be getting the message that you are going to college; it shouldn't be that you're not smart enough. You are going, and these are the things you need to get ready and we're going to help you do them. And that's the message kids need to hear.

MR. T Yeah, yeah, there's a lot of things that need to be changed and I think that what we need is leadership that's willing to implement it and leaders willing to do the research needed to figure out what is working in my organization and what isn't working. Thankfully, I think we have some amazing leaders at a national level right now who are really starting to talk about these questions at a little bit deeper level and starting to do things about them.

DR. H   There are people at the national level who've worked in child welfare at the local level and are willing to advocate and to push for systems change.

MR. T   Yeah, and I think I'm really excited to see what's going to happen, especially with serving youth who are disproportionately represented in the system.

DR. H   I mean it's an exciting time to be doing this work; that's why I'm doing this work. Well, I've been doing it my entire career.

MR. T   I'm a big fan of the point of the whole trickle-down thing. I think when we apply it to social services in training I think that is a brilliant concept of taking leadership. Leaders need to demonstrate the type of behaviors that we want. To conclude my last thought I watched this video; have you heard of TED talks? So, it's like this lecture program where they hire, not hire, but guest speakers will come out and give little lectures. I remember I was watching this one by Melinda Gates and she was lecturing on NGOs, She stated that nonprofits need to learn from Coca-Cola and I was like, this is interesting. I just sat down and I was kind of like stuck on it for a minute. I was like, this is interesting. I have to hear what she says, and what she said was that Coca-Cola is very . . . they're very . . . what was the word that she used? Um, God, it was brilliant. They're very deliberate about the way that they go about their marketing. And they're very anthropological about it. They don't just read about a culture; they experience it. And what they do is that they really understand a culture before they start marketing to it. And that they're some of the most brilliant market-ers out there. What they do is that they go into a community in Nigeria and they learn about their cultural norms and what they value as a culture and they use that as a way to sell Coca-Cola and what she said is that NGOs need to learn that you don't market safer sex the same way in Sudan that you do in Har-lem; that cultures are different about sex and that you don't just go in with an HIV prevention program and expect everyone to jump on board in a village in Sudan, just because it has lowered HIV rates in Harlem. And that we're wasting a lot of money for one thing by doing it that way. And that we could be saving lives, time, and money if we were more culturally aware of certain populations and how they function, and how they're different and what their experiences are. For me that clicked for a second and I was like this is how the child welfare system is. It's like different countries and we all have a common humanity, like we share humanity with people who live in Europe, Asia, and Africa, but we have different worldviews and cultures and learning how to deliver services that are culturally competent I think relates to what she was talking about so much. We need to be able to realize that a foster kid that lives in this home and a foster kid in that home are going to need services delivered in different ways. That is why we need skilled service providers who know how to deliver stuff out of the box and to look at kids as being unique.

DR. H   And it gets back to the fact that there is not one size that fits all. For example, there should be different parenting practices based on the background of a child when a child is placed in a foster home.

MR. T   Yeah, yeah, I mean and there's so much that goes into it. I mean when we talk about it. Because I was thinking maybe if social workers understood their foster parent population a little bit better, like who provides services for them, maybe we can be a little bit more strategic in the way that we place kids; but when we have an overload of caseloads, who wants to think about that; the goal of the day is to place a kid without very little thought.

DR. H   And I was talking earlier about the fact that I had a caseload of fifteen. I worked for a private agency. It was unheard in a private agency that you were going to have a caseload of forty or fifty kids; you really can't do anything with that many children.

MR. T   Hence the reason why I said earlier that A and I was easy. There were no issues; we got a visit once every six months instead of once every month which is what we were supposed to get. And it baffles me to think that we were so easy that we never got seen, but also resources were gone. So there's this loss, this disconnect between they are doing so well, but we didn't get access to the resources. I did get access to them, but it took a lot of work by me and A.

DR. H   Right, it took a lot of proactive work on your part and on A's part.

MR. T   Right, yeah, that's my experience. Today what I get to do is I get to do a job that I love that is not really in child welfare. I get to spend time outside of it as an expert on the field and when I say an expert I mean someone who has lived in the system and someone who understand it, and someone who has a solid education.

DR. H   Well, you bring a strong voice to this experience.

MR. T   Like I said A and I have become really . . . like we've become recognized as having some sort of experience in this and, especially related to LGBT kids. I can't speak on behalf of all the people, but when it comes to that, I think that we've been well respected. I have the honor today to get to work with organizations who are trying to do what we are talking about right now who are really interested in how can I tell my community that I am able to provide services to these kids and how can I make sure LGBT foster kids have the same access to resources and have that same or better outcome than they had five or ten years ago. I get the opportunity to work with these organizations to help them restructure their curriculums and even develop (laughing) curriculums around education on these issues. The agencies are so warm and welcoming to us, but it's typically the staff that are hesitant to have these types of conversations. That is why I know from qualitative experiences as well as professional experiences that there's a lot of miseducation around certain populations. It's never the administration that is hesitant; it's more the line staff.

DR. H   And these are the people who are having direct interaction with kids and families.

MR. T   Um, like I said, we create a culture and if that culture isn't affirming, we can only throw out statistics about what is going to happen to these kids.

DR. H   I agree. Well, thank you so much for talking to me. Is there anything else you would like to say?

MR. T   No, that's it. I think that we talked a lot.

DR. H   We did. Thank you.

MR. T   Yes, you are welcome.

REFERENCES

American Humane Association. (1994, December). Cultural competence in child protective services. *Child Protective Leader,* 1–2.

American Public Human Services Association. (2008). *Disproportionality Diagnostic Tool.* Washington, DC: Author.

Billingsley, A., & Giovannoni, J. M. (1972). *Children of the storm: Black children and American child welfare.* New York, NY: Harcourt Brace Jovanovich.

Cross, T. L. (2008). Disproportionality in child welfare. *Child Welfare, 87*(2), 11–20.

Cross, T. L., Bazron, B. J., Dennis, K. W., & Isaacs, M. R. (1989). *Toward a culturally competent system of care.* Washington, DC: Georgetown University Child Development Center.

Flicker, B. D. (1982). *Standards for juvenile justice: A summary and analysis* (2nd ed.). Cambridge, MA: Ballinger.

Gibelman, M., & Furman, R. (2008). *Navigating human service organizations* (2nd ed.). Chicago, IL: Lyceum Books.

Graman, K. (2007, April). Child welfare system biased, experts claim: Disproportionate number of minorities affected. *The Spokesman-Review,* pp. 1–7. Retrieved from http://spokesmanreview.com/ourkids/stories/?ID=182615

Harris, M.S., & Hackett, W. (2008). Decision points in child welfare: An action research model to address disproportionality. *Children and Youth Services Review, 30*(2), 199–215.

Hill, R. (2004). Institutional racism in child welfare. In J. E. Everett, S. P. Chipungu, & B. R. Leashore (Eds.), *Child welfare revisited: An Africentric perspective* (pp. 57–76). New Brunswick, NJ: Rutgers University Press.

King County Coalition on Racial Disproportionality. (2004). *Racial disproportionality in the child welfare system in King County, Washington.* Seattle, WA: Author.

Leonard, E. (1972). A history of the Riverdale Children's Association. In A. Billingsley & J. M. Giovannoni (Eds.), *Children of the storm: Black children and American child welfare* (pp. 27–28). New York, NY: Harcourt Brace Jovanovich.

Lewis, J. A., Packard, T. R., & Lewis, M. D. (2012). *Management of human service programs* (5th ed.). Belmont, CA: Thomson Brooks/Cole.

McRoy, R. (2004). The color of child welfare. In K. E. Davis & T. B. Bent-Goodley (Eds.), *The color of social policy* (pp. 37–63). Alexandria, VA: The Council on Social Work Education.

Miller, J., & Garran, A. M. (2008). *Racism in the United States: Implications for the helping professions.* Belmont, CA: Thomson Brooks/Cole.

Miller, K. M., Cahn, K., Cause, A., Bender, R., & Cross-Hemmer, A. (2010). *What we know about disproportionality and disparity in Oregon's child welfare system: Decision point analysis qualitative report.* Portland, OR: The Child Welfare Partnership, Portland State University School of Social Work.

Padilla, J., & Summers, A. (2011). *Disproportionality rates for children of color in foster care.* Reno, NV: Council of Juvenile and Family Court Judges.

Sue, D. W. (2010). *Microaggressions in everyday life: Race, gender, and sexual orientation.* Hoboken, NJ: Wiley.

Weaver, H. N. (2005). Social work history and cultural diversity. In *Explorations in cultural competence: Journeys to the four directions* (pp. 6–14). Belmont, CA: Thomson/Brooks Cole.

5

Social Work Curriculum

IN THIS CHAPTER THE READER will learn why curriculum is significant for students planning to work in the child welfare system. Syllabi for five courses are presented. These courses should be required in schools of social work that are training students to work in child welfare organizations/ agencies. Information for field instruction, including the importance of home visits and respect for family cultural practices, will be explored.

According to the Council on Social Work Education (CSWE 2011a), which is the accrediting organization for social work education in the United States, there are 472 accredited undergraduate (BASW) social work programs and 213 graduate (MSW) social work programs. These programs are accredited based on CSWE's Educational Policy and Accreditation Standards (Council on Social Work Education 2001). CSWE requires that all accredited schools of social work demonstrate a commitment to diversity (e.g., age, class, color, culture, disability, ethnicity, gender, gender identity and expression, immigration status, political ideology, race, religion, sex, and sexual orientation) in all facets of their programs. All accredited schools of social work tend to have one or more courses in their curriculum that focus on diversity content; therefore, a syllabus for a diversity course is not included in this chapter. However, diversity content, including content about institutional racism, must be an integral part of the social work curriculum. According to the National Association of Social Workers (2007):

> In education institutions, effectiveness in addressing institutional racism will involve making a commitment to the incorporation of content related

to institutional racism curriculum and all forms of education. The goal is to graduate social workers who are on the road toward competency in addressing institutional racism throughout their careers. It also means examining ways in which the current curriculum promotes and supports values, beliefs, and practices that foster institutional racism and then engaging in change process as indicated. Leadership is needed from deans and directors, chairs of educational committees, as well as from admissions and field work departments and field work supervisors. (18)

The profession of social work is not as ethnically diverse as the population in the United States. Findings from a 2006 study by the Center for Health Workforce Studies and the National Association of Social Workers Center for Workforce Studies (2006) revealed that 85 percent of the licensed social workers in the study were non-Hispanic white, 6.8 percent were African American, 0.5 percent were American Indian, 1.4 percent were Asian American, and 4.3 percent were Hispanic. According to a report by Shrestha and Heisler (2011), the following are percentages of the total U.S. population by race: White 74.46 percent; Black or African American 12.36 percent; Asian 4.38 percent; American Indian and Alaska Native 0.80 percent; and Native Hawaiian and Other Pacific Islander 0.15 percent. The findings from a 2011 Council on Social Work Education survey revealed percentages regarding racial/ethnic identification of the following graduates by program: Baccalaureate (White 52.4 percent; African American/ Other Black 19.2 percent; Asian American/Other Asian 1.9 percent; American Indian/Native American 1.1 percent and Pacific Islander 0.4 percent); Masters (White 55.3 percent; African American/Other Black 15.5 percent; Asian American/Other Asian 3.2 percent; American Indian/Native American 0.8 percent; and Pacific Islander 0.3 percent); Doctoral (White 60.7 percent; African American/Other Black 12.1 percent; Asian American/ Other Asian 11.5 percent; American Indian/Native American and Pacific Islander are excluded because their number in this category was less than five). The Council on Social Work Education survey (2011b) also identified the percentage of full-time faculty by race/ethnicity (White 66.6 percent; African American/Other Black 15.5 percent; Asian American/Other Asian 2.5 percent; American Indian/Native American 0.6 percent; and Pacific Islander 0.3 percent). These figures are troubling and speak to the urgent need to increase the number of students and faculty of color in schools of social work across the country. Many of these graduates will work with the disproportionate number of children of color and their families in the child welfare system.

Although diversity content, including content about institutional racism, is very important for social work students, there is additional content that should be included in the curriculum for students who are planning to work in the child welfare system. The following are syllabi for five courses that should be required in schools of social work for any student who plans to work in the child welfare system.

The first syllabus is for a Child Development course (Harris 2013a) developed for students in the MSW Program at the University of Washington Tacoma. Regardless of a child's racial, ethnic, or cultural background she or he will have physical, cognitive, social, and emotional stages of development. Child welfare workers need to have a strong knowledge base in all of these stages of development prior to actually working with children and adolescents in the child welfare system. If social work students do not learn what constitutes a "normal" process of growth and development for children and adolescents, they will be unable to determine if a child or adolescent is experiencing some type of developmental problem and/or delay.

The second syllabus is for a Family Theories course (Harris 2013c) developed for students in the MSW Program at the University of Washington Tacoma. Students must have knowledge of family theory in order to work with children and families in the child welfare system. Families in society, including the families involved in the child welfare system, are diverse; they are also always changing. Child welfare workers need a theoretical base in order to engage in the best child welfare practice with the children and families of color who are continuously entering the child welfare system. Theory is the driving force behind social work practice. The third course syllabus is for Children of Incarcerated Parents (Harris 2013b); this course is taught in the Social Work and Criminal Justice Programs at the University of Washington Tacoma. Thousands of children across the country have a birth parent or parents who are incarcerated in jail or prison. Many of these children are involved in the child welfare system because they are in some type of out-of-home placement. Social work students who plan to work in child welfare need knowledge regarding the problems and issues experienced by these children and their parents, including the difficulty of parent–child visits when birth parents still have their parental rights. These visits are important for children and parents to maintain their attachment relationship.

The fourth syllabus is for Disproportionality Across Systems (Harris 2013d); this course is taught in the Social Work and Criminal Justice Programs at the University of Washington Tacoma. Many children and families are involved with multiple systems in our society (criminal justice, education, health, juvenile justice, and mental health) in addition to the child welfare system. Children of color and their families are disproportionately represented in these systems and also experience disparities in these systems. Course content covers all of the aforementioned systems, including disparities and other issues encountered by children and families involved in these systems. The final syllabus is for an Assessment of Mental Disorders (Harris 2009) course. This graduate course is taught in the MSW Program at the University of Washington Tacoma. This course content is very important because many children who enter the child welfare system have a history of prior traumatic experiences that have resulted in mental health problems. Some children will require a thorough mental health assessment, as well as culturally appropriate mental health treatment. In many private child welfare agencies across the country mental health assessments, as well as treatment, are provided within the agency rather than via referral to an outside agency.

UNIVERSITY OF WASHINGTON SCHOOL OF SOCIAL WORK

UNIVERSITY OF WASHINGTON TACOMA, SOCIAL WORK PROGRAM

Child Development

COURSE DESCRIPTION

The early years of a child's life are crucial for his or her growth and development. Many factors impact the child's development during these early years; however, the family has the most significant impact. This course will examine major theories of child development and research findings to give students a look at the trajectory of child development. Theories are essential elements in human development, and those theories that demonstrate reliability via research serve as a guide to our observations and give a solid foundation for useful procedures required to maximize the development of children. Diverse environmental and/or other experiences will be explored that provide an understanding of why some children are more resilient than others. The role of heredity in child development will be explored. The child's growth and development will be traced through the following periods: prenatal, birth, infancy and toddlerhood (the first two years), early childhood (two to six years), middle childhood (six to eleven years), and adolescence. There will be a focus on understanding the whole child's development (physical, cognitive, emotional, and social).

TABLE OF COUNCIL ON SOCIAL WORK EDUCATION COMPETENCIES
AND PRACTICE BEHAVIORS TARGETED IN THIS COURSE

Competency #3: Apply critical thinking to inform and communicate professional judgment.

3a. use critical thinking to distinguish, evaluate, and integrate multiple sources of knowledge, including research-based knowledge, practice wisdom, and client/constituent experience.

Competency #4: Engage diversity and difference in practice.

4b. develop and demonstrate sufficient critical self awareness to understand the influence of personal biases and values in working with diverse clients.

4c. recognize and dialogue with others about the role of difference and the multiple intersections of oppression and privilege in shaping a person's identity and life experiences.

Competency #7: Apply knowledge of human behavior and the social environment.

7a. apply theories and conceptual framework relevant to understanding people and environments across systems levels.

7b. critique and apply human behavior and social environment theories and conceptual frameworks to assessment, intervention, and evaluation at multiple systems levels.

Competency #10: Engage, assess, intervene, and evaluate individuals, families, groups, organizations, and communities.

10b. engage with families and groups in the context of diverse and multidisciplinary settings.

ASSESSMENT

10h. assess client/constituent strengths, stressors, and limitations.

10i. identify and select appropriate and culturally responsive strategies.

INTERVENTION

10k. implement prevention interventions that enhance client/constituent capacities.

COURSE OBJECTIVES

(Related CSWE Competencies Delineated in Parentheses)
After completing this course, students will be able to:

1. Understand the evolution of child development from historical and contemporary viewpoints via the use of varied theories and concepts. (3a, 7a, 7b)
2. Describe and critically analyze the major child development theories. (7a, 7b)
3. Demonstrate the ability to recognize, describe, and compare developmental milestones for infants, children, and adolescents across the life span.
4. Understand the relationship between heredity and environment in child development. (7a)
5. Describe and compare the physical, cognitive, emotional, and social development of infants, toddlers, and children in early childhood, middle childhood, and adolescence. (10h)
6. Describe and discuss the strengths and weaknesses of research methodologies utilized in the study of child development.
7. Understand the necessity for utilizing an empowerment lens when developing practices and/or courses of action for the developing child. (10i, 10k)
8. Understand the role of family in child development. (10b)
9. Demonstrate an understanding of child development from a cultural context that is affected by race, sex, sexual orientation, and social class. (4b, 4c)
10. Understand and discuss ethical and value dimensions of child development.

COURSE REQUIREMENTS

1. Learning in this course relies heavily upon active involvement. Student and instructor responsibilities include being present and participating fully in the learning experience to gain the greatest benefit from the course.

2. As part of professional responsibility, the expectation is that all assignments will be completed by the deadline. The *Publication Manual of the American Psychological Association* (6th ed.) guidelines will be used for all assignments. If for any reason you will not be able to submit an assignment, you *must* discuss this reason with the professor prior to the due date.

3. The "Standards for Essential Abilities and Attributes for Admission and Continuance in the MSW Program" in your *Program Manual* mandate commitment to professional social work education, values, and ethics. Attendance and class participation are indications of professional commitment and are an expectation in all classes. Failure to participate in at least 70 percent of class sessions for any given course will result in a faculty review of the student's appropriateness for continuation in the program. *Class participation* is demonstrated through your involvement in class discussions and experiential activities. Students are expected to complete required readings prior to class and should be well prepared to participate in discussion and experiential learning assignments. Failure to regularly attend class and demonstrate through discussions that one has comprehended the readings will be considered in assigning the final grade. Class participation will be evaluated by relevance of questions and comments; evidence of reading required materials; ability to work cooperatively with peers; and quality and not quantity of questions and comments. Recognizing that we come from different backgrounds with different *worldviews,* students are encouraged to dialogue with others in a meaningful way that respects the opinions of others and provides opportunities to learn from one another. Your presence and engagement throughout the term—verbally and bodily—will allow us to establish an intellectually and emotionally vital and safe climate for learning (15 percent of your grade). Students are responsible for any material missed due to absences.

4. Students are expected to both learn and demonstrate knowledge of child development theories. This requires a search of the literature in a defined area in order to develop specialized knowledge concerning the physical, cognitive, social, and emotional development of child from conception to adolescence. In addition, students will demonstrate their level of applied knowledge of child development on one mid-term examination, a child observation assignment/paper, and a critical reflection/research paper.

All written assignments must adhere to the format of the *Publication Manual of the American Psychological Association* (6th ed.). Do not exceed page limits in the assignment, as they provide ample opportunity for discussion. Assignments must be double-spaced and typed (12 pt. font). Include an alphabetized reference page to indicate sources you read to prepare each assignment. Check your paper for syntax, grammar, punctuation, spelling, etc., prior to submission. Poor form will lower your grade. Plagiarism or any other kind of scholarly misconduct will be reported and may result in disciplinary action, including failing the class. If accepted, late assignments will be assessed point penalties at the rate of 5 points for each day late. Please make *advance* arrangements with the professor for any due date that you miss or need to change.

Course Requirements for the Quarter

1. Mid-Term Examination

One short examination based on readings, lectures, and discussions will be given in the course. This examination is 20 percent of your final grade in this course.

2. Observation of a Child Assignment/Paper

This assignment requires that you observe a child or adolescent between the ages of birth and eighteen in his or her natural environment. There will be variation in the observations based on the child's age and developmental level. You must get permission from the child's parents or any other individual who is identified as the child's caregiver. Please inform parents or caregivers that this observation is a required class assignment. Assign a pseudonym to the child for use in taking notes and writing your paper (4 to 5 pages). You must assure the child, parents, and caregivers that confidentiality will be maintained; no child, adolescent, parent, or caregiver will be identified by name or use of any type of identifiable information in your paper. It is important for you to monitor your internal feelings during this assignment; your feelings must be discussed in your paper. A detailed discussion of this assignment has been posted on Canvas for your perusal. This assignment is 25 percent of your final grade.

3. Reflection/Research Paper
Select a facet of child development that you would like to explore in depth. Write a 15- to 20-page paper about this area of child development that is of interest to you. You must discuss a theory that is most applicable to your selected area. This paper should address the physical, cognitive, emotional, and social development of the child. A discussion of the heredity and environmental factors that impact the child or adolescent is an integral component of this paper. You must demonstrate an understanding of culture and its relevance to child development. Your paper must include a thorough review of the literature. Discuss any issues of diversity that impact child development—i.e., race, sex, sexual orientation, social class, etc. Also, include those actions and/or strategies that can be utilized to nurture and support children and adolescents to maximize their growth and development. A detailed discussion of this assignment has been posted on Canvas for your perusal. An alphabetized list of references must be included in your paper. This assignment is 40 percent of your total grade.

SUMMARY OF COURSE REQUIREMENTS

Mid-Term Examination	20%
Observation of Child Assignment/Paper	25%
Reflection/Research Paper	40%
Participation	15%
Total	100%

REQUIRED TEXTBOOKS

Robinson, L. (2007). *Cross-cultural child development for social workers.* New York, NY: Palgrave Macmillan.
Santrock, J. W. (2012). *Life-span development* (14th ed.). New York, NY: McGraw-Hill.
All other required reading has been placed on Canvas.

Week One:

Introduction to the Course
Review of Syllabus and Course Requirements

REQUIRED READING

Robinson, L. (2007). Introduction. In *Cross-cultural child development for social workers* (pp. 1–18). New York, NY: Palgrave Macmillan.

Week Two:

Theories of Child Development

REQUIRED READING

Berk, L. (2001). History, theory, and research strategies. In *Development through the lifespan* (2nd ed., pp. 3–43). Needham Heights, MA: Allyn & Bacon.

Robinson, L. (2007). Cognitive development: Cross-cultural perspectives. In *Cross-cultural child development for social workers* (pp. 82–106). New York, NY: Palgrave Macmillan.

Week Three:

Beginning Life

REQUIRED READING

Santrock, J. W. (2012). Biological beginnings. In *Life-span development* (14th ed., pp. 78–109). New York, NY: McGraw-Hill.

Santrock, J. W. (2012). Prenatal development and birth. In *Life-span development* (14th ed., pp. 110–143). New York, NY: McGraw-Hill.

Week Four:

The Family and Child Development

REQUIRED READING

Gullotta, T. P. (2008). How theory influences treatment and prevention practice with the family. In T. P. Gullotta & G. M. Blau (Eds.), *Family influences on childhood behavior and development* (pp. 1–20). New York, NY: Routledge, Taylor & Francis Group.

Osher, T. W., Osher, D., & Blau, G. M. (2008). Families matter. In T. P. Gullotta & G. M. Blau (Eds.), *Family Influences on childhood development* (pp. 39–61). New York, NY: Routledge, Taylor & Francis Group.

Williams-Washington, K. N., Melon, J., & Blau, G. M. (2008). Childhood growth and development within a family context. In T. P. Gullotta & G. M. Blau (Eds.), *Family influences on childhood behavior and development* (pp. 21–38). New York, NY: Routledge, Taylor & Francis Group.

Week Five:

Infant Development

REQUIRED READING

Santrock, J. W. (2012). Cognitive development in infancy. In *Life-span development* (14th ed., pp. 180–203). New York, NY: McGraw-Hill.

Santrock, J. W. (2012). Physical development in infancy. In *Life-span development* (14th ed., pp. 145–179). New York, NY: McGraw-Hill.

Santrock, J. W. (2012). Socioemotional development in infancy. In *Life-span development* (14th ed., pp. 204–229). New York, NY: McGraw-Hill.

Week Six:

Early Childhood Development
Mid-Term Examination

REQUIRED READING

Robinson, L. (2007). Attachment theory: Cross-cultural perspectives. In *Cross-cultural child development for social workers* (pp. 19–35). New York, NY: McGraw-Hill.

Santrock, J. W. (2012). Physical and cognitive development in early childhood. In *Life-span development* (14th ed., pp. 230–265). New York, NY: McGraw-Hill.

Santrock, J. W. (2012). Socioemotional development in early childhood. In *Life-span development* (14th ed., pp. 266–297). New York, NY: McGraw-Hill.

Week Seven:

Middle and Late Childhood Development
DUE: Child Observation Paper

REQUIRED READING

Goode, T. D., & Jones, W. A. (2008). Cultural influences on child development: The middle years. In T. P. Gullotta & G. M. Blau (Eds.), *Family influences on childhood behavior and development* (pp. 63–95). New York, NY: Routledge, Taylor & Francis Group.

Robinson, L. (2007). Racial/ethnic identity development. In *Cross-cultural child development for social workers* (pp. 36–81). New York, NY: McGraw-Hill.

Santrock, J. W. (2012). Physical and cognitive development in middle and late childhood. In *Life-span development* (14th ed., pp. 298–333). New York, NY: McGraw-Hill.

Santrock, J. W. (2012). Socioemotional development in middle and late childhood. In *Life-span development* (14th ed., pp. 334–365). New York, NY: McGraw-Hill.

Week Eight:

Adolescent Development

REQUIRED READING

Santrock, J. W. (2012). Physical and cognitive development in adolescence. In *Life-span development* (14th ed., pp. 366–401). New York, NY: McGraw-Hill.

Santrock, J. W. (2012). Socioemotional development in adolescence. In *Life-span development* (14th ed., pp. 402–435). New York, NY: McGraw-Hill.

Week Nine:

Child Development and Poverty
DUE: Reflection/Research Paper

REQUIRED READING

Lipina, S. J., & Colombo, J. A. (2009). Conceptualization and measurement of poverty. In *Poverty and brain development during childhood* (pp. 11–29). Washington, DC: American Psychological Association.

Lipina, S. J., & Colombo, J. A. (2009). Effects of poverty on development I: Health, educational, and psychometric perspectives (pp. 51–74). Washington, DC: American Psychological Association.

Lipina, S. J., & Colombo, J. A. (2009). Effects of poverty on development II: Cognitive neuroscience perspectives (pp. 75–91). Washington, DC: American Psychological Association.

Lipina, S. J., & Colombo, J. A. (2009). Experimental models: Effects of physical and social privation on brain development. In *Poverty and brain development during childhood* (pp. 31–49). Washington, DC: American Psychological Association.

Lipina, S. J., & Colombo, J. A. (2009). Overview. In *Poverty and brain development during childhood* (pp. 3–10). Washington, DC: American Psychological Association.

Week Ten:

Communication and Socialization
Course Evaluation

REQUIRED READING

Robinson, L. (2007). Communication: Cross-cultural perspectives. In *Cross-cultural child development* (pp. 107–137). New York, NY: Palgrave Macmillan.

Robinson, L. (2007). Socialization: Cultural-racial influences. In *Cross-cultural child development* (pp. 138–167). New York, NY: Palgrave Macmillan.

UNIVERSITY OF WASHINGTON SCHOOL OF SOCIAL WORK

UNIVERSITY OF WASHINGTON TACOMA, SOCIAL WORK PROGRAM

Family Theories

COURSE DESCRIPTION

This course focuses on students' developing a knowledge base in family theories and the underpinnings for these theories. Family theories are frameworks that can be utilized to understand families. There will be an emphasis in this course on development of skills for critical analysis of family theories and their applicability to the varied types of families that make up society today. There is no one model of family life today; there is a wide range of diverse configurations. The course will focus on varied factors that impact families today, including race, class, gender, sexual orientation, age, culture, and ethnicity. Family theories will be examined on the basis of time perspectives—i.e., static, episodic, biographical, and epochal. Family differences as well as similarities will be explored. Families will be viewed in their historical context. A look at families over time reveals that many families as well as family members have been dominated and oppressed by dominant members and/or groups in society. We will look at family theories and their applicability to social work practice with several diverse populations.

TABLE OF COUNCIL ON SOCIAL WORK EDUCATION COMPETENCIES AND PRACTICE BEHAVIORS TARGETED IN THIS COURSE

Competency #3: Apply critical thinking to inform and communicate professional judgments.

3a. use critical thinking to distinguish, evaluate, and integrate multiple sources of knowledge including research-based knowledge practice wisdom, and client/constituent experience.

Competency #4: Engage diversity and difference in practice.

4b. develop and demonstrate sufficient critical self-awareness to understand the influence of personal biases and values in working with diverse groups.

4c. recognize and dialogue with others about the role of difference and the multiple intersections of oppression and privilege in shaping a person's identity and life experiences.

Competency #7: Apply knowledge of human behavior and the social environment.

7a. apply theories and conceptual frameworks relevant to understanding people and environments across systems levels.

Competency #10: Engage, assess, intervene, and evaluate with individuals, families, groups, organizations, and communities.

ENGAGEMENT

10b. engage with families and groups in the context of diverse and multidisciplinary settings.

ASSESSMENT

10i. identify and select appropriate and culturally responsive strategies.

INTERVENTION

10l. help and empower clients/constituents to resolve problems.

COURSE OBJECTIVES

(Related CSWE Competencies Delineated in Parentheses)
After completing this course, students will be able to:

1. Critically analyze a wide range of family theories.
2. Conceptualize the dynamics of relationships between family members.
3. Trace the development of individuals across the life span within the context of their families.
4. Demonstrate an understanding of vulnerable families that have been oppressed by dominant members and/or groups in society. (4b, 4c)
5. Demonstrate the role of research in the formulation of family theories. (3a)
6. Demonstrate an understanding of families based on time perspectives—i.e., static, episodic, biographical, and epochal.
7. Demonstrate an understanding of families as dynamic systems that are impacted by social and environmental factors. (7a)
8. Demonstrate an understanding of the diverse family types/forms.
9. Identify the roles and functions of families.
10. Demonstrate skills in utilizing family theories in social work practice with diverse families across multiple systems. (10b, 10i, 10l)

COURSE REQUIREMENTS

1. Learning in this course relies heavily upon active involvement. Student and instructor responsibilities include being present and participating fully in the learning experience to gain the greatest benefit from the course.
2. As part of professional responsibility, the expectation is that all assignments will be completed by the deadline. The *Publication Manual of the American Psychological Association* (6th ed.) guidelines will be used in all assignments. If for any reason you will not be able to submit an assignment, you *must* discuss this reason with the professor prior to the due date.
3. The "Standards for Essential Abilities and Attributes for Admission and Continuance in the MSW Program" in your *Program Manual* mandate commitment to professional social work education, values, and ethics. Attendance and class participation are indications of professional commitment

and are an expectation in all classes. Failure to participate in at least 70 percent of class sessions for any given course will result in a faculty review of
the student's appropriateness for continuation in the program. *Class participation* is demonstrated through your involvement in class discussions and
experiential activities. Students are expected to complete required readings prior to class and should be well prepared to participate in discussion
and experiential learning assignments. Failure to regularly attend class and
demonstrate through discussions that one has comprehended the readings
will be considered in assigning the final grade. Class participation will be
evaluated by relevance of questions and comments; evidence of reading required materials; ability to work cooperatively with peers; and quality and
not quantity of questions and comments. Recognizing that we come from
different backgrounds with different *worldviews,* students are encouraged
to dialogue with others in a meaningful way that respects the opinions of
others and provides opportunities to learn from one another. Your presence
and engagement throughout the term—verbally and bodily—will allow
us to establish an intellectually and emotionally vital and safe climate for
learning (10 percent of your grade). Students are responsible for any material missed due to absences.
4. Students are expected to both learn and demonstrate the knowledge of
family theories and skills needed for family assessment, engagement, and
intervention. This requires a search of the literature in a defined theoretical
area. In addition, students will demonstrate their level of applied knowledge of family theories and skills on one mid-term examination and in a
critical analysis paper.

ASSIGNMENTS AND GRADING

Course Assignments for the Quarter

Your course grade will reflect your score based on the number of points
you accumulate from the assignments, examination, and participation in
the class.

1. Mid-Term Examination

One short examination based on readings, lectures, and discussions will be
given in the course. It will be worth 20 percent of your final grade. *Make-up
exams will not be given unless there are unusual extenuating circumstances.*

2. Family Theory Paper

The purpose of this assignment is for you to explore a family theory in detail. Your paper must include a thorough review of the literature. You should use the literature to provide the historical context for the theory that is explored in your paper and to discuss what is known and what is not known about the theory. Your review should be selective and include the most relevant literature. You must also apply the theory that is explored in your paper to a family with a focus on the dynamics inherent in the family's relationships. A detailed structure for this assignment is on Canvas. This assignment is worth 30 percent of your total grade.

3. Family Development Paper

The purpose of this assignment is for you to examine yourself and reflect on how the values, beliefs, rules, rituals, and customs/traditions of your own family have shaped your behavior and thinking in the adult phase of your life span. In this paper you should do a comprehensive assessment of your family system and culture, including a description of your family of origin. You must select and discuss a theory that is most applicable in order for one to understand the development of your family system. A detailed structure for this assignment is on Canvas. This assignment is worth 40 percent of your total grade.

SUMMARY OF COURSE REQUIREMENTS

Mid-Term Examination	20%
Family Theory Paper	30%
Family Development Paper	40%
Participation	10%
Total	100%

REQUIRED TEXTBOOKS

Bregman, O. C., & White, C. M. (Eds.). (2011). *Bringing systems thinking to life: Expanding the horizons for Bowen Family Systems Theory.* New York, NY: Routledge, Taylor & Francis Group.

White, J. M. (2005). *Advancing family theories.* Thousand Oaks, CA: Sage.

All other required readings have been placed on Canvas.

Week One:

Introduction to the Course
Review of Syllabus and Course Requirements
Overview of Family Theories

Week Two:

Understanding Theory

REQUIRED READING

White, J. M. (2005). Family theory and social science. In *Advancing family theories* (pp. 13–29). Thousand Oaks, CA: Sage.

White, J. M. (2005). Introduction. In *Advancing family theories* (pp. 1–12). Thousand Oaks, CA: Sage.

White, J. M. (2005). Science and its critics. In *Advancing family theories* (pp. 30–50). Thousand Oaks, CA: Sage.

Week Three:

Theory and Theoretical Method

REQUIRED READING

Goldenberg, H., & Goldenberg, I. (2008). Strategic models. In *Family therapy: An overview* (7th ed., pp. 212–228). Belmont, CA: Thomson Brooks/Cole.

Goldenberg, H., & Goldenberg, I. (2008). The structural model. In *Family therapy: An overview* (7th ed., pp. 236–261). Belmont, CA: Thomson Brooks/Cole.

Turner, F. J. (2011). Theory and social work treatment. In *Social work treatment: Interlocking theoretical approaches* (5th ed., pp. 3–14). New York, NY: Oxford University Press.

White, J. M. (2005). Functions and types of theory. In *Advancing family theories* (pp. 70–93). Thousand Oaks, CA: Sage.

White, J. M. (2005). Theory, models, and metaphors. In *Advancing family theories* (pp. 51–69). Thousand Oaks, CA: Sage.

Week Four:

Families and Family Theories

REQUIRED READING

Goldenberg, H., & Goldenberg, I. (2008). Adopting a family relationship framework. In *Family therapy: An overview* (7th ed., pp. 1–24). Belmont, CA: Thomson Brooks/Cole.

Goldenberg, H., & Goldenberg, I. (2008). A comparative view of family theories and therapies. In *Family therapy: An overview* (7th ed., pp. 428–444). Belmont, CA: Thomson Brooks/Cole.

Goldenberg, H., & Goldenberg, I. (2008). Family development: Continuity and change. In *Family therapy: An overview* (7th ed., pp. 25–53). Belmont, CA: Thomson Brooks/Cole.

Week Five:

Mid-Term Examination

Week Six:

Family Phenomenon

REQUIRED READING

McGoldrick, M., & Carter, B. (2003). The family life cycle. In F. Walsh (Ed.), *Normal family processes* (3rd ed., pp. 375–399). New York, NY: Guilford Press.

McGoldrick, M., Gerson, R., & Shellenberger, S. (1999). Developing a genogram to track family patterns. In *Genograms: Assessment and intervention* (2nd ed., pp. 13–61). New York, NY: Norton.

Walsh, F. (2003). Changing families in a changing world: Reconstructing family normality. In *Normal family processes* (3rd ed., pp. 3–26). New York, NY: Guilford Press.

White, J. M. (2005). Rational choice and the family. In *Advancing family theories* (pp. 95–114). Thousand Oaks, CA: Sage.

White, J. M. (2005). Transition theory. In *Advancing family theories* (pp. 115–144). Thousand Oaks, CA: Sage.

Week Seven:

Theoretical Considerations and Bowen Theory

REQUIRED READING

Bourne, G. M. (2011). Various points people miss: A training session by Dr. Murray Bowen at the Minnesota Institute of Family Dynamics. In O. C. Bregman & C. M. White (Eds.), *Bringing systems thinking to life: Expanding the horizons for Bowen Family Systems Theory* (pp. 31–59). New York, NY: Routledge, Taylor & Francis Group.

Comella, P. A. (2011). Observing emotional function in human relationship systems: Lessons from Murray Bowen's writings. In O. C. Bregman & C. M. White (Eds.), *Bringing systems thinking to life: Expanding the horizons for Bowen Family System Theory* (pp. 1–30). New York, NY: Routledge, Taylor & Francis Group.

Papero, D. V. (2011). Responsibility for self. In O. C. Bregman & C. M. White (Eds.), *Bringing systems thinking to life: Expanding the horizons for Bowen Family System Theory* (pp. 67–73). New York, NY: Routledge, Taylor & Francis Group.

Week Eight:

DUE: Family Theory Paper
Self and Bowen Theory

REQUIRED READING

Howard, L. (2011). Clarifying principles for investing in self. In O. C. Bregman & C. M. White (Eds.), *Bringing systems thinking to life: Expanding the horizons for Bowen Family Systems Theory* (pp. 137–158). New York, NY: Routledge, Taylor & Francis Group.

White, C. M. (2011). Learners without teachers: The simultaneous learning about self-functioning and Bowen Theory by supervisor, staff interns, and clients in an outpatient program. In O. C. Bregman & C. M. White (Eds.), *Bringing systems thinking to life: Expanding the horizons for Bowen Family Systems Theory* (pp. 117–136). New York, NY: Routledge, Taylor & Francis Group.

Wilgus, A. J. (2011). Incorporating Bowen Theory into an undergraduate social work curriculum: An exercise in the responsible use of self. In O. C. Bregman & C. M. White (Eds.), *Bringing systems thinking to life: Expanding the horizons for Bowen Family Systems Theory* (pp. 159–171). New York, NY: Routledge, Taylor & Francis Group.

Week Nine:

Exploring Diversity in Families

REQUIRED READING

Boyd-Franklin, N. (2003). Race, class and poverty. In F. Walsh (Ed.), *Normal family processes* (3rd ed., pp. 260–279). New York, NY: Guilford Press.

Falicov, C. (2008). The cultural meaning of family triangles. In M. McGoldrick (Ed.), *Re-visioning family therapy* (pp. 37–49). New York, NY: Guilford Press.

Hardy, K., & Laszloffy, T. (1995). The cultural genogram: Key to training culturally competent family therapists. *Journal of Marital and Family Therapy, 21*(3), 227–237.

Lee, M. Y. (2003). A solution-focused approach to cross-cultural clinical social work practice utilizing cultural strengths. *Families in Society: The Journal of Contemporary Social Services, 84*(3), 385–439.

Pinderhughes, E. (2008). Black genealogy revisited: Restoring an African American family. In M. McGoldrick (Ed.), *Re-visioning family therapy* (2nd ed., pp. 114–134). New York, NY: Guilford Press.

Zinn, M. B., & Eitzen, D. S. (1999). The historical making of family diversity. In *Diversity in families* (5th ed., pp. 59–89). New York, NY: Longman.

Week Ten:

Reflections on Family Theories
Course Evaluation
DUE: Family Development Paper

UNIVERSITY OF WASHINGTON TACOMA, CRIMINAL JUSTICE PROGRAM

UNIVERSITY OF WASHINGTON TACOMA, SOCIAL WORK PROGRAM

Children of Incarcerated Parents

COURSE DESCRIPTION

This course is intended to introduce students to the complexity of issues that touch the lives of millions of children whose parents have been arrested and incarcerated. It will provide an in-depth exploration of a variety of theoretical perspectives that are relevant to this topic and can be utilized to provide guidelines for future research, intervention, and policy. Students will gain detailed knowledge regarding the trauma experienced by children because of sudden separation from their sole caregiver and vulnerability to feelings of fear, anxiety, anger, sadness, depression, and guilt. The course will explore issues of abandonment and loss, weakened attachment caused by separation, and the possibility of inadequate ongoing care resulting from movement from caregiver to caregiver. The impact of parental arrest and incarceration on key developmental tasks will be examined. The course will provide an overview of how imprisonment alters family dynamics and affects parents, children, and youth involved with the foster care system. Students will learn about programs that are designed for children to maintain regular contact with parents. Finally, students will learn the challenges and problems encountered when the parent and child are reunited after the incarceration ends.

TABLE OF COUNCIL ON SOCIAL WORK EDUCATION COMPETENCIES AND PRACTICE BEHAVIORS TARGETED IN THIS COURSE

Competency #1: Identify as a professional social worker and conduct oneself accordingly.

1a. advocate for just social structures (institutions & systems).

1b. advocate for equitable client/constituent access to social work services, in the context of diverse and multidisciplinary settings.

Competency #3: Apply critical thinking to inform and communicate professional judgments.

3a. use critical thinking to distinguish, evaluate, and integrate multiple sources of knowledge, including research-based knowledge, practice wisdom, and client/constituent experience.

3d. critically analyze models of intervention, especially in relation to their cultural relevance and applicability and their promotion of social justice.

Competency #4: Engage diversity and difference in practice.

4a. recognize and articulate the ways in which social and cultural structures— including history, institutions, and values—oppress some identity groups while enhancing the privilege and power of dominant groups.

Competency #7: Apply knowledge of human behavior and the social environment.

7a. apply theories and conceptual frameworks relevant to understanding people and environments across systems levels.

7b. critique and apply human behavior and social environment theories and conceptual frameworks to assessment, intervention, and evaluation at multiple systems levels.

Competency #8: Engage in policy practice to advance social and economic well-being and to deliver effective social work services.

8c. collaborate with colleagues, clients/constituents, and others to advocate for social and economic justice to affect policy change.

Competency #10: Engage, assess, intervene, and evaluate with individuals, families, groups, organizations, and communities.

ASSESSMENT

10i. identify and select appropriate and culturally responsive intervention strategies.

EVALUATION

10o. critically analyze, monitor, and evaluate interventions.

COURSE OBJECTIVES

By the end of the quarter, the student will be able to:

1. Identify the consequences of imprisonment for individual prisoners; their families, especially their children; and the communities to which these prisoners return.

2. Understand the psychological impact of parental incarceration on children and parents.

3. Understand the significance of personal visits, as well as regular contact in the form of telephone calls and letters for children and parents during incarceration.

4. Think critically about current justice policies related to children and incarcerated parents and ways in which these policies could be improved. (1a, 1b, 2c)

5. Identify the short-term and long-term effects of parental incarceration on children.

6. Understand the importance of focusing on the family unit when parents are incarcerated.

7. Understand and apply relevant theoretical perspectives to this topic, including developmental theory, ecological theory, risk and resilience theories, life-span theory, and cumulative risk models in cross-level analyses of

the individual child and parent, the parent–child dyad, the family network, the community, the institution, and the culture. (3a, 7a, 7b)

8. Understand the disparate impact of parental incarceration on children and families of color.

9. Identify and analyze relevant programs and services that have been empirically validated for children whose parents are incarcerated. (3d, 10i, 10o)

10. Understand the significance of race, class, and gender in the many facets of the criminal justice system for parents who are incarcerated and how these factors are used to oppress parents, especially mothers. (1a, 1b, 4a)

COURSE REQUIREMENTS AND ASSESSMENT METHODS

1. Participation (20 percent). In this course, attendance is critical because the class interaction stimulates ideas. I expect you to attend every class meeting, including a field trip. I also expect you to be prepared and participate in discussion. I have scheduled a tour of a women's prison for the class. I expect you to do your best to attend. It is part of the learning experience. Each student is responsible for all academic work missed during absences. Class participation will be evaluated by the relevance of questions and comments; evidence of reading required materials; ability to interact and work cooperatively with peers; and the quality not quantity of questions and comments. If you can't ask questions or answer them, then you aren't prepared or aren't paying attention. *All required readings must be read.* Recognizing that we come from different backgrounds with different *worldviews,* students are encouraged to dialogue with others in a meaningful way that respects the opinions of others and provides opportunities to learn from one another. As an institution of higher education, the University of Washington Tacoma has an obligation to combat racism, sexism, and other forms of bias and to provide an equal educational opportunity. All members of the University must treat one another as they would wish to be treated themselves, with dignity and concern. Your presence and engagement throughout the term—both verbally and bodily—will allow us to establish an intellectually and emotionally vital and safe climate for learning.

2. As part of professional responsibility, the expectation is that all assignments will be completed by the deadline. The *Publication Manual of the American Psychological Association* (6th ed.) guidelines should be used in all assignments. If for any reason you are unable to submit an assignment on time, you must discuss this with the professor *prior* to the due date.

3. Mid-Term (30 percent). The mid-term examination will specifically focus on the understanding of theoretical perspectives and the short-term and long-term effects on children of incarcerated parents.

4. Three Quizzes (30 percent). The three quizzes will focus on material covered in class lectures and assigned reading.

5. Reflection Paper (20 percent): Write a 2-page paper, and reflect on your internal and external reactions to the Mission Creek Corrections Center for Women field trip. Your paper must include citations and a list of references (minimum of four references) from the required reading and/or other sources.

ASSIGNMENTS AND GRADING

All written assignments must adhere to the format of the *Publication Manual of the American Psychological Association* (6th ed.). Do not exceed the page limits specified in the assignments, as they provide ample opportunity for discussions. All assignments must include citations in the text of the paper. All assignments must be typed (12 pt. font); include your name, date, assignment name, and title. Include an alphabetized reference page(s) to indicate sources you read to prepare each written assignment. Check your paper for proper syntax, grammar, punctuation, spelling, etc., prior to submission. Poor form will lower your grade. *Spell check.* Plagiarism or any other kind of scholarly misconduct will be reported and may result in disciplinary action, including failing the class. Assignments are to be submitted at the beginning of class on the due date.

SUMMARY OF COURSE ASSIGNMENTS

Your course grade will reflect your score based on the number of points you accumulate from the mid-term examination, three quizzes, written assignment, and participation in the class.

Three Quizzes	30%
Mid-Term Examination	30%
Reflection Paper	20%
Participation	20%
Total	100%

Reflection Paper (20 percent)

Write a 2-page paper, and reflect on your internal and external reactions to the Mission Creek Corrections Center for Women field trip. This written "reflection" is a personal response to the experience of visiting a women's prison. Show the learning that has taken place because of your experience. This paper is an emotional journey of several paragraphs that connect your impressions, observations, emotions, or ideals that take.the reader to a conclusion that is designed to compel more in-depth thinking about what it means to women to be incarcerated, especially if they are mothers.

Your paper must include citations and at least four scholarly references. Such scholarly references can be relevant articles from professional journals or reports; books or book chapters on children of incarcerated parents, their families, communities, and issues; etc. Your references may include, but must not be limited to, the course readings. You must include an alphabetized list of references. You must adhere to the guidelines in the *Publication Manual of the American Psychological Association* (6th ed.) when writing your paper.

Mid-Term Examination (30 percent)

The mid-term examination is designed to evaluate your understanding and comprehension of assigned reading, content presented and discussed during class lectures, and content discussed by guest speakers. This examination will consist of thirty multiple-choice questions.

Quizzes (30 percent)

You will be given three quizzes during this quarter. The maximum number of points for each quiz is 10 points. These multiple-choice quizzes are designed to evaluate your understanding and mastery of course content.

Participation (20 percent)

You are expected to attend class and actively engage in class discussions. The following guide will be utilized to evaluate your interaction in class:

A+—A– (20%) Present for all sessions; prepared with readings and initiates thoughtful questions and insightful observations.

B+—B– (15%) Present for all sessions; prepared with readings and responds when called on with thoughtful questions and insightful observations.

C+—C– (10%) Present . . . quiet . . . probably engaged, but I can't tell.

REQUIRED TEXTBOOK

Harris, Y. R., Graham, J. A., & Carpenter, G. J. O. (2010). *Children of incarcerated parents: Theoretical, developmental, and clinical issues.* New York, NY: Springer.

Session One:

Introduction to the Course
Scope of the Problem
Complete Information for Security Clearance for Class
    Field Trip to Mission Creek Corrections Center for Women

REQUIRED READING

Graham, J. A., Harris, Y. R., & Carpenter, G. J. O. (2010). The changing
    landscape in the American prison population: Implications for children of
    incarcerated parents. In Y. R. Harris, J. A. Graham, & G. J. O. Carpenter
    (Eds.), *Children of incarcerated parents: Theoretical, developmental, and
    clinical issues* (pp. 3–19). New York, NY: Springer.

Session Two:

Attachment Theory
Developmental Theory
Ecological Theory

REQUIRED READING

Christian, S. (2009). *Children of incarcerated parents* (pp. 1–18). Washington,
    DC: National Conference of Legislatures.
Holmes, T. R., Belmonte, K., Wentworth, M., & Tillman, K. (2010). Parents
    "in the system": An ecological systems approach to the development of
    children with incarcerated parents. In Y. R. Harris, J. A. Graham, & G. J. O.
    Carpenter (Eds.), *Children of incarcerated parents: Theoretical, developmen-
    tal, and clinical issues* (pp. 21–43). New York, NY: Springer.

Session Three:

Reunification Issues/Problems

REQUIRED READING

Harris, Y. R., Harris, V., Graham, J. A., & Carpenter, G. J. O. (2012). The chal-
    lenges of family reunification. In Y. R. Harris, J. A. Graham, & G. J. O. Car-
    penter (Eds.), *Children of incarcerated parents: Theoretical, developmental,
    and clinical issues* (pp. 255–275). New York, NY: Springer.

Phillips, S. D., & Erkanli, A. (2008). Differences in patterns of parental arrest and the parent, family, and child problems protective service workers encounter in working with families. *Children and Youth Services Review, 30*(2), 157–172.

Poelhmann, J., Dallaire, D., Loper, A. B., & Shear, L. D. (2010). Children's contact with their incarcerated parents: Research findings and recommendations. *The American Psychologist, 65*(5), 575–598.

Session Four:

Incarcerated Parents, Their Families and Communities
Quiz #1

REQUIRED READING

Chung, H. L., & McFadden, D. (2010). The effects of incarceration on neighborhoods and communities. In Y. R. Harris, J. A. Graham, & G. J. O. Carpenter (Eds.), *Children of incarcerated parents: Theoretical, developmental, and clinical issues* (pp. 105–126). New York, NY: Springer.

Foster, H. (2010). Living arrangements of children of incarcerated parents: The roles of stability, embeddedness, gender, and race/ethnicity. In Y. R. Harris, J. A. Graham, & G. J. O. Carpenter (Eds.), *Children of incarcerated parents: Theoretical, developmental, and clinical issues* (pp. 127–157). New York, NY: Springer.

Session Five:

The Impact of Incarceration and Reentry on Parents

REQUIRED READING

Beyer, M., Blumenthal-Guigui, R., & Krupat, T. (2010). Strengthening parent–child relationships: Visit coaching with children and their incarcerated parents. In Y. R. Harris, J. A. Graham, & G. J. O. Carpenter (Eds.), *Children of incarcerated parents: Theoretical, developmental, and clinical issues* (pp. 187–214). New York, NY: Springer.

Toth, K., & Kazura, K. (2010). Building partnerships to strengthen families: Intervention programs and recommendations. In Y. R. Harris, J. A. Graham, & G. J. O. Carpenter (Eds.), *Children of incarcerated parents: Theoretical, developmental, and clinical issues* (pp. 161–186). New York, NY: Springer.

Session Six:

Children's Rights and Other Issues

REQUIRED READING

The Annie E. Casey Foundation. (2011). *When a parent is incarcerated: A primer for social workers*. Baltimore, MD: Author.

Boudin, C. (2011). Children of incarcerated parents: The child's constitutional right to the family relationship. *The Journal of Criminal Law and Criminology, 101*(1), 77–118.

The Sentencing Project. (2009). *Incarcerated children and their parents: Trends 1991–2007*. Washington, DC: Author.

Session Seven:

Guest Speaker: Wanda McCrae, Superintendent, Mission Creek Corrections Center for Women, Belfair, WA

Session Eight:

The Child Welfare System and Incarcerated Parents

REQUIRED READING

Beckerman, A. (2010). Child welfare legislation and policies: Foster children with a parent in prison. In Y. R. Harris, J. A. Graham, & G. J. O. Carpenter (Eds.), *Children of incarcerated parents: Theoretical, developmental, and clinical issues* (pp. 217–235). New York, NY: Springer.

Hayward, R. A., & DePanfilis, D. (2007). Foster children with an incarcerated parent: Predictors of reunification. *Children and Youth Services Review, 29*(10), 1320–1334.

Phillips, S. D. (2010). Service planning and intervention development for children of incarcerated parents. In Y. R. Harris, J. A. Graham, & G. J. O. Carpenter (Eds.), *Children of incarcerated parents: Theoretical, developmental, and clinical issues* (pp. 237–253). New York, NY: Springer.

Session Nine:

Children of Incarcerated Fathers

Video: *A Sentence of Their Own*

REQUIRED READING

Bushfield, S. (2004). Fathers in prison: Impact of parenting education. *The Journal of Correctional Education, 55*(2), 104–116.

Mazza, C. (2002). And then the world fell apart: The children of incarcerated fathers. *Families in Society: The Journal of Contemporary Social Sciences, 83*(5/6), 521–529.

Santos, F. (2010, December 8). "Daddy, read for me." *The New York Times.* Retrieved from http://www.nytimes.com2010/12/26rikers.html?_r=1&sq=ricersisland&st= . . .

Swisher, R. R., & Waller, M. R. (2008). Confining fatherhood: Incarceration and paternal involvement among nonresident white, African American, and Latino fathers. *Journal of Family Issues, 29*(8), 1067–1088.

Session Ten:

Guest Speakers: Libby Compton and Kiara St. John, Girl Scouts Beyond Bars, Seattle, WA

Session Eleven:

Mid-Term Examination

Session Twelve:

Guest Speaker: Carrie Kendig, MSW, Child and Family Welfare Program Manager, DSHS Children's Administration, Olympia, WA

Session Thirteen:

Mentors and Children of Incarcerated Parents
Video: *Girl Scouts Beyond Bars*
Quiz #2

REQUIRED READING

Davies, E., Brazzell, D., La Vigne, N. G., & Shollenberger, T. (2008). *Understanding the experiences and needs of children of incarcerated parents: Views from mentors* . Washington, DC: Urban Institute Justice Policy Center.

Grant, D. (2006). Resilience of girls with incarcerated mothers: The impact of Girl Scouts. *The Prevention Researcher, 13*(2), 11–14.

Session Fourteen:

Adolescent Children of Incarcerated Parents

REQUIRED READING

Adalist-Estrin, A. (2006). Providing support to adolescent children with incarcerated parents. *The Prevention Researcher, 13*(2), 7–10.

Eddy, J. M., & Reid, J. B. (2003). The adolescent children of incarcerated parents: A developmental perspective. In J. Travis & M. Waul (Eds.), *Prisoners once removed: The impact of incarceration and reentry on children, families, and communities* (pp. 233–258). Washington, DC: Urban Institute.

Murray, J., & Farrington, D. P. (2005). Parental imprisonment: Effects on boys' antisocial behaviour and delinquency through the life course. *Journal of Child Psychology and Psychiatry, 46*, 1269–1278.

Newby, G. (2006). After incarceration: Adolescent–parent reunification. *The Prevention Researcher, 13*(2), 18–20.

Session Fifteen:

Reentry Challenges for Incarcerated Women

REQUIRED READING

Berman, J. (n.d.). *Women offender transition and reentry: Gender responsive approaches to transitioning women offenders from prison to the community.* Washington, DC: National Institute of Corrections.

Covington, S. S. (2001). *A woman's journey home: Challenges for female offenders and their children.* Retrieved from http://aspe.hhs.gov/hsp/prison2home02/Covington.htm

National Institute of Justice. (2005, July). Reentry programs for women inmates. *NIJ Journal, 252*, 1–8.

Session Sixteen:

Parental Challenges
Quiz #3

REQUIRED READING

Berstein, N. (2005). Grandparents. In *All alone in the world: Children of the incarcerated* (pp. 109–142). New York, NY: New Press.

Berstein, N. (2005). Visiting. In *All alone in the world: Children of the incarcerated* (pp. 71–107). New York, NY: New Press.

Session Seventeen:

Field Trip: Mission Creek Corrections Center for Women, Belfair, WA

Session Eighteen:

Long-Term Impact of Parental Incarceration on Children

REQUIRED READING

Berstein, N. (2005). Legacy. In *All alone in the world: Children of the incarcerated* (pp. 211–255). New York, NY: New Press.

Carpenter, G. J. O., Graham, J. A., & Harris, Y. R. (2010). Research and intervention issues for moving forward with development in children of incarcerated parents. In J. R. Harris, J. A. Graham, & G. J. O. Carpenter, (Eds.), *Children of incarcerated parents: Theoretical, developmental, and clinical issues* (pp. 277–286). New York, NY: Springer.

Session Nineteen:

DUE: Reflection Paper
Guest Speaker: Sierra Raynor, Boys and Girls Club, Tacoma, WA

Session Twenty:

Course Evaluation
Reflections on Children of Incarcerated Parents

UNIVERSITY OF WASHINGTON SCHOOL OF SOCIAL WORK

UNIVERSITY OF WASHINGTON TACOMA, SOCIAL WORK PROGRAM

UNIVERSITY OF WASHINGTON TACOMA, CRIMINAL JUSTICE PROGRAM

Disproportionality Across Systems

COURSE DESCRIPTION

Disproportionality occurs when the percentage of a group of people in any system is higher than the percentage of that group in the general population. It refers to the overrepresentation of a given population group, often defined by racial and ethnic backgrounds. This course will examine disproportionate representation of people of color, including children and adolescents, in the following systems: child welfare, criminal justice, economic, education, health, juvenile justice, and mental health. These systems are not altogether separate or unrelated. Rather, they form a network of practices, traditions, policies, and discourses that mutually inform one another and together produce symptomatic, racially disparate outcomes. A special focus of this course will be on how each of these systems interacts with the criminal justice system, where disproportionality is a particularly serious social problem.

This interactive course examines the language of disproportionality, the continuous problem of structural racism in all of the aforementioned systems, and the impact of racial disparity on people of color involved in the various systems. Racial disparity occurs when the rate of disproportionality of one racial group (e.g., African American) exceeds that of a comparison group (e.g., white American). The language of racial disparity will be examined in this course in order to come to some common understanding of what the term means; key measures of disparity and common issues faced in measuring disparity will also be explored. There is an explicit emphasis on racial disparity in the child welfare, criminal justice, economic, education, health, juvenile justice, and mental health systems and on how these systems engage with the wider policies, practices, and institutions that impact the lives of people of color. The course will explore implications for research, policy, and practice, including an increased emphasis on building capacity to challenge public policies and system practices that reproduce racial disparity. Promising practices to address and/or eradicate disproportionality will be explored.

COURSE OBJECTIVES

The objectives of this course are aimed at preparing students to:

1. Understand the meaning of disproportionality across systems and why children, youth, adults, and families of color are involved with multiple systems.
2. Provide a literal definition of the term *disparity*.
3. Distinguish between the terms *disproportionality* and *disparity*.
4. Critically analyze the trends in the specific rates of racial and ethnic disproportionality in the criminal justice system.
5. Define, assess, and understand the health status of populations, determinants of health and illness, factors contributing to health disparities, and factors influencing the use of health services.

6. Think critically about current policies in the education, child welfare, crim-inal justice, juvenile justice, mental health, health, and economic systems that result in service disparities for people of color and ways in which these policies could be improved.

7. Think critically about and articulate the extent and ramification of dispro-portionality in varied systems for people of color.

8. Articulate the disparate impact for people of color once they become involved with the child welfare, mental health, health, criminal justice, juvenile justice, education, and economic systems.

9. Identify and analyze relevant research regarding disproportionality and dis-parities in varied systems and the limitations of research.

10. Analyze the significance of race, class, and gender in the many facets of the criminal justice, juvenile justice, child welfare, mental health, economic, health, and education systems and how these factors are used to oppress people of color who are involved with the aforementioned systems.

COURSE METHODOLOGY

The class format will include a mixture of lecture and dialogue, guest speakers, short presentations, and videos. Real-world examples illustrate concepts, and carefully planned and thought-out exercises help build knowledge. Emphasis is focused on active participation, experiential learn-ing, critical thinking, and reflection on course content.

COURSE REQUIREMENTS

1. Participation in class is essential. It is the professional responsibility of the social work or criminal justice student to participate in class in order to gain the greatest benefit from the course. Class participation is demon-strated through your involvement in class discussion and experiential exer-cises. It will be evaluated by the following: (a) relevance of questions and comments—i.e., the *quality* of your questions and comments and not the *quantity* of your questions and comments; (b) evidence of reading the required materials; and (c) evidence of ability to apply course materials to human services/social work and criminal justice practice situations. Atten-dance and participation are indications of professional commitment and an expectation in all classes.

2. Learning in this course relies heavily upon active involvement. Student and instructor responsibilities include being present and participating fully

in the learning experience to gain the greatest benefit from the course. You are expected to thoughtfully engage in discussions and to share your understandings of and questions about the readings. Participation in the course is worth 20 percent of your grade.

3. As part of professional responsibility, the expectation is that all assignments will be completed by the deadline. The *Publication Manual of the American Psychological Association* (6th ed.) guidelines will be used in all assignments. If for any reason you will not be able to submit an assignment, you *must* discuss this with the instructor prior to the due date.

ASSIGNMENTS AND GRADING

All written assignments must adhere to the format of the *Publication Manual of the American Psychological Association* (6th ed.). Do not exceed page limits specified in the assignments, as they provide ample opportunity for discussion. All assignments must be double-spaced and typed (12 pt. font). Include an alphabetized reference page to indicate sources you read to prepare each assignment. Check your paper for syntax, grammar, punctuation, spelling, etc., prior to submission. Poor form will lower your grade. Plagiarism or any other kind of scholarly misconduct will be reported and may result in disciplinary action, including failing the class.

SUMMARY OF COURSE REQUIREMENTS

Your course grade will reflect your score based on the number of points you accumulate from the assignments, mid-term examination, and participation in class. The mid-term examination is designed to evaluate your understanding, comprehension, and mastery of course content via assigned reading, videos, presentations, lectures, and discussions. The course grade is calculated as follows:

Brief Discussion Essays	30%
Mid-Term Examination	20%
Critical Literature Review	30%
Participation	20%
Total	100%

Assignment #1—Brief Discussion Essays (30 percent)

Each student will be responsible for preparing three discussion essays for three specific articles from the assigned readings, which you will distribute to the class for review. Based on this document, you should be prepared to lead three discussions on the articles.

Discussion essays include a summary and discussion points. Your summary should be a 2-page abstract of the article that touches on the main argument, key concepts and theories, and data and key findings (if applicable). Discussion points should take the form of critique or reaction (e.g., strengths and limitation of the article, what it adds to our understanding, next steps). You should post your essay to the weekly discussion board on Canvas by Monday at 6:00 P.M. if your discussion is for a Tuesday class and by Wednesday at 6:00 P.M. if your discussion is for a Thursday class. Please remember to proofread. Late posts will be penalized. And remember, just because you are posting to a discussion board does not mean you can be casual or cavalier in your work. Your essays must be professional.

In order to be prepared for class discussion, students should read through all the posts prior to Tuesday or Thursday class.

Assignment #2—Critical Literature Review (30 percent)

Each student is responsible for preparing a critical literature review (6–8 pages) of a topic relevant to some area of disproportionality. You will need to be highly selective in identifying and citing references—usually choosing those that are the most important and/or most current. You should establish two main goals for your literature review. First, attempt to provide a comprehensive and up-to-date review of your selected topic regarding disproportionality. Second, try to demonstrate that you have a thorough command of the area you are reviewing. You should clearly identify the topic of the review and indicate its delimitations. (For example, is it limited to a certain period of time? Does it deal only with certain aspects of the problem?) Your review should be cohesive and guide the reader through the literature from subtopic to subtopic. You must interpret and critique each article that you review and not merely summarize articles. Finally, state whether each article that you review makes an important contribution to knowledge based on your synthesis of the literature. A typical search of the literature in the social and behavioral sciences will yield primarily original reports of empirical research because these types of documents dominate academic journals. Theoretical articles that relate directly to your topic should be included in your literature review. It is important to identify the landmark studies and theorists on your topic (i.e., those of *historical importance* in developing an understanding of a topic or problem). Near the beginning of the review, state explicitly what will and will not be covered. Your literature review should be written in the form of an essay that has a particular point of view in looking at the reviewed research and theoretical articles. Use subheadings, especially in long reviews. Aim for a clear and cohesive essay; avoid annotations. Use transitions to help trace your argument. Write a conclusion for the end of the review. Check the flow of your argument for coherence. An alphabetized list of references is required.

REQUIRED READINGS

Readings for this course are accessible via the UWT and/or UW library system. Three of the required readings from books in PDF are posted on my Canvas site. The professor will disseminate copies of the 2008 *Washington State Racial Disproportionality Report* during the first class session.

Session One:

Introduction to the Course
Scope of the Problem
Selecting and Searching Databases
Guest Speaker: Erica Coe, UWT Library

Session Two:

Culturalized and Immigrant Groups

REQUIRED READING

Anderson, E. (1994, May). The code of the streets. *Atlantic Monthly,* 81–94.
Esposito, A., & Favela, A. (2003). Reflective voices: Valuing immigrant students and teaching with ideological clarity. *Urban Review, 35*(1), 73–91.
Grinde, D. A. (2004). Taking the Indian out of the Indian: U.S. policies of ethnocide through education. *Wicazo Sa Review, 19*(2), 25–32.
Ogbu, J. (1998). Voluntary and involuntary minorities: A cultural-ecological theory of school performance with some implications for education. *Anthropology and Education Quarterly, 29,* 155–188.

Session Three:

Race, Class, and Dropout Groups

REQUIRED READING

Patton, J. M. (1998). The disrepresentation of African Americans in special education. *Journal of Special Education, 32*(1), 25–31.

Rumberger, R. W. (2004). *Why students drop out of school and what can be done?* Retrieved from http://www.civilrightsproject.harvard.edu/research/dropouts/rumberger.pdf

Skiba, R. J. (2001). When is disproportionality discrimination? The overrepresentation of black students in school suspension. In W. Ayers, B. Dohrn, & R. Ayers (Eds.), *Zero tolerance in our schools* (pp. 176–187). New York, NY: New Press.

Stanton-Salazar, R. D., & Sanford, M. D. (2004). Social capital and the reproduction of inequality: Information networks among Mexican-origin high school students. *Sociology of Education, 68*(2), 116–135.

Turnbull, R. H. (2005). Individuals with Disabilities Education Act reauthorization: Accountability and personal responsibility. *Remedial and Special Education, 26*(6), 320–326.

Session Four:

Poverty in America

REQUIRED READING

Cancian, M., Meyer, D. R., & Reed, D. (2010). Promising antipoverty strategies for families. *Poverty and Public Policy, 2*(3), Article 8.

Cellini, S. R., Signe, M. M., & Radcliffe, C. (2008). The dynamics of poverty in the United States: A review of data, methods, and findings. *The Journal of Policy Analysis and Management, 27*(3), 577–605.

Hunt, M. O. (2004). Race/ethnicity and beliefs about wealth and poverty. *Social Science Quarterly, 85*(3), 828–853.

Rector, R. (2008). *Understanding and reducing poverty in America: Testimony before Joint Economic Committee, U.S. Senate.* Retrieved from http://www.heritage.org/research/welfare/tst040209b.cfm

Session Five:

Poverty, Race, and Policy Making

REQUIRED READING

Clampet-Lundquist, S., & Massey, D. S. (2008). Neighborhood effects on economic self-sufficiency: A reconsideration of the moving opportunity experiment. *American Journal of Sociology, 114*(1), 107–143.

Jens, L., Liebman, J. B., Kling, J. R., Duncan, G. J., Katz, L. F., Kessler, R. C., & Sanbonmatsu, L. (2008). What can we learn about neighborhood effects from the moving to opportunity experiment? *American Journal of Sociology, 114*(1), 144–188.

Sampson, R. J. (2008). Moving to inequality: Neighborhood effects and experiments meet social structure. *American Journal of Sociology, 114*(1), 189–231.

Sawhill, I., Thomas, A., & Monea, E. (2010). An ounce of prevention: Policy prescriptions to reduce the prevalence of fragile families. *Future of Children, 20*(2), 133–155.

Session Six:

Racial Disproportionality in the Child Welfare System
Guest Speaker: Deborah Purce, JD, Executive Staff Director, DSHS Children's Administration, Olympia, WA

REQUIRED READING

Washington State Racial Disproportionality Advisory Committee. (2008). *Racial disproportionality in Washington State.* Olympia, WA: Author.

Session Seven:

UWT Library—Conduct Research for Assignment #2, Critical Literature Review

Session Eight:

Guest Speaker: Judge Frank Cuthbertson, Pierce County Superior Court, Tacoma, WA

Session Nine:

Racial Disproportionality in the Child Welfare System (Continued)

REQUIRED READING

Bowser, B. P., & Jones, T. (2004). *Understanding the over-representation of African Americans in the child welfare system*. San Francisco, CA: Urban Institute.

Cahn, K., & Harris, M. S. (2005). Where have all the children gone? A review of the literature on factors contributing to disproportionality: Five key decision points. *Protecting Children, 20*(1), 4–14.

Harris, M. S., & Courtney, M. E. (2003). The interaction of race, ethnicity, and family structure with respect to the timing of family reunification. *Children and Youth Services Review, 25*(5/6), 409–429.

Harris, M. S., & Hackett, W. (2008). Decision points in child welfare: An action research model to address disproportionality. *Children and Youth Services Review, 30*(2), 199–215.

Johnson, E. P., Clark, S., Donald, M., Pedersen, R., & Pichott, C. (2007). Racial disparity in Minnesota child protection system. *Child Welfare, 86*, 7–17.

Libby, A. M., Orton, H. D., Barth, R. B., & Burns, B. J. (2007). Family service needs: Alcohol, drug, and mental health service needs for parents and children involved with child welfare. In R. Haskins, M. Webb, & F. Wulczyn (Eds.), *Child protection: Using research to improve policy and practice* (pp. 107–119). Washington, DC: Brookings.

Session Ten:

Mid-Term Examination

Session Eleven:

Race: Metrics and Disparities

REQUIRED READING

Blackwell, A. G., Kwoh, S., & Pastor, M. (2010). Color lines. In *Uncommon common ground: Race and America's future* (pp. 55–102). New York, NY: Norton.

Katz, M. B. (2008). Why don't American cities burn very often? *Journal of Urban History, 34*(2), 185.

Passel, J. S., & D'Vera, C. (2010). *U.S. population projections: 2008–2050*. Washington, DC: Pew Research Center.

Passel, J., & Taylor, P. (2009). *Who's Hispanic?* Washington, DC: Pew Hispanic Center.

Session Twelve:

Race/Ethnicity, Crime, and Justice

REQUIRED READING

Cernkovich, S. A., Giordano, P. C., & Rudolph, J. L. (2000). Race, crime, and the American dream. *Journal of Research in Crime and Delinquency, 37,* 131–170.

Peterson, R. D., & Krivo, L. J. (2005). Macrostructural analysis of race, ethnicity, and violent crime: Recent lessons and new directions for research. *Annual Review of Sociology, 31,* 331–356.

Stewart, E. A., & Simons, R. L. (2010). Race, code of the street, and violent delinquency: A multilevel investigation of neighborhood street culture and individual norms of violence. *Criminology, 48,* 569–605.

Wright, B. R. E., & Younts, C. W. (2009). Reconsidering the relationship between race and crime: Positive and negative predictors of crime among African American youth. *Journal of Research in Crime and Delinquency, 46,* 327–352.

Session Thirteen:

Race/Ethnicity in the Justice System

REQUIRED READING

Eitle, D., & Monahan, S. (2009). Revisiting the racial threat thesis: The role of police organizational characteristics in predicting race-specific drug arrest rates. *Justice Quarterly, 26,* 528–561.

Feld, B. (2003). The politics of race and juvenile justice: The "due process revolution" and the conservative reaction. *Justice Quarterly, 20,* 765–800.

Harris, C. T., Steffensmier, D., Ulmer, J. T., & Painter-Davis, N. (2009). Are blacks and Hispanics disproportionately incarcerated relative to their arrests? Racial and ethnic disproportionality between arrest and incarceration. *Race and Social Problems, 1,* 187–199.

Romero, M. (2003). Racial profiling and immigration law enforcement: Rounding up of usual suspects in the Latino community. *Critical Sociology, 32,* 447–473.

Session Fourteen:

Race/Ethnicity and Crime

REQUIRED READING

Freng, A., & Esbensen, F. A. (2007). Race and gang affiliation: An examination of multiple marginality. *Justice Quarterly, 24*, 600–628.

McNulty, T. L., & Belfair, P. E. (2003). Explaining racial and ethnic differences in serious adolescent violent behavior. *Criminology, 41*, 709–749.

Phillips, J. A. (2002). White, black, and Latino homicide rates: Why the difference? *Social Problems, 49*, 349–373.

Shihadeh, E. S., & Barranco, R. E. (2010). Latino employment and black violence: The unintended consequences of U.S. immigration policy. *Social Forces, 88*, 1393–1420.

Session Fifteen:

Race/Ethnicity in the Criminal Justice System

REQUIRED READING

Bontrager, S., Bales, W., & Chirocos, T. (2005). Race, ethnicity, threat, and the labeling of convicted felons. *Criminology, 43*, 589–622.

Harris, D. A. (2006). U.S. experiences with racial and ethnic profiling. *Criminology, 14*, 213–239.

Schlesinger, T. (2005). Racial and ethnic disparity in pretrial criminal processing. *Justice Quarterly, 22*, 170–193.

Ulmer, J. T., Kurlychek, M., & Kramer, J. H. (2007). Prosecutorial discretion and the imposition of mandatory minimum sentences. *Journal of Research in Crime and Delinquency, 44*, 427–458.

Session Sixteen:

Health Disparities

REQUIRED READING

Gakidou, E. E., Murray, C. J., & Frenk, J. (2000). Defining and measuring health inequality: An approach based on the distribution of health expectancy. *Bulletin of the World Health Organization, 78*, 42–54.

Krieger, N., Chen, J. T., Waterman, P. D., Rehkopf, D. H., & Subramanian, S. V. (2005). Painting a truer picture of U.W. socioeconomic and racial/ethnic health inequalities: The public health disparities geocoding project. *American Journal of Public Health, 95*(2), 312–323.

U.S. Department of Health and Human Services. (2010). *Disparities-Healthy people 2020: Improving the health of Americans.* Washington, DC: Author.

Wagstaff, A. (2002). Inequality aversion, health inequalities and health achievement. *Journal of Health Economics, 21*(4), 627–641.

Session Seventeen:

Mental Health Disparities

REQUIRED READING

Atdijan, S., & Vega, W. A. (2005). Disparities in mental health treatment in U.S. racial and ethnic minority groups: Implications for psychiatrists. *Psychiatric Services, 56*(2), 1600–1602.

Miranda, J., McGuire, T. G., Williams, D. R., & Wang, P. (2008). Mental health in the context of health disparities. *American Journal of Psychiatry, 165*, 1102–1108.

Miranda, J., McGuire, T., Williams, D., & Wang, P. (n.d.). *Reducing mental health disparities: General vs. behavioral health policy.* Chicago, IL: MacArthur Foundation on Mental Health Policy Research.

National Alliance on Mental Illness. (n.d.). *Eliminating disparities in mental health: An overview.* Arlington, VA: Author.

Session Eighteen:

Health Disparities (Continued)
Guest Speaker: Ben Danielson, MD, Director, Odessa Brown Clinic, Seattle, WA

Session Nineteen:

Mental Health Disparities (Continued)
Guest Speaker: Mary O'Brien, Clinical Services Manager, Yakima Valley Farm Workers Clinic—Behavioral Health Services, Yakima, WA

Session Twenty:

DUE: Critical Literature Review
Course Evaluation
Reflections on Disproportionality

UNIVERSITY OF WASHINGTON SEATTLE SCHOOL OF SOCIAL WORK

UNIVERSITY OF WASHINGTON TACOMA, MASTER OF SOCIAL WORK PROGRAM

Assessment of Mental Disorders

COURSE DESCRIPTION

This foundation-level course will provide students with a pragmatic set of skills needed to successfully assess mental disorders and to establish the medical necessity for treatment that is required under managed mental health care. The course will inform students of the manifestations of psychopathologies, with emphasis on *Diagnostic and Statistical Manual of Mental Disorders* (4th ed., text revision; DSM-IV-TR) diagnostic classifications. Cultural definitions of mental health and mental illness will be addressed in the context of the ways in which cultural belief systems affect the delivery of mental health services. A historical overview will trace the ways in which social expectations have influenced perceptions of mental well-being and development of treatment standards. Conflicts between some cultural belief systems and dominant American mental health paradigms will be explored, and assessment will be approached from person-in-environment and psychiatric rehabilitation perspectives. The course will draw upon readings, instructor and participant experiences, case examples, and group discussion to provide an effective introduction to the DMS-IV-TR and its use in various mental health settings.

COURSE OBJECTIVES

Given regular class attendance and participation and completion of required readings and assignments, the student will be able to:

1. Explain the diagnostic classification system provided by the DSM-IV-TR and understand its relevance to generalist social work practice. This includes the history of the DSM-IV-TR and its application within the social work profession.
2. Identify the major categories and subcategories of psychopathology primarily oriented to child populations in order to conduct the most efficacious assessments to guide the most appropriate intervention.

3. Identify the essential features and diagnostic criteria for multiaxial diagnosis to facilitate the application of person-in-environment perspective.
4. Demonstrate the ability to apply evidence-based interventions for empowerment of underserved and disempowered clients.
5. Discuss values and ethical controversies associated with the medical paradigm employed with the DSM-IV-TR.
6. Identify the strengths and weaknesses of the DSM-IV-TR as applied to diverse populations and gain an understanding of cultural competence in assessment.
7. Apply principles of social and economic justice to mental health services provided within the current sociopolitical climate.
8. Demonstrate the importance of advocacy in mental health work in order to empower clients and their families.
9. Describe the relationship between policy and the social construction of mental illness.
10. Apply newly developed skills in assessment and demonstrate an understanding of the professional language necessary for team involvement with other mental health care professions in order to maximize the effectiveness of interventions with families facing mental illness complications.

INCOMPLETES

Students are expected to complete all course work by the last day of class. Those who are unable to do so because of illness or circumstances beyond their control must negotiate an incomplete with the instructor. Please see a more detailed explanation of the guidelines under which an incomplete may be given and the resulting restrictions in the *Program Manual* under the "Grading System."

COURSE REQUIREMENTS

1. Participation in class is essential. It is the professional responsibility of the social work student to participate in class in order to gain the greatest benefit from the class. The ability to think critically is essential, and students are expected to demonstrate such ability. *Class participation* is demonstrated by analyzing, synthesizing, and evaluating concepts, information, and ideas presented, as well as by contributing to class presentations, discussions, and exercises. It will be evaluated by the following: (1) relevance of questions and comments—i.e., the *quality* of your questions and comments and not

the *quantity* of your questions and comments; (2) evidence of reading the required materials; and (3) evidence of ability to apply course materials to social work practice with children.

2. Learning in this course relies heavily upon active involvement. Student and instructor responsibilities include being present and participating in the learning experience to gain the greatest benefit from the course. Participation in the course is worth 10 percent of the final grade.

3. The "Standards for Essential Abilities and Attributes for Admission and Continuance in the MSW Program" in your *Program Manual* mandate commitment to professional social work education, values, and ethics. Attendance and class participation are indications of professional commitment and an expectation in all classes. Program policy states that failure to participate in at least *70 percent* of class sessions for any given course will result in a faculty review of the student's appropriateness for continuation in the program.

4. As part of professional responsibility, the expectation is that all written assignments will be completed by the deadline. The *Publication Manual of the American Psychological Association* (6th ed.) guidelines will be used for all assignments. If for any reason you will not be able to submit an assignment, you *must* discuss this with the instructor prior to the due date.

ASSIGNMENTS AND GRADING

All written assignments must adhere to the format of the *Publication Manual of the American Psychological Association* (6th ed.). Do not exceed the page limits specified in the assignments, as they provide ample opportunity for discussion. All assignments should be double-spaced and typed (12 pt. font). Include an alphabetized reference page to indicate sources you read to prepare each assignment. Check your paper for syntax, grammar, punctuation, spelling, etc., prior to submission. Poor form will lower your grade.

SUMMARY OF COURSE REQUIREMENTS

Mid-Term Examination	20%
Diagnostic Formulations	30%
Assessment Assignment	40%
Participation	10%
Total	100%

ASSIGNMENTS

Assignment A: Diagnostic Formulations

Students will be expected to practice diagnostic formulations throughout the course. These will be done within the class. Case studies will be presented, and students will be given an opportunity to make assessments and diagnoses. In addition to making an assessment, students will be asked to justify and explain their diagnostic conclusions. Assessments and diagnoses for two case studies will be completed in class; these assessments will be graded. Students can earn a maximum of 15 points for each assessment/diagnosis.

The purpose of this assignment is to allow students the opportunity to think critically about a case study and present their conclusions utilizing the language of the DSM-IV-TR. Each diagnostic formulation must address the following:

1. What are the presenting symptoms in the case study?
2. What clinical impressions have you formed based on the case study?
3. What other clinical syndromes and/or personality disorders did you consider in your decision making—i.e., differential diagnosis?
4. What cultural factors/issues may be significant that impact both the client's perception of his or her symptoms and your impression of the client's symptoms—i.e., cultural formulation?
5. What are your final diagnostic impressions on all five axes? *Note: Include both code numbers and narrative labels on Axis I and Axis II.* The diagnostic formulations are worth 30 percent of the final grade.

Assignment B: Assessment

A family comes to see you and your treatment team with their child who is having some kind of problem. The child can be a preschooler, an elementary school–age child, or an adolescent. An introduction and conclusion must be included with this assignment. The assignment must be typed (12 pt. font, double-spaced). The maximum length for this assignment is 8 pages. The rubric for grading this assignment will be posted on Canvas. Demonstrate your knowledge of assessment by creating a scenario that encompasses the following:

-   Develop a story about the family that sets the context and underscores the relevant issues.

- Describe the nature of your "team" and who will add what to the assessment (e.g., medical, social work, school).
- Explain how you would distinguish between "normal" and "problem" behavior using developmental theory.
- Indicate where you would use an ecological model to guide your assessment and why.
- Identify three issues that may result from multiple professions working together.
- Do a multiaxial assessment using the five axes in the DSM-IV-TR multiaxial classification (include both code numbers and narrative labels on Axis I and Axis II).
- State your tentative hypothesis about the problem and how you arrived at that conclusion.
- Include an alphabetized list of references to support your assessment.

This assignment is worth 40 percent of the final grade.

REQUIRED TEXTBOOKS

American Psychological Association. (2000). *Diagnostic and statistical manual of mental disorders* (4th ed., text revision). Washington, DC: Author.

Greenspan, S. I., & Greenspan, N. T. (2003). *The clinical interview of the child* (3rd ed.). Washington, DC: American Psychiatric Publishing.

COURSE OUTLINE

Session I:

Introduction and Course Overview
Introduction to DSM-IV-TR

REQUIRED READING

American Psychological Association. (2000a). Introduction. In *Diagnostic and statistical manual of mental disorders* (4th ed., text revision, pp. 1–12). Washington, DC: Author.

Session II:

Utilizing the DSM-IV-TR
Basics and Application
Documentation and the Multiaxial Diagnostic Assessment

REQUIRED READING

American Psychological Association. (2000b). Additional codes. In *Diagnostic and statistical manual of mental disorders* (4th ed., text revision, pp. 743–757). Washington, DC: Author.

American Psychological Association. (2000c). DSM-IV-TR classification. In *Diagnostic and statistical manual of mental disorders* (4th ed., text revision, pp. 13–26). Washington, DC: Author.

American Psychological Association. (2000d). Glossary of technical terms. In *Diagnostic and statistical manual of mental disorders* (4th ed., text revision, pp. 819–828). Washington, DC: Author.

American Psychological Association. (2000e). Multiaxial assessment. In *Diagnostic and statistical manual of mental disorders* (4th ed., text revision, pp. 27–37). Washington, DC: Author.

American Psychological Association. (2000f). Other conditions that may be a focus of clinical attention. In *Diagnostic and statistical manual of mental disorders* (4th ed., text revision, pp. 731–735). Washington, DC: Author.

Session III:

Lines of Development for Children
Observation of Children

REQUIRED READING

Greenspan, S. I., & Greenspan, N. T. (2003a). Chronological age- and phase-appropriate illustrations for each observational category. In *The clinical interview of the child* (3rd ed., pp. 75–98). Washington, DC: American Psychiatric Publishing.

Greenspan, S. I., & Greenspan, N. T. (2003b). Conceptual foundations: An overview. In *The clinical interview of the child* (3rd ed., pp. 1–33). Washington, DC: American Psychiatric Publishing.

Greenspan, S. I., & Greenspan, N. T. (2003c). Framework for systematic observation of the child. In *The clinical interview of the child* (3rd ed., pp. 35–74). Washington, DC: American Psychiatric Publishing.

Session IV:

Initial Assessment—Children and Adolescents
Handout: Initial Assessment Form: Children and Adolescents

REQUIRED READING

American Psychological Association. (2000g). Disorders usually first diagnosed in infancy, childhood, or adolescence. In *Diagnostic and statistical manual of mental disorders* (4th ed., text revision, pp. 39–84). Washington, DC: Author.

Greenspan, S. I., & Greenspan, N. T. (2003d). Clinical illustrations of interviews with children. In *The clinical interview of the child* (3rd ed., pp. 99–165). Washington, DC: American Psychiatric Publishing.

Greenspan, S. I., & Greenspan, N. T. (2003e). Conducting the interview. In *The clinical interview of the child* (3rd ed., pp. 167–186). Washington, DC: American Psychiatric Publishing.

Session V:

Mid-Term Examination

Session VI:

Using a Developmental Approach for Diagnostic Formulations
Experiential: Diagnostic Formulation for Selected Case Studies
Handout: Personal History Form: Children and Adolescents
DUE: Diagnostic Formulation #1

REQUIRED READING

Greenspan, S. I., & Greenspan, N. T. (2003f). Constructing a formulation based on a developmental approach. In *The clinical interview of the child* (3rd ed., pp. 187–233). Washington, DC: American Psychiatric Publishing.

Greenspan, S. I., & Greenspan, N. T. (2003g). A developmental biopsychosocial model for assessment and treatment. In *The clinical interview of the child* (3rd ed., pp. 257–286). Washington, DC: American Psychiatric Publishing.

Greenspan, S. I., & Greenspan, N. T. (2003h). Interviewing the parents: Selected comments. In *The clinical interview of the child* (3rd ed., pp. 235–255). Washington, DC: American Psychiatric Publishing.

Session VII:

Feeding and Eating Disorders of Infancy or Childhood
Eating and Substance Abuse Disorders of Adolescence

REQUIRED READING

American Psychological Association. (2000h). Eating disorders. In *Diagnostic and statistical manual of mental disorders* (4th ed., text revision, pp. 583–595). Washington, DC: Author.

American Psychological Association. (2000i). Feeding disorders of infancy or early childhood. In *Diagnostic and statistical manual of mental disorders* (4th ed., text revision, pp. 107–108). Washington, DC: Author.

American Psychological Association. (2000j). Substance-related disorders. In *Diagnostic and statistical manual of mental disorders* (4th ed., text revision, pp. 191–295). Washington, DC: Author.

Session VIII:

Anxiety and Personality Disorders
Experiential: Diagnostic Formulation for Selected Case Studies
DUE: Assessment Assignment

REQUIRED READING

American Academy of Child and Adolescent Psychiatry. (2007). Practice parameter for the assessment and treatment of children and adolescents with bipolar disorder. *Journal of the American Academy of Child and Adolescent Psychiatry, 46*(1), 107–125.

American Psychological Association. (2000k). Anxiety disorders. In *Diagnostic and statistical manual of mental disorders* (4th ed., text revision, pp. 429–484). Washington, DC: Author.

American Psychological Association. (2000l). Personality disorders. In *Diagnostic and statistical manual of mental disorders* (4th ed., text revision, pp. 686–729). Washington, DC: Author.

Session IX:

Relational Problems
Problems Related to Abuse and Neglect
Video: *Play Therapy for Severe Psychological Trauma*
DUE: Diagnostic Formulation #2

REQUIRED READING

American Psychological Association. (2000m). Outline for cultural formulation and glossary of culture-bound syndromes. In *Diagnostic and statistical manual of mental disorders* (4th ed., text revision, pp. 897–903). Washington, DC: Author.

American Psychological Association. (2000n). Problems related to abuse and neglect. In *Diagnostic and statistical manual of mental disorders* (4th ed., text revision, pp. 738–739). Washington, DC: Author.

American Psychological Association. (2000o). Relational problems. In *Diagnostic and statistical manual of mental disorders* (4th ed., text revision, pp. 736–737). Washington, DC: Author.

Yasui, M., & Dishion, T. J. (2007). The ethnic context of child and adolescent problem behavior: Implications for child and family interventions. *Clinical Child and Family Psychology, 10*(2), 137–179.

Session X:

Other Disorders of Infancy, Childhood, or Adolescence

REQUIRED READING

American Psychological Association. (2000p). Other disorders of infancy, childhood or adolescence. In *Diagnostic and statistical manual of mental disorders* (4th ed., text revision, pp. 121–134). Washington, DC: Author.

Davies, D. (2004). Attachment as a context of development. In *Child development: A practitioner's guide* (2nd ed., pp. 7–38). New York, NY: Guilford Press.

The author hopes that the five syllabi presented in this chapter will be valuable contractual resources that faculty will utilize to increase communication effectiveness and facilitate the learning process for students. Finally, social work students should be required to do a self-assessment of their level of cultural competency at the beginning of any diversity courses and again at the end of the courses. Lum's (1999, illus. 3.6) Social Work Cultural Competencies Self-Assessment instrument can be used by students to measure their level of cultural competency.

An integral part of social work education for students is their social work practicum. Any student planning to work in the child welfare system needs to have a field experience that entails home visits. Home visits have always been significant to the social work profession. The social worker is able to see and observe the children and families in their own environment when he or she makes a home visit. According to Ebeling and Hill (1983), an individual's home reflects one's distinct personality:

> Within the walls of a home, people experience the intimate moments of their lives. They sleep, wake up, bathe, eat, drink, make love, raise children. They fight, scream, and rejoice; they cry, laugh, and sing. They may experience the warmth of positive object relationships, the anguish of negative ones, or isolation and loneliness. Their outer space reflects their inner space. The way the homes are decorated and furnished can reveal either the chosen life-style of the occupants or their economic position. It can also indicate depression, despair, and disorganization. (64)

Social work students need to know that it is important to respect cultural differences as well as family cultural practices when making home visits. Home is the sanctuary for children and families. In particular, it is a place where children and families of color can seek refuge from the ongoing oppression, discrimination, racism, and bias that they repeatedly experience in their interaction with individuals, organizations, and social service systems in the outside world, including the child welfare system. Students need to learn that culture should not be a barrier to good child welfare practice. However, social work students need a sound knowledge base as well as skills in intercultural communication, tripartite cultural assessments, and cultural interventions that they can use in their work with children and families of color in the child welfare system. Making a visit to the homes of children and families of color in the child welfare system can be a significant part of establishing the client–worker relationship when the worker is culturally sensitive and demonstrates this sensitivity via appropriate interactions in the family's home.

Students also need to learn to be cognizant of their own cultural background and life experiences in order to provide ethically and culturally relevant services to the disproportionate number of children and families of color in the child welfare system today. Students have to learn new patterns of behaviors and develop the ability to effectively apply them when their practicum experience entails making home visits that will at some point in time include visiting the homes of children of color and their families. For these home visits to be successful the students must be able to demonstrate cultural sensitivity, as well as some level of cultural competence, in their interactions with children and families of color.

REFERENCES

Center for Health Workforce Studies & National Association of Social Workers Center for Workforce Studies. (2006). *Licensed social workers in the United States, 2004: Demographics.* Rensselaer, NY: Center for Health Workforce Studies, School of Public Health, University of Albany; Washington, DC: National Association of Social Workers Center for Workforce Studies.

Council on Social Work Education. (2011a). *Accreditation—current number of social work programs.* Retrieved from http://www.cswe.org/Accreditation .aspx

Council on Social Work Education. (2011b). *2011 statistics on social work education in the United States.* Alexandria, VA: Author.

Ebeling, N., & Hill, D. (1983). *Child abuse and neglect.* Boston, MA: John Wright, PSG.

Harris, M. S. (2009). *Assessment of mental disorders: Children.* Tacoma: University of Washington Tacoma, Social Work Program.

Harris, M. S. (2013a). *Child development.* Tacoma: University of Washington Tacoma, Social Work Program.

Harris, M. S. (2013b). *Children of incarcerated parents syllabus.* Tacoma: University of Washington Tacoma, Social Work Program & Criminal Justice Program.

Harris, M. S. (2013c). *Family theories.* Tacoma: University of Washington Tacoma, Social Work Program.

Harris, M. S. (2013d). *Disproportionality across systems syllabus.* Tacoma: University of Washington Tacoma, Social Work Program & Criminal Justice Program.

Lum, D. (1999). *Culturally competent practice: A framework for growth and action.* Pacific Grove, CA: Brooks/Cole.

National Association of Social Workers. (2007). *Institutional racism and the social work profession: A call to action.* Washington, DC: Author.

Shrestha, L. B., & Heisler, E. J. (2011). *The changing demographic profile of the United States. CRS report for Congress.* Washington, DC: Congressional Research Services.

6

Future Directions for Research and Policy

THIS CHAPTER WILL HIGHLIGHT AREAS of research that need to be explored, including referrals by mandated reporters. Future research is especially important in this area because the number of referrals for children of color continues to be very high and the largest percentage of these children enters the child welfare system because of child neglect; however, the definition of *child neglect* continues to be quite nebulous. Changes to current social welfare policy that are needed, as well as new policies that appear to be warranted, will also be addressed in this chapter.

There are a number of areas that need to be examined in future research studies. As noted above, one of these areas is individual bias in decision making by mandated reporters and child welfare caseworkers. It would be most beneficial to design a longitudinal study covering several states with a large sample. Qualitative studies that have been conducted have been limited in their scope and have included descriptive data collected from participants in focus groups. Research (Harris & Courtney 2003) has shown that race and family structure impact the exit rates of children of color involved in the child welfare system, especially African American children from single-parent families in California. Are children of color that are involved in the child welfare system in other states affected by these two study variables?

Other research that is needed includes a study of proactive steps that have been taken to address racial disproportionality and disparities in those states that have enacted legislation mandating the child welfare system to examine the overrepresentation of children of color in the system.

Among the states with disproportionality legislation are California, Connecticut, Florida, Illinois, Indiana, Iowa, Massachusetts, Michigan, Minnesota, Texas, and Washington. How many of the aforementioned states have implemented family group decision making (FGDM)? Do children and families of color experience better outcomes as a result of the implementation of FGDM? For example, are African American and Native American children exiting the system sooner when their families have been involved in FGDM? Has there been a decrease in the disproportionate number of children of color entering the child welfare system in those states with disproportionality legislation?

Another relevant research study is one that examines what practices have been implemented to include birth fathers of color in permanency planning for their children. Do children experience better outcomes when their fathers are included in permanency planning? How often are fathers used as a placement resource for children of color involved in the child welfare system? Are fathers included in family group conferences?

Differential response or alternative response has been used to keep children from entering the system when they are not at risk of harm or in imminent danger. Have the entry rates for children of color, especially the rates for African American and Native American children, decreased in states that have implemented differential response systems? In those states that have implemented differential response was this alternative the result of some type of legislative action? Are families of color more trusting of the child welfare system when differential response is utilized if their children are not in imminent danger?

It is also time to collect data from the children of color and their families who are directly affected by racial disproportionality and disparity at each key decision point in the child welfare system. Why do they think this problem is so pervasive? What ideas do they have for ameliorating racial disproportionality in the child welfare system? Have they experienced bias in decision making at key decision points in the child welfare system? What types of disparities have they experienced?

Research that examines the child welfare system with the goal of making systemic change is long overdue. "As long as disproportionality is viewed as an individual or personal issue of African American and Native American children or other children of color, the solutions to disproportionality will not be focused in the public domain of the child welfare system, a system that created and has continued to perpetuate disproportionality" (Harris & Hackett 2008, 202). Who benefits from racial disproportionality? Children and families of color certainly receive no benefits; they are adversely affected by racial disproportionality and disparity in the child welfare system. For example, the following was reported about the child welfare system in South Dakota:

> Critics say foster care in South Dakota has become a powerhouse for private group home providers who bring in millions of dollars in state contracts to care for kids. Among them is Children's Home Society, the state's largest foster care provider, which has close ties with top government officials. It used to be run by South Dakota's Gov. Dennis Daugard. An NPR investigation has found that Daugard was on the group's payroll while he was lieutenant governor-and while the group received tens of millions of dollars in no-bid state contracts. It's an unusual relationship highlighting the powerful role money and politics play in South Dakota's foster care system.
>
> (Sullivan & Walters 2011, 2)

One tribal social worker, Juanita Sherick, stated, "They make a living off of our children" (Sullivan & Walters 2011, 2). It certainly appears that Native American children in foster care are not receiving any benefits from being disproportionately represented in the South Dakota child welfare system.

What types of outcome measures are currently being used to track whether or not there have been reductions in the disproportionate numbers of children of color at key decision points in the child welfare system? Data collection and analyses have to be done continuously at each key decision point in the system to determine where disparities occur, and a proactive approach must be taken to eradicate identified disparities. If new services and/or supports are implemented, they must be evaluated to determine their effectiveness for all children in the system, with a special emphasis on the disproportionate number of children of color in the system. It is important for the child welfare system in each state in this country to continue to collect reliable and valid data in order to determine what system changes are required to eliminate racial disproportionality and disparity.

Section 1123A of the Social Security Act requires the U.S. Children's Bureau to conduct Child and Family Services Reviews (CFSRs) of each state's child welfare system. The purposes of the CFSRs are to:

- Ensure conformity with federal child welfare requirements,
- Determine what is actually happening to children and families as they are engaged in child welfare services, and
- Assist states to enhance their capacity to help children and families achieve positive outcomes. (U.S. Children's Bureau 2011)

However, no CFSRs are required for Indian tribes that have Title IV-E programs. Since Indian children continue to be disproportionately represented in the child welfare system at all key decision points, Section 1123A of the Social Security Act needs to be amended to mandate CFSRs for all Indian tribes that have implemented Title IV-E programs. There also needs to be an amendment that will require the Children's Bureau to determine each state's conformity with provisions in the Indian Child Welfare Act whenever the Children's Bureau conducts a CFSR. Although many Indian children, as well as Indian tribes, have participated in CFSRs, the current law does not focus on child welfare services that are being provided for Indian children by tribes. The mere fact the Indian tribes with Title IV-E programs are not included in Section 1123A of the Social Security Act is a disparity in policy that needs to be changed.

Many children of color in the child welfare system have a birth mother and/or father who is incarcerated in a jail or prison. According to Glaze and Maruschak (2008), among minor children in the United States 484,100 white non-Hispanic children, 768,400 black non-Hispanic children, and 362,800 Hispanic children had an incarcerated parent; approximately half of these children were nine years of age or younger. These figures show that children of color and their families are disproportionately represented in another system. Many of these minor children are cared for by grandparents or other relatives when a birth parent and/or parents are incarcerated. For example, when incarcerated mothers and fathers were asked about the caregivers for their children 10 percent stated grandparents were providing care, 6 percent stated their children were with other relatives, and 3 percent stated their children received care through a foster home, agency, or institution. However, the majority of parents, i.e., approximately 81 percent stated that care for at least one of their children was provided by the other parent (Christian 2009).

There are two federal policies that directly impact children of incarcerated parents that need to be examined and changed. The first policy that should be changed is the 1997 Adoption and Safe Families Act (ASFA)—specifically, the section regarding termination of parental rights if a child has been in out-of-home care for 15 of the last 22 months. The average sentence for birth parents who are incarcerated is from 80 to 100 months; consequently, many incarcerated birth parents face the risk of having their parental rights terminated (Christian 2009). According to Lee, Genty, and Laver (2005), there has been an increase in the number of cases involving birth parents who are incarcerated since the ASFA was enacted. The ASFA does have three exceptions that can be used at the discretion of the state when making decisions regarding termination of parental rights for children who have been in out-of-home care for 15 of the most recent 22 months. These exceptions are as follows: (1) the child is in kinship/relative placement; (2) documentation indicates that termination of parental rights is not in the best interest of child; and (3) the state failed to provide services needed by the family for the child to safely return home.

The second policy involves the Mentoring Children of Prisoners Program. When the Child and Family Services Improvement and Innovation Act, Pub. L. No. 112–34, was enacted in October 2011, it did not extend or further authorize funds for the Mentoring of Children of Prisoners Program. In fact, although the program had been authorized to receive funding from fiscal year 2007 through fiscal year 2011, no funds were appropriated for this program in fiscal year 2011. Mentors are social capital for children of incarcerated parents. Mentoring can help facilitate many positive outcomes for these children. Mentors can function in the following roles:

- A consistent adult presence. What children of incarcerated parents need, above all, is stable, reliable care from adults. A mentor has the ability to provide continuity when other circumstances in a child's life may be in flux.
- Advocacy for youth in court settings or with social services. Mentors can serve as impartial voices for young people, helping to represent their best interests in proceedings involving placements or the court system.
- Support for the relationship with the incarcerated parent and assistance with reentry. When it is determined to be an appropriate goal, mentors may engage children in activities that help nurture the parental relationship (writing letters, making cards, assisting with visits, etc.). In some programs, mentors may also assist the parent when she or he reenters the community, helping forge connections with an array of positive supports.

- Exposure to community support systems. Mentoring is one support among many that children of incarcerated parents need. Involvement with other organizations can help surround these children with a web of care, concern, and positive experiences.
- An adult friend. The caring adults who interact most with children of incarcerated parents (social workers, case managers, foster parents, etc.) are often paid professionals. A mentor is there for the children alone, extending friendship that builds trust and self-esteem.

In essence, a mentor can serve as an island in the storm. While this requires real commitment from both the mentor and the program, the support that lies at the heart of mentoring can greatly benefit children of incarcerated parents.

(LEARNS 2004, 2)

Children of incarcerated parents need to know that they have not been abandoned because they have a birth mother and/or father who is in jail or prison. They need to know and feel that they have caring adults in their lives; mentors can be those caring adults who make a difference in the lives of children of incarcerated parents.

Grandparents (4.5 million) and other relatives (1.5 million) are the caregivers for many of the children involved in the child welfare system. They are often clueless about what services and supports are available in the system and how to gain access to these services and supports. In 2005 Senator Hillary Rodham Clinton and several other members of the U.S. Congress introduced/sponsored the Kinship Caregiver Support Act (S. 958); however, it was never enacted into law. The purpose of this bill was as follows:

- To establish kinship navigator programs in states, large metropolitan areas, and Indian tribal organizations to help kinship caregivers navigate existing programs and services and to help them learn about and obtain assistance to meet the needs of the children they are raising, as well as their own needs.
- To promote effective partnerships among organizations, private not-for-profit agencies, and community and faith-based organizations to help them more effectively and efficiently serve kinship care families and address the fragmentation that creates barriers to meeting their needs.

- To provide funding for kinship navigator programs that can help kinship care families use existing programs and services and to increase the capacity of government, private not-for-profit, community, and faith-based agencies and related federal programs, such as the National Caregiver Support Program, to better serve the needs of kinship care families. (Child Welfare League of America n.d., 1–2)

Passage of federal legislation to support kinship caregivers would be most beneficial to all of these caregivers, especially the large number of kinship caregivers of color. A higher number of African American and Native American children are in kinship care placements, and prior work has shown that a disparity in services exists between foster parents and kinship care providers (Berrick, Barth, & Needell 1994; Harris & Skyles 2008).

Finally, there needs to be a federal policy that mandates all states to have policies and procedures that are specifically developed and implemented to address and eliminate the problem of racial disproportionality and disparities in the child welfare system. Institutional racism and individual racism must be eradicated from all key decision points in the child welfare system. All children and families must receive equitable treatment for the problem of racial disproportionality and disparity in the child welfare system to be eradicated. Currently, disproportionality continues to be the norm for African American and Native American children in the child welfare system.

REFERENCES

Berrick, J. D., Barth, R. P., & Needell, B. (1994). A comparison of kinship foster homes and family foster homes: Implications for kinship foster care as family preservation. *Children and Youth Services Review, 16*(1/2), 33–63.

Child Welfare League of America. (n.d.). *Kinship Care Support Act.* Washington, DC: Author.

Christian, S. (2009). *Children of incarcerated parents.* Washington, DC: National Conference of State Legislatures.

Glaze, L., & Maruschak, L. (2008). *Parents in prison and their minor children.* Washington, DC: Bureau of Justice Statistics.

Harris, M. S., & Courtney, M. E. (2003). The interaction of race, ethnicity, and family structure with respect to the timing of family reunification. *Children and Youth Services Review, 25*(5/6), 409–429.

Harris, M. S., & Hackett, W. (2008). Decision points in child welfare: An action research model to address disproportionality. *Children and Youth Services Review, 30*(2), 199–215.

Harris, M. S., & Skyles, A. (2008). Kinship care for African American children: Disproportionate and disadvantageous. *Journal of Family Issues, 29*(8), 1013–1030.

LEARNS. (2004). *Mentoring children of incarcerated parents: A toolkit for senior corps directors.* Portland, OR: Author.

Lee, A., Genty, P. M., & Laver, M. (2005). *The impact of the Adoption and Safe Families Act on children of incarcerated parents.* Washington, DC: Child Welfare League of America.

Sullivan, L., & Walters, A. (2011). *Native foster care: Lost children, shattered families.* Retrieved from http://www.npr.org/2011/10/25/141672992/native-foster-care-lost-children-shattered-families

U.S. Children's Bureau. (2011). *The Children's Bureau requesting public comments.* Retrieved from http://www.nrc4tribes.org/announcements/thechildresbur eaurequestingpubliccomments

Child Welfare Laws

1. Washington State Indian Child Welfare Act (SB 5656)
2. Personal Responsibility and Work Opportunity Reconciliation Act of 1996 (Pub. L. No. 104–193)
3. Multiethnic Placement Act of 1994 (Pub. L. No. 103–382)
4. Adoption and Safe Families Act of 1997 (Pub. L. No. 105–89)
5. Indian Child Welfare Act of 1978 (Pub. L. No. 95–608)
6. Adoption Assistance and Child Welfare Act of 1980 (Pub. L. No. 96–272)
7. Child Abuse Prevention and Treatment Act of 1974 (Pub. L. No. 93–247)
8. Fostering Connections to Success and Increasing Adoptions Act of 2008 (Pub. L. No. 110–351)
9. Child and Family Services Improvement and Innovation Act of 2011 (Pub. L. No. 112–34)

WASHINGTON STATE INDIAN CHILD WELFARE ACT (SB 5656)

The Washington State Indian Child Welfare Act was passed in April 2011. It is designed to codify as state law the provisions of the federal Indian Child Welfare Act, which ensures (1) that every effort will be taken to place Indian children in homes with their extended families or their respective tribes in order to maintain the rights and preserve the unique values and culture of Native American children who are unable to reside with their biological parents, and (2)that, if the children are unable to reside with their tribe, then the state will make every effort to place the children in foster homes that will respect and foster the children's cultural, social, and spiritual needs for their specific development. The state act also clarifies key terms within the federal act. The Washington act was a reaction to what was deemed a disproportionate number of removals of Indian children from their families and tribes by state courts and welfare agencies. This led to unnecessary levels of cultural disorientation and child vulnerability, an accusation that has become less common since the passage of the act.

The Washington State Indian Child Welfare Act is essentially an attempt to keep displaced Indian children within their own families or extended families. For example, it dictates that when a child is domiciled within an Indian reservation or has been made a ward of a tribal court, the state court must transfer the child's case to the tribal court. If an Indian child is not domiciled within an Indian reservation and there is no objection from either parent or cause for alternate action, the act obligates the state court to transfer the child's case to the appropriate tribal court upon the motion of either of the child's parents, the child's Indian custodian, the child's tribe, or the child, if he or she is at least twelve years of age. If the state court does not transfer the child's case to an appropriate tribal court, it must do everything in its power to reunite the family. If the state court should deem an out-of-home placement is necessary, it must give preference to the child's extended family and then to other tribal and Indian homes.

Other provisions in the act cover the right of the Indian child, the child's tribe, or the child's Indian custodian to intervene in child custody proceedings; court-appointed counsel for the parent or Indian custodian; and notification of the Indian tribe when emergency removal has been evidenced and occurs. In cases of involuntary foster care placement, a qualified expert witness will be called upon to confirm and support the determination that the continued residence of the Indian child with his or her parents or tribe will cause serious emotional or physical harm to the child. The act provides a list of placement preferences, including a setting that most approximates a family situation, that is in close proximity to the Indian child's home, and in which the Indian child's special needs can be met. Preference is given to members of the child's extended family, Indian foster homes, foster homes approved by the child's tribe, and non-Indian families that are either approved by the child's tribe or committed to promoting family and tribe visitation, maintaining the child's relationship with the tribe, and participating in cultural events pertaining to the child's heritage. The Washington State Department of Social and Health Services, Children's

Administration is to consult with Indian tribes to establish standards and procedures for its review of cases subject to the act, as well as methods for monitoring its compliance with the federal and state acts. These standards, procedures, and methods are to be integrated into the child welfare contracting and contract monitoring process.

PERSONAL RESPONSIBILITY AND WORK OPPORTUNITY RECONCILIATION ACT OF 1996 (PUB. L. NO. 104-193)

The Personal Responsibility and Work Opportunity Reconciliation Act (PRWORA) was drafted and introduced in Congress in response to the rising opposition to and criticism of the Aid to Families with Dependent Children (AFDC) program. AFDC was widely recognized as being ineffective and causing cyclical patterns of poverty, with a high percentage of cases involving welfare fraud. Congress had identified dependency, out-of-wedlock birth, and intergenerational poverty as the main contributors to a welfare system in need of reform. The welfare reforms in PRWORA became law when President Bill Clinton signed the act on August 22, 1996. At the time President Clinton stated that PRWORA "is the best chance we have fir a long time to complete the work of ending welfare as we know it" (Kilborn & Verhovek 1996, 1). The act was also a fulfillment of the Republican Contract with America, a document released by the Republican Party outlining a series of issues that Republican congressional representatives would resolve should they become the House majority.

The PRWORA took effect on July 1, 1997. Title I replaced the AFDC program and the Job Opportunities and Basic Skills Training program with Temporary Assistance for Needy Families (TANF) block grants to states. The grants were available to those states that passed a basic set of requirements evidencing the ability to design their own systems, and these states were required to use 80 percent of their funding with activities related to TANF. As part of PRWORA's effort to end welfare as an entitlement program, it declared the following persons ineligible to receive TANF funding: those who had received a cumulative lifetime total of five years of assistance, those who had been convicted of drug-related felonies, those who don't cooperate with child support enforcement requirements, and unmarried teen parents, who are required to stay in school and live in an adult-supervised household. TANF also includes a series of work requirements for those receiving aid, including participation in community service two months after the person begins receiving welfare benefits and participation in employment after two years of receiving these benefits.

The act is also a reaction to an opinion prevalent at the time that America's welfare system constituted a pull factor for potential immigrants that had detrimental domestic effects. As a result, the act reduces funding for all immigrant welfare programs and withholds professional and occupational licenses from illegal immigrants. It has instituted measures to discourage births out of wedlock and encourage two-parent families, including reducing aid for unmarried parents under age eighteen. A key aim of the act is to enhance efforts to collect child support and preclude attempts by noncustodial parents to avoid making child support payments. The act has also improved existing procedures for ensuring that custodial parents received child support.

The House Ways and Means Committee declared that the act does not intend to abolish "the function of welfare as a safety net for families experiencing temporary financial problems," but rather it aims to "reduce the length of welfare spells by attacking dependency" (Debate Politics, 11). Over six years, PRWORA cut $55 billion from funding for low-income programs, including basic programs for low-income children and families, the elderly, immigrants, and those with disabilities. Its passage was followed by a period of decline in both welfare and poverty rates in the late 1990s that has been said to be an effect of PRWORA.

MULTIETHNIC PLACEMENT ACT OF 1994 (PUB. L. NO. 103-382)

Congress observed that, with nearly 500,000 children in foster care in the United States and tens of thousands of them waiting an average of two years and eight months for adoption, something needed to be done to broaden and expedite the process of both recruiting foster parents and processing adoptions. A key obstacle to the effectiveness of the foster care and adoption systems identified by Congress was racial, ethnic, and national origin constraints placed on the process of selecting foster and adoptive families and pairing them with children in need of care. Children of color—who made up over 60 percent of those in foster care nationwide in 1994—were waiting twice as long for permanent homes as were other foster children because of the tendency to match the racial and ethnic backgrounds of the child and foster parents. In the Multiethnic Placement Act (MEPA) Congress proposed to remove all such constraints from U.S. foster care and adoption systems in the hope that such action would speed up the process, thus reducing the length of time children needed to wait for foster and adoptive placement. It leveraged this policy by denying federal assistance to any agency or entity that denies parents or children the opportunity to become adoptive or foster parents or find placement in a foster or adoptive home, respectively. Congress's suggested alternative to racial and ethnic discrimination in child placement is that foster and adoptive families be identified and recruited based on the needs of each specific child.

MEPA was enacted October 20, 1994. The first major provision of this act prevents state agencies from delaying, denying, or otherwise discriminating when making a foster care or adoption placement decision on the basis of the parent's or child's race, color, or national origin. This rule applies to state agencies and other entities that receive federal funding and are involved in foster care or adoption placements. These agencies are also prohibited from selecting foster parents solely on the basis of race, color, or national origin. The act, however, does allow for consideration of the cultural, ethnic, or racial background of a child in relation to the capacity of potential adoptive or foster parents to meet the needs of a child with that background when making a placement decision. These factors are considered only if required, in particular cases, to serve the best interest of the child in need of placement. Lastly, MEPA requires state agencies to develop plans to recruit adoptive and foster parents who can carry out the act—specifically, families that reflect the racial and ethnic diversity of the children in need of placement. By doing so, there will be families that can care for the children of diverse racial and ethnic backgrounds. The act intends to provide stable homes for children according to their individual needs and to allow for more parents of color to become adoptive or foster parents in order to meet those needs. Some problems in implementation have included (1) harmonizing the act with caseworkers' and practitioners' beliefs about the role of racial and ethnic background in the placement of children in adoptive or foster care and (2) developing an effective federal compliance monitoring system.

ADOPTION AND SAFE FAMILIES ACT OF 1997
(PUB. L. NO. 105-89)

The Adoption and Safe Families Act (ASFA) was signed by President Clinton in order to promote the adoption of more children in foster care, while increasing the focus on the health and safety of the child. For example, it reauthorized the Family Preservation and Support Services Program and renamed it the Safe and Stable Families Program. The act's first goals are to ensure safety for abused and neglected children and to accelerate the adoption process for children. Means to meet these goals include adding the clause "safety of the child" to every step of the case plan and requiring more criminal background checks of the potential foster parents. The state will then ensure removal of children from dangerous homes and their placement in safe ones. The act also requires states to initiate court proceedings to free a child for adoption if the child has been in foster care placement for at least fifteen of the most recent twenty-two months. This way the state will be responsible for expediting efforts to find permanent homes for children.

Much of this act was a response to the Adoption Assistance and Child Welfare Act of 1980, which influenced many decisions to preserve families and keep children with their biological parents. ASFA demonstrates the shift in thinking to the health and safety of the child rather than keeping parents and children together, regardless of prior abuse or neglect. With this shift, the state has to focus on removal of children from unsafe homes or abusive parents. The act ensures either that the children's homes will stabilize sooner or that the adoption of the children will not be delayed. One lead sponsor of the act, Republican Senator John H. Chafee, said, "We will not continue the current system of always putting the needs and rights of the biological parents first. . . . It's time we recognize that some families simply cannot and should not be kept together" (Seelye 1997, 1). In greeting the final measure, President Clinton said that the act "makes clear that children's health and safety are the paramount concerns" (Access America Government Services 1998, 1).

INDIAN CHILD WELFARE ACT OF 1978 (PUB. L. NO. 95-608)

The Indian Child Welfare Act (ICWA) aims to protect the rights of Indian tribes, promote the health of their children, and restrict the unfair treatment of the tribes by giving more voice to the tribal governments concerning the removal of children from Indian homes. Many Indian children were being removed from their homes, which, with or without justification, were deemed unsafe for them, and then adopted into new homes—without adequate consideration of the cultural differences or the relationships among the child, family, and tribe. Some studies showed that around one in four Indian children was being placed into a non-Indian home—which potentially harms the child, as well the culture and health of the tribe. ICWA establishes minimum federal standards for the removal of Indian children from their families and requires that Indian children be placed in foster or adoptive homes that reflect Indian culture.

The intent of the act is to give due respect to the Indian tribes and prevent the breakup of Indian families and culture. Removing children from their family culture and from their tribal culture risks damaging both the child (personally) and the tribe (culturally). The act also is actively aimed at improving the relationship between the tribal and state governments, creating exclusive tribal jurisdiction over all Indian child custody proceedings at request of American Indian tribes and requiring courts to give full faith and credit to tribal court decrees. The act further is intended to provide proper notice, communication, and respect across the cultural barriers in order to do what is best for the children in need, while not dismissing or disregarding those cultural barriers.

ADOPTION ASSISTANCE AND CHILD WELFARE ACT OF 1980 (PUB. L. NO. 96-272)

The Adoption Assistance and Child Welfare Act aims to reunite children and parents or to have children adopted if family reunification is not in their best interests. There is special reference to children identified as "special needs"—those who cannot be returned to their parents' care and cannot be placed in care without assistance. President Jimmy Carter, who signed the act in June 1980, said that there were 500,000 children in foster care at the time and that half of them had been away from their families for over two years, though their foster care placements were meant to be temporary. This major federal legislation is one of the first child welfare acts that recognizes the need for permanency planning and discourages long-term placement of children in foster care.

The act requires the state to make "reasonable efforts" and plan for reunification and preventative programs to expedite family reunification because of the lack of accountability by those who are responsible for either reuniting children with their parents or finding them other permanent placements when family reunification is no longer the permanency goal. If the biological parents are unable to be reunited with their child, then the state is required to place the child close to his or her home. The act also ensures a written case plan for the child, as well as court reviews regarding the status of the child every six months to determine what is in the child's best interest. Specific permanency plans have to be made for the eighteen-month dispositional review; permanency goals include family reunification, adoption, and continued foster care placement. The act also included provisions to help states provide funds for adoption expenses for children identified as "special needs." In many cases children who had been abused and neglected in their own homes were removed from the care of their biological parents and placed in out-of-home care. The act also refines the foster care system so that children will not have multiple foster care placements but rather alternative permanent placements when family reunification is no longer a viable permanency goal. However, the act does stipulate that reasonable efforts must be made to reunify a child with his or her biological parents.

CHILD ABUSE PREVENTION AND TREATMENT ACT OF 1974 (PUB. L. NO. 93-247)

The creation and passage of the Child Abuse Prevention and Treatment Act (CAPTA) took over a decade, resulting from growing concern over child abuse, which had received increasing coverage in the media and which was the subject of more research into scope of the problem, especially after lawyers, judges, hospitals, social workers, and others began discussing increasing reports of abuse. It was signed into law by President Richard Nixon on January 31, 1974, and has been amended several times since its enactment.

CAPTA provides federal funding to support the prevention of child abuse through research and demonstration projects on the causes, prevention, identification, assessment, and treatment of child abuse and neglect;

the development and implementation of evidence-based training programs; and technical assistance to grantees and communities through national resource centers and the Child Welfare Information Gateway. These funds are provided to state and local agencies and organizations, as well as university- and hospital-affiliated programs. The act also established the Office on Child Abuse and Neglect and mandated the National Clearinghouse on Child Abuse and Neglect Information.

CAPTA sets forth a minimum definition of child abuse and neglect. The act defines child abuse and neglect as "at a minimum, any recent act or failure to act on the part of a parent or caretaker, which results in death, serious physical or emotional harm, sexual abuse or exploitation, or an act or failure to act which presents an imminent risk of serious harm" (Goldman, Salius, Wolcott, & Kennedy 2003, 1).

FOSTERING CONNECTIONS TO SUCCESS AND INCREASING ADOPTIONS ACT OF 2008 (PUB. L. NO. 110-351)

On October 7, 2008, President George W. Bush signed into law the Fostering Connections to Success and Increasing Adoptions Act. This act improves health care and education for children in foster care and promotes their long-term stability by encouraging relative guardianship and adoption. Additionally, in reaction to the charge that children in foster care are forced out of care at age eighteen with connections and resources inadequate to ensure their success as adults, the act extends federal support for children in foster care to age twenty-one. It also authorizes grants to state, local, and tribal child welfare agencies for use in helping children at risk of needing foster care reconnect with their families. States can claim federal reimbursement of costs incurred while training guardians, agency personnel, neglect court agents, attorneys, and court-appointed special advocates. In addition, the act extends Title IV-E funding opportunities for foster care, adoption assistance, and kinship guardianship assistance to Native American tribes that apply. The act requires fingerprint-based criminal records checks of all relative guardians and of other adults living in the guardian's home, and it doubles the incentives for special needs and older child adoptions. The crux of the act is its institution of guardianship assistance payments for relatives of children in foster care who decide to assume legal guardianship for those children.

CHILD AND FAMILY SERVICES IMPROVEMENT AND
INNOVATION ACT OF 2011 (PUB. L. NO. 112-34)

On September 30, 2011, President Barack Obama signed the Child and Family Services Improvement and Innovation Act. Title I of this act extends through fiscal year 2016 the authorization of appropriations for the Stephanie Tubbs Jones Child Welfare Services Program, initially put in place by the Child and Family Services part of the Social Security Act. The act also requires that each state include in any attempt to coordinate health care services for children in foster care an outline of how it proposes to monitor psychotropic medications and emotional trauma in maltreated children, as well as a description of the measures taken to reduce the time children under the age of five are without a permanent home. The act requires that such explanations also address how states will identify and treat the developmental needs of children using services provided by the Child and Family Services Program. Title I requires that caseworkers complete 90 percent of the number of visits they would have completed if they had visited each child in foster care at a rate of once monthly.

Title I also extends the Safe and Stable Families Program through fiscal year 2016 and requires that states provide peer-to-peer parent and caregiver mentoring and support group services. It requires that state reports—including tables on planned and actual spending, among other things—be compiled by the secretary of the U.S. Department of Health and Human Services (DHHS) and published online for public viewing. Title I extends specified reservations of funding for monthly caseworker visits through fiscal year 2016 and requires that a portion of those funds be used to improve the quality of such visits and the analysis resulting from them.

Title II of the act renews through fiscal year 2014 the authority of the secretary of DHHS to authorize states to conduct child welfare program demonstration projects likely to promote the objectives of the act and specifies conditions under which states may be eligible to conduct new demonstration projects. It also authorizes states to establish programs that address domestic violence and other preconditions for the placement of children in foster care.

REFERENCES

Access America Government Services. (1998). *President Clinton announces expansion of the Internet to increase adoptions.* Retrieved from govinfo.library.unt.edu/accessamerica/docs/adoption.html

Debate Politics. (2013). *Welfare: Keep, reform or end.* Retrieved from http://www.debatepolitics.com

Goldman, J., Salius, M. K., Wolcott, D, & Kennedy, K. Y. (2003). *A coordinated response to child abuse and neglect: The foundation for practice* (p. 1). Washington, DC: U. S. Children's Bureau, Office on Child Abuse and Neglect.

Kilborn, P. T., & Verhovek, S. H. (1996, August 2). Clinton's welfare shift ends tortuous journey. *The New York Times,* p. 1.

Seelye, K. Q. (1997, November 9). Clinton to approve sweeping shift in adoption. *The New York Times,* p. 1.

Mrs. F. *See* executive director of private
child welfare agency and adoptive
mother
Mrs. T. *See* female foster care alumnus
Ms. B. *See* adoptive mother
Ms. K. *See* birth mother
Ms. T. *See* foster parent and kinship
caregiver
MSW programs. *See* graduate social work
programs
multiaxial assessment, 291
multicultural organization, 115
Multiethnic Placement Act of 1994
(MEPA), 7–9, 310–11
multiple foster care placements, 52, 163,
207, 228–29
multiracial children, 198, 235
Murray, Martha, 92

National Association of Public Child
Welfare Administrators (NAPCWA),
98–100. *See also* Disproportionality
Diagnostic Tool
National Council of Juvenile and Family
Court Judges, 40–41
Native American children, 31, 95, 304; ASFA
and, 13; in birth father's interview, 138;
boarding schools for, 93–94; CFSRs and,
301; court system and, 41; exposure/visi-
bility bias and, 38; Fostering Connections
to Success and Increasing Adoptions Act
and, 14–16; in history of child welfare
system, 93–94; ICWA and, 4–5, 41, 60,
307–9, 312–13; in kinship care, 44–45,
308; programs for, 60, 62; in South
Dakota, 300; Washington State Indian
Child Welfare Act for, 5, 60, 307–9.
See also female foster care alumnus
navigator programs, kinship, 303–4
neglect: in Australia, 25; CAPTA and, 2;
defined, 298, 315; ICWA and, 4; investigation of, 36; Office on Child Abuse
and Neglect for, 315; substance abuse
and, 13–14, 41, 76, 78–80, 82, 211. *See
also* reporting, abuse and neglect
New Zealand: CPS in, 30–31; kinship care
in, 31–32; racial disproportionality in,
30–32

Nixon, Richard, 314
no contact order, 137, 140, 144–45
notifications, in Australia, 25, *26*

OAACS. *See* Office of African American
Children's Services
Oasis youth center, 234
Obama, Barack, 3, 16, 316
objective criteria, in child welfare, 37–38, 55
objectives, course. *See* course objectives
observation, of children, 251, 292
Odessa Brown Children's Clinic, 62–63
Office of African American Children's
Services (OAACS), 129, 131
Office on Child Abuse and Neglect, 315
Olive Crest, 216, 221
One Church One Child: executive director
of, 188–97; kinship and, 191–92
orphanages, 92–94
orphan boats, 33
Orphan Foundation of America, 219
out-of-home care: in Australia, *26*, 27–28;
child development and, 46; decision
point of, 36, 39, 43; institutional racism
and, 94–95; risk factors, 51–52
overdose, 145

Pacific Islander children, 31
parental incarceration: adolescents and,
274; of birth mother, 122, 125–28; child
development influenced by, 265, 270;
foster care and, 265; mentors and, 273,
302–3; reunification after, 265, 270–71;
statistics, 301. *See also* Children of Incarcerated Parents syllabus
parental rights: of birth mother, 118, 120;
kinship care and, 302; termination of,
12–13, 118, 135, 137, 200–201, 206, 302;
visitation, 246–47
parenting courses, 59, 121, 142
parents: in best practices/promising practices case study, 75–83; childhood abuse
of, 77, 79, 82; depression in, 76; step-
parents, 225; visitation with, 78, 80–81,
246–47, 266. *See also* Children of Incarcerated Parents syllabus; fathers; foster
parent and kinship caregiver; mothers
permanency planning, 6–7, 14, 313–14